Paul Howse

A FIELD GUIDE TO THE MAMMALS OF CENTRAL AMERICA & SOUTHEAST MEXICO

A FIELD GUIDE TO

THE MAMMALS OF

CENTRAL AMERICA &

SOUTHEAST MEXICO

Written & Illustrated by
FIONA A. REID

New York   Oxford
Oxford University Press
1997

Oxford University Press

Oxford   New York
Athens   Auckland   Bangkok   Bogota   Bombay   Buenos Aires
Calcutta   Cape Town   Dar es Salaam   Delhi   Florence   Hong Kong
Istanbul   Karachi   Kuala Lumpur   Madras   Madrid   Melbourne
Mexico City   Nairobi   Paris   Singapore   Taipei   Tokyo   Toronto   Warsaw

and associated companies in
Berlin   Ibadan

Published by Oxford University Press, Inc.
198 Madison Avenue, New York, New York 10016

Oxford is a registered trademark of Oxford University Press

Library of Congress Cataloging-in-Publication Data
Reid, Fiona A.
    A field guide to the mammals of Central America and Southeast Mexico /
written and illustrated by Fiona A. Reid.
        p.   cm.
    Includes bibliographical references and index.
    ISBN 0-19-506400-3; 0-19-506401-1 (pbk)
        1. Mammals— Central America.   2. Mammals— Mexico.
    3. Zoological illustration.   4. Mammals in art.   I. Title.
    QL723.A1R545   1997
    599.0972— dc20   96-15540

9 8 7 6 5 4 3 2

Printed in the United States of America
on acid-free paper

To my friend and mentor

Guy Tudor,

whose unmatched artistic talent

rests on a profound love and knowledge

of natural history

PREFACE

When I first considered writing and illustrating a field guide to mammals, I was motivated by several factors. Although I studied biology as an undergraduate and graduate student, I had been working for several years as a natural history illustrator, specializing in Neotropical mammals. I was frustrated by having to create lifelike renderings of mammals based solely on museum specimens, and I wanted the opportunity to study and draw live mammals. I also wanted to get to know the entire mammal fauna of one area in depth, not only from an artist's perspective. At that time, no field guides were available for mammals throughout the Neotropics. I decided to focus on Central American mammals largely because the fauna was a little better known than that of South America, and it seemed to be a more manageable unit for a field guide. I later decided to include southeastern Mexico as a compromise between political and ecological boundaries, and as a convenient cutoff point for range maps.

At the outset of this project, I knew very little about Central America and its mammals; I had taken a few short trips to the region and seen some of the larger species. My goal was to see as many species of mammals as possible, and to draw from life most of the small mammals. I moved to Costa Rica in 1988 and spent the next two years, and portions of the subsequent four years, traveling throughout most of Central America and southeast Mexico. I supported myself during this time by leading nature tours for Questers Tours and Travel, New York. Questers helped me on many occasions with complicated travel arrangements and reduced fares.

During my field work, I observed in the wild or captured for study more than 85% of the mainland species of mammals included in this book. I initially drew field sketches of species new to me, but after the first year I planned out the color plates and carried them with me, painting each species directly onto the plates as I encountered them. Field conditions are not optimal for detailed and precise painting; paint and paper (and artist) react differently in the cold, humid environment of montane oak forest and the sweltering hot weather of Yucatán in summer. Some species I painted while sitting in a truck, using the steering wheel as an easel, and some while in a tent with a headlamp at night, but most were done outside during the day, sitting on the ground or on a log.

The white background of the plates suffered from a continuous onslaught of dust, sweat, and grime, drops of urine or feces from the subject being painted, squashed mosquitoes, rain, and other indefinable debris. Carrying the plates throughout Central America involved some harrowing experiences, one of which was a short flight to Tortuguero in Costa Rica. The pilot had at length persuaded me to put my portfolio in the front baggage hold in the nose of the plane, and after we took off he realized that the door to this hold had come open. While the other four passengers agonized over the possibility of the plane going down if luggage became tangled in the propellors, I was trying to follow our coordinates so I could search for my plates if they fell to the swampy ground below. Fortunately, we landed at a small airfield, corrected the problem, and lost nothing but peace of mind.

On my travels through Central America and southeastern Mexico, I was greatly aided by numerous individuals and organizations. These are outlined roughly chronologically below.

In Costa Rica, permits for capture and collection of small mammals were granted by Servicio de Vida Silvestre, Ministerio de Recursos Naturales Energía y Minas, and by Servicio de Parques Nacionales, with the help of Carlos Salas-A., Fernando Cortés, and Roberto Aviles-B. Assistance, advice, and/or companionship in the field were provided variously by Horst and Ursula Korn, Cathy Langtimm, Alex Wilson, Richard and Meg LaVal, Bob Timm, Amos Bien, Luis Torres, Marcelo Aranda, and others. John and Doris Campbell and Stella Wallace kindly allowed me to set traps and nets on their land at Monteverde. Field trips with graduates from the Universidad Nacional Autonoma de Heredia, students taking Organization for Tropical Studies courses, and undergraduates from the Universidad de Costa Rica helped me encounter several mammal species new to me in areas of the country that I was not familiar with. Lily and Werner Hagenour kindly gave me access to their land and allowed me to sketch and obtain tracks from their excellent collection of captive cats. As a Questers Tour leader, I worked with several Costa Rican Expeditions (CRE) naturalist guides, Jorge Fernandez in particular, and benefited from their help and knowledge. CRE also provided generous hospitality at their excellent facility, Tortuga Lodge, which borders some of the best habitat for bats in the country.

In Panama, I obtained permits for small mammal studies from INRENARE, facilitated by Nick Smythe and Gloria Maggiore of the Smithsonian Tropical Research Institute (STRI). Nick and Tanis Smythe provided much-needed help and hospitality during several trips to Panama. Bob Brown introduced me to nighttime stream walking in Soberania National Park; he and Brian Fisher accompanied me to the Darién. Bill Adsett gave much help and hospitality at Cerro Azúl. Permits to visit Cerro Azúl were granted by the Melo Group. Dodge Engleman provided helpful information for the Panama section of "Where to find mammals."

In Belize, staff at the Belize Zoo and Tropical Education and Conservation Center, particularly Amy Bodwell and Sharon Matola, provided help, hospitality, and logistic aid on several mammal-watching trips.

In Guatemala, permits were kindly granted by Consejo Nacional de Areas Protegidas (CONAP), with particular help from María José González, Juan Carlos Villagrán, and Gerda María Huertas. Margaret and Michael Dix of the Universidad del Valle helped with logistics, including vehicles and drivers. Centro de Estudios Conservacionistas (CECON) staff, especially Milton Cabrera, facilitated our visits to several Biotopos in northern Guatemala.

In El Salvador, permits were granted (to Mark Engstrom) by Servicio de Parques Nacionales y Vida Silvestre, with the cooperation of Carlos Roberto Hasbún. Staff from the Museo de Historia Natural de El Salvador assisted in the permit application process. Victor Hellebuyck helped with logistic arrangements and field work. Francisco Serrano allowed us to work on his land and provided help and hospitality.

In Mexico, permits (issued to Mark Engstrom and Bob Dowler) were granted by Dirección General de Conservación Ecologica de los Recursos Naturales. Fernando Cervantes helped with logistics and sent some very capable students to accompany us, including Yolanda Hortelano-M. In Guatemala, El Salvador, and Mexico, I worked with Mark Engstrom and Burton Lim from the Royal Ontario Museum, and on some of the Mexican trips we enjoyed the additional company and expertise of Bob Dowler, Duke Rogers, Terry Maxwell, and Karen Peterson.

Throughout Central America and southeastern Mexico, I received enormous support from local people, not all of whose names I learned. Park guards, in particular, willingly cooperated in locating bat roosts, nests, and so forth. Special thanks to Pizarro Melendez and Alipio Flaco in Darién National Park. To the women who brought tortillas when our truck broke down, the man who let me pitch my tent under his tin roof in the pouring rain, the farm hand who arrived one morning clutching a live mouse opossum inside its nest, and for all the other acts of help and kindness shown to me, thank you all.

Most of the field work for this book was conducted in Middle America, although some illustrations were made in other areas. Several bat species are very uncommon or poorly known in Central America, yet are common in the United States or South America. The Arizona Game and Fish Department kindly gave me a permit to catch and release small mammals in southeastern Arizona, which enabled me to study from life several vespertilionids, a glossophagine, and two small rodents that I had not encountered elsewhere. A few of the phyllostomine bats were sketched in Guyana and Ecuador.

My own field work provided me with the opportunity to observe and draw live mammals and obtain limited information on distributions or natural history of some species. This contributed only a small part to the complete text of this field guide, which, as with all other natural history works, is based on museum collections and the study of those collections. Museum specimens are essential for the verification of species identifications made in the field, and as a foundation for all field studies. In fact, the determination of what constitutes a species is based entirely on material housed in museum collections. Series of specimens both from a single locality and from throughout the range of a species are necessary for such basic information as the average color and body size of the species, as well as for more detailed studies of the identity and distributional limits of species and subspecies. On several occasions I caught a single individual of a species and illustrated this individual on a color plate, only to find on a subsequent visit to a museum that the color of the individual was atypical of the species as a whole. Without the reference material of museum collections, it would be impossible for any one person to compile a useful field guide on virtually any biological topic (for an excellent discussion on the value of museum collections see Emmons, 1990). During my field work, I collected specimens of species whenever I was doubtful of the field identification or when I thought the specimen might provide additional information on distribution of the species.

Several museum collectors who worked in Middle America in the past and at present have provided an invaluable legacy, both in the specimens they obtained and in their accompanying field notes. Particularly noteworthy were the early expeditions of E. W. Nelson and E. A. Goldman in Mexico and Guatemala, and Goldman's later work in Panama; W. W. Dalquest's fieldwork in Veracruz and San Luis Potosí; and the continuing work of B. Villa-R. and T. Alvarez in Mexico, C. O. Handley Jr. in Panama, and T. J. McCarthy in northern Central America. These workers not only obtained large and important collections, but also took the time to record habitat and natural history information. Such notes often provided the only information available for the "Habitat" and "Habits" sections of many of the species accounts.

I am grateful for being allowed access to the mammal collections at a number of museums. Most of the museum research for this book involved three institutions. At the American Museum of Natural History, I would like to thank the staff of the Department of Mammalogy, especially Karl Koopman, Rob Voss, Nancy Simmons, and Wolfgang Fuchs. Staff of the Division of Mammals, United States National Museum of Natural History, helped me from the outset of my field work. Special thanks to Don Wilson, Bob Fisher, Al Gardner, Mike Carleton, Louise Emmons, Charles Handley, Claudia Angle, Linda Gordon, and others for their help on numerous visits. The Department of Mammalogy at the Royal Ontario Museum (ROM) has been my home base for several years, and much of the data in this book are derived from their excellent collections. Special thanks to Jim Borack for his painstaking preparation of new material and to Mark Engstrom, Burton Lim, Judith Eger, and Chris Pankewycz for their help and friendship. Thanks also to ROM library staff for much help with references.

Tim McCarthy and Phil Myers reviewed the entire text and provided many helpful comments and much additional data. I am very grateful for their efforts. Bernd Würsig and Randall Davis kindly reviewed the marine mammal texts. Neal Woodman reviewed the shrew accounts and allowed me to use data he had collected from visits to several museums. Fernando Cervantes and Duke Rogers provided measurements of specimens in their care. Don Wilson, Brock Fenton, and Phil de Vries reviewed portions of the manuscript and provided helpful comments. Thanks also to Oxford University Press editors Lisa Stallings and Judith May. For proofreading help, I thank Pat Ross, Lorelie Mitchell, and Jenna Dunlop.

Thanks to friends and family for encouragement, support, and basement space during my homeless years.

This book might never have come to fruition without the input of two people, Guy Tudor and Mark Engstrom. Guy suggested that I write and illustrate my own field guide and has generously given support and friendship throughout the process. He reviewed the color plates and loaned photos from his extensive photo files. Guy also reviewed earlier drafts for all large mammal texts and gave an especially detailed critique of the facing plate texts. His input gave me a much-needed balance between the demands of the general naturalist and those of the professional mammalogist. Guy has always given freely of his time and energy to me and many others in the shaping of their field guides. His unmatched knowledge of what makes a good guide has contributed to the caliber of books on a wide range of natural history topics, including, I hope, this one.

I would like to thank my husband, Mark Engstrom, for his unflagging enthusiasm and support. In the field, his determination and zeal as rat trapper extraordinaire led us to find several very rare small rodents. He goaded me into painting everything we found, even under the adverse conditions regularly encountered in field work. He read and commented on the entire manuscript, and willingly partook of many long and often boring discussions concerning various decisions I had to make as the project developed.

In a project of this kind, there is always one more species to see in the wild, one more collection of specimens to examine, or a new species revision to await. I credit the imminent arrival of my daughter Holly for giving me a deadline by which to finish the first draft of the manuscript. Her cheery companionship brightened, if not hastened, subsequent text revisions.

Toronto, Ontario   F.A.R.
May 1996

CONTENTS

CONTENTS

PLATES

TEXT FIGURES

A FIELD GUIDE TO

THE MAMMALS OF

CENTRAL AMERICA &

SOUTHEAST MEXICO

HOW TO USE THIS BOOK

SCOPE OF THE BOOK

This guide includes all living species of native mammals south of the Isthmus of Tehuantepec, Mexico, through the Mexican states of Chiapas, Tabasco, Campeche, Quintana Roo, and Yucatán, and all Central American countries: Guatemala, Belize, Honduras, El Salvador, Nicaragua, Costa Rica, and Panama (Plate 49). This region comprises most of the Neotropical Zoogeographic Realm of Middle America, which also extends northward up both coasts of Mexico and southward into South America along the Pacific Slope of northern Colombia and northwest Ecuador. Marine mammals found in the waters surrounding Central America and southeastern Mexico and most islands associated with these countries are also included. Isla del Coco, Costa Rica, is not included. Non-native mammals that may form feral populations are not included, with the exception of three widespread introduced rodents, the house rats and mouse.

CLASSIFICATION OF MAMMALS

Mammals are warm-blooded animals that give birth to live young (with the exception of egg-laying monotremes from Australia and New Guinea) and feed their young on milk. Most mammals have fur or hair, although for some species this may be limited to a few bristles or sparse hairs, as in whales, dolphins, and manatees. Marine mammals also differ from the standard mammal design in having forelimbs modified into flippers, and no external hind limbs (vestigial hind limbs may be visible on the skeleton or in embryos). Bats are another group of mammals with modified limbs. Their wings are formed by thin skin extending between the feet and the elongated finger and hand bones. The hard shell of an armadillo superficially resembles a turtle shell; however, these mammals have hair on the belly and suckle their young like other mammals.

Scientists classify plants and animals based on features that they have in common with one another. Mammals are a group of animals in the Class Mammalia. Within this broad category, mammals are grouped into orders, families, genera, and species.

The scientific classification of a species has been based on whether or not a group of animals could interbreed and produce viable offspring. This is known as the "biological species concept" and can be difficult to apply when two populations of a species do not contact one another in nature. For this and other reasons, the concept of what constitutes a species is hotly debated (see Engstrom et al., 1994). Each species has a scientific name that is used by scientists throughout the world, regardless of language. The species name has two parts—the genus name, with the first letter capitalized, and the specific epithet, which is not capitalized. The names are written here in italics. For example, the scientific name for the Mantled Howler is *Alouatta palliata*, the genus is *Alouatta*, and the specific epithet is *palliata*. Both names constitute the species name. A subspecies is a population of a species that differs from another population of the same species. In most cases, intermediate forms of the two populations or subspecies can be found, suggesting interbreeding. "Subspecies" is the formal term for a geographic race of a species. Sometimes further study reveals that a subspecies is actually a separate species. In the case of the Mantled Howler, the subspecies *Alouatta palliata pigra* (abbreviated to *A. p. pigra*) was known from the Yucatán Peninsula, Mexico, based on the large size and dark color of the monkeys from this region. Subsequent studies indicated that these monkeys were distinct from other howler populations in Mexico and Central America, and where the two groups came together intermediate forms were not found, suggesting that they did not interbreed. The subspecies was then elevated to a species, the Yucatán Black Howler, *Alouatta pigra*. This case may reflect a trend that will be seen in many groups of mammals in Central America in the future, as more detailed studies of species and subspecies is likely to increase the known number of species and decrease the number of subspecies.

The reverse can also occur, as has happened with some squirrels in the region. The Variegated Squirrel, *Sciurus variegatoides*, varies enormously in color throughout its range (see Plates 20 and 21). When a few specimens were first examined by biologists, they assumed that each color pattern represented a distinct species. As more specimens became available and intermediate forms were found, the different populations were reclassified as subspecies within the species *S. variegatoides*. Scientific analyses of species limits are based on external morphology, internal morphology (particularly features of the skull and teeth), and, increasingly, on biochemical studies of chromosomes, DNA, and proteins.

Related species are placed in the same genus. These species share characteristics that are not found in other genera. Genera with features in common are grouped into families. For example, all the howler monkeys are in the genus *Alouatta*, and all the spider monkeys are in the genus *Ateles*. These and several other genera of monkeys are grouped in the Family Cebidae, based on shared, derived characters indicating a shared history. Other monkeys that do not share the same morphological features are placed in other families; for example, marmosets and tamarins are in the Callitrichidae. All the families of monkeys are grouped together in the Order Primates.

ACCOUNTS FOR ORDERS AND FAMILIES

The main text of this book consists of accounts for the orders, families, and species of mammals found in Central America and southeastern Mexico. The family and order accounts outline features common to all members of the group considered. In some cases, two or more families may be described together, or a subfamily of a large family may be described. Most family accounts include the dental formula (if it is highly variable within the family, it may be given in the genus summaries at the end of the family account). The dental formula is a short-hand enumeration of the number and types of teeth on one side of the jaw, with upper teeth/lower teeth. It contains the following abbreviations: incisors = i, canines = c, premolars = p, molars = m. Brief descriptions of genera follow the family or subfamily account for those families with several easily confused genera.

SPECIES ACCOUNTS

The bulk of the text consists of species accounts. The accounts are arranged taxonomically and contain the following information:

ENGLISH NAME   Plate #
Scientific name   Map #
Alternate English and regional names.

The English common name is given first. Many species have more than one common name, and some alternate English names are listed on the second line but are not used in text comparisons. I have tried to select the most widely used English name, derived from a number of different sources. Common names are not normally used by scientists for most small mammals, and I have made up a few names, or modified seldom-used or inappropriate names. When these species are referred to in other accounts, their scientific names are used, in addition to, or in place of, their common names. Scientific names change over time as more is learned about a species and its relationships with other species. The scientific names and taxonomy used in this book follow Wilson and Reeder (1993) for most species. Where I do not follow this source, justification and/or a reference is given in the "Comment" section. This section also lists scientific names that have been widely used in previous publications.

Alternate English names and examples of regional names are given in the following order: English names; Spanish names used in more than one country in the region; other local names and the country or indigenous group of origin, arranged from north to south, in Spanish, Creole English (for Belizean and Caribbean coastal names), or indigenous languages. Many of the Spanish names are derived from indigenous words for the animal and are not truly of Spanish origin. Only the more widely used local names are noted. Principal references for regional names include Aranda and March (1987); Marineros and Martínez Gallegos (1988); Méndez (1970); Mora and Moreira (1984).

The color plate and map numbers on which the species appears are indicated on the right.

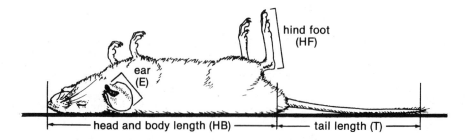

FIGURE 1. Measurements of small mammals.

MEASUREMENTS

The measurements use the following abbreviations:

HB: head and body length, measured from tip of nose to base of tail, with the animal in a flat, but not stretched position (see Figure 1).

T: length of tail, measured from base of tail to tip of last vertebra, not including tufts of hair at the tip.

HF: length of hind foot, measured from heel to tip of longest claw.

E: length of ear, measured from notch inside ear to tip.

SH: height at shoulder (given for some larger mammals only).

TL: total length (for marine mammals only) from tip of beak to notch in tail flukes (see Figure 2).

FA: length of forearm (for bats only), from elbow to wrist, measured on the dorsal surface with the wing closed.

Wt: weight of nonpregnant adults of the species, in grams (g), kilograms (kg), pounds (lb), or tons.

Unless otherwise indicated, length measurements are in millimeters (mm). Abbreviations for other units are meters (m), inches ("), feet (').

Figures 1 and 2 show the measurements and body parts of a rodent and a marine mammal. Note that many small mammals appear to have shorter bodies and relatively longer tails when alive than when laid out and measured, although for the squirrels and other hairy-tailed mammals, the reverse is true because the long hairs at the tip of the tail are not included in the tail measurement.

I have not been consistent in the measurements given throughout the book. For small mammals, the first four measurements listed above are noted, plus the weight (and forearm for bats). These are given in metric units only. For large mammals, head and body length, tail length, and weight are given, in both metric and nonmetric units (and shoulder height where appropriate). The rationale for this discrepancy is that many small mammals may be more easily identified by reference to hind foot and ear measurements, and since most of these species can only be identified when being hand-held, the body parts can be measured as easily in metric units as in nonmetric. Large mammals, on the other hand, are usually identified at a distance, and absolute measurements of ear or foot are seldom useful for identification. In these cases, it may be helpful to know that a species is about 2 feet at the shoulder, or that the tail is 8 inches

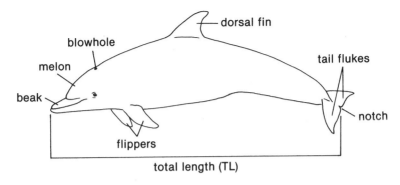

FIGURE 2. Measurements and parts of marine mammals.

long, and so both metric and nonmetric units are given (an average rather than a range of sizes is given in nonmetric units).

The measurements for small mammals were, with few exceptions, taken from a sample of 20 or more museum specimens, compiled directly from data on specimen tags written by the collector. Adult male and female specimens collected from several localities throughout the region covered by this book were used wherever possible. These measurements are on the conservative side: I did not include any individuals that might have been subadult or juvenile, any measurements that may have reflected collector error, or even in some cases measurements that just seemed odd (too large or too small). Therefore, the range of measurements given approximates the normal range of variation in adults of the species but may not include the extremes. Some mammals occur throughout a large geographic area and may be larger or smaller in other parts of their range, but wherever possible, measurements in this book are limited to individuals from Central America and southeastern Mexico. For a few small mammals and several species of larger mammals, measurements were taken from the literature.

Figure 3a illustrates the parts of a bat. All bat accounts include measurements of the forearm. This is the most useful field measurement and the easiest measurement to take accurately from a live animal. Additional measurements are given in some of the bat species accounts, including measurements of the calcar (the cartilage which extends from the ankle along the edge of the tail membrane) and the tibia (the leg bone between knee and ankle). Tibia measurements are taken by gently pressing the foot in toward the body and measuring, as shown in Figure 3e. Fur length may be helpful for identification and should be measured on the upper back or shoulder. Leaf-nosed bats are sometimes identified by details of the noseleaf, which consists of two parts, the spear and the horseshoe (Figure 3b). Free-tailed bats have a fold of skin at the base of the ear known as the antitragus, and the shape of this structure may be helpful in identification (Figure 3c). The tragus, a fold of skin inside the ear, is measured by some collectors; however, tragus length alone is seldom diagnostic and is not included in these accounts.

Measurements are given for adults only. It is important to distinguish juveniles from adults whenever possible. Young bats can be recognized by the appearance of the wing

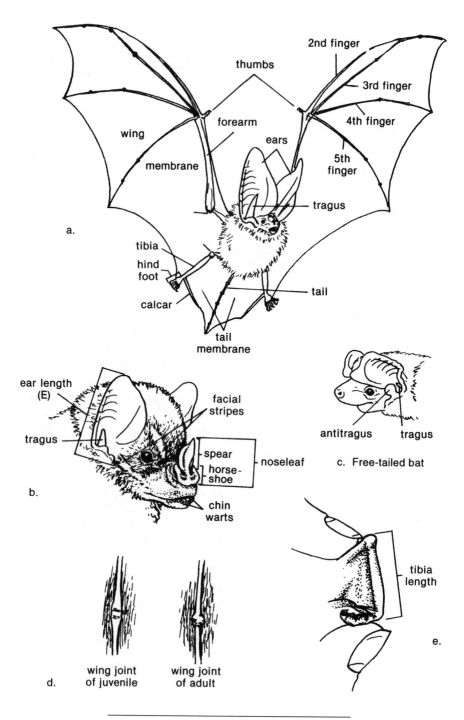

FIGURE 3. Measurements and parts of bats.

joints between finger bones: in adults the joints are knobby and not elongated; in juveniles the joints are smooth, elongated; and have a midsection of cartilage that appears transparent when held up to the light (Figure 3d). Young of most small mammals are grayer or darker in color than adults and have dull, fuzzy fur. Young of many mammals have disproportionately large heads and feet. A few species have distinctively colored young that are illustrated on color plates, but most are similar to or duller in color than the adults. Differences between males and females of most species of mammals in Central America are mainly in body size. Differences between sexes are outlined in the text or are illustrated in a few cases (for example, White-tailed Deer, *Odocoileus virginianus*, and howler monkeys, *Alouatta* spp.).

DESCRIPTION

This section describes the important external characteristics of the species. The first sentence is a thumbnail sketch, outlining the size, shape, or other salient features of the species. Descriptions of body color, face, tail, legs, and feet follow. Differences between the sexes, between juveniles and adults, and geographic variation are noted where appropriate. Subspecies are generally not named, although variation between populations of the species is discussed when it may cause problems in identification. The degree of detail given differs with the identification problems posed by the species. Generally, accounts are more detailed when there are a number of similar-looking species, as in most of the bats and rodents, and less detailed for many of the large-mammal accounts. The most important characteristics for identification of the species are italicized. **Similar Species.** This section considers only species that occur in the region covered by the book and only those that overlap in geographic range with the species in question.

DISTRIBUTION

The entire geographic range of the species is outlined. This statement complements the range map, which shows details of the range within Central America and southeastern Mexico only. Principal references for this section include Hall (1981) and Wilson and Reeder (1993). Other published information used in this section is usually cited, although some range maps may include data from museum specimens or unpublished field work. The known elevational range is given in meters (m). Entries that state "lowlands only" indicate that the species is found only below 500 m.

STATUS AND HABITAT

If a species has been listed by the Convention on International Trade in Endangered Species of Wild Flora and Fauna (CITES), the listing is given, followed by a note on whether the animal is abundant, common, locally common, uncommon, or rare. These are subjective terms; the relative abundance of a species should be considered within the context of the family to which it belongs. A Gray Fox (*Urocyon*) and a Mexican Deer Mouse (*Peromyscus mexicanus*) may both be listed as common, but there will not be as many Gray Foxes per square kilometer of suitable habitat as there are Mexican Deer Mice. The status of a species may also reflect its secretiveness or difficulty of capture, rather than its actual abundance. Shrews are seldom seen or trapped in Central America, but they are probably not uncommon. Some shrews are important components of the diet of owls, which seem to be more adept than people at finding these small mammals. Most species have a preferred habitat and may be more common in one habitat than another.

Habitat types referred to in this book are:

Thorn scrub and dry, deciduous forest.   Very dry, mainly lowland regions. The driest are characterized by cacti, agaves, and other thorny plants, while less arid regions have a low, open-canopy forest with mixed undergrowth including thorn brush and grass. These habitats are found in the central valleys of Chiapas, Guatemala, and Honduras, on the northwest coast of the Yucatán Peninsula, and along parts of the Pacific coast (see Plate 51). Patches of dry, deciduous forest may result from logging in deciduous regions.

Deciduous forest.   Forested regions with a long, pronounced dry season during which most trees lose their leaves. Trees are not very tall and do not form a closed canopy. Characteristic tree species include *Crescentia alata*, *Bombacopsis quinatum*, and *Enterolobium cyclocarpum*. Some of the plants in the understory and shrub levels may remain evergreen during the dry season. Woody vines are common, but other vines and epiphytes are sparse. Deciduous forests are found on the Pacific Slope from El Salvador to central Costa Rica and parts of Panama, and on the northern portion of the Yucatán Peninsula.

Semideciduous forest.   Forested regions with a shorter dry season than deciduous forests, during which some, but not all, trees lose their leaves. Trees are moderately tall and may form a closed canopy. There are some epiphytes and a dense shrub layer. This type of forest is found on the foothills of the Pacific Slope and in other regions where deciduous forest gives way to evergreen forest.

Evergreen forest.   Tall forest where most of the canopy trees are green throughout the year. Evergreen forest has several distinct layers: tall canopy trees, subcanopy trees, understory trees, shrubs, and undergrowth. Palms are common in the understory and shrub layers. In the Caribbean lowlands south of Honduras, rainfall follows a seasonal pattern, but there is no prolonged dry season as in the Pacific lowlands. Evergreen forest in these regions may be wet year-round. Characteristic trees of this very wet forest are *Pentaclethra macroloba* and *Pterocarpus officinalis*. Some areas on the Pacific Slope are subject to a short dry season but have heavy rainfall throughout the rest of the year and are covered by tall, wet evergreen forest. Examples are found in southern Costa Rica and southeastern Panama. Patches of evergreen or semi-deciduous forest may be found within otherwise dry regions along rivers or in low-lying areas. I have not used the term "rainforest," which includes both evergreen and semievergreen forest and is sometimes used to describe any tropical forest.

Mangroves.   Mangroves are found in several coastal regions, mainly on the Pacific coast. Mangroves consist of a few tree species (*Rhizophora* and others) with characteristic aerial roots that can survive in soil inundated with salt water.

Disturbed forest.   Most forests in the region have been altered by humans at some time, and "virgin" or "primary" forest is unlikely to be encountered. Forests may also be greatly altered by natural events such as hurricanes. Tall forest with an unbroken canopy is considered to be a climax forest and is referred to in the text as *mature forest.* Forest that has been selectively logged, or that was logged some time ago but now contains some tall trees is called *secondary forest.* This forest is generally lower, with a denser understory, than mature forest. *Second growth* is an earlier stage of regeneration, often in an area that was entirely cut over. The tallest trees are fast-growing species such as *Cecropia* and *Ochroma* spp., which are scattered among dense, viney shrubs. *Gallery forest* refers to strips of forest along rivers in areas that are otherwise mostly open. This type of forest is natural in savannahs of South America, but it is a result of deforestation in Central America. *Lowland pine forest*, with scattered pines, low palms, and grassy areas, predominates in central Belize and parts of Honduras. *Open woodland* is a rather dry habitat resulting from disturbance of deciduous forest (although in parts of northwestern Costa Rica, a dry, open woodland may be natural on some soils).

Highland forest.   A number of forest types are found in highland regions. *Cloud forest* is a term used for forests perpetually enshrouded in cloud. Although no forest is always in such a state, this is a convenient description for the cool, moist broadleaf forests that predominate on mountain slopes between about 1000 and 2000 m. Drier forest is found on some slopes. From Honduras northward, dry mountain slopes are usually clothed in *coniferous forest*, primarily pines or firs. Montane forest, at about 2000–3000 m elevation, may be coniferous on dry slopes and broadleaf on wet slopes. *Montane oak forest* contains huge *Quercus* oaks, numerous ferns and epiphytes, and is very wet and cold. Mountain tops, although sometimes not at high elevations, may be covered by *elfin forest*, which consists of stunted, gnarled trees, mosses, bamboo, and other shrubs.

Páramo.   Above the treeline on the highest mountains in the region, cold, open areas with grasses, bamboo, and shrubs occur. The northernmost extension of Andean Páramo is found in the Talamanca mountains of Costa Rica. Vegetation on the high peaks of Guatemala and Chiapas appears similar to true páramo, but is often the result of deforestation.

Savannah and grassland.   Most of the grassland in Central America is man-made and is maintained by grazing, clearing, and burning. Much of the original deciduous forest has been converted to pasture for beef cattle.

Swamps and marshes. Swamps are flooded areas in forests; marshes are wet areas in open habitats.

Agricultural areas. Included in this general category are croplands (such as corn, sugar cane, and cotton), plantations (such as coffee, African oil palm, and banana), and pastures.

Gardens and urban parks. Suburban gardens, hotel grounds, city parks, and similar areas may have scattered tall trees and various shrub plantings.

All habitat designations are approximate and merge into one another to some degree. For more information on specific forest types in Central America, see Hartshorn (1983).

HABITS

This section gives information on the behavior and ecology of the species. The time of day the animal is active, the place in which it may be seen (if arboreal, the height it prefers in the trees), and the types of movements usually seen are described. Its den, roost, or nest is described and diet outlined. Social behavior, including whether it is found in groups or alone, the calls likely to be heard, and breeding biology of the species are noted. The habits of many mammals are poorly known, so this section may be brief.

WHERE TO SEE

This section is not included for all species. It is based almost entirely on my own experiences in Central America and southeastern Mexico and so is strongly biased toward places where I have spent the most time. Localities where the species in question may be easily seen are given. Details of the sites may be found in the Introduction, in the section "Where to find mammals." Populations of mammals change from year to year, with or without human interference; therefore, the places listed may not be ideal sites for the species in the future. This section may include some tips about how to locate the species in the wild.

COMMENT

This section outlines taxonomic changes, previous scientific names, and other differences of opinion of a mainly taxonomic nature. If the name used in the account is different from that of Wilson and Reeder (1993), the standard taxonomic reference for my book, the rationale will be explained here and a reference given where possible.

References to scientific publications are given, primarily in the "Habits" and "Comment" sections, and sometimes in the "Distribution" section. The author's name and date can be looked up in the bibliography at the back of the book for the full citation. Not all sources used in the accounts are cited, and some general references for a group of mammals are given under the family or order accounts and not repeated when used in species accounts. Some references are given mainly to provide additional sources of reference for the reader (as in many of the Mammalian Species accounts cited, which seldom contain original research, but do have extensive bibliographies). A reference is cited only once in an account, even if several pieces of information from the same reference are used in different sections of the account.

RANGE MAPS

The geographic scope of the book is from the Isthmus of Tehuantepec, Mexico, to the Panama/Colombia border. This includes all the countries of Central America and the Mexican states of Tabasco, Chiapas, Campeche, Quintana Roo, and Yucatán (Plate 49). Range maps are given for this region only. The text section "Distribution" gives the entire range of the species. Four base maps are used: the entire region, the Yucatán region, the northwestern Pacific region, and the southern region. For each species the range is indicated by shading (a dot is used only when the species is known from a single locality). The scale of the maps does not allow an entirely accurate picture of the range. Areas with unsuitable habitat for the species may be shaded, although I have tried to eliminate montane regions from the ranges of strictly lowland species, and vice versa. Where a species has not yet been recorded from a broad area but is expected to occur there based on its presence elsewhere, a question mark is shown on the map. Arrows on the map indicate a discontinuous distribution of the species north or south of the region mapped.

COLOR PLATES

Plates are arranged roughly by taxonomic order, although some unrelated groups are combined based on space and design considerations. Within families of mammals, species are grouped by size and similarity, not always by taxonomic relatedness. The species on a plate are drawn to scale with one another unless a line appears on the plate, in which case two scales are used. Almost all the small mammals were illustrated directly from live animals in the field. The remainder were based on museum specimens, sketches, and photographs.

INTRODUCTION

HOW TO FIND MAMMALS

Mammals are not always easy to see in natural conditions, and some are extremely elusive. Although mammal watchers will not have the same success as birdwatchers in terms of numbers of individuals or species seen, there are ways to increase one's chances of seeing mammals in their natural environment. This chapter is a summary of some of the tricks of the trade.

EQUIPMENT　The basic piece of equipment for mammal-watching is a pair of good binoculars. Because diurnal mammals are almost always more active at dawn and dusk, and most species in the region live in forests where light levels are low at those hours, choose a pair of binoculars that have good light-gathering capacity. At night, when binoculars are used in combination with flashlights, the light-gathering capacity is even more critical. I use a Zeiss 7 × 42, close-focusing model; many other brands with a magnification of 7 or 8 and a wide angle are also acceptable. Compact, mini-binoculars are generally not very useful for mammal-watching, as the field of view is small and the brightness is low. Binoculars, a pocket notebook and pencil (and of course, this guide!) are all the equipment you need for daytime trips.

The majority of Neotropical mammals are nocturnal. A few of these species can be found at their daytime sleeping sites, but most are best observed when active, during the night. To find mammals at night, a headlamp is an indispensable piece of equipment. You soon get used to looking like a coal miner, and the advantages of a headlamp over a hand-held flashlight are enormous. First, both hands are free (great for untangling bats from mist nets, setting up tents after dark, or fighting off Jaguars). Second, the light moves with your eyes, and the night becomes less spooky and alien as a result; and third and most important, you can see eyeshine of mammals. The eyes of nocturnal mammals have a reflective surface in front of the retina which causes their eyes to appear to glow when a light is shone at them (they do not glow in the dark). The glow is only visible to the onlooker if the light source is close to the onlooker's eyes. If the mammal has highly reflective eyes, eyeshine may be seen even when the light comes from a hand-held flashlight or a car headlight, but for small mammals or those with less reflective eyes, many will be missed if a headlamp is not used.

Headlamps can be bought at most stores for campers or spelunkers, or through catalogs for biological supplies. There are numerous models to choose from. I prefer the Justrite brand, which holds four D-cell batteries in a pack that clips onto a belt. Other models have the battery pack on the head strap; these usually take fewer batteries and are less powerful, or the power is short-lived. Unless you are willing to carry a large supply of batteries on a field trip, it is best to get a headlamp that takes a widely available battery. Spend the extra money for long-life, alkaline batteries. Your light will be much brighter and you are less likely to end up lost in the dark, far from camp. Of course, it is a good idea to always carry a second flashlight, or mini-light, in case the bulb or batteries of your headlamp expire during the night.

There are a few headlamps that use rechargeable batteries. These may be cheaper and more ecologically acceptable, but they have two disadvantages: electrical power is not always available or adequate for recharging, and, when the battery power runs low, the light fades out completely in a matter of minutes, whereas other batteries usually give you time to get out of the woods before they die out entirely. Solar rechargers may be useful, especially for long-term studies in areas without electricity.

Some mammal watchers rely entirely on headlamps at night, and I have spent many hours out at night with only a headlamp and seen numerous mammals. In tall forest, however, a second, more powerful light is very useful. A handheld flashlight or lantern that has a halogen or xenon bulb and a narrow beam can produce a powerful spotlight, allowing a better view of a mammal in the canopy. The most powerful lights are the Q-Beams and related spotlights, which may be powered by car batteries (through the cigarette lighter attachment) or with "portable" batteries. These rechargeable batteries weigh about 5 kg (12 lb), which is a bit daunting on long hikes, but the light power is terrific. I use either a Q-Beam with its hefty battery or a lantern that takes four D-cells and has a xenon bulb and a highly focused spot beam. It is important to use the second light *only* when you have already spotted eyeshine reflected by your headlamp. You do not want to illuminate the entire forest, scare off distant mammals, or run down the spotlight batteries; the brighter light is also more of a hindrance than an aid for finding eyeshine. A headlamp will keep your eyes more night-adapted than the spotlight, and you will get the full benefit of the spotlight's power if it is used only sporadically. For night trips you will need binoculars, of course. They are easily used in conjunction with a headlamp if the light beam is angled slightly downward. Holding the beam of a large spotlight on a distant mammal while focusing with binoculars takes a little practice, but it can be done.

A red filter used with the light causes less disturbance to mammals and can be helpful when observing small mammals at close range. I have not found red lights very useful for night walks, as the light intensity is much reduced and eyeshine of some species may be missed.

Some mammals are attracted to certain sounds. Predators may investigate distress calls of smaller mammals and can sometimes be seen by using an Audubon Bird Call or a hunter's whistle. The "spishing" sound made by birdwatchers, a rough imitation of a young bird's distress call, sometimes attracts weasels. The effectiveness of whistles and calls is highly variable, and they seldom bring large and elusive predators into view. A tape recorder can be used to record sounds made by mammals. If the calls are played back to the mammal, it may approach more closely, call more, or it may leave. Good-quality recordings of poorly known mammals should be copied and sent to the Cornell Sound Library in Ithaca, New York, if possible.

Bat detectors are modified transducers that make the bats' ultrasonic echolocation calls audible to humans. Models that faithfully record all the variation in pitch given by the bat are excellent but expensive. Cheaper models are sensitive to a narrower frequency band (they can be adjusted to respond to high, middle range, or lower frequencies). They will not pick up all wavelengths at one time, but they can be interesting to use. Near a wet area, cave mouth, or on a forest trail, one can pick up the calls of a number of bat species with a detector. It is even more interesting to use a detector in a place where the calling bat can be identified. Several species of sac-winged bats roost in fairly exposed areas and are active when there is sufficient natural light to allow their movements to be followed while they call. Males often sing and display to females before leaving to feed at dusk, or when settling in at the roost at dawn (some of the calls are audible, but more are heard with a detector). Fishing bats (*Noctilio*) sometimes hunt near lights of boat docks, as the light attracts small fish and stimulates them to break the surface of the water. When the bats fly in these illuminated areas, a bat detector enables one to both see and hear them home in on prey, their calls speeding up as they rake the water.

GETTING AROUND   Mammals can be seen when on foot or horseback, by car, or by boat. Walking gives greater access to most areas where mammals are found. One person will see more mammals than a group of people, but even groups can see mammals. Although many biologists and ecotourists select khaki or camouflage-style clothes, I do not think color of clothing has much effect on most mammals. Many mammals are color-blind and rely on their senses of smell and hearing at least as much as vision. Appropriate clothing should be lightweight, strong, and fast drying. Keeping quiet and still is more important than any dress requirement. Mammals appear to be less threatened by humans if they remain motionless. A Tayra (*Eira*), Gray Fox (*Urocyon*), or group of Collared Peccaries (*Tayassu tajacu*) may give every indication of being aware of your presence, but will walk calmly by, keeping their eyes on you, if you do not move. The slightest movement will cause most mammals to flee. By standing absolutely still, not only have I had good views of mammals as they walked close by me, but I have had a Northern Tamandua (*Tamandua mexicana*) step on my feet and start to climb my legs, a Variegated Squirrel (*Sciurus variegatoides*) jump onto my head from a fence post, and a Paca (*Agouti paca*) sniff my shoes. Walking slowly and quietly, stopping frequently to look and listen for mammals, and freezing when a mammal is sighted will allow the best views of many different species, both during the day and at night.

Boats and canoes can be excellent means of traveling in search of mammals. Many species that occur chiefly high in the forest canopy are found lower in trees along waterways. During the dry season, especially in deciduous forest, wildlife concentrates along forested streams and rivers. Trees along rivers may remain evergreen during the dry season, providing an important food source for some species. Howler monkeys, sloths, squirrels, and otters may be seen during the day. At night, (with a powerful spotlight) a canoe or motor boat should be helpful for finding several species of opossum (especially Gray Four-eyed Opossums, *Philander opossum*), Kinkajous (*Potos*), Olingos (*Bassaricyon*), Pacas (*Agouti*), Mexican Porcupines (*Coendou*), and other species. Rivers and small streams can also be explored on foot. It is usually easiest to get in a shallow stream and walk along the stream bed, rather than try to keep on the bank. At night a forested stream or creek can be the best place to find small mammals. It can be slightly unnerving to wade through dark water of varying depths, but no great health risks are involved unless the water is stagnant. Be aware that the water will rise rapidly if there is a storm upriver.

Driving narrow roads or trails is a good way to cover a broad area when looking for mammals, especially the larger species. At night, a Q-Beam or other strong spotlight is necessary. One person should lean out of the window or sit on top of the car so that the light can be held close to their eyes (to detect eyeshine) and directed in front of the vehicle, illuminating tree branches and the ground on both sides of the road. Keep a flashlight available so you can quickly follow mammals that dash into the brush. Obtain permission from landowners or park personnel before spotlighting, and check locally regarding personal safety.

FRUITING AND FLOWERING TREES   Many Neotropical mammals are fruit eaters, and a few hours spent sitting under a fruiting tree can be more worthwhile than a day-long hike. Trees that are visited by a variety of birds during the day often attract mammals at night. Good trees to check when fruiting are figs, *Cecropia*, *Inga*, and *Dipteryx* spp., although numerous other species are visited by mammals. Some mammals such as agoutis (*Dasyprocta* spp.) and Paca (*Agouti*) listen for the sounds of falling fruit and may appear if one climbs a tree and drops stones at intervals (dropping pieces of banana or other edible fruit instead of stones may give visiting mammals reason to stay around longer). Some mammals feed on nectar, and others may be attracted to flowering trees to feed on the insects or bats pollinating the tree. During the day, monkeys and squirrels may be found in flowering trees. At night, Olingos (*Bassaricyon*), Kinkajous (*Potos*), Woolly Opossums (*Caluromys*) and Night Monkeys (*Aotus*) may feed on nectar in flowering balsa (*Ochroma*) and other trees. Many trees flower and fruit during the dry season, when fallen leaves make it difficult to walk quietly. By sitting near a food source, you can hear approaching mammals but they may not hear you, and so you may have excellent views of shy species.

WATER HOLES   Almost all mammals drink water. Some may obtain sufficient water from their food to drink only rarely, and others may drink from small pools of water collected in leaves or flowers in the canopy, but most find water on the ground. During the dry season, many water supplies dry up and the remaining sources are heavily used and can be excellent places to see mammals. This is particularly true in dry, deciduous regions such as the Pacific Slope lowlands, but it also applies to areas with evergreen forest on a limestone substrate, such as the southern portion of the Yucatán Peninsula and northern Guatemala, where standing water is limited. Specific localities of certain water holes are given in the next chapter. Dawn is often *not* the best time to sit and wait for

17

mammals at a water hole. Later in the morning (8–10 AM) can be a good time, but late afternoon is usually best. Keeping watch for an hour or so after sunset can also be worthwhile. White-faced Capuchins, White-nosed Coatis, White-tailed Deer, Collared Peccaries, and Central American Agoutis are frequently seen at water holes.

GARBAGE DUMPS Although not very pleasant places to spend time, some dumps can be worth visiting at night. Most national parks and lodges dig small holes for garbage and food waste in areas surrounded by natural vegetation. After dark, these sites will undoubtedly attract opossums (especially *Didelphis* spp.) and are good places to find skunks, raccoons, foxes, and sometimes spider monkeys or Ocelots.

BAITING MAMMALS Mammals can be attracted to an area by leaving food for them, although in some regions (especially lowland evergreen forest) ants will quickly clear away most of the food. Large piles of fruit or corn should be left every day for several days with minimal disturbance. When tracks and other signs of activity are evident, the area can be watched from a nearby tree or hide of some kind (climbing a fallen tree or branch is often quicker and easier than setting up a hide). Small rodents will often come to piles of seeds. They are usually shy and nocturnal and so can be difficult to observe even when attracted to a food source. Occasionally, a ready supply of food prompts a nocturnal species to become active during the day. I have seen pocket mice (*Heteromys* spp.) collecting seeds in the middle of the afternoon, and in Monteverde, Costa Rica, an Olingo regularly visits hummingbird feeders during the day. This individual has learned to leap onto the feeder and lap up the nectar that spills out as the feeder sways from side to side. Most baiting efforts are best if carried out for an extended period, but this practice can result in the animals' dependence on the food source. For several years scientists on Barro Colorado Island, Panama, provided food for Baird's Tapirs (the food supply attracted spider monkeys and coatis also). When feeding was discontinued, some of the animals starved.

TRACKS AND SIGNS Looking for and identifying tracks is the most practical way of assessing the presence of many large mammals. Finding areas with tracks also provides clues as to the preferred habitat and habits of the mammal. In wet forest, tracks are easily found along trails, in ditches, near streams, and so forth. In dry areas, look for tracks in dusty ground, near any sources of water, or in loose dirt on roadsides. A tray filled with sand and smoothed over every day will give a record of mammals passing by. If bait (for cats, urine of other cats is more effective than meat) is placed nearby, additional species may be recorded. Not all tracks are easy to identify. By following the path of the tracks, a clear and typical print may be found. Before touching the track, make a rough sketch of the shape. Measurements of the width and length can then be taken, and the track can be preserved in several ways.

The easiest method to preserve a track was described by Emmons (1990). A sheet of acetate paper or mylar is put over the track and the outline traced. Tracing over this outline onto tracing paper will reduce the possibility of smudges. Shallow tracks on a hard surface can be accurately recorded in this way, although tracks in deeper mud will be distorted if only the surface impression is noted. Mixing up a solution of plaster of

Paris (dental quality is best) and pouring this into the track will provide a more detailed record. Tracks of larger mammals are given opposite the color plates in this book. Shape and measurements of tracks taken in the field can be compared with those shown here.

Even if perfect-looking tracks are found and recorded, they may not be easy to identify. Young animals make smaller tracks than adults, tracks appear larger or smaller depending on the surface (tracks in deep, wet mud look very different from those made on nearly dry mud), and tracks differ as the gait of the mammal changes. Footprints may often overlap and produce what looks like a single track. Nevertheless, with experience, many species can be identified from their tracks. Excellent references for tracks and tracking are Aranda Sánchez (1981) and Murie (1974). The latter North American guide covers most of the larger species in Central America.

DENS, NESTS, AND BURROWS Some mammals can be found by searching for their homes. Burrows in the ground should be examined carefully. Fresh dirt near the entrance, fresh tracks or trails, and hairs in the rim of the burrow indicate recent or active use, while cobwebs across the opening or leaves on the floor of the burrow indicate abandonment. Hairs and tracks may help identify the burrow owner. Smoothing the surface or adding loose dirt may help in obtaining clearer tracks of the occupant. Small, rodent-sized burrows may belong to land crabs, tarantulas, or puffbirds. If you find a burrow that appears to be in active use by an unknown mammal, wait near the burrow at dusk to see the animal emerge. A more radical approach used by hunters is to block up all the exits and put smoking wood into the burrow to smoke out the animal.

Hollow trees and branches are frequently used as sleeping sites by mammals. During the day, a flashlight is useful for examining hollows. Of course, not all residents of hollows are furry: snakes, ants, bees, and wasps also occupy hollows. Some mammals such as porcupines return every day to the same hollow, and their droppings accumulate at the base in a characteristic (and odoriferous) manner. The whereabouts of dens or roosts may be known to park guards and other local people. Nests of mammals are usually well concealed; they may be in hollow trees or under logs, but some are located in vine tangles and other dense vegetation. Squirrels make familiar leaf nests that are easily seen in dry, open forest but are inconspicuous in tall, evergreen forest.

BAT ROOSTS Bats are difficult to identify at night, but many species can be seen, and some can be identified, at their daytime roost. Sac-winged bats roost in relatively exposed situations such as the junction under a thick branch and the trunk of a large tree, under a chunk of loose bark, or on rocks near water. These bats can often be examined through binoculars without an additional light source. Many species in the Neotropics use hollow trees for roosts, and some favor large, hollow, horizontal logs. Some of the tailless, leaf-nosed bats create a "tent" from a large leaf by chewing the veins of the leaf so that the sides collapse. These tents can be found easily with practice. They are most numerous and diverse in evergreen, lowland forest. Palms of several varieties are used, especially those with fishtail- or fan-shaped leaves. Heliconia and banana, some arums, philodendron, and melastome leaves are also used for tents. To find tents, look for live, green leaves that are hanging in an odd way. Leaf surfaces usually project horizontally to maximize light gathering, but when modified into a tent, most of the leaf surface hangs vertically. Only about 1 in 10 tents found will contain bats. Some bats are extremely wary in tents and fly out when approached, but most will stay in the tent if the surrounding vegetation is not disturbed. A flashlight and binoculars are useful for identifying bats in their tents. Other places to look for bats are in small depressions among the complex trunks of fig trees, under overhanging vegetation on banks, and in culverts under roads. Bats often use a different roost during the night. The undersides of bridges that are unoccupied by day should be checked again at night. In the daytime, some species of bats may be found clustered into dark corners under one end of the bridge, while at night other species may be found hanging anywhere under the bridge. Caves, mine tunnels, and cenotes (sinkholes in limestone substrate) may be used by day, as are modern and ancient buildings, especially Maya ruins. Termite nests, woodpecker holes in coconut palm trees, and unmodified leaves are also used as roosts. Groups of bats often betray their presence by squeaking before they emerge from an inconspicuous opening at dusk. Roost entrances are usually marked by dark stains of urine or feces.

STUDYING MAMMALS

In Mexico and all Central American countries, permits are legally required for any mammal-related activity other than observation. Live mammals cannot be trapped and released, bones or road-killed mammals cannot be collected, and wild animals cannot be marked without special permits. Scientific justification, university affiliation (both within and outside the country of study), payment of a fee, and other conditions may be necessary for a successful permit application. Collecting permits usually require that a portion of the specimens collected remain in the host country.

CATCHING BATS   Bats can be easily seen at night in most lowland regions, but most are difficult to identify in flight. Many species can be found at their day roost and observed without causing them much disturbance. To fully appreciate the incredible diversity and abundance of bats in lowland forest, however, one needs to catch bats in mist nets or other specialized traps. Mist nets for bats are the same as those used for birds. They are not easily obtained and are only available to institutions such as museums or universities and their affiliates. It is helpful to learn about bats and bat netting from someone with experience. An excellent source of information for the prospective bat netter is Kunz (1988). Nets set over water, across streams or trails, near roosts, or around fruiting trees will be effective in lowland forest. Some species of bats may be attracted by distress calls of other bats (the loud squeaks given by captive *Artibeus*, for example), insect trills, Audubon Bird Calls, or hunters' whistles. Recordings of these sounds can be played near mist nets to increase the number and diversity of bats caught. Raising nets well above ground (using ropes or pulleys) may catch a different array of species than those caught at ground level. Bat diversity is greatest in mature evergreen forest in the lowlands, but large numbers can also be found in secondary or deciduous forest and in forested regions of the foothills and middle elevations. Only a few bat species occur in montane forest.

Bats can also be caught in hand nets used for insects, or in a hand net constructed from coat hangers and a portion of an old mist net. Harp traps can be useful for small bats with highly developed echolocation systems. These traps are free-standing structures with two or more rows of closely spaced wires or monofilament line attached to a frame, with a bag suspended below the wires. Bats navigate through the first set of wires but often hit the second set and fall into the bag. Most harp traps are not easily carried and set up by one person.

Bats can be safely carried in soft cloth bags with drawstring tops. Even if bats are to be released soon after capture, they should be offered food and water. Fruit-eating bats will usually accept a piece of banana; nectar feeders will take sugar water or fruit juice from a spoon or eyedropper; insectivorous bats are often difficult to feed, but may take katydids, cockroaches, or other insects.

TRAPPING SMALL MAMMALS To identify and study most species of small mammals other than bats, it is usually necessary to catch them in live traps so that they can be examined in the hand. This is not to say that small mammals cannot be observed under natural conditions. Many arboreal mice and opossums are more easily seen than trapped, and some terrestrial species can also be observed without too much difficulty. Trapping, however, provides an opportunity to become familiar with a variety of species, so that they can be more easily identified in the field, and it is the best way to find the more secretive species. Permits are needed to set traps throughout Mexico and Central America, regardless of whether or not specimens will be retained.

The most practical traps to use are folding Sherman live traps. They are relatively light and portable and are usually effective. Locally made live traps can also be useful but are not as compact as Sherman traps. Larger wire traps, such as Havahart or Tomahawk traps, work well for slightly larger mammals. To catch a number of different species, traps should be set in different situations: on the ground and in trees or vines (secure traps with string on branches) in forest, in second growth and forest edge, in open, grassy areas, and near water. Avoid areas where people pass by because the traps may be stolen. Also avoid fields with cows, as cows invariably step on traps. Baits containing fruit (such as fresh or dried banana) are best for traps sent in trees or vines. On the ground, sunflower seeds, peanut butter, oats, corn, bacon, banana, and dried or burnt coconut can be used in various combinations.

To be a good mouse trapper, one must think like a mouse, anticipating likely corridors of movement, refuges, and so on. Mice avoid predators by keeping close to cover. They do cross open areas, but spend much more time near or under shelter. Therefore, traps set under fallen logs and near rocks or tree buttresses will be more effective than those placed in the open. Arboreal species will be more likely to travel along a vine that connects two trees than along a vine that dips to the ground, and a fallen log across a stream may be a runway for both terrestrial and arboreal species. Despite the generally high level of biodiversity in mature, lowland evergreen forest, trap success for small rodents is often poor in these regions, particularly in the wetter Caribbean Slope forests. Rodent populations and species diversity are often higher in deciduous forest, dry scrub, or second growth than in lowland evergreen forest. Cool, wet highland forests are usually excellent for rat trapping.

21

Trap sites should be marked with flagging tape so the traps can be retrieved easily. They should be baited in the late afternoon and checked early in the morning. If you do not release your catch immediately, the animals should be provided with food, bedding (cotton or paper towels are fine) and a source of water (a piece of cabbage or slice of raw potato provides sufficient water for a day). Animals not retained for museum specimens should be released at the place of capture as soon as possible. Their behavior on release can be informative; some will go directly to a burrow, others may climb a nearby branch. Most mice behave differently when released at night as opposed to when they are released during the day. They are less likely to run off in a seemingly random panic if it is dark and can often be watched for some time as they wander around or feed.

Some small mammals, such as shrews, are not easily captured in mousetraps. They are more likely to be caught in pitfalls. Pitfall traps are made by digging a hole for a smooth-sided container. The container is sunk so that the rim is below the surface of the ground or leaf litter. A small board suspended a few centimeters above the trap (use nails or stones to leave a gap between trap and board) may increase trap success. Shrews often run under boards, and the board will shield the trap from rainwater. In tropical forest, the best place for pitfall traps is at the base or sides of fallen logs or other natural runways. Artificial runways or drift fences can be constructed by placing planks on their sides, leading to the trap. Drift fences usually increase trap success. Vessels used for pitfalls need to be quite deep, so the animals cannot escape, and should have holes punched near the base to drain out rainwater. Shrews often die when left in a pitfall trap overnight; therefore, these traps should only be used by scientific collectors with the necessary permits. If pitfall traps are to be ued for ecological studies involving releae and recapture of marked animals, the traps should be checked at intervals throughout the night.

Specialized traps are also required to catch pocket gophers. Leg-hold traps are commonly used, which usually do not kill the gopher, but often cause trauma to the trapped limb. These traps should only be used by scientific collectors.

THE NEED FOR FURTHER RESEARCH

Despite considerable interest in the fauna of Central America and southeastern Mexico, the mammals remain poorly known in many respects. There have been few long-term studies of ecology or behavior of most species, especially of the small mammals, in the region. Detailed ecological studies of bats have been conducted for only two species, Seba's Short-tailed Bat (*Carollia perspicillata*) and Jamaican Fruit-eating Bat (*Artibeus jamaicensis*). Basic information is lacking for a number of common and widespread bats; for example, the roosts of yellow-shouldered bats (*Sturnira* spp.) are unknown. Several larger species such as Kinkajous, Olingos, and most of the squirrels warrant studies of ecology, population dynamics, and behavior.

In addition to studies of individual species, complete inventories of mammal species are available for only a few sites in the region, in southeastern Mexico (Selva Lacandona), Costa Rica (La Selva), and Panama (Barro Colorado Island). Basic inventories are essential for assessing conservation priorities in areas threatened with development.

Taxonomic studies have been conducted for a number of groups, and several studies are under way. Further work on biogeography and systematics is needed for various small rodents (for example, *Tylomys, Oryzomys,* and *Peromyscus*) and shrews. Museum collections are an integral part of taxonomic studies, and the collection of new material throughout the region, particularly in less well known areas, is essential. The number of species recognized in Central America and southeastern Mexico will undoubtedly increase as more comprehensive collections are developed and the material obtained is studied using modern systematic methods. Even basic taxonomic information for larger mammals such as the number of species of howler monkeys or olingos in Central America is unresolved.

WHERE TO FIND MAMMALS

Some good sites for finding mammals in the region are described in this section. The text is biased toward the countries and sites within those countries where I have spent the most time. This section may be expanded in future editions, and any comments or input from readers would be most welcome.

Mammals can be found in all but the most urban or most disturbed parts of Central America, but to find a good diversity of species, natural habitats and parks or reserves should be explored. Unprotected natural habitat can be found (although it is dwindling rapidly), mostly in small patches throughout the region, and a few mammals such as howlers, squirrels, sloths, and Kinkajous may be seen if hunting pressure is low. Many species of mammals occur at low density or they are extremely wary (and thus appear rare) in unprotected areas, and some, such as spider monkeys, agoutis, deer, and Pacas, may be strongly affected or even locally eliminated by hunting. Parks and reserves provide natural habitat and protection from hunting and thus are better places to find mammals.

National parks in Central America and southeastern Mexico range in size from tiny, well-protected areas such as Manuel Antonio National Park, Costa Rica, to extensive wilderness in Darién National Park, Panama. Several large mammal species, such as Baird's Tapir, Jaguar, and White-lipped Peccary, only occur in the larger parks and reserves. These areas are often difficult to visit, and the results of a visit may be disappointing. Indigenous groups may be permitted to hunt (or local hunting may not be controlled due to an insufficient number of park guards), so many medium-sized and large mammals will be wary and difficult to see, although their tracks may be found. Smaller parks and reserves usually do not contain sufficient habitat for "wilderness" species, but often contain an array of medium-sized and small mammals that may be easily seen. These small areas are often well protected, and the mammals may be habituated to humans, so that sightings of both numbers of individuals and numbers of species are higher than in most large parks.

In the northern part of the region, numerous Maya sites can be found. Many of these have some protected forest around them and can be very good for sighting mammals (some are described in more detail below). Forget the artifacts of ancient cultures and explore the buildings for the bats that currently occupy them. Most Maya sites can only be entered at night by special permission or with a scientific collecting permit.

The following regional guide gives information on some of the larger or more accessible parks and reserves and includes all areas mentioned in the "Where to see" section of the species accounts. Principal parks and reserves mentioned are mapped on Plate 50 (small parks and Maya sites are not mapped). An excellent reference to parks in Central America is Wallace (1995).

Southeastern Mexico

Chiapas State

Palenque. This Maya site is surrounded by tall evergreen forest and is a good place (the most accessible in Mexico) to see Yucatán Black Howlers, both around the ruins and on the grounds of the local campground. Small, brown Deppe's Squirrels (*Sciurus deppei*) are fairly common, while the strikingly colored Mexican Gray Squirrels (*S. aureogaster*), with gray heads and rumps and deep red shoulders and bellies (the all-black squirrels are also of this species), are shy and difficult to see. Numerous bats roost in the ruins or in nearby caves and hollows: above the sarcophagus there may be a colony of Common Mustached Bats (*Pteronotus parnellii*). The stream crossing the site can be followed upriver to a waterfall that has a cavern behind it; several species of leaf-nosed bats may be here. For scientific permit holders, Palenque is also a good place to trap rodents, both in the forest and in grassy areas nearby.

Montes Azules Biosphere Reserve. This reserve in the Selva Lacandona of eastern Chiapas contains the most extensive lowland evergreen forest in Mexico. The Chajul Biological Station is located in the reserve; the Maya sites of Yaxchilán and Bonampak are nearby. Montes Azules is the northernmost refuge for viable populations of several large mammals such as White-lipped Peccary, Baird's Tapir, and Jaguar. Medellín (1994) recorded 112 species of mammals here, most of which were found near the Chajul Biological Station.

El Triunfo Ecological Reserve. Located in the Sierra Madre del Sur, El Triunfo is one of several interesting highland sites in Chiapas. Access is difficult; there is a very rough road to Prusia from the central valley, and from Prusia one may have to walk 8 km uphill to the reserve. Most visitors to El Triunfo come in search of highland birds such as Horned Guan and Resplendent Quetzal, but the reserve is also home to mammals that favor cool evergreen forest. Many rodents, bats, and shrews have been recorded here; larger mammals include Red Brocket, Mexican Porcupines, and Whitenosed Coatis. Among the more interesting nocturnal mammals are Cacomistles, which may be heard or seen at night.

ZOOMAT. This zoo, located on the edge of Tuxtla Gutiérrez, is one of the best in the Neotropics. Established by Miguel Alvarez del Toro, the zoo houses only species native to Chiapas. The attractive layout and natural habitats in and around the enclosures provide good photographic opportunities. Mantled Howlers, Mexican Gray Squirrels, and Central American Agoutis roam freely on the zoo grounds. This zoo has been the center for conservation and ecological studies of several Mexican mammals.

Tabasco State

Unfortunately, most of the natural habitats of Tabasco have been destroyed in the development of agricultural lands. Viable populations of manatees have been reported from along the Usumacinta River in the vicinity of Emiliano Zapata (Colmenero-R., 1986), and other semiaquatic mammals such as the Water Opossum (*Chironectes minimus*) may occur in this region.

Campeche State

Campeche has a lower population density than most states of Mexico and has some fairly extensive forest. Central American Spider Monkeys can be found in patches of mangroves along the coast, and Yucatán Black Howlers may be heard (mostly at night) in forests inland. Grassland and marshy areas are found in the southwest corner of the state. Several species of open-country mice, Northern Raccoons, and Northern Tamanduas are common in this habitat.

Calakmul Biosphere Reserve. Located in southeastern Campeche, this area provides an important corridor between the Maya Biosphere Reserve in Petén, Guatemala, and reserves in Quintana Roo. This large park has suffered from inadequate protection and from incursions by loggers and hunters in the past, but it may be better protected at present. The road from Escárcega to Chetumal passes through this reserve, and dirt roads heading north or south provide entries to the forest. The dirt road south from Constitución is close to the western boundary and passes through interesting habitat (ask for the road to La Esperanza). Access to the interior of the park is difficult, especially during the wet season. Mammals that may be seen here include Yucatán and Deppe's Squirrels, White-nosed Coati, Gray Fox, Central American Agouti, and Kinkajou. Jaguars, Pumas, and other cats occur near the southern border but are unlikely to be seen. Rodent trapping and bat netting (with scientific permit) are both productive; in addition to many common species, Wrinkle-faced Bats (*Centurio senex*), often rare, can be abundant here (especially in low, seasonally flooded scrub). The beautiful Yucatán Vesper Mouse (*Otonyctomys hatti*) also occurs in Calakmul, but it is not easily trapped. Mexican Mouse Opossums (*Marmosa mexicana*) are very common and quite easy to catch in tree traps.

Quintana Roo State

This state has several Maya sites such as Kohunlich and Cobá, which are surrounded by forest. The pale gray race of Yucatán Squirrel can be seen at Cobá; the dark race and the smaller Deppe's Squirrel occur in the wetter forest at Kohunlich. These and other Maya sites in Quintana Roo are good for bats, both in and around the buildings.

Sian Ka'an Biosphere Reserve. Located north of Felipe Carrillo Puerto on the east coast, this reserve encompasses a variety of habitats, from swamps and lagoons to semideciduous forest. A dirt road runs north–south through the reserve, passing through low, scrubby forest with patches of taller trees. A few West Indian Manatees occur in coastal lagoons, although they are more easily seen elsewhere. Gray Foxes are abundant; White-nosed Coatis and Long-tailed Weasels may also be seen. At night, attractive Big-eared Climbing Rats (*Ototylomys phyllotis*) can be located by eyeshine, on the ground or in trees. Gaumer's Spiny Pocket Mice (*Heteromys gaumeri*) and Yucatán Deer Mice (*Peromyscus yucatanicus*) are also common, but are more easily trapped than seen in the wild. A variety of leaf-nosed bats can be netted here (with appropriate permits).

Puerto Morelos Botanical Garden. This small park is just outside the town of the same name and is easily reached by heading south from Cancún. Fires in adjacent forests a few years ago may have affected populations of mammals in the gardens, but in the past this has been a good site for Central American Spider Monkeys, which have used a large tree near the entrance as their sleeping site. White-nosed Coatis are worth looking for, as they are a brilliant rusty orange color in this region. Central American Agoutis can also be seen here. For several years, a colony of Common Big-eared Bats (*Micronycteris microtis*) have roosted under the concrete steps outside the warden's house. After dark, these small bats hunt around the street lamps in the parking lot, flying very close to the ground, while larger Common Mustached Bats (*Pteronotus parnellii*) fly higher, circling the lamps. Bat netting and rodent trapping (with permits) are quite successful; the orangish race of the Yucatán Deer Mouse (*Peromyscus yucatanicus*) is common here (the illustration on Plate 27 was done in this garden).

Cozumel Island. Despite the fact that Cozumel is overrun with beach-going tourists and associated hotels, it is of interest to mammal watchers owing to the presence of several endemic species or races. The diminutive Cozumel Raccoon (*Procyon pygmaeus*) seems to be increasingly scarce on the main island, but occurs on Isla la Pasión on the north coast. This small, protected islet is also home to a large population of Cozumel Coatis (currently considered to be a subspecies of the White-nosed Coati, *Nasua narica*). Several hotels offer tours to Isla la Pasión, which can only be reached by boat. Traveling south from the town of San Miguel, several dirt roads branch off to the left from the paved coastal road (one turnoff is near the 15-km marker). These roads provide access to the low, deciduous forests of the interior. Much of the habitat is secondary, entirely cut over, or damaged by hurricanes, but some forest remains. Some Cozumel Coatis can be found here, and the endemic Cozumel Harvest Mouse (*Reithrodontomys spectabilis*) is common in vine tangles, where it is usually trapped above ground. At dusk these mice can be heard giving a high-pitched, two- or three-note whistle. Other rodents that can be trapped in the interior are the White-footed Mouse (*Peromyscus leucopus*), Coues' Rice Rat (*Oryzomys couesi*), and the Roof Rat (*Rattus rattus*). The latter are common in forested regions on the island as well as in urban areas. Nine-banded Armadillos are sometimes seen (they are also smaller than the mainland race) in forest and second growth, and locals report that Collared Peccaries and White-tailed Deer still occur, but both appear to be scarce. Virginia Opossums (*Didelphis vir-*

giniana) are abundant on the island, especially near the airport dump on the north coast.

Yucatán State

Less interesting to the mammal watcher than the remainder of the peninsula, Yucatán State's dry forest and thorn scrub habitats have largely been modified by human activity. Gray Foxes and Eastern Cottontails are often seen on roads at night. The region is good for bats, both at Maya sites and caves. Uxmal has a colony of Broad-eared Bats (*Nyctinomops laticaudatus*) in one of the temples. Lol'Tun cave (located 8 km southwest of Oxkutzcab) contains 12 species of bats. Grutas de Balankanché, east of Chichén Itzá (and a popular stop for tourists) houses not only Maya artifacts but also a large colony of Mexican Funnel-eared Bats (*Natalus stramineus*), which are wonderful to watch as they emerge at dusk, swirling and fluttering close to the ground. Several poorly known species of free-tailed bats have been caught in mist nets set over swimming pools of hotels and colleges in the vicinity of Mérida.

Guatemala

Western Guatemala

The volcanoes and high mountains of southern Guatemala are of particular interest to small-mammal trappers, as several endemic or local species of rodents and shrews occur here. Large tracts of land have been proposed as national parks in the Sierra Cuchumatanes of Huehuetenango and around Cerro Bisís in Quiché. Infrastructure to maintain and protect these parks is not yet in place. In these regions, forests on even the highest slopes are being cleared rapidly by the large rural population. Peaks of most of the active volcanoes in western Guatemala are protected, and some are forested.

Atitlán National Park. This park encompasses two volcanoes, Atitlán and San Pedro. Cloud forest and highland oak forest can be found on the higher slopes, but are rather inaccessible. Mammal species are probably similar to those at El Triunfo in Chiapas. On the dry hills north of Lake Atitlán, Mexican Gray Squirrels are abundant and their leaf nests are conspicuous. Jaguarundis are sometimes seen crossing roads in this region.

Central Guatemala

Biotopo Mario Dary Rivera (Quetzal sanctuary). This cloud forest reserve is a few kilometers from the town of Purulhá, near Cobán in central Guatemala. The reserve is well-maintained, with excellent trails. Deppe's Squirrels are common, and Cacomistles apparently occur in the higher, more inaccessible parts of the park. Mexican Harvest Mice (*Reithrodontomys mexicanus*) can be heard singing at dusk. I have not trapped in the Biotopo itself, but a few kilometers away, in similar habitat, we caught numerous rodents including the endemic Giant Deer Mouse (*Peromyscus grandis*), Vesper Rat (*Nyctomys sumichrasti*), Forest Spiny Pocket Mouse (*Heteromys desmarestianus*), and Alfaro's Rice Rat (*Oryzomys alfaroi*).

Lanquín Cave. This cave is located northeast of Cobán, about 1 km from the small town of Lanquín. This large limestone cave is much visited, but still maintains a huge population of bats which are impressive to watch as they emerge at dusk. Lanquín Cave is one of only a few deep, hot, and humid "bat caves" known in Central America. Bat caves are characterized by the presence of mormoopid bats, and all five species in the region have been reported here. The Ghost-faced Bat (*Mormoops megalophylla*) and three of the four Central American species of mustached bats (*Pteronotus davyi, P. personatus,* and *P. gymnonotus*) are common, as is the tiny Least Sac-winged Bat (*Balantiopteryx io*), which hangs individually spaced on cave walls.

Sierra de las Minas Biosphere Reserve. This reserve protects one of the largest tracts of cloud forest in northern Central America. Steep slopes rise from the dry Motagua valley to over 3000 m on the mountain tops. Access is difficult; even with a four-wheel-drive vehicle the roads are impassable in the wet season. The reserve is managed by Fundacíon Defensores de la Naturaleza. Permits should be obtained from this organization for overnight visits or scientific study. Several uncommon species of large mammals occur in the reserve, but they are difficult to see in the dense forest. Rodent trapping is productive.

Northern Guatemala

Maya Biosphere Reserve. The entire northern portion of Petén Department is included in the Maya Biosphere, the largest reserve in Central America. This region is well forested, but is inadequately protected from logging, hunting, and development. Protected areas within the Biosphere include Tikal National Park and three Biotopos: Laguna del Tigre in the west, Dos Lagunas to the north, and El Zotz, adjacent to Tikal. The mammals in the Biotopos are similar to those in Tikal, which is the most accessible.

Tikal National Park. This deservedly famous archaeological site in Petén is also one of the best localities in the region for mammals. Tall evergreen forest is broken by clearings around the temples, creating a mosaic of habitats. Numerous human visitors and rigid control of hunting on the site has resulted in some mammals losing their fear of humans. From the tops of the temples one can sometimes look down on arboreal species in the surrounding trees. Central American Spider Monkeys are extremely common; Yucatán Black Howlers are much less common, but will be heard and can usually be found. The dark gray to black race of Yucatán Squirrel and small, brown Deppe's Squirrel are both common, as are Central American Agoutis. White-nosed Coatis are often seen in forest around the site, sometimes in large groups (I counted 64 crossing the road into the site early one morning). Gray Foxes may be seen on the site (especially near Temple 1) and can easily be found on or near the airstrip at night. Tayras (the striking yellow-headed race) may be seen in forest nearby, but they seem to avoid the more traveled sections of the park. At night, Kinkajous are fairly easy to find, Red Brocket can be seen in the forest and White-tailed Deer along the airstrip. Common Opossums are abundant, especially near garbage dumps. During the day, the dumps are visited by Gray Foxes and spider monkeys. There are numerous bat species at Tikal, some of which can be found roosting in the ruins. On the walls in dimly lit rooms there may be

Greater White-lined Bats (*Saccopteryx bilineata*). Bats on the ceiling that are quick to take flight when disturbed are usually short-tailed bats (*Carollia* spp.). The small pond near the entrance to the site is a good place to listen for bats with a bat detector.

Belize

Belize has a lower human population than surrounding countries, and although the British plundered the forests for mahogany and other timbers, extenive forest can still be found in several parts of the country. Large mammals such as Baird's Tapir and Jaguar, which are scarce in other parts of Central America, are quite common in Belize.

Río Bravo Conservation Area.   Located between Gallon Jug and San Felipe, in northwestern Belize, this is a private reserve managed by The Programme for Belize. The exclusive (and expensive) Chan Chich Lodge near Gallon Jug has similar habitat. Red Brocket are common, as are Central American Spider Monkey, Deppe's Squirrel, and Central American Agouti. Yucatán Black Howlers occur here but are more common elsewhere. Several species of cats are seen quite regularly in this area, including Jaguar and Margay.

Community Baboon Sanctuary.   Northwest of Belize City, the town of Bermudian Landing created this sanctuary to protect Yucatán Black Howlers (locally known as Baboons). Strips of forest along the Belize River support an amazing number of howlers, and ladders over roads have been installed to help them get around. This is the best place to see this species, which may also be found at Lamanai and Crooked Tree Wildlife Sanctuary (the last site is easily reached by road, off the Northern Highway).

Belize Zoo and Tropical Education Center.   Located west of Belize city on the Western Highway, this zoo is the center for conservation and environmental education in Belize. The zoo houses only native Belizean species, including all the cats and many other mammals. The cages and displays are well designed and set among natural habitat. Special arrangements can be made for photographers, with advance notice.

Southern Lagoon.   This lagoon can be entered by boat from Gales Point or via the Belize River and Northern Lagoon from Belize City. Aerial surveys have shown that Southern Lagoon has the highest population of West Indian Manatees in Central America. Manatee-watching trips can be arranged from Gales Point, although the animals are seldom seen well in the rough, murky water.

Maya Mountains.   Located in southern Belize, these mountains are relatively low, the highest peak being only 1120 m. Much of the region is poorly known biologically and is rather inaccessible. The southern mountains consist of subtropical evergreen forest, from which many of the mature hardwoods were removed some time ago, resulting in dense, tall secondary forest. Several reserves are included within the Maya Mountains.

Mountain Pine Ridge Forest Reserve.   This reserve is located in the northern portion of the Maya Mountains. It can be reached via the Chiquibul Road from Georgeville. The forest is largely conferous, with some broadleaf forest along rivers. Baird's Tapirs are common along rivers and streams.

Chiquibul National Park. This is the largest national park in Belize. It encompasses the southwestern portion of the Maya Mountains and extends west to the Guatemalan border. Several forest reserves north, south, and east of the park extend the protected zone to Mountain Pine Ridge and the Cockscomb Basin Sanctuary. A system of caverns in Chiquibul National Park may be the largest in Central America. One cave within the system has the largest chamber in the Western Hemisphere. Undoubtedly numerous bats roost in these caves.

Cockscomb Basin Wildlife Sanctuary. Located on the eastern side of the Maya Mountains, this reserve was established to protect Jaguars. This is the most accessible protected region in the Maya Mountains. To enter the sanctuary, follow the coast road south from Dangriga to Maya Centre (just south of Kendal), and turn right on the dirt road to the reserve. There is a dormitory in the reserve, but all food and supplies should be carried in. Jaguars are not easily seen here, although their tracks may be found along the road or trails. Red Brocket are very common, as are Deppe's Squirrels. At night, Kinkajous and Pacas are easily found.

El Salvador

El Imposible National Park. Located near the Guatemalan border in Ahuachapán Department, the name of the park may refer to the difficulty in finding it. The nearest town is San Francisco Menéndez; someone in the town may know the way. Most of the forest in this park is secondary, ranging from deciduous to semideciduous on higher slopes. Human presence is evident, but there are a few surprises: Cacomistles (*Bassariscus*) are common; Kinkajous and White-nosed Coatis can also be seen. Bat netting and rodent trapping (with a Salvadorean permit) are productive.

Montecristo National Park. This highland park is located in the northwest corner of the country and includes elevations of more than 2000 m. It is linked with Trifinio National Park in Honduras. Cloud forest and pine–oak forests occur here, but most appear to be secondary. Special permission from park authorities is needed for overnight visits, and scientific permits are, of course, also required for trapping or netting. Rodent trapping is productive away from the pines, and as in El Imposible, Cacomistles appear to be common (in fact, we found this seemingly rare mammal to be common in all the forested regions we visited in El Salvador).

Honduras

Honduras has the potential to match Costa Rica as an ecotourist destination, although at this time it is far less well known. There are more than 50 parks and reserves in the country.

Copán. This Maya site in western Honduras is easily reached from San Pedro Sula or from Guatemala. There are many bat roosts in hollow trees and in some of the buildings on the site, but it is difficult to get permission to visit the site after dark. A nature trail near the entrance to the site passes through tall, humid forest where Central American Spider Monkeys and Variegated Squirrels can usually be found.

Celaque National Park. This park encircles Mount Celaque (2850 m), the highest peak in Honduras. Cloud and pine-oak forest give way to fir forest on the upper slopes. Forest Rabbits and Red Brocket may be seen at forest edge. Long-tailed Weasels occur in pine-oak and fir forest. Puma and Jaguar have been recorded in the park.

Santa Bárbara National Park. The habitat and mammals in this park are similar to those of Celaque. The limestone bedrock is pitted with sinkholes and caves, some of which are used as roost sites by bats.

Cuero y Salado Wildlife Refuge. Located near La Ceiba on the Caribbean coast, this reserve was established to protect West Indian Manatees. Mantled Howlers and White-faced Capuchins can also be seen here.

Pico Bonito National Park. Habitats included in this park range from arid thorn scrub in valleys south of the mountains, to cloud and pine forests on the peaks, and wet, evergreen forest in the Caribbean lowlands. Several endangered species of mammals have been recorded in the park (Baird's Tapirs may be fairly common here). The steep, rugged terrain that provides a refuge for these mammals remains largely inaccessible except to the serious hiker.

La Tigra National Park. This park is near Tegucigalpa, to the northeast. Much of the forest is secondary, but some cloud forest is intact. There are two visitor centers in the park, with basic accommodations. Collared Peccaries and Mantled Howlers may be seen in the forest.

Sierra de Agalta National Park. This park includes the highest peak (2590 m) in eastern Honduras. Habitats include pine-oak and cloud forest. Elfin forest occurs on the peaks and ridgetops. Access is difficult.

Río Plátano Biosphere Reserve. This large reserve protects the watershed of the Patuca River. Most of the habitat is wet, evergreen forest; there are also extensive swamps and marshes. Access is difficult and expensive.

Laguna de Caratasca Wildlife Refuge. Coastal lagoons, mangroves, and wetlands are included in this refuge, located east of Río Plátano. The refuge can be reached from Puerto Lempira.

Río Kruta Biological Reserve.   This reserve extends from Río Kruta to Río Coco on the Nicaraguan border. The habitat is seasonally flooded savannah and wet, evergreen forest. Access is by river only.

Nicaragua

The largest country in Central America, Nicaragua still has extensive tracts of forest, especially on the Caribbean Slope and lowlands. Several national parks and many reserves have been established, but there is little infrastructure available to develop or protect these regions.

Masaya National Park.   This small park, located south of Managua, surrounds Masaya Volcano. There is a paved road to the park and a visitor center. Large mammals are unlikely to be seen, but numerous bats roost in lava tube caves.

Bosawas National Resource Reserve.   This huge reserve may be linked with reserves in Honduras to form La Solidaridad International Reserve. Bosawas is managed in part by The Nature Conservancy. This important reserve is poorly known biologically and is inadequately protected from logging and hunting. Access is difficult and there are no facilities for visitors at present.

Wawasang Forest Reserve.   Located north of Bluefields on the Caribbean coast, this reserve may protect a sizeable population of West Indian Manatees. Access is difficult.

Río Indio-Maíz Biological Reserve.   This large reserve borders Costa Rica to the south. Two forest reserves north of Río Indio-Maíz extend the protected zone to Bluefields. The habitat and mammals are similar to those of Barra del Colorado and Tortuguero in Costa Rica. The forest is more extensive in Nicaragua than to the south, but hunting is not controlled, so large mammals may be scarce or wary. The Si-a-Paz Biosphere Reserve encompasses these protected areas in southeast Nicaragua and northeast Costa Rica.

Costa Rica

Pacific Slope

Santa Rosa National Park.   Santa Rosa is easily reached by road by driving north on the Pan-American Highway from Liberia and following signs to the park. The principal habitat in the park is deciduous forest, with some grassland, dry second growth, and patches of tall, evergreen forest in lowlying areas. White-faced Capuchins are often seen near the administration area or near the hacienda, Mantled Howlers and Central American Spider Monkeys (a golden-colored subspecies) are usually found in evergreen forest (about halfway to the administration area on the road in, or near the beach). Several species may be seen at water holes during the long dry season (December–May): Collared Peccaries, White-tailed Deer, White-nosed Coatis, and Central American Agoutis are regular visitors. Park guards can provide maps of water holes. Look out for the beautiful black and white race of Variegated Squirrel in open, deciduous forest. Gray Sac-winged Bats (*Balantiopteryx plicata*) roost in the farm buildings of the hacienda; Common Long-tongued Bats (*Glossophaga soricina*) and Seba's Short-tailed Bats (*Carollia perspicillata*) often hang in the chapel or kitchen. Some bat roosts at Santa Rosa have suffered from too much human disturbance; biologists may be able to get information on additional sites from park guards. After dark, a small, dark race of Hooded Skunk can be found near the campgrounds or buildings, and at the dump behind the dining room. Nine-banded Armadillos and Salvin's Spiny Pocket Mice (*Liomys salvini*) can be found by the sounds they make rummaging in leaf litter. Large carnivores including Coyote, Puma, and Jaguar sometimes visit Nancite beach during the turtle-nesting season.

Guanacaste National Park. This park provides a corridor between the dry lowlands of Santa Rosa and cool, evergreen forest on the Cordillera de Guanacaste. Maritza Biological Station is located at middle elevation in the park, bordering tall, semideciduous forest. Central American Spider Monkeys are abundant near Maritza; other mammals likely to be seen are similar to those at Rincón de la Vieja.

Rincón de la Vieja National Park. This park is reached via a dirt road heading northeast from the town of Liberia. Habitats include grassy areas, low brush, and tall, semideciduous forest. Nine-banded Armadillos are abundant, and White-nosed Coatis are also common. White-faced Capuchins, Mantled Howlers, and Central American Spider Monkeys can be seen fairly easily, as can Northern Tamanduas, Central American Agoutis, and Common Opossums. Kinkajous may be seen or heard at night in the forest. Under Costa Rican permit and a special permit to work in a national park, rodent trapping is very productive, although most traps will be filled by Mexican Deer Mice (*Peromyscus mexicanus*). Forest Spiny Pocket Mice (*Heteromys desmarestianus*), Vesper Rats (*Nyctomys sumichrasti*), and Big-eared Climbing Rats (*Ototylomys phyllotis*) may also be trapped. Bat netting is reasonable if it is not too windy; Salvin's Big-eyed Bat (*Chiroderma salvini*), a rather uncommon species in Costa Rica, can be netted over streams.

Palo Verde National Park. A dirt road to this park leaves the Pan-American highway at Bagaces, between Cañas and Liberia. The habitat consists of dry deciduous forest, limestone hills, and marshland along the Tempisque River. Common mammals are similar to those at Santa Rosa, although spider monkeys are not found at Palo Verde. Gray Fox and, less often, Jaguarundi may be seen crossing the road leading to the park. Tayra are sometimes seen near the water tanks. Groups of Lesser White-lined Bats (*Saccopteryx leptura*) roost in the intersections below large branches and tree trunks upstream from the water tanks. There are some limestone caves in the park, which are home to several species of bats including Woolly False Vampire Bats (*Chrotopterus auritus*), but beware of killer bees. Check a stand of coconut palms near the administration area for occupied tents of the Common Tent-making Bat (*Uroderma bilobatum*). The Organization for Tropical Studies (OTS) maintains a station in the park, and arrangements can be made to use the dormitory. OTS may also be able to help obtain the necessary permits for scientific study. Bat netting is very productive near water sources.

Centro Ecológica La Pacífica.   This hotel is located 5 km north of Cañas. Look for Lesser White-lined Bats on the trunk of the large fig tree by cabin 15. A trail along the Corobicí River beside the hotel can be a good place to sight mammals in the dry season. Howlers and Variegated Squirrels are common; Neotropical River Otters are seen fairly frequently in the river or on the banks. At night, Mexican Porcupines, Kinkajous, and several species of opossum may be found.

Monteverde Cloud Forest Reserve.   This reserve and the adjoining Quaker community have become very well known. They are reached by heading north on a dirt road from Lagartos, on the Pan-American highway. Along this road, one is likely to see a red-bellied race of Variegated Squirrel. In the cloud forest, the medium-sized, brown squirrels are Red-tailed Squirrels (*Sciurus granatensis*), not Deppe's Squirrel (*S. deppei*), despite local lists to the contrary, and the small ones with tiny ears and scraggly tails are Alfaro's Pygmy Squirrels. Red Brocket may be seen on the trail through the reserve at dusk. One of the mammal highlights in recent years has been an Olingo (*Bassaricyon*), which regularly drinks from hummingbird feeders at the Hummingbird Gallery. It often shows up in the middle of the afternoon. Both Olingos and Kinkajous can be seen at night in scattered trees around pastures in the community (especially in fruiting figs). Other nocturnal mammals commonly seen in the farmland and forest edges are Gray Fox, Northern Raccoon, Striped Hog-nosed Skunk, and Central American Woolly Opossum. A Mexican Porcupine den may be found at Finca de las Aves. Tayras and Central American Agoutis are sometimes seen. With scientific permit and permission from local landowners, bat netting and rodent trapping are productive.

Manuel Antonio National Park.   Located on the Pacific coast, near the town of Quepos, this tiny park has the disadvantage of being on an attractive beach and so is overrun by tourists. Access to the park has been strictly controlled in recent years, which is unfortunate. Nonetheless, it is one of the best places to see a variety of mammals in a short space of time. Many of the mammals may be found nearby, although it is best to arrange special access to the park at night or in the early morning. Red-backed Squirrel Monkeys are common in secondary forest in and around the park (the subspecies here is much paler than those farther south). White-faced Capuchins and Mantled Howlers are both fairly common. Brown-throated Three-toed Sloths are abundant and can be seen by day or night. During the day, the blackish race of Variegated Squirrel and the Central American Agouti can be found. At night, Pacas are often seen, as are Nine-banded Armadillos. Striped Hog-nosed Skunks, Central American Woolly Opossums, and Northern Raccoons may also be encountered at night.

Corcovado National Park.   Located on the Osa Peninsula, Corcovado is more inaccessible than most Costa Rican parks. It is possible to fly to Sirena, where one can camp or stay in basic accommodations. Other entries to the park involve long hikes; similar habitat may be more easily reached at several lodges on the periphery of the park. The common species are similar to those at Manuel Antonio, although Variegated Squirrels are found only in the periphery, and Paca and agoutis are less easily seen. Red-backed Squirrel Monkeys are common near Sirena and are much more brightly colored here than at Manuel Antonio. Corcovado really is worth the effort to visit for a few days, as it is probably the only place in Central America where one stands a chance of seeing Baird's Tapir, Jaguar, or White-lipped Peccary (all are regularly sighted near Sirena). With the appropriate Costa Rican permit, bat netting is great, but trap success for small rodents is usually low.

Atlantic Slope

Barra del Colorado National Wildlife Refuge.   Located in the northeast corner of the country, this large refuge can be reached by boat or plane. Principal habitats in the refuge are raffia palm swamps and wet evergreen forest. Mammals seen here are similar to those at Tortuguero. Illegal logging and colonization may have affected some populations of larger mammals in the refuge.

Tortuguero National Park.   This park is south of Barra del Colorado and can be reached by boat or plane. Much of the evergreen forest here is flooded and is most easily explored by boat. Mantled Howlers are extremely common; White-faced Capuchins and Central American Spider Monkeys are less common but often seen. Both species of sloth that occur in the region can be found in trees near the water. Night boat trips have become increasingly popular and consequently less productive; night walks near lodges or on the National Park trails may be better. Mammals that can be seen at night include Kinkajous, Central American Woolly Opossums and Gray Four-eyed Opossums, Northern Raccoons, and occasionally Olingos. During the day, Neotropical River Otters and Ocelots are sometimes seen. This is a great place to look for bat tents: check fishtail palms, fan palms, heliconia, philodendrons, and other large leaves. Spix's Disk-winged Bats (*Thyroptera tricolor*) are easy to find in rolled up heliconia leaves. For permit holders, bat netting is as good as it gets, but rodent trapping is a waste of time.

La Selva.   This OTS station is near Puerto Viejo in the lowlands of Heredia Province. Although La Selva has the largest list of mammal species of any site in the country, it may not be the best place to see a lot of mammals in a short time. Central American Agoutis are easily seen, and Tayras can be found with a little effort. At night, Kinkajous are common near the clearing, and a Striped Hog-nosed Skunk may be found on the bridge across the river or near the dining room. Bats can be found on buildings (check the old rooms near the river for sac-winged bats) and in tents (check heliconia for Honduran White Bat tents). Bats are well known at this site; 66 species have been recorded here. Bat netting (with appropriate permits) is productive, but rodent trapping is almost as unproductive as it is at Tortuguero, although it is quite easy to see Tomes' Spiny Rats (*Proechimys semispinosus*) and Forest Spiny Pocket Mice (*Heteromys desmarestianus*) in the forest at night.

Braulio Carrillo National Park.   This is a large park located near San José. The main road to Limón passes through the park. Numerous mammals occur in the park (see Timm et al., 1989), although not many will be seen in a short visit. Just before the road crosses a river and emerges from the park, a small road bears off to the left. In this area,

Collared Peccaries may be seen, and numerous bat tents can be found. Braulio Carrillo extends north to La Selva, providing a corridor for elevational migration.

Rara Avis. This private reserve with good accommodations borders Braulio Carrillo on the Caribbean Slope. Northern Tamanduas are abundant at Rara Avis, as are White-nosed Coatis. Lucky guests may see the rare Watson's Climbing Rat (*Tylomys watsoni*) at night, as it gallops across their bed. Tapir tracks are evident all around Rara Avis, but the animals are not easily seen.

Cahuita National Park. This park has good populations of monkeys and numerous bats. On the way to the park, after the turnoff to Limón, head south and look out for sloths. Both species are very easy to find in second growth along the road.

Central Highlands

Volcán Poás National Park. This is one of the most accessible parks in the country. Many species of mammals have been recorded in the park, but they are seldom seen along the main road and trails. Red-tailed Squirrels (*Sciurus granatensis*) are common and are often seen at picnic areas. The less well known Montane Squirrel (*Syntheosciurus brochus*) is sometimes seen in oak forest or in trees bordering pastures near the park entrance.

Chirripó National Park and La Amistad Biosphere Reserve. Linked with La Amistad National Park in Panama and adjacent forest reserves in both countries, these protected areas span a significant portion of the Talamanca Mountains. Habitats include oak forest and páramo. Access is difficult and mostly limited to the serious hiker. Common mammals include Coyotes and Red-tailed Squirrels. Dice's Rabbit (*Sylvilagus dicei*), a species endemic to these mountains, is common in some grassy valleys.

Panama

Western Panama

Volcán Barú National Park. The summit of Barú Volcano, at almost 3500 m, can be reached by road. The lower slopes have been largely deforested, but patches of oak forest remain at higher elevations. Elfin forest and páramo are found near the summit.

Cerro Hoya National Park. This small park is located on the largely deforested Azuero Peninsula. Lowland deciduous forest gives way to evergreen forest on the hills. The endemic Yellow Deer Mouse (*Isthmomys flavidus*) may occur on the slopes. The Mantled Howler (*Alouatta palliata*) in this region may be a different species, *Alouatta coibensis*.

Central Panama

Barro Colorado Island. Located in the Panama Canal and reached by boat from Gamboa, this island is the best place to see a large number of mammals in a short time. All visits must be arranged through the Smithsonian Tropical Research Institute in Panama City, and permission to stay overnight is usually only granted to scientists. Mantled Howlers, Central American Spider Monkeys, and White-faced Capuchins are extremely common; Geoffroy's Tamarin is scarce. Central American Agoutis, White-nosed Coatis, and Red-tailed Squirrels are abundant, Northern Tamanduas can be found fairly easily, and Tayras are also seen. There are a few White-tailed Deer, but Red Brocket are more common. Collared Peccaries are mostly seen at night. Also at night, Kinkajous, Pacas, Nine-banded Armadillos, Central American Woolly Opossums, and Gray Four-eyed Opossums are easily seen. Tomes' Spiny Rats are abundant and Rufous Tree Rats (*Diplomys labilis*) can be found with some effort. Several species of bats roost on the walls or in roof crevices of the buildings, and numerous species have been netted on the island (see Handley et al., 1991, for a complete list). There are almost no small rodents.

Soberanía National Park.   This park can be entered from Gamboa, and a variety of habitats are seen by traveling along Pipeline Road. All the mammals on Barro Colorado occur here, although tamarins are unlikely to be found. At night the small streams are excellent places to look for Armored Rats (*Hoplomys*). Western Night Monkeys, Olingos, and Kinkajous may be seen in the trees, especially in flowering balsa.

Metropolitan Park.   This park is within the Panama City limits and has good forest. Geoffroy's Tamarins are common in secondary forest in the park, and several other mammals may be seen.

Fort Sherman and vicinity.   Forests on the Caribbean side of the canal, such as those around Fort Sherman, are great for sloths. Both species can be easily found in second growth and mature forest. Western Night Monkeys can be found after dusk or before dawn by spotlighting along some of the smaller roads such as Blacktop Road and Skunk Hollow Road. Mangroves in the area are good places to look for Crab-eating Raccoons.

Chagres National Park.   This park borders Portobelo National Park to the north. Much of the park is inaccessible except by boat; Cerro Azúl and Cerro Jefe, on the southern border of the park, can be reached by car. Common mammals are similar to those in the Canal Area. Some highland species have been recorded on the cerros.

Eastern Panama

Darién National Park.   The Darién is difficult and expensive to reach and explore, but worth the effort. Special permits are needed to visit the park, in addition to permits for scientific study or collecting. There are flights from Panama City to El Real. From El Real one can hire a boat to Boca del Cupe, then hike about 8 hours to Cruce de Mono Station in the park. From here it is another long hike to Cana, where there is a place to stay and a trail up Mount Pirre. It is also possible (but expensive) to schedule flights directly to Cana from Panama City. From El Real a boat can also be taken to Pijibasal (sometimes known as Pirre Village), and from this village it is a short walk to the ranger station known as Rancho Frio or Pirre Station. There is a steep, muddy trail from this station to the top of Mount Pirre, which takes about 5 hours to walk. At Cruce de Mono, Geoffroy's Tamarins, Tayras, and Forest Rabbits can be seen, in addition to many common mammals, and White-lipped Peccaries may be encountered here and on Mount Pirre. I did not find Brown-headed Spider Monkeys on my trip, although they should be present. Bat netting is excellent near Cruce de Mono and at Rancho Frio. On the slopes of Pirre, rodent trapping is very productive; the endemic Mount Pirri Deer Mouse (*Isthmomys pirrensis*) is common on the ridge top, and three species of rice rat are easily caught (*Oryzomys albigularis* on the top; *O. bolivaris* and *O. talamancae* at 800 m). Pygmy squirrels can be seen from 800 m up, but the two species found here may be indistinguishable in the field.

CONSERVATION OF MAMMALS IN CENTRAL AMERICA

There are no land masses in tropical or temperate parts of the world where the natural environment is not being eroded by humans, and Middle America is no exception. Population pressure and exploitation of natural resources have resulted in tremendous losses in forest cover throughout the region (see Plate 52). Deforestation in Central America and southeastern Mexico is proceeding at such a pace that many experts have predicted that all forests, except a few remnants, will be cleared by the end of this century.

Some of the problems specific to the region include human poverty coupled with an inadequate diet. Protein from wild game is important in many regions, and populations of mammals ranging from monkeys to agoutis suffer as a result. Hunting for sport and for hides has a serious impact on big cats and other large mammals. Unlike in northern regions, where growing populations are centered in urban or suburban areas, in Middle America the rural population is also expanding rapidly. Subsistence farmers practice slash-and-burn agriculture for their corn milpas, while large landholders clear tracts of land for export crops such as coffee, cotton, banana, citrus fruits, and sugar. Both of these farming practices exert a heavy toll on natural habitats. The development of pasture lands for beef cattle has resulted in the loss of much of the original deciduous forest of the Pacific lowlands. Population density in El Salvador is the highest on the mainland of the Western Hemisphere. The population of this small country was estimated at 2 million in 1950, 3.7 million in 1972, and 5.9 million in 1995, an increase of almost three times in 45 years. Habitat loss and other factors resulting from the burgeoning human population in El Salvador has led to the extirpation of many species, including all hoofed mammals except White-tailed Deer and possibly all native cats and monkeys (Daugherty, 1972).

Despite the many environmental problems facing Middle America, the outlook is not entirely bleak. The efforts of governmental and nongovernmental conservation organizations and local biologists have led to the establishment of numerous parks and preserves throughout the region. The government of Costa Rica recently announced that it will increase the amount of preserved land from 24% to 34% of its entire territory, a far greater proportion than is preserved in the United States or Canada. The influx of foreign funds through ecotourism continues to provide a strong incentive for conservation efforts in Costa Rica and elsewhere in Central America. Local initiatives such as reforestation using native tree species, sustainable harvesting of forest products, and "farming" of forestdwelling animals such as Paca and Green Iguana are ongoing in several Central American countries. Dedicated individuals and groups have worked to save representative habitat throughout the region, but there is a continuing need for financial aid for the protection and maintenance of these areas. Financial and technical support from international sources is essential for conservation initiatives throughout Central America and southeastern Mexico.

Endangered Species

Several mammal species in the region may be in danger of extinction. Some of the larger mammals have been placed on lists of threatened or endangered species by CITES, International Union for Conservation of Nature and Natural Resources (IUCN), and the U.S. Endangered Species Act. Only CITES listings are given in the species accounts. The status of almost all the small mammals is not sufficiently well known to allow such classification. The problems faced by endangered species are different in each case. Some mammals that may be in danger of extinction and the particular problems that they face follow. This list does not include all endangered species in the region, but serves to exemplify the types of problems different mammals face.

White-lipped Peccary (*Dicotyles pecari*). CITES Appendix II. This species lives in herds of up to 200 animals. The herds occupy huge ranges in areas with low human populations. When threatened, the adults defend the young and do not flee. This behavior makes them highly vulnerable to hunting pressure, and their need for large tracts of wilderness has added to their increasing rarity in the region. White-lipped Peccaries have disappeared from many parts of their former range and may be entirely extirpated in Central America if efforts are not made to protect them. They do, however, range through much of South America and are unlikely to become extinct throughout their entire geographic range in the immediate future.

Puma and Jaguar (*Puma concolor* and *Panthera onca*). CITES Appendix I (Jaguar and some Puma subspecies); Appendix II (Puma). Big cats require large areas of undisturbed land. As farmland encroaches on their habitat, some individuals may start to hunt domestic animals. This behavior, coupled with the value of their hides, provides strong incentives for killing these cats. Cats, like most carnivores, are generalists and will take whatever prey items are most abundant. These species would probably survive in altered habitats if hunting pressures were removed. Both Pumas and Jaguars range into southern South America, and although their distribution in Central America is patchy and diminishing, they do not appear to be in danger of extinction throughout their entire range.

West Indian Manatee (*Trichechus manatus*). CITES Appendix I. Manatees suffer principally from hunting for meat; they are also frequently maimed or killed by motor boats. Pollution and environmental degradation also have an adverse effect on manatee populations. These slow-moving, aquatic mammals have a restricted distribution and have already disappeared from many parts of their former range. A slow reproductive rate prevents fast recovery of overhunted populations.

Red-Backed Squirrel Monkey (*Saimiri oerstedii*). CITES Appendix I. Habitat loss within the limited geographic range of this species has placed it in an extremely precarious position. Although these monkeys favor secondary forest and so can survive some human disturbance, they disappear when forests are cleared. Populations of this species also suffer from excessive use of insecticides on remnant forest and adjoining farmland, which may kill them directly or reduce their insect prey populations. Many are captured and kept illegally as pets. The fragmentation of their habitat has led to small, isolated populations that are highly vulnerable.

Central American Spider Monkey (*Ateles geoffroyi*). CITES Appendix I (two subspecies); Appendix II (all other populations). Spider monkeys are considered to be the best-tasting monkeys, and hunting for meat has eliminated or severely reduced populations in Mexico and parts of Central America. These monkeys breed slowly, and hunted populations have little hope of recovery. Their apparent requirement for mature, undisturbed forest may be more a function of reduced hunting pressure in such regions than a need for specific habitat, as they do in fact survive in secondary forest when hunting is controlled. Maintenance of some type of forest is also essential for the survival of these arboreal, fruit-eating monkeys.

Maya Mouse (*Peromyscus mayensis*). Not listed. This mouse is known only from a single montane region in the Sierra Cuchumatanes of Western Guatemala. It appears to be restricted to highland oak forest with considerable accumulation of leaf litter (as is found in forests where nightly frosts occur). When we visited this region in 1990, we found the forest disappearing with alarming speed. The huge oaks were being cut for lumber or firewood, and the land was being converted to pasture for goats and sheep. This species exemplifies the situation of several small mammal species with highly restricted ranges, mostly on mountain tops (other possibly threatened small rodents include *Heteromys nelsoni, H. oresterus, Reithrodontomys tenuirostris,* and some of the shrews). Unlike the larger mammals, small rodents and shrews do not require huge tracts of forest, as most of them occupy small home ranges; viable populations may exist in areas of only a few hectares. They also do not suffer from direct persecution by humans, as local people are generally unaware of their existence. Without habitat protection, however, these species will soon become extinct. Scientific studies of the ecology, systematics, and distribution of these small mammals are necessary to establish conservation priorities and provide data for regulatory agencies and conservation groups. Collections of series of museum specimens provide the basis of all study of small mammals and should be an integral part of conservation efforts for these species.

Extinct Species

Two species of mammals have become extinct in the region in recent time; others may be locally extirpated in Central America.

Honduran Hutia (*Geocapromys thoracatus*).   This species was known from Little Swan Island, a small island off northeastern Honduras. It became extinct in the 1950s, possibly as a result of goats and feral cats being introduced on the island (Morgan, 1989).

West Indian Monk Seal (*Monachus tropicalis*).   This seal was last seen in 1952 at Seranilla Bank in Honduran waters. Aerial surveys in 1973 did not yield any definite evidence of its survival (Kenyon, 1977). It formerly ranged through the Caribbean Sea from the Bahamas south to Jamaica, Cuba, and Hispaniola, and west to the Yucatán Peninsula and coast of Honduras. Monk seals were hunted to extinction for oil and skins.

AMERICAN OPOSSUMS

Order Didelphimorphia, Family Didelphidae

All marsupials were formerly considered to belong to the order Marsupialia; however, this large group has recently been split into 7 orders. New World opossums are represented by 3 orders and Australian marsupials by 4 orders. The Didelphimorphia contains a single family, which includes all Central American opossums. The family Didelphidae consists of about 15 genera and 63 species, with 8 genera and 13 species in Central America and SE Mexico.

Central American opossums range in size from mouse opossums weighing about 40 g to the more familiar Virginia Opossum with a weight of about 2 kg. In most species of opossums, growth continues throughout life, so the adult weight of any one species may vary considerably. Male mouse opossums are usually larger than females. New World opossums have 5 toes on each foot, and the thumbs of the hind feet are opposable. The tail is usually long, naked, and prehensile. Arboreal species use their prehensile tails to grip branches as they move, and they can hang from the tail tip, grasp the tail like a rope, and climb up it when necessary. A well-developed pouch is present in *Didelphis, Chironectes,* and *Philander.* In other genera the pouch is absent or reduced to 2 longitudinal folds of skin around the nipples. The dental formula for all species is: i 5/4, c 1/1, p 3/3, m 4/4. The larger opossums are unlikely to be confused with other mammals in Central America, but the small mouse opossums superficially resemble some rodents (*Tylomys* spp., especially). In the hand, mouse opossums are easily distinguished from rodents by their opposable thumbs and dentition (small incisors, large canines, and a continuous row of teeth without a large gap). In the field, their strongly prehensile tails and distinct eye rings are usually visible.

All Central American opossums are nocturnal. They have bright, reddish eyeshine, and the eyes appear widely spaced. Several arboreal species freeze in response to illumination at night and may be easily observed. If encountered on the ground, they are more likely to run off or climb up to a safe distance. Opossums are silent unless threatened, when they usually hiss, and some species may squeal or produce loud clicks in defense. Other threat behavior includes opening the mouth wide, drooling, and raising a clenched fist, the "opossum salute." Most species are solitary outside the breeding season. Leaves and grasses are used to build nests; these materials are carried in coils of the tail. Gestation is short; after birth the tiny young crawl unassisted to the mother's nipples where they attach themselves for several weeks or months. There are often more young produced than nipples available, so several die immediately. Most species are short lived and may not survive longer than one breeding season. A good general reference for opossums is Hunsaker (1977).

COMMON OPOSSUM
Didelphis marsupialis

Plate 1
Map 1

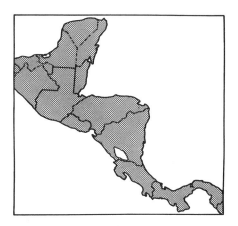

Map 1. Common Opossum, *Didelphis marsupialis*

Spanish: zorr(o/a); Mexico: tlacuache común, tacuazín; Honduras: guazalo; Miskito: kiski tara; Costa Rica: zorro pelón.

HB 263–430 (13"), T 295–450 (14"), HF 42–69, E 45–60, Wt 0.6–2.4 kg (3 lb).

Description. Large and unkempt looking. Upperparts blackish, gray, or, less commonly, whitish (depending on relative extent of long, black or white guard hairs); underparts yellow, orange, or cream. Fur long, coarse, and shaggy. Ears naked, entirely black (in adult). Face pale with narrow black eye rings and blackish median line on forehead; *cheeks cream or yellowish orange*, sometimes lightly peppered with black hairs, not pure white. Eyeshine bright, reddish. *All long whiskers on muzzle and cheeks are black. Tail slightly longer than head and body length*, base haired like the body, naked portion black near base with a *long, white tip*; usually 1/3 black, 2/3 white, sometimes half black, half white, or all-black. Legs and feet black. **Similar Species.** Virginia Opossum (*D. virginiana*) has pure white cheeks and some long, white whiskers on muzzle and cheeks; usually has tail shorter than head and body; black portion of tail longer than white portion. Difficult to distinguish with certainty at night.

Distribution. Tamaulipas, Mexico, throughout Central and South America to Peru, Bolivia, and NE Argentina. Lowlands to 2000 m.

Status and Habitat. Common to abundant in a variety of habitats; favors secondary forest or somewhat disturbed lowland regions, stream banks, and rural garbage dumps. Also found in mature evergreen forest.

Habits. It is mainly nocturnal, but occasionally may be seen early in the morning. This species usually travels on the ground, but climbs well and usually rests on a branch at night. If disturbed, it often climbs to escape, stopping when 3–5 m above ground to look back at an observer. When cornered or trapped, the Common Opossum is much more aggressive than the Virginia Opossum and shows little or no tendency to "play dead." Aggressive behavior includes hissing open mouthed and rocking from side to side, shifting the weight from one forefoot to the other. It may spray urine and feces as it twists and turns. Den sites are often above ground in hollow trees or vine tangles. Nests may also be located at or below ground level in caves, rock crevices, hollow logs, and in burrows made by other mammals. Males may change nest sites every day, but females tend to return to the same site for about 5 days. During the night, individuals travel distances of

1–3 km, but remain in well-defined home ranges. The home range size during the dry season in Venezuela is about 122 ha for males and 11 ha for females (Sunquist et al., 1987). The Common Opossum eats almost anything and is a successful, if slow-moving, predator. The diet includes small vertebrates, invertebrates, carrion, fruit, nectar, and vegetable matter. It feeds heavily on fruit and nectar in the dry season (Janson et al., 1981). It visits garbage dumps in rural areas and often raids chicken houses, killing chickens and eating eggs. This species can be the bane of the small mammal trapper, as it attacks rodents captured in live traps, often following an entire trap line, and it also may kill and eat bats held in mist nets. Females produce 2 or more litters per year, with birth peaks in February and July in Costa Rica. Litter size may be 20 or more at birth, but only 9 young are accommodated on the nipples, and further mortality leads to an average of about 6 pouch young. Young are weaned at 3 months, and females can reproduce at 7 months. Life span is usually less than 2 years. Natural history reviewed by Gardner (1983a).

VIRGINIA OPOSSUM

Didelphis virginiana

Plate 1
Map 2

Local names as for Common Opossum.

HB 374–451 (16"), T 282–370 (13"), HF 50–65, E 49–63, Wt 1.1–2.5 kg (3.5 lb).

Description. Large and unkempt looking, with a relatively short tail. Upperparts gray or whitish (rarely blackish; long, white guard hairs usually present); underparts white, cream or yellowish. Fur long, coarse, and shaggy. Ears naked, black, sometimes with narrow white tips. Face white, with narrow black eye rings and blackish median line on forehead; *cheeks pure white;* long whiskers on muzzle and cheeks mixed black and white. *Tail equal to or shorter than head and body length,* base furred like the body, naked portion usually half black, half

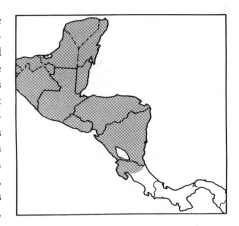

Map 2. Virginia Opossum, *Didelphis virginiana*

white, or 2/3 black, 1/3 white, sometimes all black. Legs and feet black. **Similar Species.** See Common Opossum (*D. marsupialis*). Note that above description applies to animals from SE Mexico and Central America, not the United States.

Distribution. SE Ontario, Canada, and United States through Mexico and N Central America to NW Costa Rica. Lowlands to 3000 m.

Status and Habitat. Common to locally abundant in a variety of habitats, including lowland deciduous forest and montane regions. Absent or much less common than Common Opossum (*D. marsupialis*) in mature, lowland, evergreen forest.

Habits. Similar to Common Opossum in most respects, the Virginia Opossum may be slightly more terrestrial in habit and is much less aggressive when captured. If threatened, it "plays dead" by rolling onto its side, open mouthed, with a fixed stare. It is often found in association with human dwellings and garbage dumps. Dens are usually made at ground level, among rocks, in brush, hollow logs, or in burrows made by other mammals. This species is seminomadic, occupying a shifting home range. Females have 13 mammae and therefore can raise larger litters than Common Opossums. Biology reviewed by Hunsaker (1977).

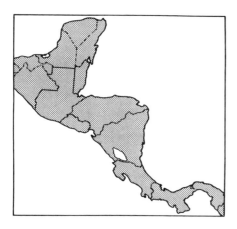

Map 3. Gray Four-eyed Opossum, *Philander opossum*

GRAY FOUR-EYED OPOSSUM Plate 2
Philander opossum Map 3

Mexico: tlacuache cuatro-ojos; Honduras: cayopolin; Costa Rica: zorro de cuatro ojos.

HB 253-315 (11"), T 273-329 (12"), HF 43–50, E 33–41, Wt 263–1400 g (1.7 lb).

Description. Medium sized. Upperparts dark gray-brown to blackish gray peppered with white hairs, imparting a slight sheen; underparts and tops of feet cream or yellow. Fur dense and slightly woolly. *Ears black,* naked; cream-colored patch of fur at bases. Head blackish, with contrasting cream spots above the eyes and cream cheeks. Eyeshine bright, reddish. *Tail haired like body for basal 30–50 mm,* then almost naked and *blackish for two-thirds or more of its length, contrasting with pure white tip.* **Similar Species.** See Brown Four-eyed Opossum (*Metachirus*) and Water Opossum (*Chironectes*).

Distribution. Tamaulipas, Mexico, through Central and South America to Peru and NE Argentina. Lowlands to 1600 m.

Status and Habitat. Locally common, sometimes abundant, in deciduous and evergreen forest, second growth, and gardens; often found near streams.

Habits. This opossum is frequently seen at night foraging along the edges of streams through partially forested areas. It is both terrestrial and arboreal, but is more often encountered on the ground than in trees. It climbs well and usually escapes by running to the nearest tree and climbing up a safe distance, then stopping to stare down at the observer. It feeds on invertebrates (crabs, shrimps, and insects) and small vertebrates (birds, mice, and frogs) and is attracted to the calls of breeding frogs or distress calls of bats held in mist nets. Fruits such as *Cecropia* and *Piper* spp. are also included in the diet. Leaf nests are usually made above ground, in vine tangles or hollow trees. Nests are occasionally placed on the ground, under tree falls or roots. Litter size is 2–7, and females produce 2 or more litters per year (Fleming, 1973).

Comment. Sometimes placed in the genus *Metachirops,* in which case *Philander* is used for the Brown Four-eyed Opossum.

WATER OPOSSUM Plate 1
Chironectes minimus Map 4

Yapok; Mexico: tlacuache acuático; Honduras: perrito de agua; Costa Rica: zorro de agua.

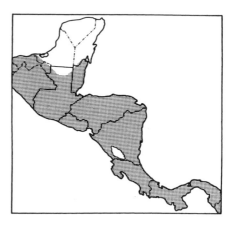

Map 4. Water Opossum, *Chironectes minimus*

HB 221–400 (12"), T 281–430 (14"), HF 55–73, E 22–32, Wt 604–790 g (1.5 lb).

Description. Medium sized, *strikingly marked*, semiaquatic. Upperparts pale gray with *4 broad, chocolate-brown to black bands across back*, joined by a narrow, dark line down spine; underparts pure white. Fur short and dense. Ears short, blackish. Eyeshine bright, reddish. Tail broad at base, furred like body for 30–40 mm, then naked, mainly black, with a short white tip. *Hind feet webbed* between all toes; forefeet broad with long, slender toes; long bone of hand projects to form a sixth "finger." Pouch present in female and male.
Similar Species. Markings are distinctive and usually easily seen in the field when out of water. No other opossums have webbed hind feet, and of those seen on the ground at the water's edge (*Didelphis, Philander*), only the Water Opossum characteristically dives to escape.

Distribution. Oaxaca and Tabasco, Mexico, through Central America (except Yucatán Peninsula) to Peru, SE Brazil, and N Argentina (absent from much of Amazon basin). Lowlands to 1800 m.

Status and Habitat. Apparently uncommon or rare; found near streams or rivers through forested regions. Favors fast-flowing, rock- or gravel-bottomed streams in hilly country.

Habits. The Water Opossum is mainly nocturnal. It is terrestrial and semiaquatic and is always found close to water. It forages for crustaceans, fish, frogs, and insects, swimming with the forepaws extended and using the long fingers to grab and manipulate prey. Rough pads on the fingers allow it to grasp slippery fish. The tip of the tail is prehensile but is only used for grasping nesting material, not for climbing. Burrows are constructed in stream banks, with entrances above or below the waterline leading to enlarged nest chambers. Nests are lined with leaves and grasses and are usually in burrows, but may be located on

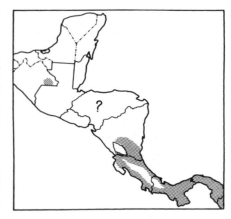

Map 5. Brown Four-eyed Opossum, *Metachirus nudicaudatus*

stream banks. If disturbed, this opossum usually jumps into water and swims to a nearby burrow or may escape on land. Females have litters of 2-5 young, which remain with the mother when she swims. The musculature of the pouch is highly developed so that when it is closed it provides a watertight compartment for the young. Males draw the scrotum into their pouch when swimming. Biology reviewed by Marshall (1978).

BROWN FOUR-EYED OPOSSUM
Metachirus nudicaudatus

Plate 2
Map 5

Costa Rica: zorricí; Panama: zorra morena.

HB 217–299 (10"), T 303–405 (14"), HF 46–53, E 32–40, Wt 254–619 g (1 lb).

Description. Medium sized, long legged. Upperparts *dull brown* grading to tan on sides and below ears; underparts pale yellow (rufous around nipples of female, which lacks a pouch). Fur coarse and rather short. Ears brown. Face dark brown, with a narrow, dark stripe extending from forehead to nape of neck; cheeks and *spots above eyes cream-colored*, rest of face dark brown. *Tail sparsely haired* (naked-looking) for its *entire length*, bicolor, brown above, white below, fading gradually to all white at tip. Feet whitish. **Similar Species.** Gray Four-eyed Opossum (*Philander*) is gray, not brown and has tail clearly divided into 3 parts: thickly furred at base, then naked, black midsection, with a well-defined white tip (tail difference more apparent at night than color difference). Other opossums lack pale spots above eyes.

Distribution. Chiapas, Mexico (Medellín et al., 1992); Nicaragua to Peru and NE Argentina. Lowlands to 1200 m.

Status and Habitat. Uncommon but widespread; usually found in mature evergreen forest of lowlands and foothills, occasionally in deciduous or dense secondary forest. Generally seems to be much less common than Gray Four-eyed Opossum (*Philander*) in Central America.

Habits. This nocturnal opossum is shy and nervous, taking off at a fast run if encountered. It is seldom seen and may be more reluctant to enter traps than other opossums (this may account for its apparent rarity in Central America). Largely terrestrial, it travels on the ground or on low logs and runs rather than climbs in response to danger. Dens are located in well-concealed nests in rock crevices, hollow logs, depressions, and under palm fronds, on or close to the ground (Miles et al., 1981). It feeds on insects, including termites, beetles, and cicadas, and small vertebrates, including birds, bird eggs, and reptiles (Medellín et al., 1992). It also eats some fruit.

Comment. This species is sometimes placed in the genus *Philander*, in which case *Metachirops* is used for Gray Four-eyed Opossum.

GRAYISH MOUSE OPOSSUM Plate 3
Marmosa canescens Map 9

HB 85–149, T 93–154, HF 16–21, E 22–30, Wt 38–41 g.

Description. *Small*, with a relatively short tail. Upperparts *pale gray*; underparts cream-white. Fur medium length, slightly woolly. Prominent black eye rings. Tail about equal to head and body length, faintly bicolor, occasionally white-tipped. **Similar Species.** *M. mexicana* is orangish in color, with a proportionally longer tail.

Distribution. Sinaloa to Oaxaca, W Mexico; Tres Marías Islands; Yucatán, Mexico. Lowlands to 2100 m.

Status and Habitat. Uncommon to locally common in desert scrub, deciduous forest, and dry hills. Known in SE Mexico from a few specimens from the dry, northern portion of Yucatán Peninsula.

Habits. This species is semiarboreal and may spend more time on the ground than other mouse opossums. It eats insects, figs, and probably cactus fruits. Ball nests of dry leaves and stems, lined with plant down, are placed in forks of small trees and bushes (Wilson, 1991). Other nest sites include hollows in cacti or tree limbs, abandoned birds' nests, and a single record of a nest among litter at the base of a fig tree (Armstrong and Jones, 1971). In W Mexico, the breeding season is from August to October, and litters of 8–13 have been recorded.

MEXICAN MOUSE OPOSSUM Plate 3
Marmosa mexicana Map 6

Mexico: ratón tlacuache; Miskito: kiski sirpi.

HB 95–202, T 118–223, HF 16–25, E 15–25, Wt 40–100 g (Nicaragua and Costa Rica), 14–47 g (Mexico, Belize, and Guatemala).

Description. Small; size varies with age, sex, and locality. Upperparts *pale brown, cinnamon*, or *orange-brown*; underparts creamy, pinkish, or buffy yellow (palest on median line). Fur medium length (7–9 mm), smooth, not woolly. Prominent black eye rings. Eyeshine moderate, reddish. Tail naked-looking, uni-

Map 6. 1. Mexican Mouse Opossum, *Marmosa mexicana*
2. Highland Mouse Opossum, *Marmosops impavidus*

formly brown or faintly bicolor. **Similar Species.** Easily confused with *M. robinsoni*, which overlaps with it in Belize, Guatemala, El Salvador, and possibly W Panama; *M. robinsoni* is usually larger (Wt 53–76 g in Belize and Guatemala) and has longer, slightly woolly fur. Body size and fur length vary with age, and field identification may not be conclusive (see Comment under *M. robinsoni*). See *M. canescens* and Alston's Mouse Opossum (*Micoureus alstoni*).

Distribution. Tamaulipas and E Mexico to Oaxaca, throughout SE Mexico and Central America to SW Panama. Lowlands to 1800 m.

Status and Habitat. Locally common in a variety of habitats, from dry deciduous to highland evergreen forest, second growth, and grassland.

Habits. This mouse opossum is mainly arboreal and much more easily caught in traps placed on vines or branches than on the ground. It is occasionally caught on the ground, probably when traveling from one foraging area to another. It is active in understory, subcanopy, and canopy levels, to at least 30 m. The diet includes insects and fruit. A nest was found inside a burrow on a bank in Veracruz (Hall and Dalquest, 1963);

however, nests may be more commonly located above ground. In Costa Rica, bird-nest boxes attached to trees are sometimes used, with ball-shaped nests constructed inside the nest box. Like other mouse opossums, this species is secretive and seldom seen, but it may be fairly common, as indicated by the predominance of its bone fragments in regurgitated pellets of Spectacled Owls (Timm et al., 1989).

ROBINSON'S MOUSE OPOSSUM
Plate 3
Marmosa robinsoni
Map 7

Panama: zorra murina.

HB 113–180, T 150–280, HF 20–29, E 23–29, Wt 36–132 g.

Description. Relatively large. Upperparts *orange-brown*, pale to medium brown, or *cinnamon*; underparts buffy yellow or cream (palest on median line). Fur long (9–12 mm) and slightly woolly. Dark eye rings usually large and prominent, sometimes reduced in extent. Eyeshine moderate, reddish. Tail naked looking, brown, faintly bicolor. **Similar Species.** See *M. mexicana* and *Marmosops impavidus*.

Distribution. Belize and Guatemala; El Salvador; Roatán Island, Honduras; Panama to

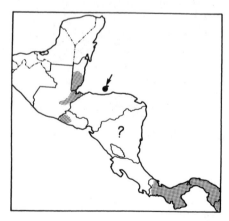

Map 7. Robinson's Mouse Opossum, *Marmosa robinsoni*

Venezuela and N Peru; Saboga and Isla del Rey, Panama; Grenada; Trinidad and Tobago. Lowlands to 2700 m (usually below 500 m in Central America).

Status and Habitat. Locally common in almost all forest types; sometimes abundant in forest gaps, dense second growth, and other edge habitats.

Habits. It is arboreal and terrestrial; about equal numbers are trapped on the ground as in trees and vines. It feeds on insects, fruit, and small vertebrates. Population density averages 0.31–2.25 per ha, and individuals appear to be solitary and nomadic (Fleming, 1972). Nests are built in hollow trees, among banana stalks, in bird-nest boxes, or in abandoned birds' nests. Nonreproductive individuals may not use a permanent nest site but rest in any available shelter encountered at daybreak. Litter size is 6–15; in Panama young are born from April to September (Fleming, 1973). Average life span is about 1 year. Biology reviewed by O'Connell (1983).

Comment. The Central American distribution of this species was previously known only from Panama, with disjunct populations in Belize and Roatán Island, Honduras. It has recently been reported in Guatemala and El Salvador (Engstrom et al., 1993, 1994b). It may be present throughout Central America, and specimens may have been confused with *M. mexicana*. These species can be distinguished by skull characters when adult, but skulls of young and subadult *M. robinsoni* are virtually indistinguishable from those of *M. mexicana*. A reappraisal of all specimens of the 2 species in Central America is needed to determine their exact distributions.

HIGHLAND MOUSE OPOSSUM
Marmosops impavidus

Plate 3
Map 6

HB 126–152, T 155–205, HF 19–24, E 21–24, Wt 36–45 g.

Description. Fairly small. Upperparts reddish brown to *dark brown*; underparts buffy with a white median line. Fur long and soft, slightly woolly. Tail dark brown. **Similar Species.** *Marmosa robinsoni* is orangish and usually larger (can be confusing). *Marmosops invictus* is dark gray and smaller.

Distribution. E Panama to Venezuela, Colombia, Ecuador, and S Peru. 1000–2700 m.

Status and Habitat. Uncommon or rare; found in evergreen, highland forest.

Habits. Arboreal and terrestrial, this species is sometimes trapped on the ground. It favors moist areas and vine tangles (Handley, 1976).

Comment. Formerly known as *Marmosa impavida*, it was placed in the genus *Marmosops* by Gardner and Creighton (1989).

SLATY MOUSE OPOSSUM
Marmosops invictus

Plate 3
Map 8

HB 106–115, T 124–147, HF 17–19, E 21–22, Wt?

Description. Small and shrewlike. *Upperparts dark gray, underparts silvery gray.* Fur short, dense, and even. Tail naked, dark brown, underside blotchy. **Similar Species.** Smaller and darker than other mouse opossums in Panama; gray underparts diagnostic. Sepia Short-tailed Opossum (*Monodelphis*) is smaller, brownish, and has tail shorter than head and body.

Distribution. Panama. 600–1100 m.

Status and Habitat. Rare; found in mid-elevation evergreen forest and second growth.

Habits. This mouse opossum appears to be more terrestrial than other species and is usu-

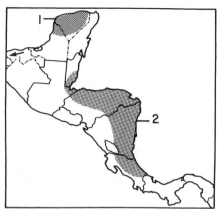

Map 8. Slaty Mouse Opossum, *Marmosops invictus*

Map 9. 1. Grayish Mouse Opossum, *Marmosa canescens*
2. Alston's Mouse Opossum, *Micoureus alstoni*

ally trapped on the ground in moist areas, near or under logs or among rocks. It is occasionally caught on logs 1–2 m above ground. The diet includes insects and plant material. A lactating female was noted in March.

Comment. Formerly known as *Marmosa invicta*, it was placed in the genus *Marmosops* by Gardner and Creighton (1989).

ALSTON'S MOUSE
OPOSSUM   Plates 2, 3
Micoureus alstoni   Map 9

HB 169–200, T 195–281, HF 27–33, E 25–32, Wt 60–150 g.

Description. Largest mouse opossum. Upperparts gray-brown; underparts white or pale orange. Fur long and woolly. Prominent, dark eye rings. *Base of tail furred like the body for 25–50 mm*, naked portion dark brown, with a *long white tip* (usually half brown, half white, sometimes all-dark or with short white tip or blotched toward tip). **Similar Species.** Other mouse opossums are usually smaller and do not have tails that are thickly furred at base or white at tip. Large adults approach Central American Woolly Opossum (*Caluromys*) and Gray Four-eyed Opossum (*Philander*) in size, neither of which have prominent, dark eye rings.

Distribution. Central Belize south along Caribbean Slope to SE Costa Rica. Lowlands to 1600 m.

Status and Habitat. Uncommon to locally common in evergreen forest, second growth, and gardens.

Habits. Chiefly arboreal, it is active in subcanopy or understory levels. It sometimes descends to the ground to feed or travel from tree to tree. It feeds on insects, small vertebrates, and fruit. This species may invade houses near forested areas and is sometimes found in groups (Timm et al., 1989), although most records are of solitary individuals. Leaf nests are built in vine tangles. A female suckling 11 young was noted (Tate, 1933).

Comment. Formerly in *Marmosa*, it was placed in the genus *Micoureus* by Gardner and Creighton (1989).

SEPIA SHORT-TAILED
OPOSSUM   Plate 3
Monodelphis adusta   Map 10

HB 74–107, T 53–66, HF 15–17, E 11–15, Wt 35 g.

Map 10. Sepia Short-tailed Opossum, *Monodelphis adusta*

Description. *Very small* and short tailed. Upperparts *dark brown*, blackish on rump and hips, reddish brown on sides; underparts buffy brown, sometimes with a pale median line. Fur short and smooth. Ears dark brown, short, and rounded. *Tail shorter than head and body*, dark brown, sparsely haired, and faintly bicolor. **Similar Species.** Much smaller and shorter-tailed than other opossums. Could be confused with a small rodent in the field.

Distribution. E Panama to Colombia, Ecuador, and E Peru on the eastern slopes of the Andes. Lowlands to 2200 m (600–900 m in Panama).

Status and Habitat. Rare and local; found in mature, evergreen forest.

Habits. Poorly known. This small opossum is terrestrial. It has been caught among rocks on a forested riverbank, and under a log on a dry gravelbar. It probably eats insects. Females have 6 mammae.

CENTRAL AMERICAN WOOLLY OPOSSUM
Caluromys derbianus

Plate 2
Map 11

Mexico: tlacuache dorado; Honduras: guazalillo dorado; Costa Rica: zorro de balsa; Panama: comadreja, zorra roja.

HB 247–321 (11"), T 271–457 (14"), HF 35–50, E 38–42, Wt 200–400 g (0.7 lb).

Description. Medium sized and long tailed. Upperparts pale gray with *orangish patches* (color varies from entirely gray to entirely orange; commonly has 3 orange patches on neck and shoulders, midback, and rump, with a gray diamond between shoulders); underparts creamy white. Fur long and *woolly*. Ears large and pale pinkish. Dark brown median line on forehead. Eyes large, brown; bright, red eyeshine. *Tail very long, upper surface haired like body for half tail length*; naked midsection mottled, dark brown and white; long, *naked tip entirely white*. Tops of feet white. **Similar Species.** No other opossums in Central America have the tail furred for half its length. At night, the long white tail tip and pale pink ears are distinctive.

Distribution. Veracruz, Mexico, to W Colombia and N Ecuador. Lowlands to 2500 m.

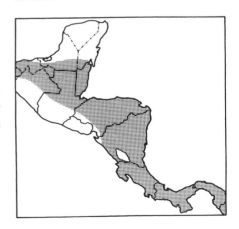

Map 11. Central American Woolly Opossum, *Caluromys derbianus*

Status and Habitat. Uncommon to locally common in evergreen and deciduous forest and second growth. Usually found at forest edge, in vine tangles, and in tall secondary forest.

Habits. This attractive opossum is strictly nocturnal and emerges late in the evening, seldom being seen until at least an hour after dark (individuals on islands are sometimes diurnal in habit). It is easily located with a headlamp by its bright, red eyeshine. When encountered, it usually freezes in response to light, with the long tail hanging vertically. This strictly arboreal species runs with fast, agile movements along vines or branches, the tail held horizontally, its tip in close contact with the substrate. When moving slowly, the tail tip may be coiled around a branch or vine. In rural areas near forest, it is sometimes seen sitting motionless on a telephone wire and can run easily along this narrow surface. A voracious insect eater, this opossum also eats fruit, including *Piper* spp., *Cecropia* spp., and figs, and it may eat small vertebrates. During the dry season it feeds on nectar, including *Ochroma pyramidale, Mabea occidentalis,* and *Trichanthera gigantea.* By visiting the flowers of several trees of a single species, woolly opossums may act as pollinators (Gribel, 1988). Leaf nests are made in vine tangles or in tree holes well above ground. Litter size is 1–6 and breeding may occur throughout the year. Biology reviewed by Butcher and Hoffmann (1980).

ANTEATERS, SLOTHS, AND ARMADILLOS

Order Xenarthra (Edentata)

This order of mammals consists of 4 families, with 13 genera and 29 species, all of which are restricted to the New World. Although anteaters, armadillos, and sloths are externally dissimilar, they share certain skeletal characteristics. The name "xenarthra" refers to extra articulations in the lumbar vertebrae, which are found only in members of this order. They are also sometimes known as "edentates," which means without teeth, although this term was originally used to group xenarthrans with the toothless Old World pangolins (Order Pholidota). Whether these New and Old World groups are related or whether their similarities result only from convergent evolution remains controversial, but the New World group is nearly always considered a separate order. The anteaters are the only toothless xenarthrans, although the teeth of sloths and armadillos are undifferentiated and peglike. These mammals diverged early from the main placental mammal lineage, when South America was an island continent. Their extinct relatives included giant ground sloths and glyptodonts.

Xenarthrans do not maintain as constant a body temperature as most other tropical mammals. Allowing the body temperature to drop slightly at night or in cool weather may be a means of conserving energy. Because of this, few species are strictly nocturnal or diurnal; instead, they adjust their behavior depending on the local climate and show great individual variation in activity patterns. Several species are common in the region, and all are relatively easy to observe once located, relying more on cryptic camouflage or external armor than speed and alertness to avoid predators. A general reference for the group is Montgomery (1985).

ANTEATERS (Spanish: hormigueros)
Family Myrmecophagidae

The Myrmecophagidae consists of four species in three genera; three species occur in Central America. Anteaters have elongated noses, very long, wormlike tongues, and no teeth. They have muscular forelegs and forefeet equipped with a large third claw for tearing open ant mounds or rotting logs. When an ant or termite nest is opened, soldiers from the colony defend the nest by biting or spraying noxious chemicals at the attacker. To collect harmless workers and larvae before the soldier insects are mobilized, anteaters feed for very short periods, often only a few seconds, at each nest (Redford, 1985). Sticky saliva on the long tongue enables them to quickly gather large numbers of insects before they move on to another nest. When on the ground, anteaters do not walk on the soles of the forefeet, but on the knuckles or sides of the feet. This results in a front track with a peculiar reversed-claw impression and a rather awkward gait. These mammals have poor vision and hearing, but a good sense of smell. When cornered or threatened, they rear up on their hind legs, brace themselves with the tail, and strike with the powerful foreclaws. The larger species are reputed to kill or maim dogs in self-defense and thus are routinely killed by hunters and farmers.

GIANT ANTEATER
Myrmecophaga tridactyla

Plate 4
Map 12

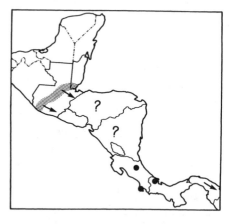

Map 12. Giant Anteater, *Myrmecophaga tridactyla*
Former range and recent sightings (●)

Spanish: oso hormiguero, oso caballo; Miskito: wingu tara.

HB 1100–2000 (4'), T 600–900 (2'6"), Wt 22–39 kg (66 lb).

Description. Large; body shape unlike any other mammal. The long, tapered snout and long, bushy tail result in an extremely elongated profile. Brownish, with a distinct black V from chest to midback; forelegs cream with black bands on wrists. Four claws on forefoot, third claw huge (track shows claws pointing backward); 5 claws on hind foot. **Similar Species.** None.

Distribution. In Central America, possibly from S Belize to E Panama; in South America west of the Andes to N Ecuador; east of the Andes to Bolivia and N Argentina. Lowlands only.

Status and Habitat. CITES Appendix II. Very rare and local in Central America, where it is known only from specimens collected in the 1900s or before. The northernmost locality in S Belize is an undocumented reference to a site near Punta Gorda. There have been a few recent sight records in Costa Rica (Timm et al., 1989) and Panama. This species may be the most endangered mammal in Central America. It suffers from habitat loss, fire, and direct persecution by farmers throughout its range. It prefers open savannah, but also occurs at lower densities in forest.

Habits. In South America the Giant Anteater may be active day and night, depending on temperature, rainfall, and human disturbance. A terrestrial species, it walks long distances with a shuffling gait. If pursued it speeds up to a rolling gallop, but when cornered it may erect the long hair on its back. The powerful forelimbs and large claws are used to break into large, terrestrial termite mounds. This anteater seems to be most common where such mounds are clearly in evidence, although it also feeds on ants in inconspicuous ground nests. Individuals are solitary except during the breeding season. Females give birth to one young, which is carried on the mother's back for 6–9 months. Young call with high-pitched whistles; adults are usually silent but may roar when attacked. Life span in captivity is up to 16 years. Biology reviewed by Redford and Eisenberg (1992).

NORTHERN TAMANDUA   Plate 4
Tamandua mexicana   Map 13

Vested anteater; Spanish: oso hormiguero común; Mexico: hormiguero arborícola, brazo fuerte; Maya: chab; Belize: ant bear; Miskito: wingku; Costa Rica: oso mielero; Panama: hormiguero bandera; Chocó: osito; Kuna: sugachu.

HB 520–770 (2'), T 400–675 (1'8"), Wt 3.8–8.5 kg (12 lb).

Description. Long, tapered snout and blotchy, *almost naked, prehensile tail.* Fur sparse, *cream to golden brown with a black vest.* Forelimbs powerful, forefoot with 2 large and 2 small claws (track shows claws facing inward or backward); 5 claws on hind foot. Eyeshine

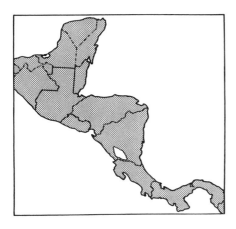

Map 13. Northern Tamandua, *Tamandua mexicana*

dull, reddish. Young usually same color as adult, rarely all black or all yellow. **Similar Species.** None in region.

Distribution. San Luis Potosí and Tamaulipas, Mexico, to NW Peru and NW Venezuela. Lowlands to 1600 m.

Status and Habitat. CITES Appendix III (Guatemala). Widespread; uncommon to fairly common in evergreen and deciduous forest, mangroves, second growth, and savannah. Sometimes hunted for its hide or for meat for dogs.

Habits. Nocturnal and diurnal; some are diurnal and may be active at any time of day, while others may be entirely nocturnal at the same locality. It may be found as it noisily shuffles along or by the sound of tearing as it rips apart decaying wood. When alarmed it usually climbs a tree or vine but seems to have a short memory of disturbance and may closely approach a motionless observer. Both terrestrial and arboreal, there is considerable variation between individuals in the amount of time spent on the ground or in trees. This anteater dens in hollow trees or logs, in holes on the ground, or it may sleep on a shaded branch during the day. The diet consists of ants, termites, and occasionally bees. Termites are taken both from large, arboreal nests and from feeding aggregations in rotting wood; ants are usually obtained on the ground. It is solitary and usually silent in the wild, although it may wheeze and salivate if threatened. Individual home range size in Panama is about 75 ha. Females give birth to one young at any time of year; young ride on the mother's back or may be left in a den. Natural history reviewed by Lubin (1983).

Where to See. Common at Rara Avis, Costa Rica, and around Gamboa, Soberanía National Park, and Barro Colorado Island, Panama. Where common, roadkills are frequently seen.

SILKY ANTEATER
Cyclopes didactylus

Plate 4
Map 14

Mexico: hormiguero dorado; Maya: kisin, woyotz; Miskito: likur; Costa Rica: ceibita, tapacara, serafín de platanar; Panama: gato balsa.

HB 123–215 (7"), T 170–242 (8"), Wt 155–275 g (8 oz).

Map 14. Silky Anteater, *Cyclopes didactylus*

Description. Tiny. Upperparts *shiny gray-gold*, dark brown stripe from shoulders to rump; underparts creamy yellow, usually with a dark brown stripe on midline of belly; fur dense and wavy. Nose not greatly elongated. *Prehensile tail long, furry*, and tapered. Forefoot with 2 large claws; 4 long, curved claws and an extra joint in hind foot. **Similar Species.** This arboreal anteater is about the size of a small squirrel; other mammals of this size do not have furry, prehensile tails or large foreclaws.

Distribution. SE Veracruz and SE Oaxaca, Mexico, through Central America (except Yucatán Peninsula) west of the Andes to S Ecuador, and east of the Andes to C Brazil and Bolivia. Lowlands to about 1500 m.

Status and Habitat. Poorly known; may be fairly common although seldom seen. Found in evergreen and semideciduous forest, second growth, and mangroves.

Habits. This small, nocturnal anteater rests during the day rolled up in a ball, 2–10 m above ground in vine tangles. Look for a furry, "golden tennis ball." Activity starts soon after sunset and continues until 1–3 hours before dawn. Strictly arboreal, it travels on pencil-thin branches and vines by gripping them tightly with the modified hind feet. It feeds chiefly on ants that live inside hollow stems and thin branches. The large foreclaws are used to split open the stems, and ants inside are licked up. Adults are solitary and require a large home range for their size; therefore, population densities are low. Males have very large home ranges that include nonoverlapping ranges of several females. Females give birth to single young and may reproduce twice yearly. Young are left behind when the mother forages and are moved to a new rest site before dawn. Natural history reviewed by Montgomery (1983b).

SLOTHS (Spanish: perezosos)
Families Megalonychidae and Bradypodidae

There is one genus with 2 species of two-toed sloths (Family Megalonychidae, formerly Choloepidae), and one genus with 3 species of three-toed sloths (Family Bradypodidae). One species from each of the 2 sloth families occurs in Central America. These species are not closely related to one another; the two-toed sloths are allied with a group of extinct giant ground sloths. Sloths are the only mammals that may be seen hanging motionless below a branch. They are specialized to exist on a low-energy diet of leaves.

They have long, curved claws that grip branches without using muscular force, enabling them to hang upside down without expending energy. The direction of fur growth is reversed so that it hangs down from the belly toward the back. Individual hairs are pitted or grooved, and in humid areas become filled with algae, giving the fur a greenish cast and providing the sloth with an effective camouflage. Certain moths feed on the algae. Sloths have simple, peglike teeth, with 5 upper and 4 to 5 lower teeth on each side of the jaw. The two-toed sloths have pointed, caninelike front teeth. The stomach has several chambers to aid in the digestion of leaves.

Sloths are common in mature forest, where they are often very difficult to see. Both species are more easily seen in second growth and pastures with scattered trees, particularly in the Caribbean lowlands. Sloths descend to the ground about once a week to defecate and urinate (when on the ground, three-toed sloths dig a small hole with the tail, tailless two-toed sloths do not). The round trip from the canopy takes more than an hour and may expose the sloth to predators on the ground. This unusual behavior has not been shown to benefit the sloth, although several dubious hypotheses, such as preferential fertilization of food trees, have been proposed. Although generally considered to be unaggressive and silent, in both species the males occasionally fight with one another, and when aroused may give high-pitched cries or whistles (Greene, 1989; H. Tiebout, personal communication).

HOFFMANN'S TWO-TOED SLOTH
Choloepus hoffmanni

Plate 5
Map 15

Spanish: perezoso de dos dedos; (others as for three-toed sloth).

HB 540–700 (2'), T 0, Wt 4–8 kg (13 lb).

Description. Hangs below branch. Fur long and shaggy; body and tops of feet *dull cream-brown*; legs usually darker, dull red-brown. Fur on head pale gray, often with a greenish cast on crown, white around face. *Snout bulbous, piglike*, with large, widely spaced nostrils. Eyes large, brown. No tail. Forelegs slightly longer than hind legs, *2 claws on forefoot*, 3 claws on hind foot. Feet long and narrow, with naked pads. Young dark brown with short, woolly fur. Dull, reddish eyeshine. **Similar Species.** See Brown-throated Three-toed Sloth.

Distribution. E Honduras (McCarthy et al., in press) and N Nicaragua to Peru and E Brazil. Lowlands to 3300 m (reported from high elevations in Costa Rica by Molina U. et al., 1986).

Map 15. Hoffmann's Two-toed Sloth, *Choloepus hoffmanni*

Status and Habitat. CITES Appendix III (Costa Rica). Fairly common and widespread in evergreen and semideciduous forest and second growth in lowlands and highlands. Rare or absent in dry, lowland forest.

Habits. Mainly nocturnal, this sloth may shift position and occasionally feeds by day. It sleeps during the day in vine tangles high in the canopy, or in the shaded crotch of a tree. In the lowlands it maintains a more constant body temperature than a three-toed sloth but may allow its temperature to drop at night in the highlands. It often rests on exposed branches at higher elevations, where it is more easily seen than in tall, lowland forest. Hoffmann's Two-toed Sloth is arboreal; it travels on narrow branches and lianas and has difficulty ascending trunks of large trees. It sometimes crosses gaps or roads on the ground; it crawls awkwardly but can support its weight in this position (unlike a three-toed sloth). It swims well. This species is more active and faster-moving than a three-toed sloth and is much more aggressive. If the vines around it are disturbed while it rests, it will advance and slash with the forelimbs or attempt to bite savagely (Montgomery and Sunquist, 1978). It feeds on leaves and some fruit, and sometimes licks and gnaws on tree trunks, probably feeding on lichen or moss growing on the bark. Females give birth to one young, which is carried on the mother's chest.

Where to See. This is the more common sloth at higher elevations; in the lowlands it is less common than Brown-throated Three-toed Sloth. Two-toed Sloths are easily seen in pastures with scattered trees at 1000–1500 m on the Pacific Slope of Cordillera de Tilarán near Monteverde, Santa Elena, and around Lake Arenal, Costa Rica. Both sloths are common at Tortuguero National Park; in scattered trees along the highway south of Limón, and in the Limón town square, Costa Rica; also on roadsides on the Atlantic Slope of the Panama Canal Area (near Fort Sherman, for example).

BROWN-THROATED THREE-TOED SLOTH

Bradypus variegatus

Plate 5
Map 16

Spanish: perezoso de tres dedos; Miskito: si-waiku; Panama: perico ligero, mono perezoso; Chocó: bucha; Kuna: ibku.

Map 16. Brown-throated Three-toed Sloth, *Bradypus variegatus*

HB 400–770 (1'9"), T 47–90 (3"), Wt 2.3–5.5 kg (8 lb).

Description. Hangs below branch. *Grizzled, grayish*, coarse-looking fur. "Cute, smiling" face, with a small dark snout, dark mask through eyes and whitish fur on forehead; throat brown. *Short, stubby tail.* Forelegs much longer than hind legs. Limbs and feet stocky, palms and soles fully furred; *3 claws on each foot.* Patch of short, orange fur with a black central line or black spots on midback of male. Eyeshine weak, reddish. **Similar Species.** Hoffmann's Two-toed Sloth has 2 claws on each forefoot, a broad, piglike snout, and face ringed with white fur. When curled up asleep, high in trees, the species can be difficult to distinguish; Hoffmann's is dull brown, not grizzled gray, and has darker fur on limbs than on back.

Distribution. C Honduras to E Peru and NW Argentina. Lowlands to 2400 m (Molina U. et al., 1986).

Status and Habitat. CITES Appendix II. Common to abundant in lowland evergreen and deciduous forest and second growth; less common in highland forest.

Habits. This sloth allows its body temperature to drop at night, relying on sunlight to warm up in the morning. In tall forest, it spends part of the day sunning itself high in the canopy, where it is difficult to see from the ground. It is much easier to see in disturbed forest and second growth, where it often suns itself in smaller, open-structure trees such as *Cecropia*. Most of the day is spent sleeping, hanging from a branch, or curled in a ball on the crotch of a tree or among vines. It often changes position and sometimes feeds by day, but is more active at night. This species is strictly arboreal and cannot support its body when on the ground, but it swims well. The diet consists entirely of leaves taken from a large number of tree species. The long arms are used to reach the end of branches to grasp young leaves, which are more digestible and are preferred. In suitable habitat, there may be five to eight individuals per hectare. Adults are solitary; although home ranges of about 1.6 ha may overlap, neighbors seldom feed from the same tree. When captured and handled, these sloths do not attempt to bite or strike. Females give birth to one young after a 6-month gestation. Young start to eat leaves at 2 weeks of age and are carried on the mother's chest for about 6 months. The female then leaves part of her home range to her offspring and moves to an adjacent area. Life span is thought to be 20–30 years in the wild. Natural history reviewed by Montgomery (1983a).

Where to See. Abundant and easily seen at Manuel Antonio and Tortuguero National Parks, Costa Rica. Refer to "Where to See" for Hoffman's Two-toed Sloth for additional localities.

ARMADILLOS (Spanish: armadillos)
Family Dasypodidae

There are 8 genera and about 20 species of armadillos, most of which are restricted to South America. Two species occur in Central America and SE Mexico. Armadillos are covered on the upper surface by bony armor. The shell, or carapace, covers the body and has moveable plates in the middle which allow the animal to bend. Scales, or scutes, also cover the top of the head, legs, and in some species, the tail. Shape of the scutes is characteristic for each genus. The soft, pink belly may be nearly naked or lightly furred. The feet are equipped with long, broad claws for digging. There are 7–10 undifferentiated, peglike teeth on each side of the upper and lower jaws.

Armadillos are found in forests and open areas. Where common, they are often killed by traffic on roads or hunted for meat. They are terrestrial and semifossorial. They dig burrows that are used for rest sites and for raising young. Abandoned armadillo burrows are often used by other mammals. Armadillos feed on insects, especially ants and termites, and occasionally eat other plant or animal foods.

NORTHERN NAKED-TAILED ARMADILLO

Cabassous centralis   Plate 5
                                             Map 17

Spanish: armadillo; Maya: wai-wech; Honduras: tumbo armado, cusuco venenoso, pitero de uña; Costa Rica: armadillo zopilote; Panama: armadillo rabo de puerco.

HB 300–400 (13"), T 130–180 (6"), Wt 2.5–3.5 kg (7 lb).

Description. Broad and flat looking. *Tail short, less than half head and body length, naked-looking* (a few small scutes present), pale pinkish gray. Upperparts mostly dark gray-brown, edge of carapace yellowish. Scutes large, roughly

Map 17. Northern Naked-tailed Armadillo, *Cabassous centralis*

The soil fills in behind the animal when it digs an escape tunnel, and after it disappears, the only sign of activity is a bare patch where the leaf litter has been disturbed. Burrows are often located on banks; the entrances are circular or oval. This armadillo sometimes dens under buildings and may draw attention to itself with surprisingly loud roars and growls. It has a strong, musty smell, and gives a low roar when handled. The diet consists mainly of ants and termites. Individuals are solitary. Females give birth to one young.

square in shape; 10–13 inconspicuous moveable bands on back. Head broad, with widely spaced, rounded ears. Five claws on each foot; claws on forefoot broad and long, *middle claw very large*, about half length of foot. **Similar Species.** Nine-banded Armadillo (*Dasypus*) is larger, with a long, armored tail and a more narrow, upright shape.

Distribution. E Chiapas, Mexico (Aranda and March, 1987), and Belize (McCarthy, 1982), patchily distributed through Central America to NE Colombia and NW Venezuela. Lowlands to 1800 m.

Status and Habitat. CITES Appendix III (Costa Rica). Apparently rare and local; poorly known. It is not hunted for meat due to its unpleasant odor. Found in deciduous and evergreen forest, second growth, and savannah. It seems to be most common in seasonally dry regions in rather open habitats or at forest edge in rocky terrain.

Habits. Probably mainly nocturnal, although occasionally seen by day. This apparently rare species may spend more time underground than other armadillos and therefore is seldom encountered. It is occasionally seen digging under rotten logs. If disturbed, it uses the powerful front claws to quickly tunnel out of view, while the body rotates from side to side.

NINE-BANDED ARMADILLO
Plate 5
Dasypus novemcinctus
Map 18

Spanish: armadillo; Mexico: mulita; Maya: mail chan, wech; Belize: dilly; Miskito: tahira; Honduras, Costa Rica: cusuco; Panama: armado; Kuna: ugsi; Chocó: tro.

HB 384–573 (19"), T 276–430 (14"), Wt 3–7 kg (11 lb).

Description. The familiar "Texas armadillo." Body shape in profile roughly semicircular, long and narrow from above. *Tail long, about 2/3 head and body length, entirely armored*; scutes on tail arranged in overlapping bands for ⅔ length from base. Dark gray, with small scutes and 8-9 conspicuous, moveable bands on back. Head and ears long and narrow; ears funnel-shaped, closely spaced. Four claws on forefoot (track often shows only 2 larger middle claws); 5 claws on hind foot (track is birdlike, with only 3 toes usually showing). No eyeshine. **Similar Species.** See Northern Naked-tailed Armadillo (*Cabassous*).

Distribution. SE and C United States, widespread through Mexico, Central and South America to Uruguay and N Argentina; Grenada, Margarita, Trinidad, and Tobago. Lowlands to 2600 m (usually below 1500 m).

Status and Habitat. Common and widespread in evergreen and deciduous forest, thorn scrub,

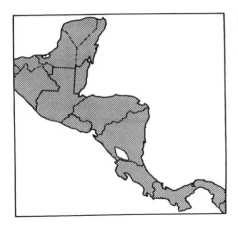

Map 18. Nine-banded Armadillo, *Dasypus novemcinctus*

and savannah. The identical young are used in medical research (particularly in studies of leprosy) in the United States. Large numbers are killed on roads by motor vehicles, and the species is heavily hunted in some areas.

Habits. Mainly nocturnal, but sometimes active by day, especially in cooler weather. The Nine-banded Armadillo is usually heard before it is seen, as it snuffles and noisily rummages through leaf litter like a small tank. Its movements are erratic; on sensing danger, it stops, sniffs, races explosively for several meters, then stops again. When alarmed at close range, it may jump straight up, with its back arched. The senses of smell and hearing are good, but eyesight is poor. This armadillo swims well; it sometimes gulps air to increase buoyancy, or may cross small streams by walking on the bottom of the streambed. It dens in burrows with multiple entries, which are often dug on banks. Burrow entrances are roughly semicircular and have well-worn paths radiating out from them. Nests are lined with grass or leaves, which are grasped between the front feet and carried backward into the burrow. It eats arthropods (mainly beetles, ants, termites, earthworms, and snails), some small vertebrates, fruit, and carrion. Rotting, flyblown carrion is favored over fresh kills. Signs of armadillo activity include disturbance of leaf litter and small, conical holes where insects have been dug out. Individuals are solitary, but not territorial. Mating takes place with the female lying on her back. Identical quadruplets are born relatively well developed and forage with the mother after a few weeks. Biology reviewed by McBee and Baker (1982) and Wetzel (1983).

Where to See. Especially common at Rincón de la Vieja National Park, Costa Rica, and Barro Colorado Island, Panama, but may be seen throughout the region.

INSECTIVORES

Order Insectivora

This group of mammals includes the shrews, moles, solenodons, hedgehogs, moonrats, and tenrecs. Some members of this order have not changed greatly from the generalized, ancestral mammal form. Although insectivores are found throughout most of the world, their diversity in the Neotropics is low, and members of only one family, the shrews, occur in Central America and SE Mexico.

Insectivores have long, tapering snouts, small eyes and ears, teeth in continuous rows, and 5 toes on each foot. Most insectivores are small in size and are among the world's smallest mammals. They are terrestrial, subterranean, or semiaquatic and eat mostly insects, other invertebrates, and small vertebrates.

SHREWS (Spanish: musarañas)
Family Soricidae

There are 22 genera and about 290 species of shrews. Shrews are found throughout most of the world, but in South America only reach the northern Andes. Two genera and about 15 species occur in Central America and SE Mexico, mostly in the highlands. Shrews are small, mouselike mammals, with long, pointed snouts and small eyes. They have 5 clawed toes on each foot (unlike mice, which have 4 toes on the front foot). The small, sharp teeth usually have reddish tips and are in a continuous row (in mice there is a large gap behind the incisors). The dental formula is: i 3/1, c 1/1, p 3/1 (*Sorex*) or 2/1 (*Cryptotis*), m 3/3. Shrews have short, velvety fur, which is usually blackish or gray-brown in color. Most shrews have a summer and a winter coat that differ slightly in length and color. Males sometimes have enlarged scent glands on the flanks that appear as hairless ovals; this feature may be helpful in distinguishing the sexes, as the external genitalia are similar in males and females.

Most of the shrews in the region are found in cold, wet highland forests and forest edges. They may enter agricultural areas, often along the banks of streams or in ditches with dense vegetation. Some are found in dry, coniferous forest, but they are usually associated with seeps or wet areas in such regions.

Shrews are terrestrial; they use runways in the leaf litter or on the soil surface under grass, and some make shallow burrows in the soil. They generally do not climb, but there are a few records of shrews trapped in trees or on logs. Most species for which information is available are active sporadically during the day and night; some are mainly nocturnal. When awake, shrews are frantically active, highly nervous, and often aggressive to one another. These diminutive mammals die of stress with little provocation. Loud noises, unfamiliar surroundings, and other stimuli can cause their demise. Shrews are reputed to have a voracious appetite and high metabolism. In captivity they can consume one half to two times their body weight in food per day and may die of starvation or stress if food-deprived for a few hours. It is unlikely that wild individuals behave in a similar fashion to captives, as shrews are often exposed to periods of food shortage. When this happens, they probably spend more time resting, and may even go into torpor. Even in captivity, short tailed shrews (*Blarina* sp.) can live for several months on a diet amounting to only 10% of their body weight per day (Martinsen, 1969). Shrews eat mainly invertebrates, including earthworms and adult and larval insects. Some small vertebrates, including other shrews and small mice, and, to a lesser extent, fungi and seeds, are also consumed.

Little is known of the ecology of shrews in Mexico and Central America. Most species appear to be rare based on numbers of specimens in museum collections. This probably more reflects the difficulty of capture than actual abundance, as the remains of shrews are often well represented in the diet of predators such as owls (skulls and partial skeletons can be identified from regurgitated owl pellets). Shrews seldom enter mouse traps; they are not attracted to the commonly used baits and may be more wary of entering traps than most rodents. Instead, pitfall traps, consisting of smooth-sided containers dug into the ground with the rim slightly below the soil surface, are used to capture shrews. Drift fences made of planks or plastic sheets, leading to the pitfall, increase trap success. It takes considerable effort to set a sufficient number of pitfalls to catch shrews; the catch rate is usually low, so only shrew specialists and a few dedicated collectors regularly set these traps. Shrews are sometimes found dead in the middle of a trail or road, often in populated areas. These individuals may have been killed by domestic cats, which find them distasteful and do not eat them.

Shrews in Central America and SE Mexico are extremely difficult to identify to species in the hand (and virtually impossible when glimpsed dashing across a path); most can only be identified based on characters of the teeth and skull. Several species have restricted geographic ranges and so may be identifiable by location. The principal taxonomic reference for short-eared shrews (*Cryptotis* spp.) is Choate (1970). Later work by Woodman and Timm (1992, 1993) has revealed additional species in this genus. Notes on Middle American *Sorex* were provided by Junge and Hoffmann (1981). Further studies will probably add to the number of species of both *Cryptotis* and *Sorex* in the region. The 2 genera are quite easily distinguished from one another, as follows:

Sorex. Tail long, about 3/4 head and body length; small external ears clearly visible; feet relatively long and narrow; most species dark brown.

Cryptotis. Tail short, less than or equal to 1/2 head and body length; ears very small, concealed in fur and not visible externally; feet relatively short and broad; most species blackish.

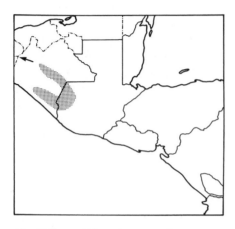

Map 19. Saussure's Shrew, *Sorex saussurei*

SAUSSURE'S SHREW
Sorex saussurei

Plate 25
Map 19

HB 65–77, T 43–60, HF 14–16, E about 5.

Description. Upperparts sandy brown to dark chocolate brown; underparts pale to dark gray-brown. Tail more than 2/3 head and body length. **Similar Species.** Other *Sorex* shrews in the region are usually darker in color, but may be difficult to distinguish in the field.

Distribution. Highlands of Mexico from Coahuila and Durango to Chiapas, and SW Guatemala. 1800–3200 m.

Status and Habitat. Uncommon to locally common in cold, coniferous and broadleaf forest. Also found in disturbed habitats, often near water.

Habits. Terrestrial; travels in shallow burrows in the leaf litter or near the soil surface.

SCLATER'S SHREW
Sorex sclateri

Map 20

HB 68–73, T 52–53, HF 15–16, E about 6.

Description. Upperparts blackish brown; underparts slightly paler, dark gray-brown. Tail long, about 3/4 head and body length. Relatively long hind feet. **Similar Species.** No other *Sorex* shrews have been taken at its locality; the other species in the region do occur in the same mountain range but are usually found at higher elevations. *S. sclateri* is the darkest species, but could be easily confused with *S. veraepacis.*

Distribution. Known only from Tumbalá, N Chiapas, Mexico. 1700m.

Status and Habitat. Apparently rare.

Habits. Unknown.

SAN CRISTOBAL SHREW
Sorex stizodon

Map 20

HB 66, T 41, HF 12, E about 5.

Description. Upperparts dark gray-brown; underparts brown with a pinkish cast. Tail almost 2/3 head and body length. **Similar Species.** *S.*

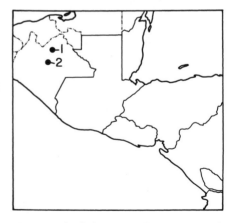

Map 20. 1. Sclater's Shrew, *Sorex sclateri*
2. San Cristóbal Shrew, *Sorex stizodon*

saussurei is slightly larger but otherwise very similar.

Distribution. San Cristóbal, N Chiapas, Mexico. 2700 m. Known only from the type locality.

Status and Habitat. Apparently rare; found in wet, montane forest.

Habits. Unknown.

VERAPAZ SHREW
Sorex veraepacis

Plate 25
Map 21

HB 67–78, T 45–57, HF 14–16, E about 5.

Description. Upperparts dark gray-brown, sometimes flecked with white hairs; underparts gray-brown. Tail more than 2/3 head and body length. **Similar Species.** *S. saussurei* and *S. stizodon* are both usually paler and browner, but the 3 species may not be distinguishable in the field.

Distribution. Mountains of Veracruz, Guerrero, Oaxaca, and Chiapas, Mexico, and C Guatemala. 1800–3100 m.

Status and Habitat. Locally common in cold, wet, pine–oak and broadleaf forest.

Habits. Terrestrial; uses shallow burrows in the leaf litter and may travel on fallen logs.

LEAST SHREW
Cryptotis parva

Plate 25
Map 22

HB 55–78, T 17–27, HF 10–13, E 0, Wt 4–8 g.

Description. Very small, with a short tail (1/3 or less length of head and body). Upperparts *brownish* (gray-brown, sandy brown, or dark brown); underparts pale silvery gray, often with a yellowish cast. Fur short, about 3 mm long on rump. Front feet very small with tiny, needlelike claws (claws about 1 mm long). **Similar Species.** This is the only *Cryptotis* in the region with brown upperparts; all others (except *C. mayensis*, which does not overlap with *C. parva*) are blackish. As the name suggests, the Least Shrew is the smallest species in the genus. Its range overlaps with 6 other species, but it is usually at lower elevations and in more open habitats than other shrews.

Distribution. SE Canada and E United States through E and C Mexico to Costa Rica. Lowlands to 2400 m (usually above 800 m in Central America).

Status and Habitat. Widespread, often common, mainly in open, grassy habitats and along streams in otherwise dry habitats. Also found in cold, wet, pine–oak and broadleaf forest.

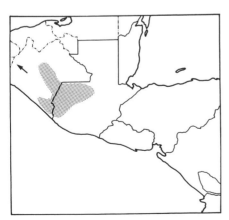

Map 21. Verapaz Shrew, *Sorex veraepacis*

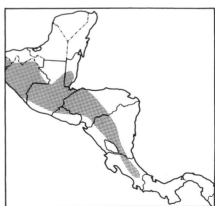

Map 22. Least Shrew, *Cryptotis parva*

Habits. The Least Shrew is active sporadically during both night and day, with greatest activity during the night. It is terrestrial and makes tiny runways through grass or uses larger runways made by rodents. Globular nests of leaves and dry grass are usually located directly below logs, rocks, or boards, but are sometimes constructed in burrows. The diet includes insect larvae, centipedes, and earthworms. It sometimes enters bee hives to eat the brood. Unlike most shrews, this species is fairly social; up to 30 adults may share a nest, and adults do not appear to fight when they encounter each other. They make a variety of calls, including clicks and birdlike chirps, audible only at close range. Ultrasonic clicks are also given, which may be used for echolocation. Litter size is 2-7, usually about 4. Biology reviewed by Whitaker (1974).

BLACKISH SMALL-EARED SHREW
Cryptotis nigrescens   Map 23

HB 55–83, T 19–37, HF 13–14, E 0, Wt 5–8 g.

Description. Small. Upperparts blackish, sometimes sprinkled with pale hairs; under-

Map 23. Blackish Small-eared Shrew, *Cryptotis nigrescens*

parts charcoal gray, almost as dark as upperparts. Fur on rump 4–5 mm long. Tail rather short, less than 1/2 head and body length. Feet small and slim, with tiny claws. Snout relatively short and broad. **Similar Species.** Usually darker, but probably indistinguishable in the field from *C. merriami* (both occur in the Cordillera de Tilarán but have not been taken together); *C. gracilis* has a relatively longer tail (1/2 head and body length) and has longer fur (6–7 mm); *C. parva* is brownish and usually smaller; see *C. endersi*.

Distribution. Mountains of Costa Rica and W Panama. 800–2900 m.

Status and Habitat. Locally common in cool, evergreen forest and forest edge, and in drier, open woodland on the Pacific Slope. Also in pastures and other open areas.

Habits. Litter size is 1–3.

HONDURAN SMALL-EARED SHREW
Cryptotis hondurensis   Map 26

HB 55–64, T 27–29, HF 11–13, E 0.

Description. Small. Upperparts blackish-brown; underparts dark brown. Fur on rump 4–5 mm long. Tail relatively long, about 1/2 head and body length, tapering to a point at the tip. **Similar Species.** Very similar to *C. merriami*, which has a slightly shorter, blunt-tipped tail. The only other *Cryptotis* in Honduras is *C. parva*, which is brownish with a shorter tail.

Distribution. Known only from 3 localities in Departamento Francisco Morazán, S Honduras, at about 1700 m.

Status and Habitat. Apparently rare; found in cool, wet pine and broadleaf forest.

Habits. Unknown.

Comment. Previously included in *C. gracilis*. See Woodman and Timm (1992).

MERRIAM'S SMALL-EARED SHREW
Cryptotis merriami   Map 24

HB 65–76, T 24–33, HF 11–14, E 0.

Description. Upperparts blackish brown or dark gray-brown; underparts gray-brown, slightly paler than upperparts. Fur on rump 3–5 mm long. Tail moderately short, less than 1/2 head and body length. **Similar Species.** See *C. nigrescens* and *C. hondurensis*; *C. goldmani* and *C. goodwini* are both larger, with bigger feet and longer fur, and are usually found at higher elevations.

Distribution. Mountains of E Chiapas, Mexico, to N Nicaragua; also NW Costa Rica. 1000–1650 m.

Status and Habitat. Apparently uncommon; occurs in evergreen, broadleaf and pine–oak forest and cultivated areas near forest.

Habits. Poorly known.

Comment. Treated as a subspecies of *C. nigrescens* by Choate (1970), but given species status by Woodman and Timm (1993).

DARIEN SMALL-EARED SHREW
Cryptotis mera   Map 24

HB 67–73, T 24–31, HF 11–13, E 0.

Description. Small. Upperparts blackish brown; underparts charcoal gray. Fur on rump about 4 mm long. Tail short, less than 1/2 head and body length. **Similar Species.** No other shrews are known from E Panama.

Distribution. Darién highlands, E Panama. 1400–1500 m.

Status and Habitat. Apparently rare; found in wet, evergreen forest.

Habits. Terrestrial. Individuals have been trapped under logs on steep banks of streams. The banks were wet and densely covered with ferns (Goldman, 1920).

Map 24. 1. Merriam's Small-eared Shrew, *Cryptotis merriami*
2. Darién Small-eared Shrew, *Cryptotis mera*

Comment. Previously considered to be a subspecies of *C. nigrescens*. See Woodman and Timm (1993).

MAYA SMALL-EARED SHREW   Plate 25
Cryptotis mayensis   Map 25

HB 61–90, T 24–33, HF 11–13, E 0, Wt 4–6 g.

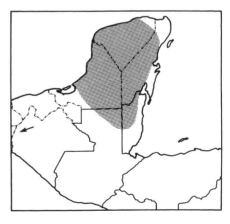

Map 25. Maya Small-eared Shrew, *Cryptotis mayensis*

Description. Small. Upperparts pale gray or gray; underparts silvery, slightly paler than upperparts. Fur short, 3–4 mm long on rump. Tail short, slightly more than 1/3 head and body length. Feet small. **Similar Species.** Paler gray than other *Cryptotis* spp. No other shrews are known from the Yucatán Peninsula; *C. parva* approaches it in Belize: *C. parva* is brownish and occurs at higher elevations in Central America.

Distribution. Yucatán Peninsula, Mexico, to NE Guatemala and C Belize; also possibly Guerrero, Mexico. Lowlands; mainly below 100 m (650 m in Guerrero).

Status and Habitat. Locally common in dry scrub, deciduous forest, and seasonally dry evergreen forest.

Habits. Poorly known. Most records are from owl pellets or archaeological sites.

Comment. Previously considered to be a subspecies of *C. nigrescens*; see Woodman and Timm (1993). Records from Guerrero, Mexico are limited to skull parts recovered from owl pellets.

MEXICAN SMALL-EARED SHREW
Cryptotis mexicana   Map 27

HB 67–80, T 22–33, HF 12–14, E 0, Wt 6–10 g.

Description. Upperparts blackish brown; underparts gray-brown. Tail short, about 1/3 head and body length. Front feet medium-sized (claws about 2 mm long). Tops of feet blackish. Snout rather long and narrow. **Similar Species.** Only 2 other *Cryptotis* occur in NE Chiapas: *C. goldmani* has larger, broader feet with thicker claws (difficult to distinguish); *C. parva* is smaller and brownish, with pale underparts.

Distribution. Tamaulipas, Mexico, through the eastern mountains to Veracruz, then throughout Oaxaca and into NE Chiapas.

2100 m in Chiapas; 500–3200 m farther north.

Status and Habitat. Uncommon to locally common in cold, wet, pine–oak forest and forest edge. Favors damp, grassy areas bordering streams or orchards.

Habits. Terrestrial. Probably breeds throughout the year. One litter of 3 has been reported. Biology reviewed by Choate (1973).

GOLDMAN'S SMALL-EARED SHREW
Cryptotis goldmani   Map 26

HB 69–85, T 25–32, HF 13–16, E 0, Wt 5–14 g.

Description. Large. Upperparts blackish brown or dark gray-brown; underparts slightly paler, silvery gray or gray-brown. Fur on rump 7 mm long. Tail relatively short, about 1/3 of head and body length. Front feet large and broad, with long, strong claws. Tops of feet paler than back. **Similar Species.** Range overlaps with 4 other *Cryptotis* species: see *C. goodwini* and *C. mexicana*; *C. merriami* is smaller, with shorter fur and smaller, narrower feet; *C. parva* is brownish and much smaller (cf. hind foot and tail measurements).

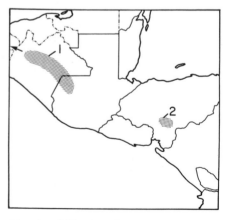

Map 26. 1. Goldman's Small-eared Shrew, *Cryptotis goldmani*

2. Honduran Small-eared Shrew, *Cryptotis hondurensis*

Distribution. Pacific Slope and mountains of S Mexico, from Jalisco to Chiapas, and into W Guatemala. Lowlands to 4100 m (usually above 2000 m; known from lowlands near Tehuantepec, Oaxaca).

Status and Habitat. Fairly common; usually found in wet, highland, pine–oak or fir forest, sometimes in dry, lowland forest.

Habits. Poorly known.

GOODWIN'S SMALL-EARED SHREW

Cryptotis goodwini

Plate 25

Map 27

HB 75–94, T 27–34, HF 14–17, E 0, Wt 12–19 g.

Description. Largest species in the region. Upperparts black or very dark brown; underparts silvery gray. Fur on rump 7–8 mm long. Tail rather short, about 1/3 of head and body length. Front feet long and broad, with powerful, long claws (claws to 4 mm). Tops of feet blackish. **Similar Species.** Range overlaps with the very similar *C. goldmani* in Huehuetenango, Guatemala: *C. goldmani* is slightly smaller, with tops of the feet usually pale, not blackish (may not be distinguishable in the field). *C. merriami* is smaller, with slim front feet and short claws; *C. parva* is brownish and much smaller.

Distribution. Mountains of SE Chiapas (near Prusia, Atlantic Slope of El Triunfo), Mexico, to S Guatemala and W El Salvador. 900–3400 m.

Status and Habitat. Uncommon to locally common; in cold, wet, pine–oak forest.

Habits. Poorly known. Biology reviewed by Choate and Fleharty (1974). Reported from Chiapas by Hutterer (1980).

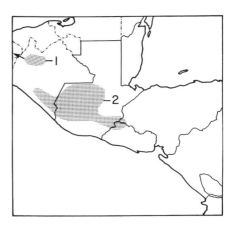

Map 27. 1. Mexican Small-eared Shrew, *Cryptotis mexicana*
2. Goodwin's Small-eared Shrew, *Cryptotis goodwini*

TALAMANCAN SMALL-EARED SHREW

Cryptotis gracilis

Plate 25

Map 28

HB 60–79, T 30–41, HF 13–15, E 0, Wt 5–10 g.

Description. Fairly small. Upperparts blackish; underparts charcoal gray. Fur long and dense, 6–7 mm on rump. Tail relatively long, about 1/2 head and body length. Long snout. **Similar Species.** *C. parva* has a much shorter

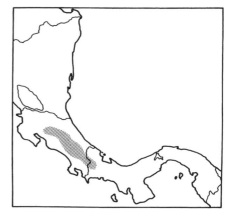

Map 28. Talamancan Small-eared Shrew, *Cryptotis gracilis*

tail and short, brown fur. See *C. nigrescens* and *C. endersi*.

Distribution. Central and Talamancan mountains of Costa Rica and W Panama. 1800–3400 m.

Status and Habitat. Fairly common in highland oak forest and páramo.

Habits. Litter size is 1-4, and breeding may occur year-round.

ENDERS' SMALL-EARED SHREW
Cryptotis endersi   Map 29

HB 89, T 49, HF 15, E 0

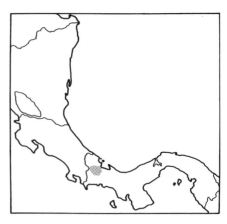

Map 29. Enders' Small-eared Shrew, *Cryptotis endersi*

Description. Upperparts blackish; underparts charcoal gray. Tail relatively long, about 1/2 head and body length. **Similar Species.** No other shrews have been taken on the Atlantic Slope of mountains in W Panama, but *C. nigrescens* and *C. gracilis* are known from the same mountain chain: *C. nigrescens* is smaller and has a shorter tail; *C. gracilis* is slightly smaller, but externally indistinguishable from *C. endersi*.

Distribution. Known only from the Atlantic Slope of the Talamanca Mountains, W Panama. 1200–1850 m.

Status and Habitat. Apparently rare; one specimen was caught in an isolated barren of stunted trees and sparse ground cover in a region mostly covered by dense, wet evergreen forest.

Habits. Unknown.

Comment. The above measurements are those of an adult male, provided by N. Woodman. Previous published measurements are those of a juvenile, the type specimen.

BATS

Order Chiroptera

With about 950 species worldwide, the diversity of bats is second only to that of rodents. Bats are more diverse in tropical than in temperate zones, and the Neotropics contain more species of bats than equivalent areas in the Paleotropics. There are 9 families, 60 genera, and about 136 species of bats in SE Mexico and Central America. At least 100 species of bats are known from Costa Rica, with a land mass of 50,700 km². In this small country, one can encounter more than 10% of all the species of bats in the world. Bats are divided into two suborders, Megachiroptera, the Old World fruit bats or flying foxes, and the cosmopolitan Microchiroptera. Names of the suborders are misleading, because there is considerable overlap in size between them, although the largest bat species are megachiropterans and the smallest are microchiropterans. In the New World, all bats belong to the Microchiroptera.

Bats are the only mammals capable of powered flight. Other mammals such as flying squirrels can glide but do not produce lift through flapping. The bat wing consists of a double layer of thin skin stretched across the legs, arms, and hands, supported by greatly elongated finger and hand bones. The thumb is not greatly enlarged and projects out of the wing membrane. The skin, or membrane, of the wing is highly elastic and expands easily when the wings are spread. Some bats roost on horizontal surfaces, but most roost upside down. This posture allows them to take flight by dropping and spreading their wings. Legs and arms work in unison during flight. Short, broad wings allow slow, highly maneuverable flight, whereas long, narrow wings are associated with greater speed and less agility. All bats in the region are nocturnal, although some are crepuscular, active at dusk and near dawn. All bats see well and use vision to detect distant objects when flying. The microchiropterans use echolocation (or biosonar) for orienting at close range and for hunting insect prey in the dark. High-pitched calls, sometimes audible, usually ultrasonic, are emitted through the mouth or nostrils. Echoes of these sounds rebound from objects, giving the bat an impression of its surroundings. Elaborate folds of skin on the mouth or nose may be used for focusing outgoing calls, and large, moveable ears increase sensitivity to faint echoes. Bats with very large ears, well-developed noseleafs, or complex folds and bumps on the face are usually predatory species that hunt in cluttered environments such as forest interiors. Fruit and nectar-feeding bats, with smaller ears and noseleafs, rely heavily on good vision and an acute sense of smell to find food.

The use of echolocation, excellent vision, and powered flight have enabled bats to dominate the Neotropical night skies, much as birds do during the day. Bats are found in virtually every habitat in the region, from urban areas to forest and desert, but they are scarce on the highest mountains. Forest species typically roost in hollow trees, but are also found under foliage, in caves, in the burrows of other animals, and in termite nests. Man-made structures such as buildings, bridges, mine tunnels, and road culverts are also used as roosts. Neotropical bats have diverse feeding habits: many are aerial insectivores, using the tail membrane or wing tip to scoop up moths, beetles, and other flying insects; others glean insects and small vertebrates from the surface of vegetation, pausing in flight to grab their prey in the mouth; a few large-footed species trawl the water surface for fish or aquatic insect larvae; long-tongued bats probe flowers and lap up nectar; the largest number of species eat fruit; and three species feed exclusively on blood.

More than 95% of all tropical plants are pollinated by animals, and the majority of these plants also rely on animals for seed dispersal. Bats play a crucial role in both pollination and seed dispersal in the tropics. Not only do they maintain the diversity of undisturbed habitats, but they are also extremely important in forest regeneration through dispersal of the seeds of pioneer plants such as *Piper, Solanum,* and *Cecropia* spp. (see Fleming, 1988). Most bats are directly beneficial to humans in several ways, particularly in controlling insect populations and in pollinating fruit trees, including cash crops such as bananas, cashews, and mangos. Only one species, the Common Vampire Bat (*Desmodus rotundus*), can be a serious pest, although several others may be rather annoying housemates.

Unfortunately, few people appreciate the importance of bats, and most do not distinguish between vampires and other species, resulting in indiscriminate destruction of roosts and unnecessary persecution of beneficial and harmless bats. Bat populations do not recover quickly when their numbers are reduced. Their reproductive rates are surprisingly low compared with other mammals of similar body size; most have only one young per birth and reproduce only once or twice each year. Life spans of up to 30 years have been recorded, but limited data suggest that 6–8 years may be more typical in tropical regions.

There are few comprehensive works on bats of the region. Barbour and Davis (1969) is the classic reference for bats in the United States and Villa-R. (1966) for bats in Mexico. Excellent general references are Fenton (1992) and Kunz (1988).

Local names for bats are: Spanish—murciélagos; Maya—zotz; Belize—ratbats; Miskito—skankis.

SAC-WINGED BATS
Family Emballonuridae

The Emballonuridae is worldwide in distribution but usually restricted to tropical zones and includes 12 genera and about 48 species. These bats are delicate and thin-boned, with curved forearms and long, soft fur. All emballonurids have a long tail membrane and a relatively short tail, the tip of which projects freely above the dorsal surface of the membrane. This feature, in conjunction with large eyes and lack of ornamentation of nose and mouth, serve to distinguish the family. Many, but not all, species of sac-winged bats possess a glandular structure in the portion of wing membrane between the leading edge and the arm bones (propatagium). The wing sac is well developed in adult males but may be rudimentary in females. Females are usually larger than males, and this size difference is most pronounced in species with wing sacs. Most of the New World emballonurids are small, although the distinctive white Northern Ghost Bat is quite large. Dental formula of Central American species is: i 1/3 (3/3 in *Cormura*), c 1/1, p 2/2, m 3/3.

Sac-winged bats are found in a variety of habitats but are usually restricted to warm, lowland regions. Several species may be seen during the day, roosting on logs or branches, walls of buildings, or entrances to caves or hollow trees. Unlike most bats, they do not seek out the darkest recesses and remain alert in their more exposed roosts. Their typical roosting posture is characteristic and unmistakable: toes and thumbs cling to vertical surfaces, the forearms are held at 45° from the body, and the head and chest are raised off the surface. The 2 genera with diminutive thumbs, *Diclidurus* and *Cyttarops*, do not roost in this manner, but hang from the feet only, often beneath palm leaves. Sacwinged bats appear to be exclusively insectivorous in diet and capture small, flying insects. Several species fly high and are almost never captured in mist nets, but even low-flying species are seldom taken due to their considerable agility and sensitive echolocation systems. Breeding usually occurs once annually, early in the rainy season. Females give birth to single young.

Distinctive characteristics of the genera are:

Rhynchonycteris.   Small; grizzled fur; pair of faint, wavy lines on back and tufts of pale fur on forearms. No wing sacs.

Saccopteryx.   Dark fur with pair of pale wavy lines on back; naked forearms. Wing sacs parallel to and along edge of forearms.

Centronycteris.   Shaggy, yellowish fur extending onto tail membrane; wings attach to base of toes. Ears sickle shaped. No wing sacs.

Peropteryx.   Brown fur; long hair on forehead, remainder of face naked; wings attach to ankles. Wing sacs start at wing edge, parallel to body, open outward.

Cormura.   Brown fur; face haired to nose; wings attach to base of toes. Large wing sacs start at wing edge, parallel to body, open outward.

Balantiopteryx.   Gray or brown; wings attach to ankles. Wing sacs do not reach wing edge, parallel to body, open inward.

Cyttarops.   Dark gray fur; short, broad ears; thumbs tiny. No wing sacs.

Diclidurus. White fur; relatively large; thumbs tiny; glandular sac in tail. No wing sacs.

PROBOSCIS BAT
Rhynchonycteris naso

Plate 6
Map 30

HB 36–48, T 11–17, HF 6–8, E 11–14, FA 36–40, Wt 3–6 g.

Description. *Tiny.* Upperparts *grizzled*, gray-brown or yellowish; 2 faint, wavy, cream-colored stripes extend from shoulders to rump; underparts pale yellow or grayish. Fur long and fluffy. *Nose long,* projecting well beyond lower lip. Membranes and facial skin blackish, with *tufts of pale fur on forearms* and tail membrane. No wing sacs. **Similar Species.** White-lined sac-winged bats (*Saccopteryx* spp.) are darker in color, with naked forearms and more prominent wavy lines on back.

Distribution. Veracruz, Mexico, through most of Central America to E Brazil, Bolivia, and Peru; Trinidad. Lowlands only.

Status and Habitat. Common in lowland forest near water (streams, rivers, mangroves, and lakes).

Habits. Roosts in groups of about 10 (range 3–45) on exposed logs, tree trunks, and rocks, always near or directly above water. When roosting, individuals usually form a single vertical line and can be difficult to see. If disturbed by day, the group flies together to a nearby roost; their small size and fluttery flight gives the impression of dark moths. Activity starts early, before sunset; groups usually forage within 3 m of the surface of slow-moving, shallow water, feeding mainly on Diptera (including mosquitoes) and other small, flying insects (Bradbury and Vehrencamp, 1976). Echolocation calls contain a constant frequency component at about 100 kHz and are less intense than those of other emballonurids. Single young are born once a year, early in the wet season.

GREATER WHITE-LINED BAT
Saccopteryx bilineata

Plate 6
Map 31

HB 47–56, T 16–23, HF 10–12, E 13–17, FA 44–48, Wt 6–9 g.

Description. Upperparts *blackish* with two prominent, buffy stripes extending from neck to rump; underparts dark gray. Membranes blackish and hairless. Wing sacs are well developed in male, opening along the forward edge of the upper side of the forearm. Females are slightly larger than males. **Similar Species.** *S. leptura* is smaller, with brown, not black, upperparts. See Proboscis Bat (*Rhynchonycteris naso*).

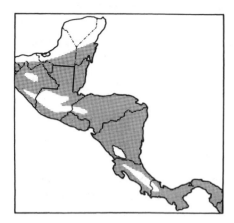

Map 30. Proboscis Bat, *Rhynchonycteris naso*

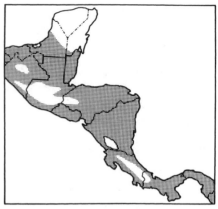

Map 31. Greater White-lined Bat, *Saccopteryx bilineata*

Distribution. Jalisco, Mexico, through Central America to Peru and E Brazil; Trinidad and Tobago. Lowlands to 600 m.

Status and Habitat. Common in lowland evergreen and semideciduous forest and forest edge. Rare in dry deciduous forest.

Habits. Roosts in tree holes, buttress cavities, and on walls of buildings in groups of 5–50. Groups are made up of several harems, with each male defending 1-9 females. Males "salt" their females with strong-smelling secretions from the wing sacs and use territorial displays and audible songs to maintain their harem. These behaviors can be observed near dawn or dusk at a roost site. Individuals leave the roost shortly before sunset and forage nearby in the lower levels of the forest. After dark, they move farther afield to forage in areas of greater insect abundance. Maximum energy of echolocation calls is about 50 kHz; a variety of audible calls are also given. One young is born annually, at the onset of the rainy season (May in W Costa Rica). Females carry the young to individual hiding sites when foraging; young are able to fly at 2 weeks but continue to suckle for several months (Bradbury, 1983).

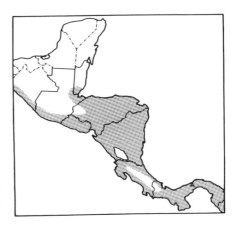

Map 32. Lesser White-lined Bat, *Saccopteryx leptura*

Status and Habitat. Uncommon to locally common in lowland deciduous and evergreen forest.

Habits. Roosts in the junction below a large branch and tree trunk, or in exposed tree boles in groups of 1–9 animals (usually a pair of adults and their offspring). Each group defends its foraging territory from neighboring groups. Group members feed together in the forest subcanopy early in the evening, then move above the canopy later in the night (Bradbury and Vehrencamp, 1976). Echolocation calls of 45–95 kHz are used (maximum energy about 55–60 kHz), and a variety of audible chirps may be heard. Births are synchronized with the onset of the rainy season (May in W Costa Rica); a second birth peak may occur in October or November.

LESSER WHITE-LINED BAT   Plate 6
Saccopteryx leptura   Map 32

HB 38–51, T 9–19, HF 6–10, E 12–15, FA 37–43, Wt 3–6 g.

Description. Similar to *S. bilineata*, but smaller, with *dark brown* upperparts and less-pronounced buff-colored back stripes; underparts gray-brown. Females slightly larger than males. **Similar Species.** See *S. bilineata* and Proboscis Bat (*Rhynchonycteris naso*).

Distribution. Chiapas, Mexico, and Belize (McCarthy, 1987b) to Peru and E Brazil; Margarita Island; Trinidad and Tobago. Lowlands only.

SHAGGY BAT   Plate 6
Centronycteris maximiliani   Map 33

HB 49–59, T 20–24, HF 7–9, E 17–19, FA 43–49, Wt 5–6 g.

Description. Body dull *yellow* or gray-brown; orange-brown on lower rump and tail membrane; fur long and thick. *Ears long, sickle shaped, and pointed.* Facial skin pink. Mem-

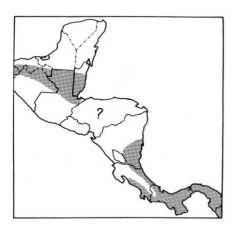

Map 33. Shaggy Bat, *Centronycteris maximiliani*

LESSER DOGLIKE BAT

Peropteryx macrotis

Plate 6

Map 34

HB 42–53, T 11–15, HF 8–10, E 14–16, FA 43–45 (males), 45–48 (females), Wt 4–7 g.

Description. Upperparts usually *reddish brown*, occasionally dark brown; underparts gray-brown. Fur dull, soft, and *moderately long* (6 mm on neck, 8–9 mm on back). Ears gray-brown; tragus rounded at the tip. Face naked with a long fringe of hair starting abruptly on forehead. Wing membranes blackish; *wings attach to ankles*; tail membrane translucent, brown. Wing sac extends to edge of wing, parallel to body, opening faces outward. **Similar Species.** See *P. kappleri* and Chestnut Sacwinged Bat (*Cormura brevirostris*). Least Sacwinged Bat (*Balantiopteryx io*) is smaller, with opening of wing-sac facing toward body.

Distribution. Guerrero and Veracruz, Mexico, through Central America to Peru, Paraguay, and S and E Brazil; West Indies; Trinidad and Tobago. Lowlands to 700 m.

Status and Habitat. Widespread but generally uncommon and local. It seems to be most common in seasonally dry areas with limestone caves (e.g., Yucatán Peninsula).

Habits. Roosts in large and small caves, shallow crevices, Maya buildings, and churches,

branes blackish; tail membrane long, well-haired at base. Calcar long; wings attach to feet at base of toes. No wing sacs. **Similar Species.** Unlike any other emballonurid in color (shape of ears and face reminiscent of *Saccopteryx* spp.). Coloration similar to yellow bats (*Lasiurus* spp.), which have shorter, rounded ears, long tails, and fully-haired tail membranes.

Distribution. Veracruz, Mexico, to N Peru, the Guianas, and the Amazon basin of Brazil. Lowlands only.

Status and Habitat. Apparently rare; known from few specimens. Found in evergreen and semideciduous forest and second growth.

Habits. Poorly known. Roosts in tree holes and on trunks of trees (Timm et al., 1989). Usually caught in mist nets set across wide paths or clearings through tall forest. Flight is slow and deliberate; individuals may patrol the same area repeatedly. When hand held, this attractive bat snarls with mouth opened remarkably wide and emits a variety of persistent, loud, chirping calls. Pregnant females have been noted in May.

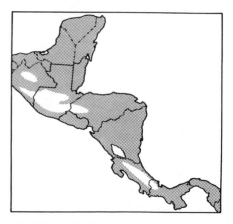

Map 34. Lesser Doglike Bat, *Peropteryx macrotis*

often near water. Groups usually number 10–20 but may be as large as 80, and several groups may occupy a large cave. Individuals hang singly on vertical or steeply sloped walls near the roost entrance (Arita and Vargas, 1995). Activity starts at sunset or soon after. Individuals foraging along tree-lined roads have been noted in Costa Rica (Starrett and Casebeer, 1968). Pregnant females have been recorded in March and April (Jones et al., 1973; Rick, 1968).

GREATER DOGLIKE BAT
Peropteryx kappleri

Plate 6
Map 35

HB 63–75, T 11–20, HF 9–11, E 13–16, FA 45–50 (males), 46–52 (females), Wt 7–13 g.

Description. Similar to *P. macrotis*, but *larger,* with upperparts usually *dark brown*, occasionally reddish brown; fur *long* (8 mm on neck, about 10 mm on back). Ears blackish. **Similar Species.** See Chestnut Sac-winged Bat (*Cormura brevirostris*).

Distribution. Veracruz, Mexico, through Central America to E Brazil and Peru. Lowlands to 1500 m.

Status and Habitat. Uncommon; usually found in mature, evergreen forest.

Habits. Roosts in groups of one to six in small caves, humid fallen logs, or damp cavities of trees within 1 m of the ground; occasionally in buildings. Individuals stack up one on top of another when roosting. This species forages in the subcanopy with slow flight and may glean insects from foliage in addition to taking prey aerially (Bradbury and Vehrencamp, 1976). Echolocation pulses have maximum energy at 20–40 kHz. Single young are born once a year, usually in June.

CHESTNUT SAC-WINGED BAT
Cormura brevirostris

Plate 6
Map 36

HB 46–58, T 10–16, HF 5–8, E 13–16, FA 45–50, Wt 7–11 g.

Description. Upperparts *rich chestnut-brown* (or blackish, mostly in subadults and young), underparts slightly paler. Fur thick and shiny. Facial skin and ears blackish, tragus broad and square topped; nose short, haired almost to tip. Membranes black; *wings attach to feet at base of toes. Wing sac large;* opening extends to wing edge and faces outward from the body. **Similar Species.** All other brown bats with wing sacs have wings attached to ankle, not foot.

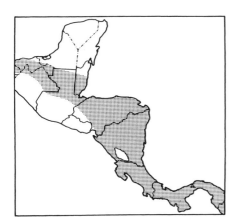

Map 35. Greater Doglike Bat, *Peropteryx kappleri*

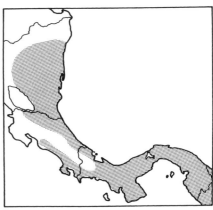

Map 36. Chestnut Sac-winged Bat, *Cormura brevirostris*

Distribution. Nicaragua to Panama; east of the Andes from Venezuela and the Guianas to Peru and Amazonian Brazil. Lowlands to 1000 m.

Status and Habitat. Uncommon and local in Central America, usually in lowland evergreen forest.

Habits. Roosts in small groups in large, rotting hollow logs, under fallen trees, or in tree hollows. Individuals stack up one on top of another when roosting. Active soon after sunset, it feeds on small, flying insects near forest edge or over water. In Guyana, loud chirps of a captive juvenile attracted a lactating adult female, which repeatedly flew into a roofed shelter and eventually landed on the cloth bag containing the young bat.

LEAST SAC-WINGED BAT Plate 6
Balantiopteryx io Map 37

HB 38–44, T 8–18, HF 7–8, E 10–13, FA 36–40, Wt 3–4 g.

Description. Very small and fragile. *Dark brown* or blackish above; underparts graybrown. Membranes black; wings attach to ankles. *Wing sac small, not extending to edge of membrane; opens toward body.* **Similar Species.** Other plain brown sac-winged bats are larger

(compare forearm length), with wing sacs opening outward.

Distribution. Veracruz and Oaxaca, through Tabasco and N Chiapas, Mexico, to Belize and Guatemala. Lowlands to 500 m.

Status and Habitat. Locally common in semideciduous or evergreen lowland forest.

Habits. Roosts in rather dark recesses of large, limestone caves. Groups may number 50 or more, with individuals widely and evenly spaced, often roosting in crevices on the ceiling of high chambers. Activity starts well after sunset, later than related species, and, as a result, flight and foraging behavior are difficult to observe. Pregnant females have been recorded between March and July. Biology reviewed by Arroyo-Cabrales and Jones (1988).

GRAY SAC-WINGED BAT Plate 6
Balantiopteryx plicata Map 38

HB 47–53, T 13–17, HF 7–10, E 13–15, FA 40–45, Wt 5–6 g.

Description. Upperparts *pale gray*, often yellowish at base of tail membrane; underparts slightly paler. Face and chin naked. Membranes brown, legs and forearms pinkish. Thumbs normal in size. Wing sac opens to-

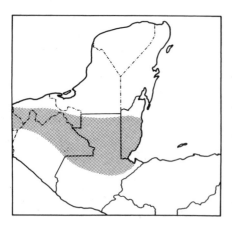

Map 37. Least Sac-winged Bat, *Balantiopteryx io*

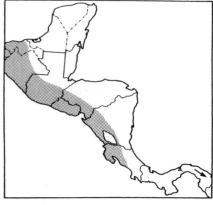

Map 38. Gray Sac-winged Bat, *Balantiopteryx plicata*

ward the body and does not extend to the edge of the wing. **Similar Species.** Few adult bats with no noseleaf are gray in color: Smoky Bat (*Cyttarops alecto*) and Thumbless Bat (*Furipterus horrens*) both have tiny thumbs and lack wing sacs.

Distribution. NW Mexico to NW Costa Rica, mainly on the Pacific Slope, but also from San Luis Potosí to Tabasco in E Mexico; also N Colombia. Lowlands to 1500 m.

Status and Habitat. Common in deciduous forest and dry thorn scrub; rare in evergreen forest.

Habits. Roosts near the entrances of caves and mines or in hollow trees and buildings. Groups may use a separate night roost, such as under a bridge. Group size is usually greater than 50, with a sex ratio of about 75% males to 25% females. Activity begins immediately before sunset; individuals fly above the canopy and forage with long, straight sallies and rapid dives after flying insects. This early flight above the relatively low, open canopy of deciduous forest can be easily observed. Echolocation calls have maximum energy at about 35 kHz. Young are born in late June in Costa Rica, well into the rainy season (Bradbury and Vehrencamp, 1976).

SMOKY BAT
Cyttarops alecto

Plate 6
Map 39

HB 47–55, T 20–25, HF 7–8, E 11–13, FA 45–47, Wt 6–7 g.

Description. Body entirely *dark gray*, fur long and fluffy. Ears broad, triangular. Chin well haired, appears bearded (noticeably so when roosting). Membranes black; feet small, *thumbs tiny*. No wing sacs. **Similar Species.** See Gray Sac-winged Bat (*Balantiopteryx plicata*).

Distribution. E Nicaragua, E Costa Rica; the Guianas and NE Brazil. Lowlands only.

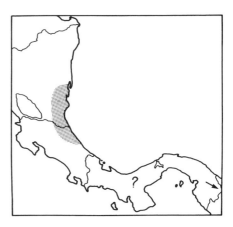

Map 39. Smoky Bat, *Cyttarops alecto*

Status and Habitat. Rare and local; known from a few specimens taken in humid lowland areas.

Habits. Roosts in groups of 1–10 under palm fronds (coconut and oil palms) usually in relatively open areas such as groves or gardens. It hangs freely by the feet when roosting, near the midrib of a frond. Activity starts about 45 minutes after sunset but is usually restricted to immediately around the roost for 15–30 minutes, after which time, in complete darkness, individuals disperse, flying at least 3–4 m above ground. Echolocation calls are loud, short, and high frequency (greater than 100 kHz), with no constant frequency component. When handled, this species makes no audible vocalizations, unlike most emballonurids. In Costa Rica, subadults and females with young have been recorded in August (Reid and Langtimm, 1993; Starrett, 1972).

NORTHERN GHOST BAT
Diclidurus albus

Plate 6
Map 40

HB 68–82, T 18–22, HF 10–12, E 16–17, FA 63–69, Wt 17–24 g.

Description. *Large; long, white fur*. Ears yellowish. Membranes pinkish; tail membrane extensive, with a glandular sac around the tip of the

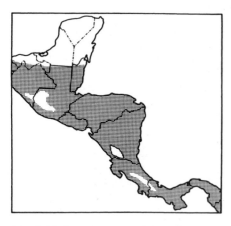

Map 40. Northern Ghost Bat, *Diclidurus albus*

Status and Habitat. Uncommon or rare; usually found in humid, lowland regions.

Habits. Roosts individually or in groups of up to 4 on the underside of palm fronds, 2–25 m above ground. Individuals hang by the feet near the rachis of the leaf. One was found on the trunk of a fig tree (McCarthy, 1987b). This species is almost never caught in mist nets. It forages high above ground and is sometimes found in villages or near street lamps, attracted to moth swarms around lights. In Guatemala, a group of about 100 were seen foraging around the lights of an oil rig (Jones, 1966), but most records are of lone individuals. Echolocation calls have not been described; when foraging, this bat makes "a unique musical twittering" (Starrett and Casebeer, 1968). Pregnant females have been recorded from January to June. Biology reviewed by Ceballos and Medellín (1988).

Comment. Some authors consider the population *D. a. virgo* to be a distinct species.

tail. Thumbs tiny. **Similar Species.** Honduran White Bat (*Ectophylla alba*) is much smaller, with a yellow noseleaf and blackish membranes.

Distribution. Nayarit, Mexico, patchily distributed through Central America to E Brazil; Trinidad. Lowlands to 1500 m.

FISHING OR BULLDOG BATS
Family Noctilionidae

The Noctilionidae consists of a single genus with 2 species, distributed from Mexico to Bolivia and E Brazil. Fishing bats are recognized by their divided and drooping upper lips, well-developed nosepad, and ridged chin. They have exceptionally large canines and have been referred to as "saber-toothed bats." Their fur is extremely short and velvety, with a pale (white or orangish) mid-dorsal stripe from shoulders to rump. Long limbed and powerful, they have large wings and an extensive tail membrane, well over twice the length of the tail. At rest the tail tip projects freely above the membrane. The feet are large and equipped with long, powerful claws. The long, narrow, pointed ears are often curled back when these bats are handled. Both species have a characteristic, strong, musty odor. The dental formula is: i 2/1, c 1/1, p 1/2, m 3/3. Fishing bats regularly forage over water; however, only the larger species preys extensively on fish.

GREATER FISHING BAT   Plate 7
Noctilio leporinus   Map 41

HB 76–107, T 27–35, HF 30–36, E 24–31, FA 82–89, Wt 49–78 g.

Description. One of the largest bats in Central America, with *large, elongated hind feet.* Upperparts orange, gray, or brown; pale back stripe (usually wide and prominent); underparts paler, sometimes bright yellow. Ears long and narrow; *upper lip split, drooping.* Membranes brown (glisten at night); wings and tail membrane very long; calcars longer than feet. Claws of hind feet elongated, orange if body is orange furred, white if body is gray or brown. **Similar Species.** *N. albiventris* is smaller, with proportionally smaller hind feet. Other large bats (forearm over 80 mm) have a noseleaf and an undivided upper lip.

Distribution. Sinaloa, Mexico, through coastal and riparian areas of Central America to N Argentina, Peru, and S Brazil; also Trinidad, West Indies, and S Bahamas. Lowlands only.

Status and Habitat. Locally common and widespread in wet lowland and coastal areas; near estuaries, lagoons, and rivers.

Habits. Roosts in hollow trees (including *Ceiba pentandra, Rhizophora mangle,* and *Manilkara bidentata*), or in sea caves. It sometimes occupies abandoned woodpecker holes in coconut palms (dark stains at the entrance indicate the presence of bats, not birds). Several hundred animals of both sexes may roost together; all individuals in a roost are similarly colored. This species may be active throughout the night or may rest in a tree hollow used exclusively as a night roost. It is usually seen foraging over water and can be recognized by its large size and long, glistening wings, relatively slow wingbeats, and habit of dipping the feet in the water (many bats drink in flight, but few trawl). It directs ultrasonic calls at the water, which allows it to detect changes made by a fish breaking the water surface. Maximum en-

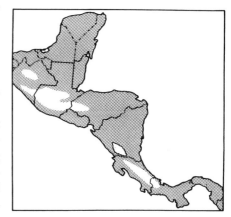

Map 41. Greater Fishing Bat, *Noctilio leporinus*

ergy of echolocation calls is 60 kHz; pulse length decreases from 14 to 1 millisecond immediately before capture of prey (a "feeding buzz"). The elongated feet and claws are then lowered to gaff small fish (3–4 cm long); by lifting the tail, the tail membrane and calcars are held clear of the water while trawling (Altenbach, 1989). Prey is quickly transferred to the mouth and swallowed in flight, or roughly chewed and held in cheek pouches to be more thoroughly masticated later at a night roost. In addition to fish, insects and other invertebrates such as land crabs are eaten. Frogs are occasionally taken. Flying insects, caught in the wing or tail membranes, make up more than half the diet during the wet season (Brooke, 1994). Birth peaks occur from April to June; occasionally a second pregnancy may follow, with young born in September–October. Young remain in the roost for a month and appear to be tended by both parents. Predators include Black-and-white Owls. Biology reviewed by Hood and Jones (1984).

Where to See. This large bat is one of the easiest species to observe in flight, and it can be found over most bodies of water in forested habitats. The best situations for observation are well-lit docks, which often attract shoals of small fish (on a seasonal basis). The bats circle repeatedly to capture fish and their calls can be picked up with a bat detector; dock lights allow good visibility. Several docks in Tortuguero, Costa Rica, and elsewhere provide these conditions.

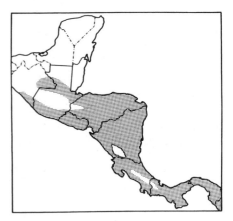

Map 42. Lesser Fishing Bat, *Noctilio albiventris*

LESSER FISHING BAT   Plate 7
Noctilio albiventris   Map 42

HB 61–81, T 14–19, HF 17–20, E 21–24, FA 54–65, Wt 15–37 g.

Description. Similar to *N. leporinus* but smaller, with powerful, but not greatly elongated feet and claws. **Similar Species.** See *N. leporinus.* Clearly divided and drooping upper lips distinguish it from all other bat species.

Distribution. Chiapas, Mexico (Jones et al., 1988; Medellín, 1994), to N Argentina, Peru, and E Brazil. Lowlands to 1100 m.

Status and Habitat. Uncommon to locally common in forested and open areas, usually near water.

Habits. Roosts in hollow trees and buildings. It leaves the roost at dusk and usually forages for 1–2 hours before returning to the day roost. One or 2 more periods of activity may occur before dawn, with a total time spent in flight of about 2 hours (Fenton et al., 1993). The diet consists of insects including Coleoptera (mainly water beetles), Lepidoptera, Diptera, and Hemiptera, some of which are gleaned from the water surface of nonturbulent rivers and streams. Fruit is occasionally eaten. Single young are born once a year, usually in April or May. Biology reviewed by Hood and Pitochelli (1983).

LEAF-CHINNED BATS
Family Mormoopidae

The Mormoopidae consists of 2 genera and 8 species, distributed from Mexico to Peru and Brazil. Several species occupy islands in the West Indies. Mormoopids are recognized by thickened and flared lips with one or more folds of skin below the lower lip. These slim-bodied bats have long, narrow wings and an extensive tail membrane. The tail is more than half the length of the tail membrane, and its tip projects freely above the membrane when the bat is resting. In flight the tail is contained within the extended tail membrane. The dental formula is: i 2/2, c 1/1, p 2/3, m 3/3.

These bats are fast and agile fliers that capture insect prey in flight. The large lips are flared to form a "megaphone" for emitting echolocation calls. Large, humid caves are preferred roost sites. Systematics and distribution reviewed by Smith (1972).

The genera can be distinguished as follows:

Mormoops.   Bizarre-looking face, several prominent chin flaps; low, rounded ears.

Pteronotus.   Thickened lips with small, single chin flap; narrow, pointed ears.

GHOST-FACED BAT   Plate 7
Mormoops megalophylla   Map 43

HB 57–70, T 19–29, HF 9–12, E 13–17, FA 51–57, Wt 12–19 g.

Description. *Peculiar face*, with an upturned nose and complex, leaflike folds of skin on the chin. Ears short and rounded, encircle eyes, and meet on forehead. Upperparts pale yellowish brown, dark brown, or occasionally orange; underparts slightly paler. Wings long and narrow; tail membrane long; tail about 2/3 length of membrane; tip of tail projects freely above surface of membrane. **Similar Species.** None in region.

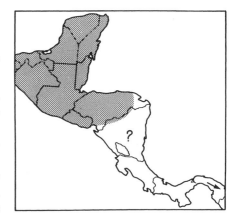

Map 43. Ghost-faced Bat, *Mormoops megalophylla*

Distribution. Disjunct populations: extreme S United States to E Honduras; N Colombia, Venezuela, and NW Ecuador; also Dutch West Indies and Trinidad. Lowlands to 2300 m.

Status and Habitat. Uncommon to locally common; usually found in dry or semideciduous lowland forest.

Habits. Roosts in large, deep caves, often in considerable numbers and with other species of bats; occasionally found in mines, culverts, or buildings. Males and females may occupy the same cave, but roost in separate groups. Individuals are spaced about 15 cm apart when roosting. Activity usually begins an hour or more after sunset, later than for other leaf-chinned bats. On leaving the roost, this species flies rather high and extremely fast (Bateman and Vaughan, 1974), foraging at heights of 3–5 m. It is seldom caught in mist nets, unlike the lower-flying mustached bats (*Pteronotus* spp.). The diet consists of moths, beetles, and flies; prey commonly have body lengths of 5–6 mm (Ceballos and Galindo, 1984). Some populations appear to be nomadic or migratory; large concentrations are found in caves in October and November, but disappear by January (Villa-R., 1966). Such movements are not always seasonal. Females produce one young per year, between April and June. Young are reared in maternity colonies.

Comment. The genus has been referred to as *Aello*, but *Mormoops* is the correct name.

COMMON MUSTACHED BAT   Plate 7
Pteronotus parnellii   Map 44

HB 58–70, T 18–25, HF 12–15, E 20–23, FA 55–63, Wt 12–26 g.

Description. Medium sized and slim bodied. Fur short, pale to dark brown, or (rarely) orange. Ears narrow and pointed, outer edge ex-

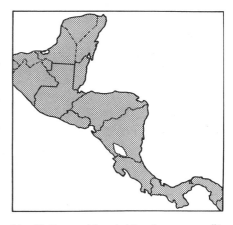

Map 44. Common Mustached Bat, *Pteronotus parnellii*

tends to mouth. Eyes tiny. Lips thickened, with a long mustache on the sides and a small leaf (fold of skin) below the flared lower lip. Membranes dark brown; wings long and narrow. Tail more than half the length of long tail membrane; tip projects above membrane at rest. **Similar Species.** See *P. personatus*. Occasionally mistaken for a free-tailed bat (Molossidae) because of the conspicuous tail tip: in free-tails, the tail is much longer than the fully extended tail membrane; in *Pteronotus* it is shorter.

Distribution. Sonora and Tamaulipas, Mexico, throughout S Mexico and Central America to Peru and E Brazil; Trinidad and Tobago, and West Indies. Lowlands to 2200 m.

Status and Habitat. Common to abundant in all types of lowland forest; also found at middle elevations and in disturbed areas.

Habits. Roosts in caves and mines; it favors large caverns, but smaller roosts, possibly including hollow trees, are also used. Activity begins at sunset (Bateman and Vaughan, 1974), although maximum mist net capture can occur 2 hours later (Bonaccorso, 1979). Individuals remain active for 5–7 hours, then return to the day roost. Some may be active again shortly before dawn. Forest trails are often used as flyways or foraging areas; streams and creeks are seldom used. A medium-sized bat flying fast and straight along a forest trail is most likely to be of this common and widespread species. It feeds primarily on moths and beetles; other types of insects and some seeds have also been found in fecal material (Whitaker and Findley, 1980). Echolocation calls consist of long (10–30 msec) pulses, with maximum energy at about 60 kHz. Single young are born at the onset of the rainy season. Biology reviewed by Herd (1983).

LESSER MUSTACHED BAT   Plate 7
Pteronotus personatus   Map 45

HB 43–55, T 15–20, HF 9–12, E 14–18, FA 42–48, Wt 5–10 g.

Description. Similar to *P. parnellii*, but much smaller and more delicate (compare forearm and weight). Orange or brown-furred individuals are equally common. **Similar Species.** *P. davyi* has a naked back.

Distribution. Sonora and Tamaulipas, Mexico, through Central America except Yucatán Peninsula to Peru and SE Brazil; also Trinidad. Lowlands to 1000 m.

Status and Habitat. Uncommon to locally common in lowland forest (in Central America it is apparently uncommon and local south of Honduras).

Habits. Poorly known. Roosts in large, humid caves, often with other mormoopids, and is usually the first species to leave at dusk (Bateman and Vaughan, 1974; Villa-R., 1966).

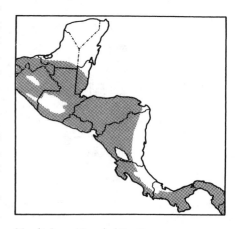

Map 45. Lesser Mustached Bat, *Pteronotus personatus*

DAVY'S NAKED-BACKED BAT   Plate 7
Pteronotus davyi   Map 46

HB 42–55, T 18–25, HF 9–11, E 15–18, FA 43–49, Wt 5–10 g.

Description. Small and delicate, with a *naked back*. The wings meet on the midback (fur extends onto the back beneath the wings).

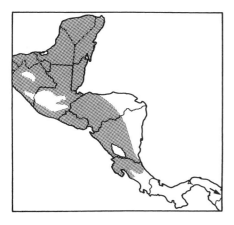

Map 46. Davy's Naked-backed Bat, *Pteronotus davyi*

Fur usually brown, occasionally orange. Face, wings, and tail similar to *P. parnellii*. **Similar Species.** *P. gymnonotus* is usually larger and is slightly stockier (compare weights) with a velvety rump.

Distribution. E and W coasts of Mexico to Oaxaca and Veracruz, through N Central America (not recorded in S Costa Rica or Panama); patchily distributed through South America to E Brazil and Peru; also Trinidad and Lesser Antilles. Lowlands to 2300 m (the highest elevational record is from El Salvador; it is usually found below 1000 m).

Status and Habitat. Locally common in dry and semideciduous lowland forest, often near water; less common in evergreen forest and highly disturbed areas. Distribution may be limited by availability of roost sites.

Habits. Roosts in large numbers in deep, humid caves or mines. Greatest activity occurs for 2 hours after sunset and shortly before dawn; most individuals return to the day roost for part of the night. Often forages over water, feeding on insects including moths, earwigs, and flies. Echolocation calls have a pulse length of about 3 msec, with maximum energy dropping from 78 to 62 kHz. Biology reviewed by Adams (1989).

BIG NAKED-BACKED BAT   Plate 7
Pteronotus gymnonotus   Map 47

HB 55–69, T 21–28, HF 10–13, E 16–21, FA 50–55, Wt 11–18 g.

Description. Back naked; wings meet on midline; the naked-looking rump is covered with very short fur and appears velvety when examined closely. Fur may be brown or orange. Face, ears, wings, and tail same shape as for *P. parnellii*. **Similar Species.** See *P. davyi*.

Distribution. Veracruz, Mexico, through Central America (absent from Yucatán Peninsula) to Peru, NE Brazil, and Guyana. Lowlands to 1600 m.

Status and Habitat. Uncommon and local from Costa Rica northward, locally abundant in Panama (Handley, 1966); usually found in lowland semideciduous or evergreen forest.

Habits. Roosts in large caves, often with other species of mormoopid bats. In caves occupied by both species of naked-backed bats, *P. davyi* considerably outnumbers *P. gymnonotus*; the absence of *P. davyi* from Panama may be a significant factor in the increased abundance of the Big Naked-backed Bat in this country. Flying insects (mainly Orthoptera, beetles, and moths) are consumed; rarely, fruit and pollen

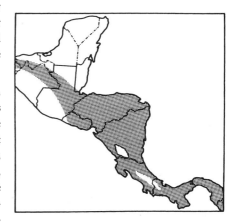

Map 47. Big Naked-backed Bat, *Pteronotus gymnonotus*

may be included in the diet (Howell and Burch, 1974; Whitaker and Findley, 1980).

This species is less well-known than other members of the genus.

LEAF-NOSED BATS
Family Phyllostomidae

The Phyllostomidae includes about 49 genera, all of which are restricted to the New World. Bat diversity in the Neotropics is extremely high as a result of the incredible variety of phyllostomids: in Central America and SE Mexico 74 of the 136 bat species are members of this family.

Leaf-nosed bats have traditionally been divided into several subfamilies based on external and skeletal morphology. In these species accounts, I follow Koopman (1993), who retained much of the traditional classification. This arrangement is not universally accepted. For example, Baker et al. (1989), using genetic and anatomical data, proposed a reclassification of the family that differs considerably from that of Koopman (1993).

Almost all phyllostomids can be recognized by the presence of a leaflike structure on the nose. The noseleaf consists of a spear, extending above the nostrils, and a horseshoe enveloping the nostrils from below. The spear may be simple or creased, and in some species the horseshoe is partially or entirely fused with the upper lip. A few leaf-nosed bats do not have a noseleaf: vampire bats are placed in their own subfamily, Desmodontinae, within the Phyllostomidae, based on genetic and anatomical similarities, but in place of a noseleaf the nostrils are surrounded by thickened folds of skin. The Wrinkle-faced Bat (*Centurio senex*) is the only other leaf-nosed bat without a noseleaf; it has a peculiarly flat, naked face, covered with complex folds and wrinkles. This tailless species is included in the subfamily Stenodermatinae.

Leaf-nosed bats show a greater range of feeding habits than any other bat family, and their division into subfamilies reflects differences in diet and feeding habits. The subfamily Phyllostominae includes gleaning and carnivorous bats. Gleaning bats pick insect or small vertebrate prey from leaves or from the ground; they usually have large ears, short, broad wings, extensive tail membranes, and are small to medium sized. Carnivorous bats prey on birds, small mammals, and reptiles and include the largest Neotropical bat (*Vampyrum spectrum*). Other members of the Phyllostominae are omnivorous, catching insects in flight or from vegetation and eating fruit. Long-tongued bats, in the subfamilies Glossophaginae and Lonchophyllinae, are specialized to feed on flower nectar and pollen. These bats are small, with long, narrow muzzles, small noseleafs, and extremely long tongues. Short-tailed and tailless bats, Carolliinae and Stenodermatinae, are fruit specialists that pluck fruit by mouth and carry it to a night roost.

Unlike other bats in the region that emit high-frequency sounds from the mouth, phyllostomids usually send echolocation calls through the nostrils and may use the noseleaf to direct the signal. They are sometimes referred to as "whispering bats," as their echolocation calls are generally given at a very low volume. Such calls are not easily picked up in the field with standard bat detectors (information on echolocation calls is not given in these species accounts). As is the general rule for Neotropical bats, fe-

Golden Bat
(*Mimon bennettii*)

Striped Hairy-nosed Bat
(*Mimon crenulatum*)

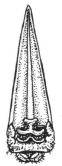

Common Sword-nosed Bat
(*Lonchorhina aurita*)

**White-throated
Round-eared Bat**
(*Tonatia silvicola*)

Fringe-lipped Bat
(*Trachops cirrhosus*)

Bartica Bat
(*Micronycteris daviesi*)

Pale-faced Bat
(*Phylloderma stenops*)

Greater Spear-nosed Bat
(*Phyllostomus hastatus*)

Woolly False Vampire Bat
(*Chrotopterus auritus*)

FIGURE 4. Noseleafs of larger gleaning bats (Phyllostominae), 1.5 × life size.

Pygmy Round-eared Bat
(*Tonatia brasiliense*)

Common Big-eared Bat
(*Micronycteris microtis*)

Silky Short-tailed Bat
(*Carollia brevicauda*)

FIGURE 5. Noseleafs of 3 small leaf-nosed bats, 2 × life size.

males give birth to a single young, although twins are occasionally reported for a few species. Many species reproduce twice annually, others once a year.

Gleaning and Carnivorous Bats
Subfamily Phyllostominae

The Phyllostominae form a diverse assemblage of species with similar feeding habits and some morphological similarities. The classification of bats in this subfamily follows Koopman (1993), although anatomical, genetic, and immunological data indicate that members of this subfamily may not be closely related, and some genera may be more closely allied to leaf-nosed bats in the subfamilies Stenodermatinae and Glossophaginae (Baker et al., 1989).

Phyllostomines range in size from tiny to very large, and include the largest Neotropical bats. They have short, broad wings and rather long legs and tail membranes. Most species have short tails that extend less than half the length of the tail membrane, although a few species have tails as long as or longer than the membrane. Several species have spectacularly large ears, and some have large, elaborate noseleafs.

Gleaning and carnivorous bats are forest species and are not usually found in highly disturbed habitats. Short, broad wings enable them to fly slowly with great agility among dense vegetation, and some may hover in flight. Gleaning bats feed on insects or small vertebrates that are grabbed by mouth from the surface of vegetation or from the ground. The large carnivorous species feed on birds, reptiles, frogs, and small mammals. The species with large ears and highly acute hearing may be attracted by the breeding calls of their prey but probably can also home in on the sound of an insect or lizard crawling across a leaf. In addition to gleaning, some flying insects are taken, and a few species are omnivorous, including fruit and other plant parts in the diet.

Important characteristics of the genera are:

Micronycteris. Very small to medium sized. Tail about half the length of tail membrane. Ears very large and rounded or moderately large and pointed. Horseshoe of noseleaf free on sides, fused below lower lip; *chin groove bordered by a smooth,* V*-shaped pad.* Dental formula: i 2/2 (1/2 in *M. daviesi*), c 1/1, p 2/3, m 3/3.

Macrotus. Medium sized. *Tail long, tip protrudes beyond shorter tail membrane.* Ears large and rounded. Dental formula: i 2/2, c 1/1, p 2/3, m 3/3.

Lonchorhina. Medium sized. Long tail reaches tip of extensive tail membrane. *Extremely long noseleaf and very large, pointed ears.* Dental formula: i 2/2, c 1/1, p 2/3, m 3/3.

Macrophyllum. Small. Long tail; rows of warts under tail membrane. *Very large feet and long legs.* Ears large, pointed; noseleaf long and broad. Dental formula: i 2/2, c 1/1, p 2/3, m 3/3.

Tonatia. Small to fairly large. Tail about half length of tail membrane. Ears large and rounded. *Horseshoe of noseleaf entirely fused to upper lip;* chin groove bordered by small warts. Dental formula: i 2/1, c 1/1, p 2/3, m 3/3.

Mimon. Medium sized to fairly large. Extensive tail membrane. *Ears large and pointed. Noseleaf long and broad, horseshoe entirely free.* Dental formula: i 2/1, c 1/1, p 2/2, m 3/3.

Phyllostomus. Fairly large to very large; muscular. Ears medium sized, pointed. Facial skin blackish. Noseleaf broad, horseshoe entirely free; *beadlike warts on chin.* Dental formula: i 2/2, c 1/1, p 2/2, m 3/3.

Phylloderma. Large; muscular. Ears medium sized, slightly pointed. Facial skin pinkish. Noseleaf broad, *horseshoe fused below nostrils*; beadlike warts on chin. Dental formula: i 2/2, c 1/1, p 2/3, m 3/3.

Trachops. Fairly large. Ears large and rounded. *Elongated warts on lips and chin.* Dental formula: i 2/2, c 1/1, p 2/3, m 3/3.

Chrotopterus. *Very large.* Very short tail. Woolly gray fur. Ears large and rounded. Horseshoe of noseleaf cup shaped. Dental formula: i 2/1, c 1/1, p 2/3, m 3/3.

Vampyrum. *Largest New World bat. No tail.* Ears large and rounded. Horseshoe of noseleaf cup-shaped. Dental formula: i 2/2, c 1/1, p 2/3, m 3/3.

COMMON BIG-EARED BAT   Plate 8
Micronycteris microtis   Map 48

HB 35–51, T 8–15, HF 8–12, E 17–22, FA 32–37, Wt 4–9 g. Calcar 10–12, fur length 8–10.

Description. Very small, with large, rounded ears. Upperparts reddish brown to gray-brown, basal 1–2 mm of hairs white; *underparts pale gray-brown, not contrasting strongly with dorsal color.* Fur long and fluffy. Ears hairy on inner edge; joined over forehead by a low, notched band of skin. Chin groove bordered by a smooth, V-shaped pad. Horseshoe of noseleaf free on sides, fused with lip at base. Wings attach to ankles; calcar equal to or longer than foot. **Similar Species.** See *M. minuta* and *M. schmidtorum* (both are much less common). Pygmy Round-eared Bat (*Tonatia brasiliense*) has small warts on median groove of lower lip, horseshoe of noseleaf entirely fused to the upper lip, and wings attached to feet at base of toes.

Distribution. Jalisco and Tamaulipas, Mexico, throughout Central America to Colombia, French Guiana, and Amazonian Brazil. Lowlands to 2600 m.

Status and Habitat. Rather common and widespread in evergreen and deciduous forest, second growth, and orchards. This species is

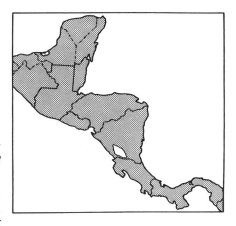

Map 48. Common Big-eared Bat, *Micronycteris microtis*

the most commonly encountered *Micronycteris* in SE Mexico and Central America.

Habits. Roosts in hollow trees, logs, caves, mines, buildings, culverts, and large mammal burrows. Shallow earthen depressions along banks and among tree roots may be occupied also. Clusters of 4–6 bats hang together from the ceiling of the roost. This small bat roosts in areas with some natural light and is alert and easily induced to take flight. The diet includes fruit and insects; insects may be gleaned from the vegetation or captured in flight. Food is usually consumed at a night roost, which may be the same as the day roost or may only be used at night. A collection of wings and legs dropped at night roosts in Costa Rica consisted of insects of 13 different orders, with small scarab beetles, grasshoppers, cockroaches, crickets, and katydids predominating. Seasonal changes in diet, probably reflecting insect abundances, were noted (LaVal and LaVal, 1980). A roost in Mexico contained wings of Lepidoptera. In Panama, flies and beetles were taken (Humphrey et al., 1983). Single young are born annually, usually at the onset of the rainy season.

Comment. This species has been treated as a subspecies of *Micronycteris megalotis*. Simmons (1996) recognized *microtis* as a distinct species, based on differences in length of hair on the ears (much longer in *megalotis*) and measurements of skull and teeth. *M. megalotis* is restricted to South America and occurs with *M. microtis* in parts of Venezuela, Colombia, French Guiana, and Brazil.

TINY BIG-EARED BAT Plate 8
Micronycteris minuta Map 49

HB 40–55, T 7–13, HF 10–13, E 18–24, FA 33–38, Wt 4–8 g. Calcar 6-8, Fur length 6–8.

Description. Very small, with *large, rounded ears* and a *white belly*. Upperparts pale reddish brown, basal 1–2 mm of hairs white; *underparts sharply contrasting with upperparts*, pure white or pale buffy gray (or, rarely, fur entirely orange). Fur rather short and even. Ears haired on inner edge, joined over forehead by a high, deeply notched band. Facial skin pinkish. Chin groove bordered by a smooth, V-shaped pad. Hind feet relatively large, *calcar shorter than foot.* **Similar Species.** Easily confused with *M. schmidtorum*, which has longer fur, calcar as long as foot, and usually has slightly shorter ears. *M. microtis* has a grayish or brownish belly, a low, notched band between ears, and longer fur and calcars.

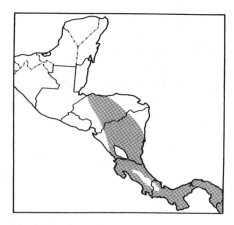

Map 49. Tiny Big-eared Bat, *Micronycteris minuta*

Distribution. NW Honduras (McCarthy et al., 1993) to Bolivia and S Brazil; Trinidad. Lowlands to 800 m.

Status and Habitat. Uncommon or rare; found in evergreen and deciduous lowland forest and agricultural areas with scattered trees.

Habits. Roosts singly or in small groups in hollow trees; occasionally found in caves or mines. The diet includes insects and plant material (Fleming et al., 1972). Pregnant females have been recorded in March and April in Costa Rica.

SCHMIDT'S BIG-EARED BAT
Micronycteris schmidtorum Map 50

HB 47–54, T 12–16, HF 9–11, E 14–20, FA 34–38, Wt 5–8 g. Calcar 10–12, Fur length 8–10.

Description. Small, with large, rounded ears and a white belly. Upperparts pale brown, basal 4 mm of hairs white; *underparts sharply contrasting with upperparts*, white or pale gray. Fur long and fluffy. Ears joined by a high, deeply notched band. Chin groove bordered by a smooth, V-shaped pad. Calcar as long as foot; tail relatively long. **Similar Species.** See the very similar *M. minuta. M. microtis* has a grayish or

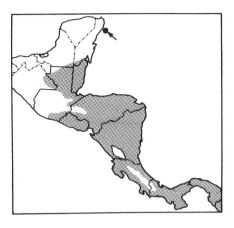

Map 50. Schmidt's Big-eared Bat, *Micronycteris schmidtorum*

brownish belly and a low, notched band between ears.

Distribution. Cozumel Island, Mexico; E Chiapas (Alvarez and Alvarez-C., 1990), N Guatemala, and Belize (McCarthy, 1987b) through Central America to Venezuela; NE Peru; NE Brazil. Lowlands only.

Status and Habitat. Apparently rare and local; found in evergreen and deciduous lowland forest and forest edge.

Habits. Poorly known. Small groups roost in hollow trees, such as *Bursera simaruba* in Tikal, Guatemala. Moths are included in the diet (Howell and Burch, 1974).

HAIRY BIG-EARED BAT   Plate 8
Micronycteris hirsuta   Map 51

HB 54–66, T 9–19, HF 10–15, E 24–28, FA 42–46, Wt 10–18 g.

Description. Relatively large for the genus. Upperparts pale to dark brown, base of hairs white; underparts gray-brown. *Fur long* and fluffy, usually with a *long tuft of hair* on the forehead of adult male. Ears *large and rounded*, joined by a low, notched band. Chin groove bordered by a smooth, V-shaped pad. Calcar about same length as foot; wings attach to feet (halfway from ankle to base of toes). **Similar Species.** Other leaf-nosed bats with large, rounded ears are either smaller (forearm less than 40 mm: *Tonatia brasiliense, M. microtis, M. minuta,* and *M. schmidtorum*) or larger (forearm greater than 47 mm: *Macrotus waterhousii,* larger *Tonatia* spp., *Trachops cirrhosus*). See these species for additional differences.

Distribution. E Honduras to the Guianas, Peru, and Amazonian Brazil; Trinidad. Lowlands to 1500 m.

Status and Habitat. Apparently rare and local; occurs in evergreen and deciduous lowland forest and forest edge.

Habits. Roosts in hollow trees, buildings, and under bridges. Feeds on insects, mainly katydids, cockroaches, June beetles, and Lepidoptera larvae, which are gleaned from vegetation. Some fruit is taken during the dry season only (Whitaker and Findley, 1980; Wilson, 1971). This bat is attracted to katydid calls and is much more likely to be caught in mist nets baited with singing male katydids than in unbaited nets (where it is seldom captured). Equal numbers of male and female (noncalling) katydid remains have been found at roosts, indicating that the bats can find prey using cues other than male songs (Belwood and Morris, 1987).

Map 51. Hairy Big-eared Bat, *Micronycteris hirsuta*

ORANGE-THROATED BAT
Micronycteris brachyotis

Plate 8
Map 52

HB 48–62, T 7–13, HF 11–14, E 13–19, FA 40–42, Wt 12–14 g. Calcar 10–11, fur length 4–5.

Description. Upperparts dark brown or orange-brown, base of hairs pale; *throat bright orange*, belly yellowish. Ears medium sized, broad, with *pointed tips*. Chin groove bordered by a smooth, V-shaped pad. *Calcar as long as foot.* **Similar Species.** Distinctive orange throat generally diagnostic. It could be mistaken for a short-tailed bat (*Carollia* spp.), which are sometimes entirely orange; *Carollia* spp. have rows of small, round warts bordering a larger central wart on chin. See *M. nicefori* and *M. sylvestris*.

Distribution. Oaxaca and Veracruz, Mexico (Medellín et al., 1983) through most of Central America to C Brazil and French Guiana; Trinidad. Lowlands to 700 m.

Status and Habitat. Rather uncommon and local; found in evergreen and deciduous lowland forest.

Habits. Roosts in hollow trees, caves, mines, and old buildings. Group size is usually small, although a sea cave in Veracruz, Mexico, contained about 300 individuals. Greatest activity occurs in the first 2 hours after sunset, with a second activity peak after midnight. Bonaccorso (1979) caught twice as many in subcanopy mist nets than in ground-level mist nets. About equal amounts of fruit and arthropods (spiders, beetles, ants, bugs, and flies) are eaten (Humphrey et al., 1983). Although occasionally caught in secondary forest and clearings, this species appears to be sensitive to habitat disturbance: the large group in Veracruz disappeared as the surrounding forest was cut and burned (Medellín et al., 1985). Births usually coincide with onset of the rainy season, and a second pregnancy may follow later in the year.

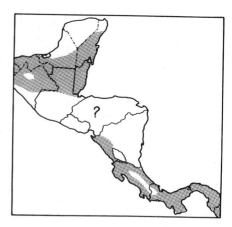

Map 52. Orange-throated Bat, *Micronycteris brachyotis*

Where to See. Surprisingly common near water sources in the dry forest of Palo Verde National Park, Costa Rica.

NICEFORO'S BAT
Micronycteris nicefori

Plate 8
Map 53

HB 51–58, T 8–15, HF 11–14, E 17–20, FA 37–40, Wt 7–11 g. Calcar 4–6, fur length 5–7.

Description. Upperparts dark brown, gray-brown, or buff, occasionally bright orange, sometimes with a very faint, pale gray stripe from mid-back to rump; fur faintly *tricolor*

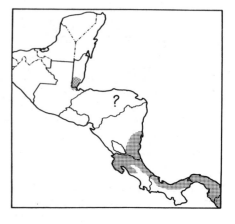

Map 53. Nicefora's Bat, *Micronycteris nicefori*

(base dark, middle pale, tip dark); underparts buffy gray. Fur short and even. Ears moderately large, *tips pointed.* Indistinct dark mask around eyes. *Chin groove bordered by a smooth, V-shaped pad. Calcar much shorter than foot.* **Similar Species.** *M. brachyotis* has an orange throat and longer calcar. *M. sylvestris* has longer, clearly tricolor fur and longer calcar. Short-tailed bats (*Carollia* spp.) are very similar, but have rows of small round warts bordering central wart on chin (see Figure 6).

Distribution. Belize (McCarthy, 1987b); E Nicaragua to Peru and Amazonian Brazil; Trinidad. Lowlands only.

Status and Habitat. Apparently rare and local in Central America; found in evergreen and dry deciduous lowland forest (more common in South America).

Habits. Poorly known. Roosts in hollow trees and buildings. This species seems to be most active for an hour after sunset and an hour before dawn.

TRICOLORED BAT   Plate 8
Micronycteris sylvestris   Map 54

HB 55–70, T 8–15, HF 11–12, E 20–22, FA 37–43, Wt 9–11 g. Calcar 6–8, fur length 7–10.

Description. Upperparts dark gray-brown, *fur clearly tricolor* (base dark, middle whitish, tip dark); underparts buffy or pale gray. Fur long and fluffy. Ears moderately large, *tips pointed.* Chin groove bordered by a smooth, V-shaped pad. Calcar shorter than foot. **Similar Species.** See *M. nicefori.* Short-tailed bats (*Carollia brevicauda* and *C. subrufa* in particular) are very similar, but have rows of small, round warts bordering central wart on chin (see Figure 6).

Distribution. Nayarit and Veracruz to Chiapas, Mexico; patchily distributed from E Honduras through Central America (McCarthy et al., 1993) to Peru and SE Brazil; Trinidad. Lowlands to 800 m.

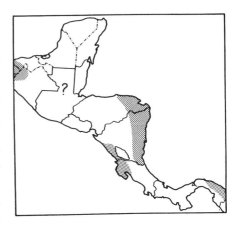

Map 54. Tricolored Bat, *Micronycteris sylvestris*

Status and Habitat. Rare and local; found in evergreen and deciduous lowland forest.

Habits. Poorly known. Roosts in hollow trees and caves, in groups of up to 75 individuals (Hall and Dalquest, 1963; Handley, 1976; Linares, 1986). Occasionally caught in mist nets or harp traps set over streams.

BARTICA BAT   Plate 9
Micronycteris daviesi   Map 55

HB 63–84, T 5–11, HF 17–20, E 27–31, FA 54–58, Wt 19–30 g.

Description. Largest species in the genus, with a single pair of *very large upper incisors* (same length as canines). Upperparts *dark gray-brown,* underparts slightly paler. Fur long and woolly. *Ears large, tips pointed.* Lips and chin well haired; chin groove bordered by a smooth, V-shaped pad. Tail short, about half the length of tail membrane. Calcar shorter than foot. Feet long and moderately haired. **Similar Species.** Much larger than all other *Micronycteris* spp. Large-eared leaf-nosed bats of similar size all have upper incisors much smaller than canines. See *Mimon* spp., large *Tonatia* spp., *Phyllostomus discolor,* and *Trachops cirrhosus* for additional differences (see Figure 4).

Map 55. Bartica Bat, *Micronycteris daviesi*

Distribution. Caribbean lowlands of E Honduras, NE Costa Rica, and E Panama to Peru, Venezuela, and the Guianas. Lowlands only.

Status and Habitat. Apparently very rare and local; probably restricted to mature, evergreen forest.

Habits. Poorly known. Three individuals were found roosting in a hollow tree in Peru (Tuttle, 1970). Occasionally caught in harp traps or mist nets set across forest trails. A small spotted frog was found in the stomach of one individual from Panama. Unlike most bats, this species is capable of chewing its way out of a cloth holding bag.

Comment. Formerly placed in a separate genus, *Barticonycteris*, in reference to the type locality, Bartica, Guyana.

WATERHOUSE'S BAT   Plate 9
Macrotus waterhousii   Map 56

HB 54–67, T 29–40, HF 12–16, E 25–34, FA 49–54, Wt 12–19 g.

Description. *Large, rounded ears and long tail.* Upperparts gray-brown or reddish brown, fur long, white at base; underparts pale gray. Edge of ears hairy. Noseleaf small, horseshoe fused below nostrils; chin groove bordered by a smooth, V-shaped pad. *Tip of long tail extends beyond shorter tail membrane.* **Similar Species.** All other leaf-nosed bats with large, *rounded ears* (*Tonatia, Trachops,* and *Micronycteris*) have tails shorter than tail membranes.

Distribution. Sonora and Hildago, to Chiapas, Mexico, and possibly Guatemala; also Greater Antilles and Bahamas. Lowlands to 1400 m.

Status and Habitat. Rare and local in SE Mexico and possibly N Central America; large aggregations found in parts of W Mexico. Usually found in dry areas, rarely in evergreen, lowland forest.

Habits. Roosts in large caves and mine tunnels, occasionally in buildings, in groups of 1–500. Individuals hang by one or both feet from high ceilings near the roost entrance and do not cluster. This species does not crawl on feet and thumbs like many bats, but can walk rapidly in an upside-down position. Activity starts 1–2 hours after sunset; when foraging, flight is slow and maneuverable, usually within 1 m of the ground. Fruit and insects are eaten, animal prey is gleaned by mouth from the ground or vegetation and carried to a night roost (Anderson,

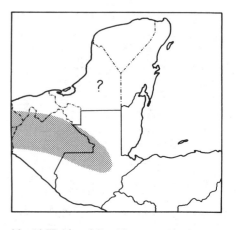

Map 56. Waterhouse's Bat, *Macrotus waterhousii*

1969). A second foraging flight occurs about 2 hours before sunrise.

Comment. This species is known from Guatemala by only 4 specimens collected over 100 years ago. These specimens have since been lost, and their identification cannot be verified (see McCarthy et al., 1993). There are similarly inconclusive reports of previous records from the Yucatán Peninsula (see Anderson and Nelson, 1965).

COMMON SWORD-NOSED BAT
Lonchorhina aurita

Plate 9
Map 57

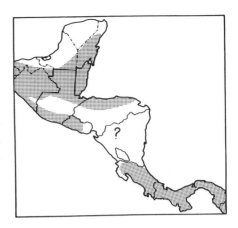

Map 57. Common Sword-nosed Bat, *Lonchorhina aurita*

HB 53–69, T 49–56, HF 13–17, E 28–35, FA 49–54, Wt 10–15 g.

Description. Rather delicate and slim bodied, with *very large, pointed ears; noseleaf almost as long as ears* with several raised folds at base. Fur long, dark brown or reddish brown. Legs and tail very long, tail extends to tip of extensive tail membrane. **Similar Species.** Other leaf-nosed bats with large ears have much shorter noseleafs, and most have tails shorter than tail membranes.

Distribution. Oaxaca, Mexico, patchily distributed through Central America (not recorded in Nicaragua) to SE Brazil and Peru; Trinidad. Lowlands to 1500 m.

Status and Habitat. Uncommon; usually found in mature, evergreen forest, occasionally in deciduous forest and agricultural areas.

Habits. Roosts in caves or mine tunnels in groups of 12–500. Activity begins well after sunset, in full darkness. This bat is an extremely agile flier and may stop and hover in front of a mist net or escape through small gaps. It is sometimes caught in nets across streams or paths through forest. Diet and behavior are poorly known; Lepidoptera and fruit were eaten by 2 individuals. Insects are probably gleaned from vegetation. Pregnant females have been found from February to April, and births may coincide with the onset of the rainy season. Biology reviewed by Lassieur and Wilson (1989).

LONG-LEGGED BAT
Macrophyllum macrophyllum

Plate 8
Map 58

HB 41–53, T 37–53, HF 10–16, E 17–19, FA 34–37, Wt 7–10 g.

Description. Small, with *long legs and tail.* Fur dark gray-brown. Ears large, with pointed tips. Noseleaf relatively large and complex, horseshoe not fused to upper lip. *Tail extends almost to the edge of extensive tail membrane; underside of membrane marked with rows of raised warts. Feet very long,* with large claws; calcar longer than foot. Wings attach halfway between knees and ankles. **Similar Species.** All other small (forearm less than 40 mm) leaf-nosed bats have much shorter tails.

Distribution. Chiapas (Medellín et al., 1986) and Tabasco, Mexico, Belize (McCarthy, 1987b), through Central America to Bolivia, SE Brazil, and NE Argentina. Lowlands only.

Status and Habitat. Uncommon; usually found near streams in mature, evergreen or semideciduous forest, occasionally in dry forest.

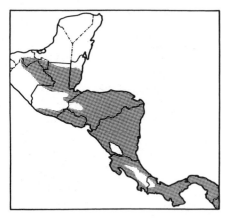

Map 58. Long-legged Bat, *Macrophyllum macrophyllum*

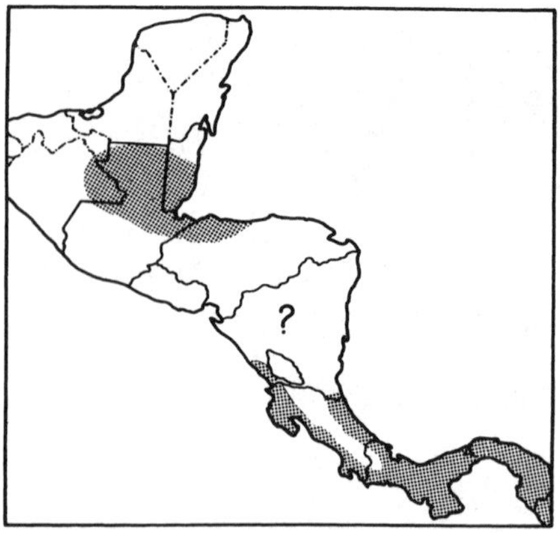

Map 59. Stripe-headed Round-eared Bat, *Tonatia saurophila*

Habits. Small groups roost together in caves, road culverts, and buildings. Records of mist-net captures are usually from nets set over streams in forest. This species appears to catch prey on the water surface; its diet includes beetles, midges, water striders, and spiders (Howell and Burch, 1974). Among New World bats, the combination of a long tail membrane, greatly elongated feet and claws, and attachment of the wings high on the legs are found only in this species and in Greater Fishing Bats (*Noctilio leporinus*). These specializations are clearly associated with hunting over water and suggest that the Long-legged Bat may trawl the water with its hind feet rather than catch prey by mouth.

STRIPE-HEADED
ROUND-EARED BAT
Tonatia saurophila

Plate 9
Map 59

HB 74–88, T 14–23, HF 15–23, E 25–35, FA 56–61, Wt 24–36 g.

Description. Large, with *long, rounded ears.* Upperparts gray-brown or dark brown (rarely deep orange); underparts slightly paler, gray or gray-brown. Fur long and slightly woolly. Indistinct, *pale median stripe extends from be-* *tween eyes to crown.* Ears not joined over forehead, haired on inner edge. Face lightly haired. Noseleaf small, *horseshoe entirely fused to upper lip* (visible only as a slight raised bump on sides of nostrils). Chin groove bordered by rows of tiny warts. Tail membrane long, tail short, less than half length of membrane. *Base of forearms thickly haired.* Short, broad wings attach to feet near base of toes; feet haired. **Similar Species.** *T. silvicola* and *T. evotis* have larger ears, naked forearms, and no stripe on the forehead. Other leaf-nosed bats of similar size with large, rounded ears are Fringe-lipped Bat (*Trachops*), which has a warty face, and Waterhouse's Bat (*Macrotus*), which has a long tail.

Distribution. Chiapas, Mexico (Medellín, 1983), patchily distributed through Central America to Peru and NE Brazil. Lowlands to 600 m.

Status and Habitat. Uncommon to rare; usually in mature, evergreen forest, occasionally in deciduous forest.

Habits. Roosts have been reported from hollow trees in Trinidad (Goodwin and Greenhall, 1961). It is usually caught in mist nets set over streams or across forest trails and usually travels in the subcanopy as opposed to the understory level. Insects (chiefly beetles, katydids, and Homoptera), arachnids, and lizards are gleaned from the foliage, carried by mouth to a night roost, and consumed (Bonaccorso, 1979; Whitaker and Findley, 1980). This bat is attracted by calling cicadas and the distress calls of small bats.

Comment. Formerly included in *Tonatia bidens*. Revised by Williams et al. (1995), who recognized 2 species, with *T. bidens* limited to southern South America.

PYGMY ROUND-EARED BAT — Plate 8
Tonatia brasiliense — Map 60

HB 42–61, T 5–10, HF 9–13, E 22–25, FA 32–36, Wt 7–13 g.

Description. Small, with *large, rounded ears*. Upperparts gray or gray-brown, base of hairs whitish; underparts slightly paler. Fur long and soft. Ears joined over forehead by a low, un-notched band of skin. Face nearly naked; noseleaf small, *horseshoe entirely fused to upper lip*. Chin groove bordered by rows of tiny warts (see Figure 5). One pair of lower incisors. Tail short, less than half the length of long tail membrane; calcars long (11–12 mm). Base of forearm sparsely covered with short fur. Short, broad *wings attach to feet* near base of toes. **Similar Species.** Much smaller than other *Tonatia* spp. Most likely to be confused with little big-eared bats (*Micronycteris* spp.), especially *M. microtis*, which have wings attached to ankles, a smooth, V-shaped pad bordering the chin groove, and 2 pairs of lower incisors.

Distribution. Veracruz, Chiapas (Alvarez-C. and Alvarez, 1991), and Quintana Roo, Mexico (Sanchez-H. et al., 1986), patchily distributed through Central America (not recorded in El Salvador or much of the Pacific Slope) to NE Brazil, Bolivia, and Peru; Trinidad. Lowlands to 600 m.

Status and Habitat. Uncommon but widespread in wet, evergreen and dry, deciduous

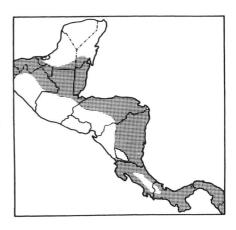

Map 60. Pygmy Round-eared Bat, *Tonatia brasiliense*

lowland forest, second growth woodland, and fruit groves.

Habits. Poorly known. Roosts in arboreal termite nests in Trinidad (Goodwin and Greenhall, 1961). Usually caught in mist nets shortly after sunset. Pregnant females were found in February and April in Costa Rica (LaVal and Fitch, 1977).

Comment. *T. minuta, T. nicaraguae*, and *T. venezuelae* are included in *T. brasiliense*.

WHITE-THROATED ROUND-EARED BAT — Plate 9
Tonatia silvicola — Map 61

HB 46–89, T 10–22, HF 15–19, E 30–39, FA 50–56, Wt 25–39 g.

Description. Rather large, with *huge, rounded ears*. Upperparts gray or gray-brown, tips of hairs frosted; belly pale gray-brown, *throat* and hair at base of ears very pale gray or *white* (rarely, the white throat patch extends to lower belly). Ears almost naked, joined by a low band across top of head. Face naked; noseleaf small, horseshoe entirely fused to upper lip (evident only as raised bumps on sides of nostrils). Chin groove bordered by rows of tiny, round warts. Tail short, less than half the length of long tail mem-

97

brane. *Forearms naked.* Wings short and broad, attached to foot near base of toes. Feet naked, calcar longer than foot. **Similar Species.** *T. evotis* is very similar, but averages smaller (forearm often less than 50 mm), distinguished in the field mainly by distribution. See *T. saurophila.* Fringe-lipped Bat (*Trachops*) has a warty face.

Distribution. Honduras to Bolivia, NE Argentina, and E Brazil. Lowlands to 600 m (in Central America).

Status and Habitat. Uncommon but widely distributed in tall forest of both the Pacific and Caribbean lowlands.

Habits. Groups of 6–10 have been found roosting in arboreal termite nests in Panama, Venezuela, and Peru (Handley, 1966, 1976; Tuttle, 1970), often in association with Greater Spear-nosed Bats (*Phyllostomus hastatus*). A group of 18 was found in a hollow tree roost in Peru. This bat is most active for 1–2 hours after sunset. It travels through the forest understory; the short, broad wings enable slow, highly maneuverable flight. Although it is largely insectivorous, fruit and pollen may be eaten during the dry season. Preferred insects are katydids, beetles, and cicadas. Whipscorpions are also important in the diet, and small vertebrates may sometimes be taken. Prey is gleaned from the vegetation, grabbed by mouth, and taken to a night roost to be eaten. This species is attracted to the breeding calls of some insects and can be captured by baiting mist nets with calling male katydids (Belwood and Morris, 1987). Birth peaks occur twice a year, in January and July in Panama. Biology reviewed by Medellín and Arita (1989).

DAVIS' ROUND-EARED BAT

Tonatia evotis Map 61

HB 49–70, T 11–18, HF 13–16, E 31–35, FA 47–54, Wt 14–23 g.

Description. Very similar to *T. silvicola*, but usually smaller; throat sometimes grayish.

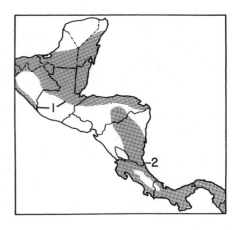

Map 61. 1. Davis' Round-eared Bat, *Tonatia evotis* 2. White-throated Round-eared Bat, *Tonatia silvicola*

Similar Species. See *T. silvicola* and Comment.

Distribution. S Veracruz, S Chiapas, and E Quintana Roo, Mexico to NE Honduras. Lowlands only.

Status and Habitat. Uncommon; found in mature and secondary lowland forest.

Habits. A group of 5 was found roosting in an inactive termite nest, 3 m above ground, and a single bat was found roosting in a building (McCarthy et al., 1993). The diet includes beetles and katydids. Flight is through the forest understory, and most records are from mist-net captures. Biology reviewed by Medellín and Arita (1989).

Comment. This species was described as distinct from *T. silvicola* by Davis and Carter (1978). Medellín and Arita (1989) noted that *T. evotis* lacks the white throat and pale patches at the base of the ears seen in *T. silvicola*. These features are quite variable in *T. silvicola*, and are evident on some specimens of *T. evotis*; therefore, they are not always useful for field identification of the 2 species.

GOLDEN BAT
Mimon bennettii

Plate 9
Map 62

HB 61–75, T 15–23, HF 16–19, E 33–38, FA 53–61, Wt 15–25 g.

Description. Fairly large. Upperparts glistening golden-brown; underparts slightly paler. Fur long and crinkly. *Ears very large and pale, tips pointed. Noseleaf long* (18 mm) and broad, horseshoe not fused to lip. Chin groove bordered by a small, V-shaped pad. Tail short, about 1/3 length of long tail membrane. Base of forearms hairy; wings attach to ankles; wingtips whitish. Calcar longer than foot. **Similar Species.** Most large-eared leaf-nosed bats of similar size have rounded, not pointed ears (*Tonatia, Trachops, Macrotus*). Pale Spear-nosed Bat (*Phyllostomus discolor*) has much shorter ears and short, velvety fur. Bartica Bat (*Micronycteris daviesi*) is dark gray with a short noseleaf and calcar shorter than foot.

Distribution. Veracruz, Mexico, through the Yucatán Peninsula and Caribbean Slope of Central America to W Panama (not recorded in Nicaragua); also N Colombia, the Guianas, and SE Brazil. Lowlands only.

Status and Habitat. Rather common in dry and semideciduous forest on the Yucatán Peninsula; rare and local southward, mainly in mature evergreen forest.

Habits. Poorly known. Usually roosts in groups of 2–20 in limestone caves (most captures are made in or around roosts). LaVal (1977) reported a roost of 15–20 in a hollow log. It probably gleans prey from vegetation. Whitaker and Findley (1980) found remains of large scarab beetles and a bird in feces of 4 individuals. Small lizards and katydids are also taken. Single young are born at the onset of the rainy season.

Comment. Includes *cozumelae* (type locality on Cozumel Island, Mexico), which is sometimes treated as a separate species.

STRIPED HAIRY-NOSED BAT
Mimon crenulatum

Plate 9
Map 63

HB 55–69, T 15–29, HF 10–14, E 21–28, FA 46–55, Wt 10–18 g.

Description. Upperparts blackish, with a prominent *white or buff stripe from crown to rump*; underparts yellowish, base of hairs dark. *Ears large,* bicolor (base pink, tip blackish), with pointed tips. *Noseleaf long and broad, sides haired and serrated.* Tail long, enclosed in extensive tail membrane. Long, slim legs. **Similar Species.** Distinctive and unmistakable. Note

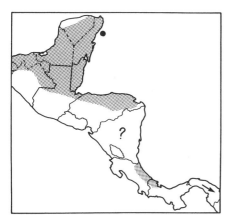

Map 62. Golden Bat, *Mimon bennettii*

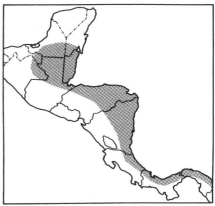

Map 63. Striped Hairy-nosed Bat, *Mimon crenulatum*

unique hairy, serrated noseleaf (see Figure 4). Other stripe-backed leaf-nosed bats of similar size are tailless.

Distribution. Chiapas, Mexico (Medellín, 1983), through Central America on the Gulf/Caribbean Slope to E Brazil, N Peru, and N Bolivia; Trinidad. Lowlands only.

Status and Habitat. Rare and local; found in evergreen and semideciduous forest, plantations, and clearings near forest.

Habits. Poorly known. Roosts in humid, rotting logs and hollow tree stumps, occasionally in buildings. Small groups cluster together in the roost. Probably gleans insects from vegetation; the diet consists mainly of beetles, with some flies, moths, whipscorpions, and small lizards (Humphrey et al., 1983). In Costa Rica, pregnant females have been recorded in April (Gardner et al., 1970; LaVal, 1977).

PALE SPEAR-NOSED BAT   Plate 10
Phyllostomus discolor   Map 64

HB 66–97, T 12–17, HF 14–18, E 16–24, FA 60–68, Wt 26–51 g.

Description. Muscular, velvety. Upperparts graybrown, brown or (less commonly) orange, often flecked with whitish hairs; *underparts notice-*

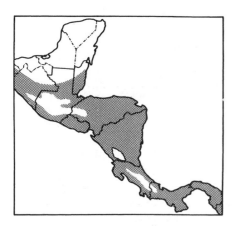

Map 64. Pale Spear-nosed Bat, *Phyllostomus discolor*

ably paler than upperparts, usually grayish, well frosted with white (pale orange if orange above). *Fur short and sleek.* Ears triangular, tips pointed, sometimes held curled back. Facial skin dark brown. Horseshoe of noseleaf not fused to upper lip. *Chin groove* bordered by *conspicuous, beadlike warts*. Membranes blackish; tail short, about half length of tail membrane, tip protrudes slightly from upper surface of membrane. Calcar shorter than foot. **Similar Species.** *P. hastatus* is much larger. See Pale-faced Bat (*Phylloderma stenops*). Other tailed, leaf-nosed bats of similar size have long, fluffy fur.

Distribution. Veracruz and Oaxaca, Mexico, through Central America (except Yucatán Peninsula) to N Argentina, SE Brazil and Paraguay; Trinidad; Margarita Island. Lowlands only.

Status and Habitat. Widespread in a variety of lowland habitats; most common in evergreen or riparian forest.

Habits. Roosts in hollow trees, occasionally in caves. Groups of up to 400 individuals are composed of small harems (1–12 females and 1 male) and small all-male clusters (Bradbury, 1977). Individuals leave the roost shortly after sunset and often fly in groups (lone individuals are seldom mist netted). These bats are frequently covered in pollen when captured and eat nectar, pollen, and flower parts of *Calliandra, Ceiba, Crescentia, Ochroma* and *Pseudobombax*. Insects, mainly beetles, may predominate in the diet during the wet season; some fruit is also eaten (Gardner, 1977; Humphrey et al., 1983). Breeding appears to occur year-round.

GREATER SPEAR-NOSED BAT   Plate 10
Phyllostomus hastatus   Map 65

HB 103–124, T 10–29, HF 19–25, E 28–34, FA 80–93, Wt 78–110 g.

Description. *Large, sleek, and muscular.* Upperparts usually blackish or dark brown, rarely bright orange; underparts slightly paler than

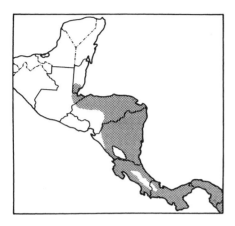

Map 65. Greater Spear-nosed Bat, *Phyllostomus hastatus*

leave the roost well after sunset; individuals forage separately (although groups may be found at fruiting trees), returning to the day roost about 2 hours later. This species flies through the forest understory and, where common, is often caught in mist nets, which it rapidly destroys. This large bat is omnivorous, feeding on insects (including swarming termites), small vertebrates (bats, mice, and birds), fruits (guava, *Cecropia*, and *Piper*), flowers, nectar, and pollen (Gardner, 1977). Synchronized reproduction occurs in Trinidad, with young born during the dry season (April–May) and weaned early in the rainy season (McCracken and Bradbury, 1981).

upperparts. Fur *short and velvety.* Ears triangular, tips pointed. Horseshoe of *noseleaf not fused to upper lip. Chin groove* bordered by *conspicuous, beadlike warts.* Membranes, ears, and facial skin black. Calcar as long as foot. **Similar Species.** One of the largest bats in the region. Other leaf-nosed bats of similar size are Woolly False Vampire (*Chrotopterus auritus*), which has huge rounded ears and woolly gray fur, and Great Fruit-eating Bat (*Artibeus lituratus*), which has facial stripes and no tail. See Pale-faced Bat (*Phylloderma stenops*).

Distribution. S Belize, E Guatemala, and N Honduras (McCarthy et al., 1993) to E Brazil, N Argentina, and Peru; Trinidad and Tobago; Margarita Island. Lowlands to 600 m.

Status and Habitat. Uncommon to locally common in lowland forest and fruit groves (in Central America it is most common in evergreen forest of E Panama).

Habits. Roosts in hollow trees, caves, termite nests, and buildings. Roosting groups are composed of several harems, each with 10–100 females and a single male grouped in a tight cluster, and aggregates of 20–50 bachelor males. Harem females form stable associations that may last several years and do not change if the harem male disappears or is replaced. They

PALE-FACED BAT   Plate 10
Phylloderma stenops   Map 66

HB 87–115, T 12–23, HF 17–25, E 24–31, FA 69–83, Wt 51–65 g.

Description. Large and muscular. Upperparts reddish brown or brown, often marked with white flecks; underparts pale gray. Fur *short and velvety. Facial skin pink; horseshoe of noseleaf fused to upper lip below nostrils.* Membranes black, often with pinkish spots; *tips of wings white.* Tail about half the length of tail membrane; tail tip projects above membrane. **Simi-**

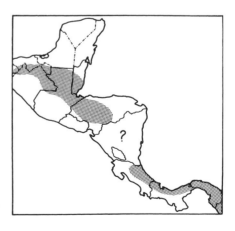

Map 66. Pale-faced Bat, *Phylloderma stenops*

101

lar **Species.** Spear-nosed bats (*Phyllostomus* spp.) have entirely black wings, dark facial skin, and horseshoe of noseleaf not fused to lip (see Figure 4).

Distribution. Chiapas, Mexico (Alvarez-Castañeda and Alvarez, 1991), and Belize (McCarthy, 1987b), patchily distributed through Central America (not recorded in Nicaragua) to Bolivia, Peru, and SE Brazil. Lowlands to 1300 m.

Status and Habitat. Rare and local; found in mature evergreen forest.

Habits. Poorly known. It is usually captured in mist nets set over streams in evergreen forest. One individual caught in Costa Rica had eaten fruit (Annonaceae) and consumed bananas and sugar water in captivity (LaVal, 1977). In Brazil, a Pale-faced Bat chewed its way into the nest of a social wasp, where it fed on larvae and pupae. It was able to extract the larvae without ingesting the thin cell walls, and was unmolested by the adult wasps while feeding inside the nest (Jeanne, 1970).

Comment. Some authors include *Phylloderma* in *Phyllostomus* (Baker et al., 1988b, but see Koopman, 1993).

FRINGE-LIPPED BAT   Plate 9
Trachops cirrhosus   Map 67

HB 65–88, T 10–20, HF 16–22, E 26–37, FA 57–65, Wt 24–36 g.

Description. Upperparts gray-brown or pale orange-brown; underparts paler. Fur long, wavy, and shiny. Ears large and rounded. *Conspicuous, elongated, papilla-like warts around mouth.* Tail membrane and calcars long, tail short. Wings broad, attached to ankles. **Similar Species.** No other leaf-nosed bat has pronounced warts on the face (see Figure 5).

Distribution. Oaxaca, Mexico, through Central America (except Yucatán Peninsula) to Ecuador, SE Brazil, and Bolivia; Trinidad.

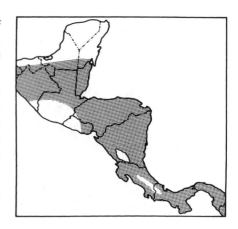

Map 67. Fringe-lipped Bat, *Trachops cirrhosus*

Lowlands to 1400 m (highland record from Monteverde, Costa Rica).

Status and Habitat. Fairly common in lowland forest; uncommon in agricultural areas and at higher elevations.

Habits. Small groups roost in caves, road culverts, buildings, and hollow trees. Larger maternity colonies are sometimes found in deep caves. This bat flies low through the forest understory to forage over streams or other wet areas. It eats frogs and can discriminate between poisonous and edible species on the basis of their calls (Tuttle and Ryan, 1981). Prey are grabbed by the mouth from the ground or substrate while the bat is in flight. Insects and lizards are also eaten. Single young are born near the end of the dry season.

WOOLLY FALSE VAMPIRE
BAT   Plate 10
Chrotopterus auritus   Map 68

HB 93–113, T 6–15, HF 21–28, E 40–48, FA 77–83, Wt 61–92 g.

Description. Very large. Upperparts *dark gray or gray-brown,* underparts silvery gray or whitish. *Fur long and woolly. Ears very long and rounded.* Horseshoe of noseleaf cup-shaped and continuous with spear. Wings attach to base of toes; wingtips white. **Similar Species.** Other large, leaf-nosed bats with long, rounded ears are smaller (*Tonatia* spp., *Trachops cirrhosus*) or larger (*Vampyrum spectrum*); compare forearm lengths.

Distribution. Oaxaca and Veracruz, Mexico, through Central America to S Brazil and N Argentina. Lowlands to 2000 m.

Status and Habitat. Uncommon to rare, but widespread; usually in mature evergreen forest, occasionally in deciduous forest or second growth.

Habits. Roosts in caves or hollow trees, in small groups hanging clustered together. These groups appear to be families, consisting of an adult pair, a juvenile, and last year's young. In large caves, groups occupy regions that are poorly lit but not entirely dark, where they are alert but reluctant to take flight if disturbed. The diet consists mainly of small mammals and birds and a few small reptiles, frogs, and insects. In captivity this large bat feeds by dropping from a resting position onto small birds or mice; prey is held with the thumbs and bitten on the head or neck. The bat then flies to a perch and eats. In the wild, prey is usually taken to a night roost (often a hollow tree)

where it is eaten, and parts of the prey and feces are dropped. Analysis of remains at such a roost found major food items to be rodents weighing 10–35 g (Medellín, 1988). It is attracted to distress calls of small bats and can sometimes be lured to a mist net by hunters' whistles. The reproductive cycle is poorly known.

GREAT FALSE VAMPIRE BAT Plate 10
Vampyrum spectrum Map 69

HB 135–152, T 0, HF 29–34, E 39–48, FA 98–110, Wt 135–235 g.

Description. *Largest bat in the New World.* Upperparts *dark brown or orangish*, with a faint pale stripe from shoulders to rump; underparts gray-brown. Fur dense, medium length. *Ears large and rounded.* Muzzle long; noseleaf cream-white, horseshoe cup-shaped. No tail. Tail membrane and calcars long; feet and claws long and powerful. **Similar Species.** Easily recognized by very large size: wingspan almost 1 m.

Distribution. Veracruz, Mexico; N Guatemala and S Belize (McCarthy, 1987b) to Peru and SW Brazil; Trinidad. Lowlands to 1650 m.

Status and Habitat. Rare and local; usually found in lowland, evergreen forest, occasionally in cloud or deciduous forest, fruit groves, pastures, or swampy areas.

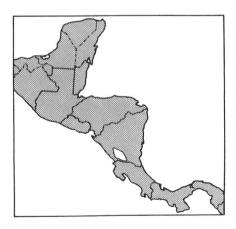

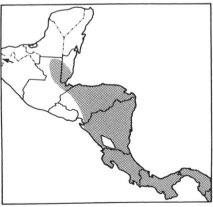

Map 68. Woolly False Vampire Bat, *Chrotopterus auritus*   Map 69. Great False Vampire Bat, *Vampyrum spectrum*

Habits. Roosts in groups of 1-5 in hollow trees (including *Ceiba pentandra, Mora excelsa,* and *Spondias mombin*). Groups usually consist of an adult pair and their offspring, which hang tightly clumped together. Activity begins at dusk; after foraging for an hour or more, the group returns to the day roost for part of the night. This huge bat is carnivorous, eating birds and small mammals. Collections of remains at a roost in NW Costa Rica revealed a diet of birds with body weights of 20–150 g. Among the 18 bird species recorded were trogons, doves, motmots, cuckoos, wrens, and orioles. Groove-billed Anis and Orange-fronted Parakeets were most frequently taken, both of which roost communally, and may be detected by odor (Vehrencamp et al., 1977). A bat (*Rhogeessa* sp.) was found in feces of an individual from Guatemala (McCarthy, 1987a); in Panama one fed on small bats held in mist nets (Peterson and Kirmse, 1969). It is often attracted to distress calls of smaller bats. Reproductive data are limited; single young appear to be born at the onset of the rainy season and are tended by both parents.

Nectar-feeding or Long-tongued Bats
Subfamilies Glossophaginae and Lonchophyllinae

There are 13 genera in these 2 subfamilies of leaf-nosed bats, 9 of which occur in Central America and SE Mexico. Most nectar bats are small and have long, narrow muzzles and greatly elongated tongues. The tip of the tongue is equipped with hairlike papillae which point backward. The lower incisors are very small or entirely absent. The noseleaf is small (when folded back onto the muzzle, it does not extend beyond the eyes) and simple, with part or all of the horseshoe fused to the upper lip. The ears are short and rounded. These bats have reduced tail membranes with very short (or no) tails and rather broad wings.

Nectar bats are among the most difficult bats to identify to species in the field. A hand lens is necessary to examine the lower incisors; when present they are small and can be overlooked and are often concealed by the tongue. It is sometimes easier to feed the bat with sugar water or dilute fruit juice before inspecting the teeth. Length of the spear of the noseleaf is given in some of the species accounts; this is measured from midpoint between the nostrils.

Long-tongued bats feed by night in much the same manner as hummingbirds feed by day, hovering in front of a bloom and probing for nectar. Less commonly, they land and crawl on the surface of a large flower. Flowers attractive to bats are often white or greenish in color, large in size, and lack a sweet odor. Many such flowers hang from long stems and are trumpet shaped. While feeding on nectar, the bats often become coated in pollen, some of which is eaten and some of which is transferred to other flowers. Flowering plants visited by bats include trees such as *Ceiba, Crescentia, Inga,* and *Bombax; Mucuna* and *Ipomoea* vines; and various cacti and agaves. Some of these plants may be dependent on bats for pollination and may be visited by other phyllostomids in addition to nectar bats. Most species of long-tongued bats also feed on fruit and insects. Little is known of the natural history of the less common bats in this group.

The following outline gives important characteristics for each genus, with more details for the smaller and easily confused species:

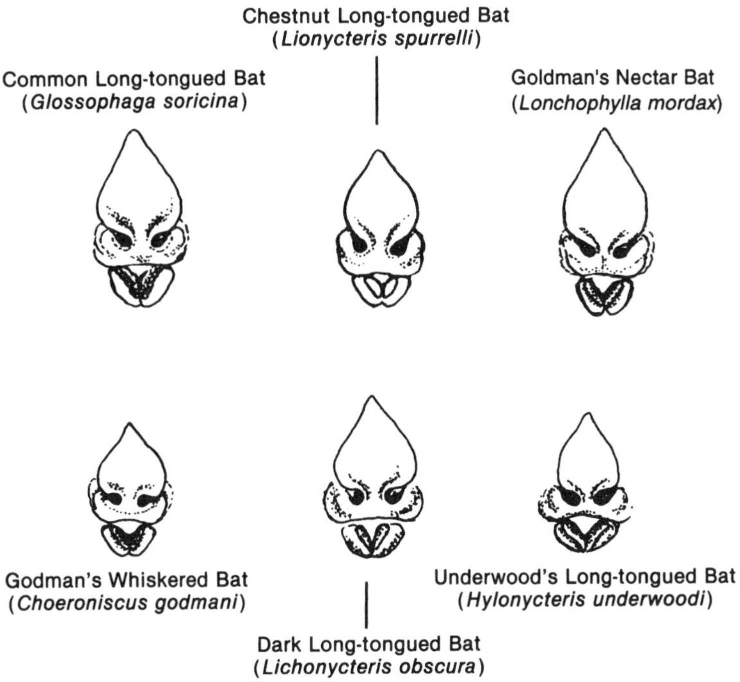

FIGURE 6. Noseleafs of long-tongued bats, 3 × life size.

Glossophaga. Small. Fur bicolor, base of hairs pale. Muzzle slightly elongated; lower jaw almost the same length as upper jaw. Forearms naked; wings attach to ankles; tail present; tail membrane naked. Lower incisors present (very small); 4 upper incisors all equal in length, barely visible without a hand lens. Dental formula: i 2/2, c 1/1, p 2/3, m 3/3.

Anoura. Medium sized. Muzzle long and narrow; lower jaw longer than upper jaw. *No tail or tiny tail; greatly reduced, hairy tail membrane.* Legs hairy. No lower incisors. Dental formula: i 2/0, c 1/1, p 3/3, m 3/3.

Lichonycteris. Very small. *Fur clearly tricolor,* base of hairs dark. Muzzle slightly elongated; lower jaw extends beyond upper jaw. Forearms well haired; *wings attach to feet near base of toes;* tail present; tail membrane naked. No lower incisors. Dental formula: i 2/0, c 1/1, p 2/3, m 2/2.

Hylonycteris. Very small. Fur faintly tricolor, base of hairs dark. Muzzle long and narrow; lower jaw extends well beyond upper jaw. Forearms well haired; wings attach to ankles; tail present; tail membrane naked. No lower incisors. Dental formula: i 2/0, c 1/1, p 2/3, m 3/3.

Choeroniscus. Very small. Fur bicolor, pale at base. Muzzle long and narrow; lower jaw slightly longer than upper jaw. Short, broad noseleaf. Forearms well haired; wings attach halfway from base of toe to ankle; tail present; tail membrane naked. No lower incisors. Dental formula: i 2/0, c 1/1, p 2/3, m 3/3.

Choeronycteris. Medium sized. Muzzle very long and narrow. Tail present; tail membrane naked. No lower incisors. Dental formula: i 2/0, c 1/1, p 2/3, m 3/3.

Leptonycteris. Relatively large. Muzzle slightly elongated. *No tail*; small, U-shaped, lightly haired tail membrane. Lower incisors present. Dental formula: i 2/2, c 1/1, p 2/3, m 2/2.

Lonchophylla. Very small to medium sized. Color varies between species. Muzzle elongated but not greatly tapered, lower jaw slightly longer than upper jaw. Ears and noseleaf more prominent than in other genera. Forearms well haired in some species, naked in others; wings attach to ankles; tail present; tail membrane naked. Lower incisors present; upper middle incisors much larger than upper outer incisors. Dental formula: i 2/2, c 1/1, p 2/3, m 3/3.

Lionycteris. Very small. Fur uniformly dark to base. Muzzle slightly elongated; lower jaw equal to upper jaw. Forearms naked; *wings attach to legs above ankles*; tail present; tail membrane naked. Lower incisors present. Dental formula: i 2/2, c 1/1, p 2/3, m 3/3.

COMMON LONG-TONGUED BAT
Glossophaga soricina

Plate 11
Map 70

HB 45–59, T 5–10, HF 7–11, E 9–15, FA 33–38, Wt 7–12 g.

Description. Small. Upperparts reddish brown to gray-brown (seldom dark brown), sometimes lightly frosted on lower back; underparts paler, gray-brown with pale frosting. Fur bicolor (or tricolor if tips frosted), *base of hairs whitish*. Muzzle elongated; lower jaw almost the same length as upper jaw. Tongue very long and narrow. Noseleaf rather small (spear about 4 mm); horseshoe of noseleaf fused to upper lip. Chin groove bordered by narrow pads with serrated edges (appears warty). Four lower incisors present, in contact with each other, forming a smooth-looking row. Four upper incisors small, almost equal in size, procumbent ("bucktoothed"). Tail short, about 1/3 length of naked tail membrane. Forearms and legs naked; wings attach to ankles. **Similar Species.** This widespread species is the most commonly encountered nectar-feeding bat in Central America. Other *Glossophaga* spp. are very similar but have gaps between lower incisors (visible with a hand lens). See Thomas' Nectar Bat (*Lonchophylla thomasi*) and Godman's Whiskered Bat (*Choeroniscus godmani*). Other small nectar bats have base of fur dark. Short-tailed bats (*Carollia* spp.) are

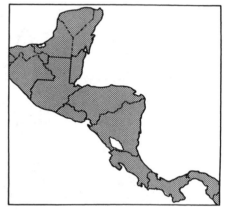

Map 70. Common Long-tongued Bat, *Glossophaga soricina*

larger, with less elongated muzzles, horseshoe of noseleaf free on the sides, and round warts on the chin.

Distribution. Sonora and Tamaulipas, Mexico, throughout Central America to S Peru, SE Brazil, and N Argentina. Lowlands to 2600 m (usually below 1000 m).

Status and Habitat. Widespread, often abundant throughout the lowlands; less common in mature evergreen forest than in seasonally dry forest and disturbed areas; uncommon in the highlands.

Habits. Roosts in small to large groups in caves, tunnels, culverts, hollow trees, and buildings, usually not in complete darkness. Individuals hang singly or in clusters. The diet varies with food availability, consisting primarily of moths and fruit (including bananas, *Muntingia*, and *Acnistes*) in the wet season and nectar and pollen (including flowers of bombacaceous and leguminous trees such as *Ceiba*, *Inga*, and *Hymenaea*) in the dry season. In Costa Rica, birth peaks occur in April–June and December–February, and young are born and raised in separate maternity colonies. Systematics and biology reviewed by Webster (1993); natural history reviewed by Howell (1983).

GRAY'S LONG-TONGUED BAT
Glossophaga leachii   Map 71

HB 47–60, T 4–10, HF 10–12, E 12–15, FA 35–39, Wt 9–11 g.

Description. Very similar to *Glossophaga soricina*, but *G. leachii* differs as follows: averages slightly larger; upper incisors not procumbent; inner lower incisors separated by a large median gap; small gap between inner and outer lower incisors (this small gap sometimes not detectable with hand lens, median gap clearly detectable). **Similar Species.** *G. commissarisi* is usually smaller and darker, with more pronounced gaps between inner and outer lower

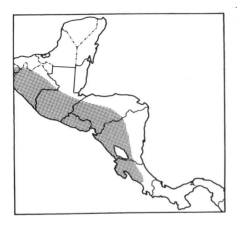

Map 71. Gray's Long-tongued Bat, *Glossophaga leachii*

incisors, but may be difficult to distinguish in the field. See *G. morenoi*; see *G. soricina* for comparisons with other nectar bats.

Distribution. Colima and Jalisco, Mexico, to Costa Rica, mainly on the Pacific Slope. Lowlands to 2400 m.

Status and Habitat. Fairly common in thorn scrub, deciduous and pine–oak forest; occasionally recorded in evergreen forest and agricultural areas.

Habits. Probably similar to *G. soricina*. Roosts in caves, buildings, and culverts. Flowers visited by this species include *Pseudobombax* and *Ipomoea* spp. Reproduction does not appear to be seasonal (Webster and Jones, 1984).

Comment. Previously known as *G. alticola*, *G. soricina alticola*, or *G. soricina leachii* (see Webster, 1993; Webster and Jones, 1980).

BROWN LONG-TONGUED BAT
Glossophaga commissarisi   Map 72

HB 42–61, T 4–11, HF 8–12, E 11–16, FA 32–35, Wt 6–11 g.

Description. Similar to *G. soricina*, but *G. commissarisi* differs as follows: averages slightly smaller with a shorter rostrum; *upperparts not frosted*, often *dark brown*; upper incisors not procumbent, middle pair smaller than outer pair; lower incisors small, clearly separated from one another, evenly spaced. **Similar Species.** This species is usually smaller and darker than other *Glossophaga* in Central America. *G. mexicana* has procumbent upper incisors. See *G. leachii*; see *G. soricina* for comparisons with other nectar bats.

Distribution. Discontinuous populations: Sinaloa to Colima, Mexico; Oaxaca, Mexico, through Central America (except Yucatán Peninsula) to E Panama; upper Amazon Basin of S Colombia to W Brazil and Peru. Lowlands to 2000 m.

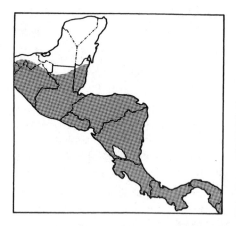

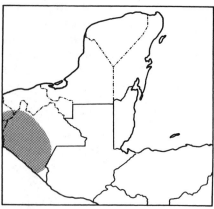

Map 72. Brown Long-tongued Bat, *Glossophaga commissarisi*

Map 73. Western Long-tongued Bat, *Glossophaga morenoi*

Status and Habitat. Common in evergreen forest (where it is often more numerous than *G. soricina*), banana groves, and clearings; less common in dry forest.

Habits. Roosts in hollow trees, caves, and tunnels. The diet includes nectar and pollen of bananas and *Mucuna,* fruit of *Acnistes,* and moths (Howell and Burch, 1974). Birth peaks have been recorded January–April and July–August (Webster, 1993).

WESTERN LONG-TONGUED BAT
Glossophaga morenoi   Map 73

HB 52–58, T 5–11, HF 10–11, E 13–15, FA 32–36, WT 7–9 g.

Description. Similar to *G. soricina,* but *G. morenoi* has a relatively long muzzle (longer than in other *Glossophaga* spp.). Upper incisors procumbent; lower incisors separated from one another by small gaps. **Similar Species.** Difficult to distinguish in the field from *G. commissarisi* and *G. leachii,* both of which do not have procumbent upper incisors. See *G. soricina* for comparisons with other nectar bats.

Distribution. Michoacán to E Chiapas, Mexico (Alvarez-Castañeda and Alvarez, 1991). Lowlands to 1500 m (usually below 300 m).

Status and Habitat. Fairly common in thorn scrub and dry, pine–oak forest, often near water.

Habits. Roosts in caves, hollow trees, culverts, wells, and buildings. It has been caught in mist nets set over rivers and creeks in arid regions and was recorded in Chiapas with the 3 other *Glossophaga* spp. found in Mexico (Webster and Jones, 1985).

Comment. The name *G. mexicana* has been used for this species (but see Webster, 1993).

GEOFFROY'S HAIRY-LEGGED BAT   Plate 11
Anoura geoffroyi   Map 74

HB 58–73, T 0, ˙HF 11–14, E 12–16, FA 40–45, Wt 13–18 g.

Description. Medium sized. Upperparts dark gray-brown, base of hairs pale; underparts gray-brown. Ears short and rounded. Muzzle elongated; lower jaw extends well beyond upper jaw. Noseleaf small. No lower incisors. *No*

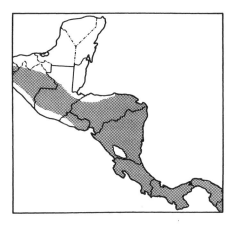

Map 74. Geoffroy's Hairy-legged Bat, *Anoura geoffroyi*

tail; *tail membrane greatly reduced and hairy.* Base of forearms well haired. *Legs hairy,* sides of feet clothed with very short hair, toes haired. **Similar Species.** *A. cultrata* has a very small tail and sides of feet naked. Other nectar bats (similar size or smaller) have tails and naked tail membranes. Long-nosed bats (*Leptonycteris* spp.) are much larger.

Distribution. Sinaloa and Tamaulipas, Mexico, through Central America (except Yucatán Peninsula) to Peru, Bolivia, and SE Brazil; Trinidad; Grenada. Lowlands to at least 2500 m.

Status and Habitat. Uncommon to locally common in evergreen forest and fruit groves; in Central America mainly on the Pacific slope at middle elevations.

Habits. Roosts in caves and tunnels. A colony of about 75 was found in a tunnel in Peru, grouped into several small clusters and hanging from the ceiling (Tuttle, 1970). Feeds on insects, pollen, fruit, and nectar, and may visit flowers primarily to obtain insects. Plant species visited in Mexico include *Agave, Ceiba, Calliandra, Eucalyptus, Ipomoea, Pinus,* and various composites (Gardner, 1977). A single birth peak occurs each year, late in the wet season (Wilson, 1979).

HANDLEY'S HAIRY-LEGGED BAT
Anoura cultrata   Map 75

HB 69–78, T 4–6, HF 12–15, E 11–14, FA 43–44, Wt 12–21 g.

Description. Medium sized. Upperparts dark gray-brown, base of hairs pale; underparts gray-brown. Ears short and rounded. Muzzle elongated; lower jaw extends well beyond upper jaw. Noseleaf small. No lower incisors. *Tail membrane very short and hairy, tail very short,* concealed in fur. Base of forearms well haired. *Legs hairy, sides of feet naked, toes haired.* **Similar Species.** See *A. geoffroyi.*

Distribution. Costa Rica to Venezuela, Colombia, and N Andes to Peru. Lowlands to 2600 m (all records are from above 600 m in Central America).

Status and Habitat. Uncommon to locally common in evergreen forest and forest edge; mainly on the Caribbean Slope.

Habits. Roosts in caves and tunnels. Feeds on insects (including Lepidoptera), pollen (including *Hibiscus luteus*), and nectar. Biology reviewed by Tamsitt and Nagorsen (1982).

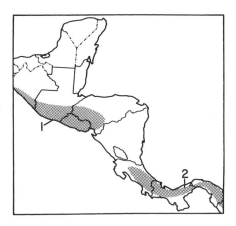

Map 75. 1. Mexican Hog-nosed Bat, *Choeronycteris mexicana*

2. Handley's Hairy-legged Bat, *Anoura cultrata*

109

DARK LONG-TONGUED BAT Plate 11
Lichonycteris obscura Map 76

HB 46–55, T 6–10, HF 8–11, E 10–13, FA 31–35, Wt 6–10 g.

Description. Very small. Upperparts *blackish* or *dark brown, hairs clearly tricolor,* base dark gray to black, middle whitish, tips dark; underparts dark gray-brown, slightly paler than upperparts. Muzzle slightly elongated; lower jaw extends just beyond upper jaw. Noseleaf small, spear 4 mm. No lower incisors. Base of forearms well haired. Tail present, shorter than naked tail membrane. *Wings attach to feet, near base of toes.* **Similar Species.** See Underwood's Long-tongued Bat (*Hylonycteris underwoodi*).

Distribution. Chiapas, Mexico, through E Guatemala and S Belize to Peru, Bolivia, and Amazonian Brazil. Lowlands to 1000 m.

Status and Habitat. Rare; usually recorded in lowland evergreen forest and plantations.

Habits. Poorly known. A specimen from Chiapas had eaten pollen of *Lonchocarpus* sp. (Alvarez and Alvarez-C., 1990).

UNDERWOOD'S LONG-TONGUED BAT Plate 11
Hylonycteris underwoodi Map 77

HB 48–60, T 3–10, HF 7–11, E 9–13, FA 31–34, Wt 6–12 g.

Description. Very small. Upperparts dark brown or blackish, *hairs faintly tricolor,* base dark gray, middle pale gray, tips dark; underparts slightly paler, dark gray-brown. Muzzle *greatly elongated,* tapering; lower jaw extends well beyond upper jaw.

Spear of noseleaf short (3–4 mm) and narrow. No lower incisors. Tail present, shorter than naked tail membrane. Base of forearms well haired. *Wings attach to ankles.* **Similar Species.** *Lichonycteris obscura* (also has tricolor fur and no lower incisors) has a less elongated muzzle and wings attached to feet, not ankles.

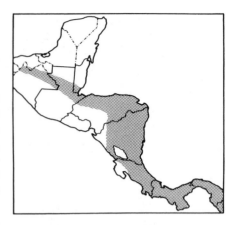

Map 76. Dark Long-tongued Bat, *Lichonycteris obscura*

Distribution. Known range discontinuous in Central America. Nayarit and Veracruz, Mexico, to W Honduras (not recorded on Yucatán Peninsula); SE Nicaragua to W Panama. Lowlands to 2600 m.

Status and Habitat. Fairly common in evergreen forest and openings on the Caribbean Slope, especially at middle elevations. Occasionally recorded in deciduous forest.

Habits. Roosts in small caves and culverts. Pollen, fruit, and insects are taken in addition to nectar (Gardner, 1977). In Costa Rica, birth peaks occur in the dry season, February–April,

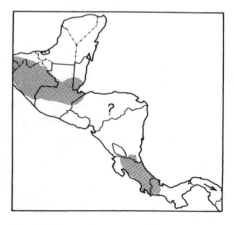

Map 77. Underwood's Long-tongued Bat, *Hylonycteris underwoodi*

and in the wet season, August–November (Wilson, 1979).

Comment. The subspecies *H. u. minor* (Nayarit to Chiapas) is considered a distinct species by some authors (but see Koopman, 1993).

GODMAN'S WHISKERED BAT   Plate 11
Choeroniscus godmani   Map 78

HB 47–58, T 5–11, HF 7–11, E 11–13, FA 31–35, Wt 5–13 g.

Description. Very small. Upperparts dark gray-brown, *base of hairs pale, tips brown,* extreme tips frosted; underparts gray-brown. Ears very short and rounded. Muzzle elongated; lower jaw extends slightly beyond upper jaw. Dense, long whiskers around mouth. Spear of *noseleaf short* (3 mm) *and broad,* horseshoe free on sides, fused below nostrils. No lower incisors. Tail shorter than naked tail membrane. *Base of forearms well haired. Wings attach to feet* (halfway from ankle to base of toe). **Similar Species.** Other small, long-tongued bats with base of fur pale (*Glossophaga* spp. and *Lonchophylla* spp.) have lower incisors, wings attached to ankles, and slightly longer noseleafs.

Distribution. Sinaloa, Mexico, patchily distributed through Central America (absent

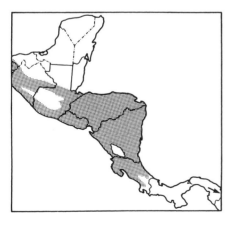

Map 78. Godman's Whiskered Bat, *Choeroniscus godmani*

from Yucatán Peninsula and Panama) to Colombia, Venezuela, and the Guianas. Lowlands to 1400 m.

Status and Habitat. Uncommon or rare; found in deciduous and evergreen forest and plantations.

Habits. Poorly known.

MEXICAN HOG-NOSED BAT   Plate 11
Choeronycteris mexicana   Map 75

HB 68–93, T 6–12, HF 10–14, E 15–18, FA 43–49, Wt 14–19 g.

Description. Medium sized. Upperparts gray-brown; underparts paler. *Muzzle greatly elongated;* lower jaw slightly longer than upper jaw. Noseleaf small. No lower incisors. *Tail membrane naked;* tail extends about 1/3 length of membrane. Base of forearms lightly haired. **Similar Species.** Larger than most nectar bats in the region. Those of similar size (*Leptonycteris* spp. and *Anoura* spp.) have greatly reduced tail membranes and tiny or no tails.

Distribution. SW United States through Mexico and on the Pacific Slope of Central America to S Honduras. Lowlands to 1900 m.

Status and Habitat. Fairly common in desert scrub, deciduous, and pine–oak forest.

Habits. Roosts in caves and mines, less commonly in buildings. Individuals are spaced 2–5 cm apart and hang near the roost entrance where they remain alert and fly out if disturbed. This species leaves the roost shortly after sunset and feeds on pollen and nectar of agaves, cacti, *Ipomoea, Ceiba,* and other plants. Cactus fruits are also eaten. In SE Arizona, this bat often visits hummingbird feeders, where it hovers in flight while lapping the nectar. Northern populations migrate south for the winter. Young are born in June-July in Arizona. Biology reviewed by Arroyo-Cabrales et al. (1987).

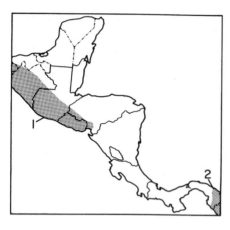

Map 79. 1. Southern Long-nosed Bat, *Leptonycteris curasoae*
2. Chestnut Long-tongued Bat, *Lionycteris spurrelli*

SOUTHERN LONG-NOSED BAT

Leptonycteris curasoae

Plate 11
Map 79

HB 67–86, T 0, HF 12–15, E 14–17, FA 53–57, Wt 20–27 g.

Description. Relatively large. Upperparts gray-brown or reddish brown, basal 2 mm of hairs white; underparts paler, frosted whitish. *Fur short (4–5 mm) and velvety.* Muzzle elongated; noseleaf very small. Lower incisors present. *No tail. Tail membrane much reduced, U-shaped, lightly haired, with a few short (2 mm) hairs along its edge.* Forearms naked; legs and feet sparsely haired. **Similar Species.** *L. nivalis* is larger and longer haired, with a fringed tail membrane. All other nectar bats are much smaller.

Distribution. Arizona, USA, to S Honduras (Lee and Bradley, 1992) and El Salvador; N Venezuela, NE Colombia, and adjacent islands. Lowlands to 2600 m (usually below 1800 m).

Status and Habitat. Endangered, U.S. Endangered Species Act. Generally uncommon; mainly in thorn scrub and deciduous forest. Its range corresponds closely to the distribution of

the mezcal plant (*Agave angustifolia*) in Mexico (Arita, 1991).

Habits. Roosts in caves and mines, often in colonies of several thousand. This bat emerges about an hour after sunset to feed on nectar and pollen of agaves and saguaro cactus in Arizona. It lands on the flowers or may hover for short periods to feed. Plant species visited in C Mexico are similar to those listed for *L. nivalis*. Some fruit and insects are also taken. Night roosts, including buildings, are used after feeding. Northern populations migrate south in September and return in May. Young are born in May–June in large maternity colonies (Barbour and Davis, 1969).

Comment. The names *L. sanborni* and *L. yerbabueni* have been used for this species. The species was revised by Arita and Humphrey (1988).

MEXICAN LONG-NOSED BAT

Leptonycteris nivalis

Map 80

HB 77–93, T 0, HF 14–19, E 17–19, FA 56–61, Wt 25–35 g.

Description. *Largest nectar bat.* Upperparts pale gray or gray-brown, basal 4 mm of hairs white; underparts paler. *Fur medium length (6–7 mm), soft, and fluffy.* Muzzle elongated; noseleaf very small. Lower incisors present. *No tail. Tail membrane much reduced, haired, and fringed with long (3–5 mm) hairs* (juveniles have a shorter fringe, hairs 2–3 mm). Base of forearms haired; legs and feet moderately hairy. **Similar Species.** See *L. curasoae.* Other nectar bats are much smaller.

Distribution. S Texas, USA, to Guerrero and Morelos, Mexico; possibly Guatemala. Lowlands to 3500 m (mostly 1000–2200 m).

Status and Habitat. Endangered, U.S. Endangered Species Act. Uncommon or rare; found in pine–oak and deciduous forest and desert scrub. This species usually favors higher and

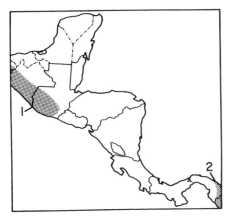

Map 80. 1. Mexican Long-nosed Bat, *Leptonycteris nivalis*
2. Thomas' Nectar Bat, *Lonchophylla thomasi*

cooler regions than *L. curasoae*, although some overlap occurs (Arita, 1991).

Habits. Usually roosts in large groups (up to 10,000) in caves or mines; occasionally found in buildings, hollow trees, or culverts. Emerges well after sunset and feeds on pollen and nectar, principally of agaves and various cacti. *Bombax, Ceiba, Ipomoea, Calliandra, Pinus,* and grasses are also important food sources in Central Mexico (Gardner, 1977). Fruit and insects are sometimes taken. Northern populations migrate south in winter; numbers found

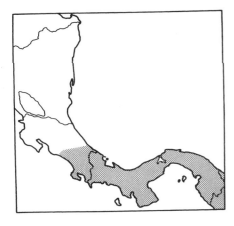

Map 81. Goldman's Nectar Bat, *Lonchophylla mordax*

in caves fluctuate greatly from year to year, indicating eruptive movements in addition to seasonal migration. Single young are born in May or June. Biology reviewed by Hensley and Wilkins (1988).

Comment. This species is known in Central America only from 2 Guatemalan specimens collected in the last century and housed in the British Museum. See Arita and Humphrey (1988) and Hall (1981) for different opinions on the identity of these specimens.

GOLDMAN'S NECTAR BAT Plate 11
Lonchophylla mordax Map 81

HB 46–65, T 6–10, HF 9–12, E 13–17, FA 32–34, Wt 7–9 g.

Description. Small. Upperparts dark brown or reddish brown, hairs slightly paler, grayish at base; underparts gray-brown. Muzzle elongated; lower jaw extends beyond upper jaw. *Spear of noseleaf prominent, 5–6 mm long*; horseshoe entirely fused to upper lip. Lower incisors present. Base of forearms well haired. Wings attach to ankles. **Similar Species.** *L. thomasi* is smaller, with base of hairs white and naked forearms. Common long-tongued bats (*Glossophaga* spp.) have less elongated muzzles and fur white at base. See Chestnut Long-tongued Bat (*Lionycteris spurrelli*). Other small nectar bats lack lower incisors and have smaller noseleafs.

Distribution. SW Costa Rica to Ecuador; E Brazil; possibly Peru and Bolivia. Lowlands to 600 m.

Status and Habitat. Fairly common in humid Pacific lowlands of SW Costa Rica; rare in Panama, known from few records, mainly in E Panama. Found in evergreen forest and banana groves.

Habits. Roosts in caves. The diet includes pollen and nectar of bananas and *Mucuna* sp. and Lepidoptera (Howell and Burch, 1974).

Comment. Sometimes known as *L. concava* (see Jones et al., 1988), which is usually treated as a subspecies of *mordax*.

ORANGE NECTAR BAT
Lonchophylla robusta

Plate 11
Map 82

HB 56–75, T 6–11, HF 11–14, E 14–19, FA 40–45, Wt 14–19 g.

Description. Medium sized. *Upperparts orange*, base of hairs white; underparts buffy. Ears relatively large. Muzzle elongated but not sharply tapered; lower jaw extends well beyond upper jaw. Spear of noseleaf prominent (6–7 mm long). Lower incisors present. Forearms almost naked. Wings attach to ankles. **Similar Species.** In its range, the only nectar bats of similar size are *Anoura* spp.; they are gray-brown with greatly reduced tail membranes and hairy legs.

Distribution. Nicaragua to Venezuela and Ecuador. Lowlands to 1000 m.

Status and Habitat. Fairly common in mid-elevation (600–800 m) evergreen forest.

Habits. Roosts in caves and cavelike structures. Timm et al. (1989) reported a roost under a jumble of huge boulders along a

stream. The few feeding records indicate that insects (including beetles and moths) may predominate in the diet; nectar, pollen, and fruit are probably included also (Gardner, 1977).

THOMAS' NECTAR BAT
Lonchophylla thomasi

Plate 11
Map 80

HB 46–57, T 4–9, HF 7–10, E 9–16, FA 29–34, Wt 6–7 g.

Description. Very small. Upperparts dark brown, *base of hairs pale gray or white*; underparts brown, slightly paler than upperparts. Muzzle elongated; lower jaw extends slightly beyond upper jaw; spear of noseleaf relatively large (5 mm). Smooth pads on sides of deep chin groove. Lower incisors present. Inner pair of upper incisors much larger than outer pair (outer pair visible only with a hand lens). Wings attach to ankles; forearms naked. **Similar Species.** See *L. concava*. Easily confused with *Glossophaga* spp., which have 4 small upper incisors roughly equal in size and serrated pads bordering chin groove. See Chestnut Long-tongued Bat (*Lionycteris spurrelli*). Other very small nectar bats lack lower incisors.

Distribution. E Panama to Bolivia and Amazonian Brazil. Lowlands.

Status and Habitat. Apparently rare in Central America; found in evergreen forest and clearings.

Habits. Poorly known. Roosts in hollow trees and small caves.

CHESTNUT LONG-TONGUED BAT
Lionycteris spurrelli

Plate 11
Map 79

HB 46–57, T 5–8, HF 8–11, E 10–14, FA 32–37, Wt 6–10 g.

Description. Very small. Upperparts dark brown, reddish brown or blackish, *hairs dark to*

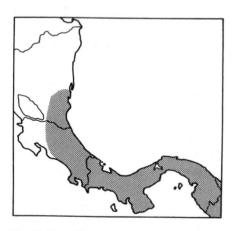

Map 82. Orange Nectar Bat, *Lonchophylla robusta*

base; underparts paler, gray-brown, tips lightly frosted. Ears short and rounded. Muzzle slightly elongated; lower and upper jaw about the same length. Chin groove shallow, *bordered by a smooth, V-shaped pad* (see Figure 6). Spear of noseleaf rather short (4 mm). Lower incisors present. Forearms naked. *Wings attach to legs, well above ankles.* **Similar Species.** All other nectar bats have wings attached to ankles or feet, not legs. Common long-tongued bats (*Glossophaga* spp.) and spear-nosed nectar bats (*Lonchophylla* spp.) have base of hairs pale and a deep chin groove bordered by serrated skin or small warts. Other small nectar bats lack lower incisors.

Distribution. E Panama to Peru and Amazonian Brazil. Lowlands to 1400 m.

Status and Habitat. Uncommon or rare; known in Central America only from evergreen forest of Darién, Panama (Handley, 1966). Also recorded in secondary forest and savannah in South America.

Habits. Poorly known.

Short-Tailed Bats
Subfamily Carolliinae

The Carolliinae includes 2 genera, one of which occurs in the region. These leaf-nosed bats are small to medium sized, with soft, fluffy fur. The short tail extends about one-third of the length of the naked tail membrane. The calcar is shorter than the foot, and the wings attach to the ankles. The ears are moderately large, with pointed tips. The horseshoe of the noseleaf is fused below the nostrils and free on the sides. There is a U-shaped row of small warts around a larger central wart on the chin. The dental formula is: i 2/2, c 1/1, p 2/2, m 3/3. Short-tailed bats can be easily confused with several species of little big-eared bats (*Micronycteris*), which have a smooth, V-shaped pad on the chin. They bear a superficial resemblance to common long-tongued bats (*Glossophaga* spp.), which have a groove at the center of the lower lip and a longer, narrower nose. Species of *Carollia* can be extremely difficult to distinguish from one another. Fur length and pattern can be helpful when body measurements are inconclusive, but are slightly variable within each species. Fur should be parted on the back of the neck or shoulder by blowing gently. I have also included tibia lengths for the 3 easily confused species, as this measurement is useful in Mexico and Central America (*Carollia* in South America are even more difficult to distinguish). To measure the tibia, gently bend the foot back toward the leg and measure from knee to ankle.

It is almost impossible to set mist nets in the lowlands anywhere in Central America and not catch a short-tailed bat. These undistinguished-looking bats are often the most abundant species in an area, and up to 3 species may occur together. They are among the few Neotropical mammals that may benefit from some human activities, as they favor second growth and somewhat disturbed forest. The diet consists primarily of fruits of pioneer plants such as *Piper, Cecropia*, and various solanaceous species. Small fruits are usually transported to a night roost to be eaten. By dropping seeds (which pass whole into the feces) at some distance from the parent plant, these common and widespread bats are important agents of seed dispersal and forest regeneration. If fruits are too heavy to carry (e.g., *Dipteryx panamensis*), they may feed directly from the fruiting

115

plant (Bonaccorso et al., 1980). Short-tailed bats will also crawl along the ground to find food, and are sometimes caught in banana-baited mouse traps set in areas too confined to allow approach on the wing. In addition to fruit, insects and nectar are consumed (Sazima, 1976). The genus was revised by Pine (1972).

CHESTNUT SHORT-TAILED BAT
Carollia castanea

Plate 8
Map 83

HB 48–60, T 7–14, HF 10–14, E 16–19, FA 34–38, Wt 11–16 g. Tibia about 14.

Description. Small. Upperparts *reddish brown, deep chestnut,* or *dull brown,* rarely grayish; underparts slightly paler. Fur about 6 mm long, *faintly tricolor,* dull brown at base. Ears moderately large, triangular, tips pointed. Muzzle rather short; horseshoe of noseleaf fused below nostrils, free on sides. Large central wart bordered by U-shaped row of small warts on chin. Tail short, about 1/3 length of naked tail membrane. *Forearms naked.* Wings attach to ankles. **Similar Species.** Usually smaller than other *Carollia* spp. *C. subrufa* and *C. brevicauda* both have clearly tricolor, grayish fur. Little big-eared bats (*Micronycteris* spp.) have a smooth, V-shaped pad on chin (see Figure 5). Long-tongued bats (*Glossophaga* spp., etc.) have a deep groove on the chin without a central wart and a smaller noseleaf.

Distribution. W Honduras to Venezuela, Bolivia, and W Brazil. Mainly on the Caribbean Slope in N Central America. Lowlands to 1100 m.

Status and Habitat. Common to abundant in evergreen forest and second growth; less common in clearings and fruit groves.

Habits. Roosts in caves, tunnels, hollow trees, mines, and under overhanging roots. Feeds on fruits, chiefly *Piper* spp. in the dry season, and fruits of various trees including *Markea panamensis* and *Dipteryx panamensis* in the wet season (Bonaccorso, 1979). Insects are occasionally taken. It is most active shortly after sunset, for 1–3 hours. In Panama, birth peaks occur

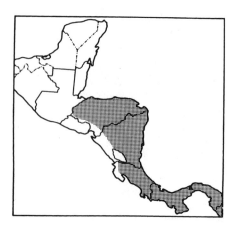

Map 83. Chestnut Short-tailed Bat, *Carollia castanea*

in March–April and July–August (Wilson, 1979).

GRAY SHORT-TAILED BAT
Carollia subrufa

Plate 8
Map 84

HB 49–61, T 5–12, HF 11–15, E 13–19, FA 37–40, Wt 10–16 g. Tibia 17–19.

Description. Moderately small. Upperparts *gray* or *gray-brown;* underparts slightly paler. Fur fairly long (6–7 mm), *clearly tricolor,* basal 1–1.5 mm dark gray, middle 2–3 mm whitish, tips gray-brown (sometimes with a faint frosting). Ears medium sized, tips pointed. Horseshoe of noseleaf free on sides, fused below nostrils. Central wart on chin bordered by U-shaped row of smaller warts. Tail short, about 1/3 length of naked tail membrane. Forearms almost naked or sparsely haired with very short hair. Wings attach to ankles. **Similar Species.** *C. brevicauda* is very similar (ranges overlap only in Honduras), but has longer fur, with a long, blackish basal section and velvety forearms. *C.*

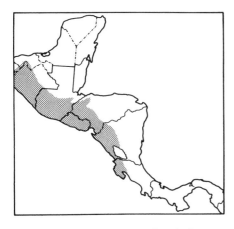

Map 84. Gray Short-tailed Bat, *Carollia subrufa*

perspicillata is almost always larger (compare forearm and tibia length). See *C. castanea.*

Distribution. Colima, Mexico, to NW Costa Rica, principally on the Pacific Slope. Lowlands to 1200 m.

Status and Habitat. Common to abundant in dry, deciduous forest and second growth woodland. Absent from wet, evergreen forest.

Habits. Roosts in caves, empty wells, culverts, hollow trees, and buildings. Feeds on fruits of *Piper, Cecropia, Muntingia,* and *Solanum* spp. in NW Costa Rica (Fleming, 1988).

Comment. Specimens of *Carollia subrufa* have been reported from evergreen forest of the Caribbean lowlands and interior of N Honduras (Lee and Bradley, 1992). On reexamination, these specimens proved to be *Carollia brevicauda* (T. J. McCarthy, in litt.).

SILKY SHORT-TAILED BAT   Plate 8
Carollia brevicauda   Map 85

HB 53–70, T 4–10, HF 11–15, E 15–21, FA 37–42, Wt 13–19 g. Tibia 16–19.

Description. Moderately small. Upperparts *gray-brown*; underparts slightly paler. Fur soft and long (7–8 mm), *clearly tricolor*, basal 2–3 mm blackish, middle 3 mm whitish, tips gray-brown

(sometimes faintly frosted with white). Ears medium sized, tips pointed. Horseshoe of nose-leaf free on sides, fused below nostrils. Central wart on chin bordered by U-shaped row of smaller warts. Tail short, about 1/3 length of naked tail membrane. Base of forearms velvety, covered with very short hair. Wings attach to ankles. **Similar Species.** See *C. subrufa* and *C. castanea. C. perspicillata* is larger (compare tibia length if forearm is 41–42 mm), and has shorter, usually less clearly banded fur.

Distribution. San Luis Potosí, Mexico, through Central America, mainly on the Gulf/Caribbean Slope, to Bolivia and E Brazil. Lowlands to 1700 m.

Status and Habitat. Abundant in second growth woodland, clearings, and plantations; less common in mature forest. This species is usually the dominant *Carollia* at middle to high elevations in evergreen forest, but also predominates in dry lowland forest of the Yucatán Peninsula. It is uncommon or absent in dry Pacific Slope lowlands.

Habits. Roosts in caves, tunnels, hollow trees, and culverts. Sexes often roost separately. This common bat eats a variety of fruits and some insects. It occasionally crawls on the ground or along tree branches and may enter mouse traps baited with fruit.

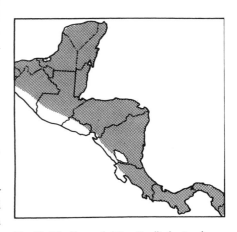

Map 85. Silky Short-tailed Bat, *Carollia brevicauda*

SEBA'S SHORT-TAILED BAT
Carollia perspicillata

Plate 8
Map 86

HB 48–70, T 8–16, HF 12–17, E 12–22, FA 41–45, Wt 15–25 g. Tibia 21–23.

Description. Medium sized. Upperparts gray-brown, dull brown, or bright orange; underparts slightly paler. Fur rather short (5–6 mm), tricolor, basal 2 mm brownish, usually not contrasting sharply with whitish middle 2 mm, tips gray-brown (sometimes faintly frosted). Ears medium sized, tips pointed. Horseshoe of noseleaf free on sides, fused below nostrils. Large central wart on chin bordered by U-shaped row of smaller warts. Tail short, about 1/3 length of naked tail membrane. Base of forearm lightly haired with very short hair. Wings attach to ankles. **Similar Species.** Other *Carollia* spp. are smaller (compare tibia length). See *C. castanea* for comparisons with other genera.

Distribution. Veracruz, Mexico, through Central and N South America to SE Brazil and Paraguay; Trinidad and Tobago; Grenada. Lowlands to 1000 m (in Central America).

Status and Habitat. Abundant and widespread throughout the lowlands in second growth, clearings, and plantations. Less common in mature, wet forest and at middle elevations.

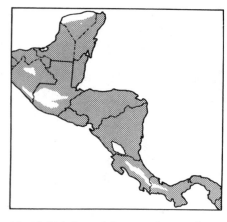

Map 86. Seba's Short-tailed Bat, *Carollia perspicillata*

Habits. Roosts in caves, tunnels, hollow trees and logs, buildings, and under bridges or culverts. Groups are usually small, but may number up to 1000. Larger roosts are arranged into clusters of bachelor males and clusters of females with a single territorial male. These associations are not stable over long periods. Fruits or flowers of at least 68 plant species are eaten, with species of *Piper* and *Cecropia* predominating in NW Costa Rica. Birth peaks occur in March–April and August–September in Costa Rica, and separate maternity colonies may form at these times. Ecology studied in detail by Fleming (1988).

Tailless Bats
Subfamily Stenodermatinae

This subfamily of leaf-nosed bats includes about 17 genera, distributed from Mexico to Argentina and Chile. About 11 genera occur in the region. Systematic studies of the relationships between genera and species among stenodermatines have reached different conclusions. Several authors have followed Owen (1987) in using *Dermanura* for small species of *Artibeus* and placing *Mesophylla* in the genus *Vampyressa* (but see Lim, 1993 and Van Den Bussche et al., 1993). The taxonomy I used for these species accounts generally follows Koopman (1993), or refers to Koopman under "Comment" when another approach is used.

Tailless bats are robust, broad-shouldered, and blunt-faced, with narrow tail membranes and no tail. Several species have white facial stripes, and some have a white stripe running down the middle of the back. The ears are small to medium sized, often with pale edges. The noseleaf is usually well developed and rather broad, with two creases running up the spear, and part or all of the horseshoe free. The wings are fairly broad, and the forearms are muscular. For a few species, I have included the length of the tail membrane, measured from the rump to the edge at its center. This measurement is approximate, as the membrane is elastic in life, but can be helpful for distinguishing certain species. The dental formulae for all members of the subfamily varies only in the number of molars. For *Sturnira*, *Uroderma*, and *Platyrrhinus*, the dental formula is: i 2/2, c 1/1, p 2/2, m 3/3; for *Vampyrodes*, *Mesophylla*, and *Ametrida*: m 2/3; for *Vampyressa*, *Chiroderma*, *Centurio*, and *Ectophylla*: m 2/2. The genus *Artibeus* shows variation in number of molars from 2/2, 2/3, to 3/3 and may vary both within and between species. Where helpful for identification, further information is given in the species accounts.

Roosts used by the group are diverse, including hollow trees, caves, and among foliage. Several species construct "tents" by chewing through veins or midribs of large leaves until the sides collapse to form a shelter. Leaves used for tents include fan-shaped, pinnate, and fishtail (or bifid) palms, heliconia and banana, various arums, philodendrons, and some large, simple pinnate leaves (see Kunz et al., 1994, for a complete list and illustrations). Different types of leaves are cut in different ways, but all result in a narrow upper, roughly horizontal section surrounded by more extensive, roughly vertical sides. Tent-making bats usually live in lowland evergreen and semideciduous forest and tall second growth, and tents are particularly numerous and diverse in wet, Caribbean Slope forest. To find tents, look for drooping and odd-shaped leaves that are still green and not withered. Most tent bats do not take flight when approached quietly, although a few species are wary and leave the tent at the slightest disturbance.

Most tailless bats fly through the forest at understory level, often following trails or stream beds, and are regularly captured in mist nets. A few species travel at the subcanopy level or higher and are encountered less often. Tailless bats are frugivorous; fruit is usually plucked by mouth and carried to a night roost, where it is eaten and the seeds and pith discarded. By carrying off fruits and discarding or defecating whole seeds away from the parent plant, these bats act as important dispersers of many trees and shrubs. Insects, nectar, and pollen may supplement the diet.

Important characteristics of the genera are:

Sturnira. Small to medium sized. Orange-brown to grayish. Fur velvety; no stripes on back or face. Orange to red patches on shoulders of large adult males. Noseleaf small and simple. Greatly *reduced tail membrane*; legs stocky and *very hairy*.

Artibeus. Small to large. Stocky. Gray, brown, or blackish. Fur faintly tricolor or bicolor. Faint to distinct stripes on face; *no back stripe*. Eyes rather small. Muzzle short and broad. Noseleaf medium sized. Tail membrane U-shaped, usually naked along edge.

Enchisthenes. Smallish. *Dark chocolate-brown.* Fur short and velvety. Narrow but distinct stripes on face; no back stripe. Eyes rather small. Muzzle short and broad. *Noseleaf short and broad,* horseshoe fused to upper lip. Tail membrane short, V-shaped, edge fringed.

Uroderma. Medium sized. Gray or brown. Fur bicolor, pale at base. *Narrow white back stripe*; bold or faint *white facial stripes*. Eyes large. Muzzle rather long and broad. Noseleaf medium sized. *Tail membrane U-shaped, naked, and not fringed.*

Platyrrhinus. Medium to large. Brown or blackish. Fur bicolor, pale at base. *Bold white back stripe;* facial stripes white or buffy; upper facial stripe broad, lower stripe narrow. Eyes fairly large. Muzzle broad, moderately long. Noseleaf medium sized. Tail membrane narrow, V-shaped, *clearly fringed on edge.*

Vampyrodes. Fairly large. Brown. Fur bicolor, pale at base. *Bold white back stripe; facial stripes prominent,* white; upper facial stripe broad. Eyes fairly large. Muzzle relatively long and broad. Noseleaf medium sized. Tail membrane narrow, V-shaped, *clearly fringed on edge.*

Chiroderma. Smallish to fairly large. Stocky build. Gray or brown. Fur thick, with prominent, long guard hairs; hairs tricolor, dusky at base. Back stripe distinct or absent; facial stripes prominent or absent. *Eyes very large. Muzzle very short.* Noseleaf medium sized. Tail membrane rather long, U-shaped, *well haired on upper surface,* but not fringed.

Vampyressa. Small. Grayish or pale brown. Fur faintly tricolor. Back stripe indistinct or absent; facial stripes prominent to indistinct. Eyes medium sized. Muzzle fairly short. Noseleaf medium sized. Ears edged yellow. Tail membrane U-shaped, short to moderately long, naked or lightly haired, with sparse hairs along edge.

Mesophylla. Small. Pale brown. Fur faintly tricolor. No back stripe; facial stripes indistinct. Eyes medium sized. Muzzle fairly short. Noseleaf medium sized, yellow. Ears yellow. Tail membrane U-shaped, medium length, edge entirely naked.

Ectophylla. Very small. *White.* Noseleaf and ears yellow. Tail membrane pale, edge naked.

Ametrida. Very small. Pale gray. *White patches on shoulders;* no stripes on back or face. Eyes large. *Muzzle very short, flat looking.* Noseleaf small and simple. Tail membrane long and well haired.

Centurio. Medium sized. Gray-brown. Fur long with conspicuous guard hairs. *White patches on shoulders;* no stripes on back or face. Eyes large. Muzzle flat. *No noseleaf; peculiarly wrinkled and folded skin on face.* Tail membrane long and well haired. Wings marked with ladderlike pattern.

LITTLE YELLOW-SHOULDERED BAT
Sturnira lilium

Plate 12
Map 87

HB 54–65, T 0, HF 12–15, E 15–18, FA 37–42, Wt 13–18 g.

Description. Small and stocky. Upperparts usually *orange-brown,* sometimes grayish or bright orange; shoulder patches deep yellow, orange, or dark red (patches present in large adult males); underparts paler than upperparts. *Fur short* (3–5 mm) and velvety. Muzzle blunt, forehead rounded. Ears and noseleaf short. *Tail membrane greatly reduced, well haired;* legs muscular, well haired on inner edge, *sparsely haired* over knees and on adjoining wing membrane. Forearms thinly haired on upper and lower surface. **Similar Species.** All other *Sturnira* average larger and have longer hair. See *S. ludovici. S. luisi* is usually dark gray-brown, with a slightly longer muzzle and longer fur. Other bats with greatly reduced tail membranes and hairy legs are Hairy-legged Vampire Bat (*Diphylla ecaudata*), which lacks a noseleaf, and hairy-legged bats (*Anoura* spp.), which have long muzzles.

Distribution. Sonora and Tamaulipas, Mexico, through Central America to N Argentina, Uruguay, and E Brazil; Lesser Antilles; Trinidad and Tobago. Lowlands to 1600 m (usually below 800 m).

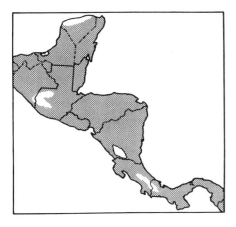

Map 87. Little Yellow-shouldered Bat, *Sturnira lilium*

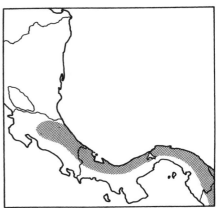

Map 88. Luis' Yellow-shouldered Bat, *Sturnira luisi*

Status and Habitat. Abundant and widespread in dry and semideciduous lowland forest and fruit groves; locally common in evergreen forest.

Habits. Very occasionally found roosting in caves, tunnels, road culverts, and under bridges; however, almost all records are from mist-net captures, and the preferred roost site of this common species is unknown. Feeds on fruit (of *Piper* spp., Melastomataceae, and Solanaceae), pollen, and nectar. In Costa Rica birth peaks are in February–March and June–July (Wilson, 1979).

LUIS' YELLOW-SHOULDERED BAT
Sturnira luisi   Map 88

HB 67–74, T 0, HF 15–19, E 14–19, FA 41–45, Wt 17–25 g.

Description. Medium sized and stocky. Upperparts *dark gray-brown*, rarely orange-brown; deep orange to red shoulder patches pronounced (mostly in adult males); underparts pale gray-brown. Fur rather long (6–7 mm), thick, and velvety. Muzzle rather short with a small, simple noseleaf. Tail membrane greatly reduced and hairy. Legs muscular and well haired; feet sparsely haired. **Similar Species.** See *S. ludovici* and *S. lilium*.

Distribution. Caribbean Slope of Costa Rica and Panama; also Ecuador and NW Peru. Lowlands to 700 m.

Status and Habitat. Status poorly understood due to confusion with *S. lilium*. Known from evergreen forest and forest edge.

Habits. Poorly known.

Comment. Previously confused with *S. lilium*, this species was described by Davis (1980). The 2 species differ mainly in cranial and dental characters. The exact limits of its distribution will not be known until all specimens of *S. lilium* are reexamined.

HIGHLAND YELLOW-SHOULDERED BAT
Sturnira ludovici

Plate 12
Map 89

HB 66–70, T 0, HF 13–16, E 12–19, FA 41–45, Wt 17–23 g.

Description. Medium sized and stocky. Upperparts usually *gray-brown*, rarely orange-brown; shoulder patches orange to dark red (on large adult males); underparts pale gray-brown. Fur long (6–8 mm) and thick. Muzzle short, forehead rounded. Noseleaf small and simple. Tail membrane greatly reduced and well haired. Base of *forearms, legs, and*

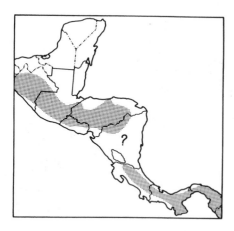

Map 89. Highland Yellow-shouldered Bat, *Sturnira ludovici*

adjoining portion of wings well haired on upper and lower surfaces; feet hairy. **Similar Species.** *S. lilium* is usually smaller, with shorter fur and less hair on legs and forearms. With a hand lens, this species can be distinguished from other *Sturnira* by dental differences: in *S. ludovici* the inner, upper edges of the lower molars are smooth; in both *S. lilium* and *S. luisi* the inner, upper edges of the lower molars are serrated. See *S. mordax*; see *S. lilium* for comparisons with other hairy-legged bats.

Distribution. Sinaloa and Tamaulipas, Mexico, through Central America (except Yucatán Peninsula, Belize, and N Guatemala) to Guyana and west of the Andes to Ecuador. Lowlands to 2000 m (usually above 800 m).

Status and Habitat. Abundant in mid-elevation evergreen forest and forest edge; also found in second growth and fruit groves. This species favors higher elevations and wetter habitats than *S. lilium*.

Habits. Roost sites are unknown. In Monteverde, Costa Rica, fruits of 27 plant species were eaten, with *Solanum* spp., *Piper* spp., and *Pothomorme umbellata* most frequently taken (Dinerstein, 1986). Birth peaks occur in April–May and September–October in Costa Rica.

Comment. The Central American population may be distinct from that in South America. The correct name would then be *S. hondurensis* in SE Mexico and Central America.

TALAMANCAN YELLOW-SHOULDERED BAT
Sturnira mordax   Map 90

HB 70–75, T 0, HF 13–15, E 15–19, FA 43–51, Wt 24–31 g.

Description. Medium sized and stocky. Upperparts usually *reddish brown*, occasionally gray-brown; shoulder patches deep red (on adult male); underparts gray-brown. Fur long (7–9 mm) and thick. *Muzzle longer* than in other *Sturnira*; forehead gradually sloping, not rounded. Noseleaf short and simple. Tail membrane greatly reduced, well haired. *Legs thickly haired, feet lightly haired.* **Similar Species.** Other *Sturnira* average smaller and have shorter muzzles with rounded foreheads. *S. ludovici* has hairier feet. The upper middle incisors of *S. mordax* are blunt (spatulate) and in contact at the tip; in all other Central American *Sturnira* the upper middle incisors are pointed and do not touch each other at the tip

Map 90. Talamancan Yellow-shouldered Bat, *Sturnira mordax*

(although worn teeth of older animals may look blunt).

Distribution. Mountains of Costa Rica and W Panama (McCarthy et al., 1993). 600–2700 m.

Status and Habitat. Fairly common in middle and high elevation evergreen forest and forest edge.

Habits. Poorly known. The diet includes fruits of *Centropogon, Anthurium, Cecropia,* and banana (Howell and Burch, 1974). Pregnant females have been recorded in April.

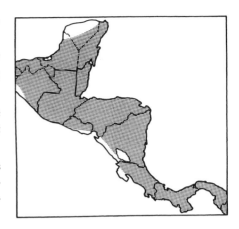

Map 91. Great Fruit-eating Bat, *Artibeus lituratus*

GREAT FRUIT-EATING BAT Plate 13
Artibeus lituratus Map 91

HB 87–101, T 0, HF 17–21, E 22–25, FA 69–78, Wt 53–73 g.

Description. Very large and stocky, with powerful, broad shoulders. Upperparts *brown* (yellow-brown, tan, or dark brown); *underparts* gray-brown, *fur not frosted.* Fur rather short and velvety. White facial stripes usually distinct, sometimes faint; upper stripe broader than lower stripe. Muzzle short and broad. Upper surface of *tail membrane and legs well haired.* **Similar Species.** *A. intermedius* is usually smaller (compare forearm length) and may be paler in color, but the 2 can be difficult or impossible to distinguish in the field. See *A. jamaicensis.*

Distribution. Sinaloa and Tamaulipas, Mexico, through Central America to S Brazil, N Argentina, and Bolivia; Trinidad and Tobago; S Lesser Antilles. Lowlands to 1700 m.

Status and Habitat. Common to abundant in evergreen and semideciduous lowland forest; uncommon or absent in very dry or highly disturbed areas.

Habits. Roosts in caves, tunnels, hollow trees, and foliage. In Panama, groups of 1–20 were found 2.7–28 m above ground under palm fronds, in vine tangles on subcanopy trees, and in recesses under branches or crowns of canopy trees (Morrison, 1980). Groups appear to be composed of a single male and several females; group size and roosting location change almost daily. Individuals leave the day roost about 45 minutes after sunset and fly mainly at subcanopy level to fruiting trees. Maximum activity occurs 2–4 hours after sunset (Bonaccorso, 1979) but is much reduced around the full moon. The diet includes figs, fruits of *Dipteryx* sp., *Piper* spp., and flowers or pollen of several canopy trees. Fruits are plucked by mouth and taken to feeding roosts; about 15–27 figs (total weight 130 g) may be carried off by one bat each night. Birth peaks occur in March–April and August–September in Panama (Wilson, 1979).

INTERMEDIATE FRUIT-EATING BAT
Artibeus intermedius Map 92

HB 80–93, T 0, HF 16–19, E 21–25, FA 61–69, Wt 40–54 g.

Description. Large and stocky. Fur usually *golden brown* (blonde to dark brown); *underparts not frosted.* Fur rather short and velvety. Facial stripes usually distinct, sometimes faint;

upper stripe broader than lower stripe. Muzzle short and broad. Upper surface of *tail membrane and legs well haired.* **Similar Species.** See *A. lituratus* and *A. jamaicensis.*

Distribution. Sinaloa and Tamaulipas, Mexico, through Central America to N South America. Lowlands to 1700 m.

Status and Habitat. Common, sometimes abundant in all types of lowland forest, pine–oak and evergreen highland forest, fruit groves, and second growth. This species tolerates drier habitats than *A. lituratus.*

Habits. Roosts singly or in small groups near the mouth of caves or in shaded crevices of cliffs (Davis, 1984). It may also roost under foliage or occupy tents in tall, palmate palms. It is often caught in mist nets set across streams, forested trails, or in banana groves.

Comment. Considered to be a subspecies of *A. lituratus* by some authors (see Koopman, 1993). Davis (1984) recognized *A. intermedius* as specifically distinct, based on external and cranial measurements of sympatric populations in Honduras.

JAMAICAN FRUIT-EATING BAT
Artibeus jamaicensis

Plate 13
Map 93

HB 70–85, T 0, HF 16–19, E 20–24, FA 55–67, Wt 29–51 g.

Description. Large and stocky. *Upperparts gray or gray-brown* (rarely tan, dark brown, or yellowish); underparts paler, tips of hairs *frosted with white or pale gray.* Fur short and velvety. *Facial stripes usually narrow and indistinct,* rarely bold. Muzzle short and broad. Upper surface of *tail membrane and legs nearly naked.* **Similar Species.** *A. lituratus* and *A. intermedius* are usually larger and browner, with hair on upper surface of legs and tail membrane and unfrosted underparts. *A. inopinatus* is smaller.

Distribution. Sinaloa and Tamaulipas, Mexico, throughout Central America to Ecuador and Venezuela; Trinidad and Tobago; Greater and Lesser Antilles; possibly Florida Keys, USA. Lowlands to 1700 m.

Status and Habitat. Abundant and widespread at lower elevations in all types of forests, plantations, and lightly disturbed habitats.

Habits. Roosts in caves, tunnels, hollow trees, logs, culverts, bridges, under tree roots, and in foliage. It has been found roosting in

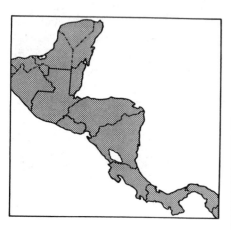

Map 92. Intermediate Fruit-eating Bat, *Artibeus intermedius*

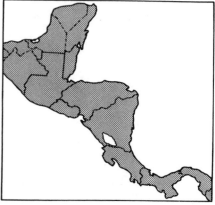

Map 93. Jamaican Fruit-eating Bat, *Artibeus jamaicensis*

tents made from modified banana, *Scheelea rostrata*, and *Pentagonia* leaves (Brooke, 1987; Timm, 1987) in Costa Rica, and in palms with palmate leaves in Trinidad (Kunz et al., 1994). Some of the occupied tents may have been cut by other species of bats, and uncut leaves (of coconut palms, for example) are also used. Cryptic roosts, with very narrow (about 6 cm), slitlike entrances into hollow trees or branches were found by radio-tagging and are occupied by harems of a single male and 4–11 females (Morrison, 1979). The harem male defends its roost against other males; it positions itself nearest the entrance, is the last to leave and forage at night, and carries each fruit back near the day roost. Activity usually begins later than in many other species and may continue throughout the night. In Panama, activity peaked 6–8 hours after sunset (Bonaccorso, 1979). This common bat is lunar phobic, being less active or inactive around the full moon. It flies 2–10 km or more each night, often following forest trails at understory level, and therefore is frequently caught in mist nets. The diet includes a variety of fruits, some flowers, pollen, leaves, and insects. Figs are often the major component of the diet. These and other small fruits are taken to a night roost to be eaten, whereas larger fruits such as *Dipteryx* may be eaten in situ. In Panama, birth peaks occur in March–April and July–August. Life span in the wild is at least 9 years. A long-term natural history study was reported by Handley et al. (1991).

HONDURAN FRUIT-EATING BAT

Artibeus inopinatus   Map 94

HB 72, T 0, HF 14–15, E 18, FA 48–53, Wt 26–36 g.

Description. Medium sized and stocky. Upperparts pale gray; underparts paler, *tips of hairs frosted whitish.* Fur very short and velvety.

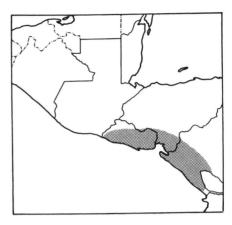

Map 94. Honduran Fruit-eating Bat, *Artibeus inopinatus*

White facial stripes faint; lower stripe sometimes absent. Muzzle short and broad. Tail membrane sparsely haired, *edge fringed near center.* **Similar Species.** Easily confused with *A. jamaicensis*, which is larger, usually darker in color, and has a naked tail membrane. See Hairy Big-eyed Bat (*Chiroderma villosum*).

Distribution. Pacific Slope of El Salvador to Nicaragua. Lowlands to 1100 m (Dolan and Carter, 1979).

Status and Habitat. Uncommon; usually found in dry thornscrub, also in deciduous forest and banana groves.

Habits. Poorly known. A small group (one male, 8 females, and 5 young) was found roosting in a building. Individuals have also been caught in mist nets set over streams and in banana groves, with both *A. jamaicensis* and *A. lituratus* (Baker and Jones, 1975; Davis and Carter, 1964). A birth peak may occur in June–July.

AZTEC FRUIT-EATING BAT

Artibeus aztecus   Map 95

HB 59–75, T 0, HF 11–14, E 15–20, FA 41–49, Wt 15–33 g.

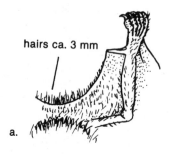
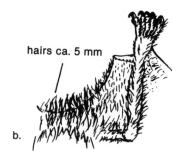

FIGURE 7. Tail membranes:
a. Toltec Fruit-eating Bat (*Artibeus toltecus*)
b. Aztec Fruit-eating Bat (*Artibeus aztecus*)

Description. Medium sized. Upperparts *charcoal-brown to blackish*; underparts slightly paler, tips of hairs faintly frosted. *Fur long* (9–10 mm) and soft. Narrow, whitish facial stripes distinct or faint. Ears and noseleaf dark brown; horseshoe of noseleaf entirely free. *Tail membrane very short* (about 6 mm), V-shaped, *upper surface well haired and edge thickly fringed* (see Figure 7); legs and feet well haired. **Similar Species.** Easily confused with *A. toltecus*, which has shorter, grayer fur and averages smaller (and usually occurs at lower elevations). See *Enchisthenes hartii*.

Distribution. There are 3 disjunct populations: Sinaloa to Oaxaca, Mexico; Chiapas, Mexico to

Honduras; Costa Rica to W Panama. 600–3000 m (usually above 1000 m).

Status and Habitat. Uncommon; found in humid broadleaf and coniferous highland forest and fruit groves.

Habits. Roosts in mine tunnels, small caves, rock crevices, and under banana leaves. Biology reviewed by Webster and Jones (1982).

Comment. This species, along with *A toltecus*, *A. phaeotis*, *A. watsoni*, and *Enchisthenes hartii*, was placed in the genus *Dermanura* by Owen (1987).

TOLTEC FRUIT-EATING BAT   Plate 12
Artibeus toltecus   Map 96

HB 59–65, T 0, HF 12–14, E 16–19, FA 39–43, Wt 14–20 g.

Description. Fairly small. *Upperparts dark gray-brown*, occasionally blackish; underparts paler, gray-brown, tips of hairs frosted. Fur medium length (6–8 mm). Narrow, whitish facial stripes distinct or faint. Ears and noseleaf brown; horseshoe of noseleaf entirely free. Tail membrane short (8–9 mm), U-shaped, *lightly haired with a short, rather sparse fringe*; legs and feet sparsely haired. **Similar Species.** See *A. aztecus* and *Enchisthenes hartii. A. phaeotis* and *A. watsoni* are paler brown, with edge of tail membrane naked.

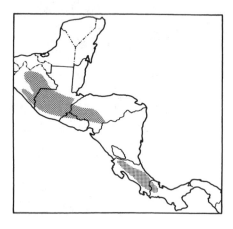

Map 95. Aztec Fruit-eating Bat, *Artibeus aztecus*

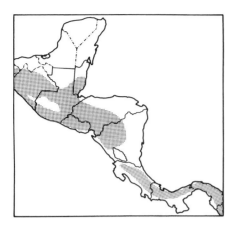

Map 96. Toltec Fruit-eating Bat, *Artibeus toltecus*

Distribution. Sinaloa and Nuevo León, Mexico, through Central America (but absent from much of the Caribbean lowlands) to E Panama. Lowlands to 2000 m.

Status and Habitat. Common to abundant in mid-elevation (600–1500 m) evergreen forest, clearings, and fruit groves.

Habits. Roosts in caves, buildings, shallow depressions under overhanging banks, and among complex trunks of fig trees. This bat also uses tent roosts made from modified anthurium and banana leaves (Timm, 1987). It feeds on fruit and favors *Solanum* spp., *Eugenia acapulcensis*, and *Ficus* spp. in Costa Rica, although fruits of 14 other plant species are also taken. Reproduction may coincide with fruit production, and birth peaks in April–May and August–September have been noted in Costa Rica (Dinerstein, 1986).

Comment. Reported from the Caribbean lowlands of E Honduras by Benshoof et al. (1984); however, the forearm measurements given (32–33mm) are too small for *Artibeus toltecus*. The specimens were later re-identified as *Vampyressa pusilla* (L. Ruedas, in litt.).

PYGMY FRUIT-EATING BAT Plate 12
Artibeus phaeotis Map 97

HB 47–59, T 0, HF 9–12, E 14–18, FA 35–40, Wt 9–15 g.

Description. Small. Upperparts *sandy brown* or *gray-brown*; underparts slightly paler. Fur moderately short and smooth (4–6 mm on upper back), faintly tricolor. *White facial stripes crisply outlined, usually prominent*; upper stripe extends to front of ear. Ears and noseleaf pale brown, sides clearly edged yellow or, rarely, white. Horseshoe of noseleaf free. Muzzle short. Tail membrane U-shaped (9–11 mm), upper surface almost naked, edge not fringed (may have a smattering of short hairs). **Similar Species.** Very difficult to distinguish from *A. watsoni*, which has longer, fluffier (often grayer) fur and less well-defined facial stripes (juveniles of both species are pale gray and may be indistinguishable in the field). *A. phaeotis* has 2 lower molars on each side, while *A. watsoni* normally has 3; the third molar is small and difficult to see in live animals, even with a hand lens. See *A. toltecus* and yellow-eared bats (*Vampyressa* spp.).

Distribution. Sinaloa and Veracruz, Mexico, through Central America to Ecuador and Guyana. Lowlands to 1200 m.

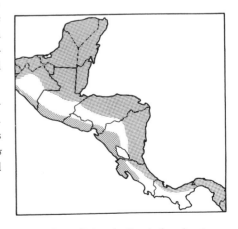

Map 97. Pygmy Fruit-eating Bat, *Artibeus phaeotis*

Status and Habitat. Common in evergreen and deciduous forest, second growth, and fruit groves. This species occurs in drier areas than *A. watsoni*; for example, on the Yucatán Peninsula.

Habits. Roosts in tents made from modified banana and heliconia leaves. Leaves are chewed along the edge of the midrib, causing the sides to collapse, forming an "upturned boat" shape (Timm, 1987). In Campeche, Mexico, it makes tents in palms with fan-shaped leaves, which are cut in a polygonal shape around the base of the frond. It feeds on fruit, including figs, *Cecropia* spp., and *Spondias* spp. in Panama (Bonaccorso, 1979), pollen, and insects. In Costa Rica, birth peaks occur in April and August–September. Biology reviewed by Timm (1985).

THOMAS' FRUIT-EATING BAT
Artibeus watsoni   Map 98

HB 50–58, T 0, HF 8–12, E 14–17, FA 35–41, Wt 9–15 g.

Description. Small. Upperparts *gray-brown* or *tan*; underparts slightly paler. Fur rather long and fluffy (6–7 mm on upper back), faintly tricolor. *White facial stripes usually prominent*, edges slightly uneven; upper stripe extends to

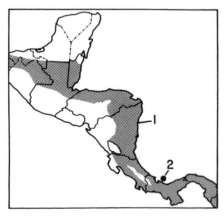

Map 98. 1. Thomas' Fruit-eating Bat, *Artibeus watsoni*
2. Escudo Island Fruit-eating Bat, *Artibeus incomitatus*

front of ear. Ears and noseleaf pale brown; base of ears sometimes edged white, cream, or, less commonly, yellow. Horseshoe of noseleaf free. Muzzle short. Tail membrane U-shaped (10–12 mm), upper surface almost naked, edge not fringed (may have a few short hairs). **Similar Species.** See *A. phaeotis*.

Distribution. Veracruz, Mexico, through Central America (mainly in the Caribbean lowlands north of Costa Rica) to Colombia, and possibly Ecuador and Peru. Lowlands to 1500 m (usually below 800 m).

Status and Habitat. Common to abundant in semideciduous and evergreen lowland forest, second growth, and fruit groves. This species favors taller, more humid forest than *A. phaeotis*.

Habits. Roosts in small groups in tents made from modified leaves of anthurium, heliconia, banana, bifid and palmate palms, and cyclanths. Leaves are cut in a variety of styles, depending on leaf shape and size (Choe and Timm, 1985; Kunz et al., 1994; Timm, 1987). This species appears to be an obligate tent-maker, as it has not been found roosting in other situations. It feeds on fruit, including *Cecropia* spp.

Where to See. Tents made from this species are easily found in the Caribbean lowlands and foothills of Costa Rica and Panama. Young palms with fishtail or fan-shaped leaves are often made into tents within a few meters of the ground. Large stands of such palms are usually located in low-lying areas.

Comment. A new species, *Artibeus incomitatus*, was recently described (Kalko and Handley, 1994). It is similar to, and probably derived from, *A. watsoni*. The new species is known only from Isla Escudo de Veraguas, Bocas del Toro, Panama. It is slightly larger (FA 41–44 mm, Wt 11–16 g) than *A. watsoni* and has slightly more hair on the tail membrane and feet. Koopman (1993) included *A. watsoni* in *A. glaucus*.

FIGURE 8. Noseleafs:
a. Velvety Fruit-eating Bat (*Enchisthenes hartii*)
b. Toltec Fruit-eating Bat (*Artibeus toltecus*)

VELVETY FRUIT-EATING BAT Plate 12
Enchisthenes hartii Map 99

HB 55–68, T 0, HF 11–14, E 14–18, FA 38–42, Wt 14–18 g.

Description. Small. *Upperparts, chin, and throat dark chocolate-brown*; belly gray-brown, tips of hairs not frosted. *Fur short* (4–5 mm), dense, and velvety. Buffy facial stripes narrow but distinct. Ears and noseleaf blackish, *horseshoe of noseleaf fused below nostrils, spear short and broad.* Tail membrane very short (4–6 mm), V-shaped, sparsely haired, edge clearly fringed; legs and feet sparsely haired. **Similar Species.** *Artibeus toltecus* and *A. aztecus* have longer fur and horseshoe of noseleaf free below nostrils (see Figure 8). All other small, stripe-faced bats are much paler in color.

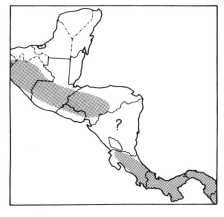

Map 99. Velvety Fruit-eating Bat, *Enchisthenes hartii*

Distribution. Jalisco and Tamaulipas, Mexico, through Chiapas and Central America (absent from Yucatán Peninsula, N Guatemala, and Belize) to Bolivia and Venezuela. Lowlands to 2600 m (usually above 1000 m).

Status and Habitat. Uncommon; usually found in evergreen, highland forest and forest edge; rare in deciduous lowland forest.

Habits. Poorly known. Feeds on fruit, including figs. This species probably flies high, through upper levels of the forest, as most mist net captures are over small streams through forest or over water in clearings, when it may be descending to drink.

Comment. This species has been placed in the genus *Artibeus* (see Koopman, 1993) and in *Dermanura* (Owen, 1987). Studies of morphology and molecular genetics indicate that it should be placed in its own genus (Van Den Bussche, 1993).

COMMON TENT-MAKING BAT Plate 13
Uroderma bilobatum Map 100

HB 59–69, T 0, HF 9–13, E 12–18, FA 40–44, Wt 13–20 g.

Description. Medium sized. Upperparts *dark gray* or *gray-brown*; hairs bicolor, pale at base; *narrow, whitish back stripe* extends from back of head or neck to rump. Underparts gray-brown. *White facial stripes prominent above and*

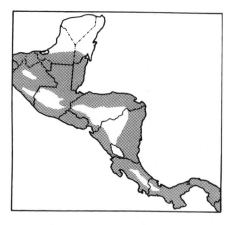

Map 100. Common Tent-making Bat, *Uroderma bilobatum*

below eye, upper stripe extends over head to back of ear. *Ears and noseleaf brown, prominently edged with yellow or white.* Muzzle relatively long and broad. Tail membrane relatively long (14–16 mm), U-shaped, nearly naked on upper surface (small, fine hairs visible under magnification), and entirely naked along its edge. **Similar Species.** *U. magnirostrum* (much less common) is brown, not gray, has little or no yellow edges on ears or noseleaf, and usually has indistinct facial stripes. Heller's Broad-nosed Bat (*Platyrrhinus helleri*) has a fringed tail membrane. Little Big-eyed Bat (*Chiroderma trinitatum*) has short facial stripes, tricolor fur, and hair on the surface of the tail membrane. All other stripe-backed bats can be distinguished by length of forearm.

Distribution. Oaxaca and Veracruz, Mexico, through Central America to Peru, Bolivia, and E Brazil; Trinidad. Lowlands to 1500 m.

Status and Habitat. Common and widespread in evergreen and deciduous lowland forest, second growth woodland, and fruit groves.

Habits. Roosts in groups of 2–59 in tents made from modified leaves. This species makes a wide variety of tent types and appears to be an obligate tent rooster. It favors large, single leaves of bananas, pinnate palms (including coconut and *Scheelea rostrata*), or palmate palms (*Sabal* sp.) for tents, but also constructs umbrella tents using several simple leaves in combination (Kunz et al., 1994). The bat's prominently striped face may function as disruptive camouflage inside a tent with multiple leaflets. The diet consists chiefly of fruit; a few insects, flower parts, or nectar may be taken. Individuals carrying small, unripe figs are sometimes caught in mist nets. Females may breed twice annually, in February and June in Panama (Fleming et al., 1972). Young stay with their mothers for about a month. Biology reviewed by Baker and Clark (1987).

BROWN TENT-MAKING BAT   Plate 13
Uroderma magnirostrum   Map 101

HB 54–70, T 0, HF 9–12, E 13–17, FA 41–45, Wt 12–21 g.

Description. Medium sized. *Upperparts brown or gray-brown;* hairs bicolor, pale at base; *indistinct, whitish back stripe* extends from neck to rump. Underparts gray-brown. *Ears and noseleaf entirely brownish* or with pale edging only near bases; *facial stripes usually indistinct*, rarely prominent, lower stripe sometimes absent. Muzzle rather broad. Tail membrane relatively

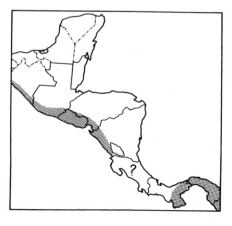

Map 101. Brown Tent-making Bat, *Uroderma magnirostrum*

long, U-shaped; naked on upper surface and along edge. **Similar Species.** See *U. bilobatum.* Hairy Big-eyed Bat (*Chiroderma villosum*) has a hairy tail membrane.

Distribution. Michoacán, Mexico (Jones et al., 1988), through the Pacific lowlands from Chiapas to Nicaragua; Panama to Peru, Bolivia, and Brazil (not recorded in Costa Rica). Lowlands (to 800 m in Peru).

Status and Habitat. Uncommon or rare; in deciduous and evergreen forest and near water in arid regions (Davis, 1968).

Habits. Poorly known. In Peru, tents similar to those made by *U. bilobatum* were constructed in large leaves of a palm, *Astrocaryum murumuru.* One tent was occupied by 5 bats (Timm, 1987). Several individuals caught in Peru were dusted with pollen, presumably after feeding on nectar or flower parts (Gardner, 1977).

HELLER'S BROAD-
NOSED BAT · · · · · · · · · · · · Plate 13
Platyrrhinus helleri · · · · · · · Map 102

HB 55–65, T 0, HF 9–13, E 13–18, FA 37–41, Wt 11–21 g.

Description. Fairly small. Upperparts *pale to dark brown* or *reddish brown*; hairs bicolor, pale at base; *prominent white back stripe* extends from crown to rump. *Upper white facial stripe distinct*, extends just beyond front of ear, lower facial stripe less prominent. Ears and noseleaf edged with cream or white. Muzzle broad and relatively elongate. *Tail membrane short* (about 8 mm), V-shaped, fringed with whitish hair. **Similar Species.** See Common Tent-making Bat (*Uroderma bilobatum*). Little Big-eyed Bat (*Chiroderma trinitatum*) and Striped Yellow-eared Bat (*Vampyressa nymphaea*) have unfringed tail membranes and back stripes not extending to crown of head.

Distribution. Oaxaca, Mexico, through Central America (except N Yucatán Peninsula) to

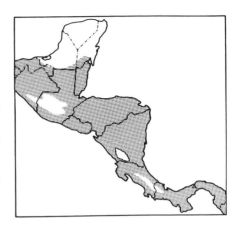

Map 102. Heller's Broad-nosed Bat, *Platyrrhinus helleri*

Bolivia and Amazonian Brazil; Trinidad. Lowlands to 1500 m.

Status and Habitat. Fairly common (sometimes abundant in Panama) in evergreen and semideciduous forest, forest edge, and fruit groves.

Habits. Roosts in small groups in caves, buildings, tunnels, and among foliage. This species is not known to make tents. It feeds mainly on fruit (including figs, *Cecropia,* and *Acnistus*), and some insects, including Lepidoptera (Howell and Burch, 1974; Bonaccorso, 1979). In seasonally dry areas, it is usually caught in mist nets set over or near streams. Birth peaks occur in March–April and July–August (Ferrell and Wilson, 1991).

GREATER BROAD-
NOSED BAT · · · · · · · · · · · · Plate 13
Platyrrhinus vittatus · · · · · · · Map 103

HB 87–103, T 0, HF 15–20, E 20–27, FA 58–62, Wt 49–60 g.

Description. *Large.* Upperparts *dark chocolate-brown*; underparts dark gray-brown. Prominent *white back stripe* from crown of head to rump. Buffy facial stripes, lower stripe indistinct or absent. Tail membrane short, V-shaped, edge clearly fringed. **Similar Species.**

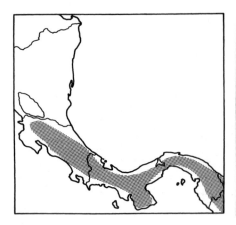

Map 103. Greater Broad-nosed Bat, *Platyrrhinus vittatus*

Map 104. Thomas' Broad-nosed Bat, *Platyrrhinus dorsalis*

All other stripe-backed bats are smaller. Great Stripe-faced Bat (*Vampyrodes caraccioli*) approaches it in size but is paler in color with white, not buffy, facial stripes. See *P. dorsalis*.

Distribution. Mountains of Costa Rica to Venezuela, Peru, and Bolivia. 600–2000 m.

Status and Habitat. Fairly common in evergreen forest, fruit groves, and second growth of foothills and highlands.

Habits. Roosts in caves and tunnels or under overhanging roots and crevices in stream banks. Feeds on fruit including figs, *Acnistus*, and *Cecropia* (Gardner, 1977).

THOMAS' BROAD-NOSED BAT
Platyrrhinus dorsalis   Map 104

HB 66–86, T 0, HF 12–17, E 18–25, FA 46–52, Wt 18–40 g.

Description. Fairly large. Upperparts *dark chocolate-brown*; underparts dark gray-brown. Prominent *white back* stripe from crown of head to rump. Buffy facial stripes, lower stripe indistinct or absent. Tail membrane short, V-shaped, edge fringed. **Similar Species.** *P. vittatus* is very similar but larger (compare forearm). All other stripe-backed bats are paler in color.

Distribution. E Panama to Peru and Bolivia. 600–1400 m (in Panama).

Status and Habitat. Uncommon; found in evergreen forest and forest edge of foothills and highlands.

Habits. Poorly known.

Comment. Some authors treat the smaller subspecies *P. d. umbratus* (which also occurs in E Panama) as a full species (see Handley, 1976; Koopman, 1993, but also see Ferrell and Wilson, 1991).

GREAT STRIPE-FACED BAT   Plate 13
Vampyrodes caraccioli   Map 105

HB 77–89, T 0, HF 12–19, E 19–23, FA 47–56, Wt 30–47 g.

Description. Rather large. Upperparts *sandy brown* or *reddish brown*; underparts gray-brown; hairs bicolor, pale at base. *Prominent white back stripe from crown of head to rump. White facial stripes prominent*, upper stripe wide, extends to back of head beyond ear. Ears and noseleaf edged yellow or cream. Muzzle relatively elongated. Tail membrane fairly short (about 10 mm), V-shaped, clearly fringed along edge. **Similar Species.** This beautiful, prominently

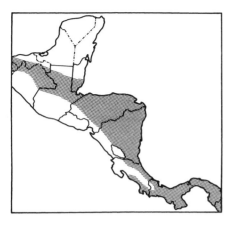

Map 105. Great Stripe-faced Bat, *Vampyrodes caraccioli*

striped bat is fairly easy to recognize. Other striped bats of similar forearm size are Salvin's Big-eyed Bat (*Chiroderma salvini*), which has short upper facial stripes, a short muzzle, and a longer tail membrane, and Thomas' Broadnosed Bat (*Platyrrhinus dorsalis*), which is blackish, with buffy facial stripes.

Distribution. Oaxaca, Mexico, through Central America, mainly on the Caribbean Slope, to Peru, Bolivia, and N Brazil; Trinidad and Tobago. Lowlands to 800 m.

Status and Habitat. Uncommon north of Panama; fairly common in mature, evergreen forest in Panama (especially in Darién).

Habits. Roosts in groups of 1–4 adults and their young under foliage of subcanopy trees, 7–12 m above ground. Group composition is stable, but roost sites change almost daily. The groups consist of small harems of 2-3 females and one male, sometimes with associated young. Bachelor males roost alone (Morrison, 1980). Although sometimes caught in ground-level mist nets, this species usually flies 3 m or more above ground. Activity is greatest 30 minutes after sunset, for 1–2 hours, and again shortly after midnight (Bonaccorso, 1979). Figs are the principal food source, other fruits and pollen or nectar may also be taken. Females may breed twice annually, in January

and July in Panama. Biology reviewed by Willis et al. (1990).

HAIRY BIG-EYED BAT   Plate 13
Chiroderma villosum   Map 106

HB 62–79, T 0, HF 10–16, E 16–20, FA 42–47, Wt 15–28 g.

Description. Medium sized. Entirely *gray or gray-brown*; fur tricolor, long and slightly woolly with *prominent, long guard hairs*. Back and facial stripes faint or absent. Ears and noseleaf pale brown, without pale edges. Tip of noseleaf creased laterally. Eyes large; muzzle short and blunt. *Tail membrane long* (about 19 mm), *well haired on upper surface, edge not fringed.* **Similar Species.** Unstriped individuals could be confused with fruit-eating bats (*Artibeus* spp.) which have shorter, velvety fur without long guard hairs and smaller eyes. See Brown Tent-making Bat (*Uroderma magnirostrum*).

Distribution. Hidalgo and Veracruz, Mexico, through Central America to S Brazil, Bolivia, and Peru; Trinidad and Tobago. Lowlands to 600 m.

Status and Habitat. Uncommon but widespread in all types of lowland forest, second growth, clearings, and fruit groves.

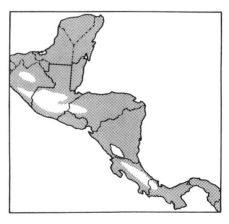

Map 106. Hairy Big-eyed Bat, *Chiroderma villosum*

Habits. Poorly known. Sometimes caught in mist nets set over pools of water or in nets placed several meters above ground.

SALVIN'S BIG-EYED BAT
Chiroderma salvini

Plate 13
Map 107

HB 70–87, T 0, HF 12–15, E 17–20, FA 48–52, Wt 30–36 g.

Description. Rather large. Upperparts *dark brown*; underparts gray-brown; fur thick with long guard hairs, tricolor, dark at base. Narrow, often inconspicuous *whitish back stripe extends from between shoulders to rump*. White facial stripes prominent, upper stripe extends to front of ears. Ears and noseleaf edged yellow at bases only. Eyes large; *muzzle short and blunt*. Tail membrane rather long (about 15 mm), U-shaped, *hairy on upper surface*, very sparsely haired on edge. **Similar Species.** See Great Stripe-faced Bat (*Vampyrodes caraccioli*) and Thomas' Broad-nosed Bat (*Platyrrhinus dorsalis*).

Distribution. Chihuahua, Mexico, patchily distributed through Central America (not reported in Nicaragua) to Venezuela and along Andean corridor to Bolivia. Usually between 600–1500 m, rarely higher or lower in Central America.

Status and Habitat. Uncommon to locally common in semideciduous and evergreen forest and forest openings; also near streams in dry areas.

Habits. Poorly known. Usually caught in nets set over streams. The diet probably includes figs and other fruit. This species is unusually noisy in captivity and has a wide repertoire of audible squeals and chirrups.

LITTLE BIG-EYED BAT
Chiroderma trinitatum

Plate 13
Map 108

HB 52–70, T 0, HF 9–12, E 13–18, FA 38–41, Wt 12–14 g.

Description. Relatively small. Upperparts *dark to pale brown*; underparts gray-brown; fur thick with long guard hairs, faintly tricolor. Indistinct to prominent *whitish back stripe extends from between shoulders to rump*. Facial stripes prominent, *upper stripe extends to front of ear*. Eyes large; muzzle short and blunt. Ears and noseleaf edged yellow or whitish at bases only. Tail membrane rather long (13–14 mm), U-shaped, upper surface sparsely haired, edge not fringed. **Similar Species.** See Heller's Broad-nosed Bat (*Platyrrhinus helleri*), Common Tent-making Bat (*Uroderma bilobatum*), and Striped Yellow-eared Bat (*Vampyressa nymphaea*).

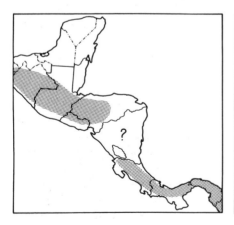

Map 107. Salvin's Big-eyed Bat, *Chiroderma salvini*

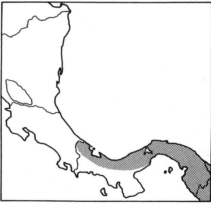

Map 108. Little Big-eyed Bat, *Chiroderma trinitatum*

Distribution. Panama to Amazonian Brazil, Peru, and Bolivia; Trinidad and Tobago. Lowlands to 700 m.

Status and Habitat. Apparently rare in Panama; found in evergreen forest and forest openings.

Habits. Poorly known. The type specimen from Trinidad was caught in a well-lit cave (Goodwin and Greenhall, 1961). It probably travels in the canopy or subcanopy, as it is seldom caught in nets set at understory level.

LITTLE YELLOW-EARED BAT   Plate 12
Vampyressa pusilla   Map 109

HB 43–52, T 0, HF 7–10, E 11–15, FA 29–34, Wt 6–11 g.

Description. Very small. Upperparts *pale brown*, hairs tricolor, brown at base. No back stripe; white facial stripes indistinct. *Tragus, entire base of ear, and upper edges of ears yellow*; noseleaf brown, edged yellow; sides of noseleaf smoothly rounded (see Figure 9). Tail membrane short (about 6–7 mm), edge *lightly fringed at center*. Forearms, fingers, and thumbs brown. **Similar Species.** Macconnell's Bat (*Mesophylla macconnelli*) has a naked tail membrane, entirely yellow ears and noseleaf, and yellowish-pink fingers and thumbs. Small fruit-eating bats (*Artibeus*

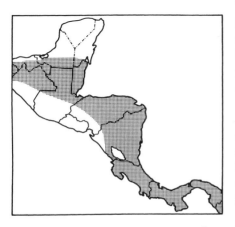

Map 109. Little Yellow-eared Bat, *Vampyressa pusilla*

spp.) are larger. See *V. nymphaea* for other differences between genera.

Distribution. Oaxaca, Mexico, through Central America (except dry Pacific Slope and Yucatán Peninsula) to the Guianas and Peru; also SE Brazil and E Paraguay. Lowlands to 1500 m.

Status and Habitat. Uncommon but widespread in semideciduous and evergreen forest.

Habits. Roosts in tents made from philodendron and other heart-shaped leaves; basal nerves and midrib are chewed near the leaf stem, causing the sides and tip of the leaf to fold down (Kunz et al., 1994). Tents are occupied by 1-5 individuals. It is usually caught in nets set across streams and prefers to fly at the subcanopy level of the forest than at understory level. Greatest activity occurs during the first 2 hours after sunset. Figs and other small fruits are eaten. Reproduction may occur twice annually, with young born late in the dry season and in the middle of the wet season. Biology reviewed by Lewis and Wilson (1987).

STRIPED YELLOW-
EARED BAT   Plate 12
Vampyressa nymphaea   Map 110

HB 54–64, T 0, HF 9–12, E 14–18, FA 35–39, Wt 11–16 g.

Description. Small. Fur gray-brown; hairs tricolor or four-banded: faint, dusky shadow at base, middle whitish, tip gray-brown, extreme tip usually frosted with white. *Very faint, pale back stripe (easily overlooked) extends from between shoulders or mid-back to rump.* Bold, *white facial stripes*; upper stripe wide at base near noseleaf, tapering as it extends over crown of head to mid-point of ear. Tragus, entire base and upper edges of ears yellow; noseleaf edged yellow or cream. Tail membrane medium length (8–11 mm), *moderately haired on upper surface, edge sparsely haired.* **Similar Species.** Easily confused with small fruit-eating

a.   b.   c.

FIGURE 9. Noseleafs:
a. Little Yellow-eared Bat (*Vampyressa pusilla*)
b and c. Macconnell's Bat (*Mesophylla macconnelli*).
In c, the noseleaf is laid forward to show a second small "noseleaf".

bats (*Artibeus phaeotis* and *A. watsoni*), which lack back stripes, have shorter facial stripes, and almost naked tail membranes. In *Vampyressa* the inner pair of upper incisors is much longer than the outer pair; in *Artibeus* the 4 upper incisors are equal in length. Little Big-eyed Bat (*Chiroderma trinitatum*) is usually larger, with shorter facial stripes, large eyes, and a short muzzle.

Distribution. SE Nicaragua to NW Ecuador. Lowlands to 900 m.

Status and Habitat. Uncommon; usually found in mature evergreen forest.

Habits. Poorly known.

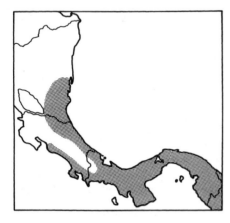

Map 110. Striped Yellow-eared Bat, *Vampyressa nymphaea*

Comment. Natural history and tents made exclusively in leaves of *Pentagonia donnell-smithii* by this species were reported by Brooke (1987). Brooke may have misidentified the bats, as all subsequent *Pentagonia* tents examined have been occupied by *Artibeus watsoni* (pers. obs.; R. M. Timm, pers. comm.), and forearm measurements given by Brooke (a mean of 39.1 mm) are too large for *Vampyressa nymphaea*.

MACCONNELL'S BAT   Plate 12
Mesophylla macconnelli   Map 111

HB 43–52, T 0, HF 8–12, E 12–15, FA 29–33, Wt 6–8 g.

Description. Very small. Upperparts *pale gray-brown* or *pale gray*, hairs tricolor, base pale brown, middle whitish, tips pale brown. No back stripe. White facial stripes indistinct or absent. *Ears and noseleaf* mostly *bright yellow*, with a brownish tinge in upper part of ears. Spear of noseleaf rough-edged; when laid forward reveals a second, tiny "noseleaf." Tail membrane pale brown, short (about 7–8 mm), *edge and upper surface naked. Forearms, fingers, and thumbs yellowish pink.* **Similar Species.** See Little Yellow-eared Bat (*Vampyressa pusilla*), which, despite its common name, has less yellow on the ears than Macconnell's Bat (also see Figure 9).

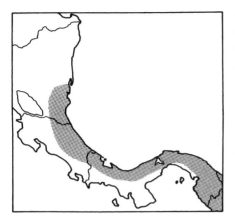

Map 111. Macconnell's Bat, *Mesophylla macconnelli*

Distribution. Caribbean Slope of Central America from Nicaragua to C Panama, throughout E Panama to Peru, Bolivia, and Amazonian Brazil; Trinidad. Lowlands to 1100 m.

Status and Habitat. Rare and local in Central America; more common in parts of South America. Usually recorded in mature evergreen forest.

Habits. Poorly known. It makes leaf tents in young bifid palms and arums (Kunz et al., 1994) and has also been found roosting in a hollow tree. In South America it is often found in low-lying areas with numerous palms.

Comment. Included in the genus *Vampyressa* by Owen (1987).

HONDURAN WHITE BAT   Plate 12
Ectophylla alba   Map 112

HB 40–47, T 0, HF 9–10, E 14–15, FA 23–31, Wt 4–7 g.

Description. *Very small.* Head and upper body *pure white*, rump and lower belly pale gray. Ears and noseleaf bright yellow. Tail membrane pale gray-brown, upper surface and edge naked. Wing membranes black; forearms, fingers, and thumbs yellowish-pink. **Similar Species.** No other leaf-nosed bats are white. Northern Ghost Bat (*Diclidurus albus*) is much larger, lacks a noseleaf, and has pinkish wings.

Distribution. Caribbean Slope from E Honduras (Benshoof et al., 1984) to Panama. Lowlands to 700 m.

Status and Habitat. Uncommon and local in wet, evergreen forest and tall second growth.

Habits. Roosts in groups of 4–8 in tents made from small to medium sized *Heliconia* spp. or other understory plants. Horizontal leaves are chewed on either side of the midrib, causing the sides to collapse and hang vertically. Old heliconia leaves assume the same form, but appear withered and dead, whereas tents in active use are in succulent, green leaves. Tents are about 2 m above ground, and some tents are used only as night feeding roosts. Fruit pulp and seeds of small, understory figs were found under a night roost. This bat is seldom caught in mist nets, except when nets are set near occupied tents. Roosting groups can be closely approached and observed. Males and females share tents until young are born (in April in Costa Rica), then males leave. Females appear to suckle each others' young on occasion (Brooke, 1990).

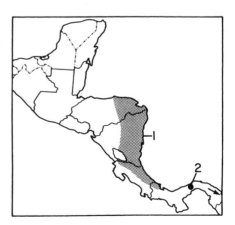

Map 112. 1. Honduran White Bat, *Ectophylla alba*
2. Little White-shouldered Bat, *Ametrida centurio*

LITTLE WHITE-SHOULDERED BAT
Ametrida centurio

Figure 10
Map 112

HB 40–55, T 0, HF 9–12, E 13–17, FA 26–34, Wt 6–12 g.

Description. *Very small.* Female (FA 31–34 mm) much larger than male (FA 26–28 mm). Fur sandy brown or gray-brown, hairs tricolor, dark at base. *White patches of fur on shoulders* at insertion point of wings and on neck at base of ears. No dorsal or facial stripes. Eyes rather large, iris yellowish. *Muzzle very short, pug-faced; noseleaf small,* squashed against face. Tail membrane moderately long, U-shaped, haired on upper surface and fringed on edge. **Similar Species.** Other tailless bats of similar size have longer muzzles and noseleafs and lack white shoulder patches.

Distribution. C Panama to Amazonian Brazil and Venezuela; Trinidad. Lowlands to 2100 m.

Status and Habitat. Known in Panama from a single record on Barro Colorado Island (Handley et al., 1991). Uncommon or rare in South America; usually found in lowland, evergreen forest near streams or moist areas, occasionally in clearings, second growth, or deciduous forest.

Habits. Poorly known.

WRINKLE-FACED BAT
Centurio senex

Plate 12
Map 113

HB 54–68, T 0, HF 11–15, E 15–17, FA 41–45, Wt 13–26 g.

Description. Medium sized; peculiar-looking face. Upperparts gray-brown or yellowish brown, with long guard hairs on head and back; underparts paler; white patches of fur on sides of shoulders. Ears yellow. Eyes large, widely spaced, iris golden. *Face naked,* pinkish or yellowish, muzzle flat and broad, *marked with complex folds and wrinkles* around nose and mouth. No noseleaf. Folds of skin on chin (small, naked and pinkish in female; large, velvety, and white, with translucent patches in male) can be pulled up to cover the face, translucent patches then cover eyes. Tail membrane relatively long and hairy. *Lattice pattern*

FIGURE 10. Little White-shouldered Bat (*Ametrida centurio*).

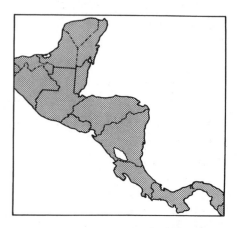

Map 113. Wrinkle-faced Bat, *Centurio senex*

on wings composed of stripes of pigmented and transparent skin (pronounced in male, subdued in female). **Similar Species.** None. Related to Little White-shouldered Bat (*Ametrida centurio*), which is smaller and has a noseleaf.

Distribution. Tamaulipas and Sinaloa, Mexico, through Central America to Venezuela; Trinidad and Tobago. Lowlands to 1400 m (at Monteverde, Costa Rica).

Status and Habitat. Generally uncommon or rare; found in deciduous and evergreen forest. Most common in dense second growth and low, seasonally flooded forest, where it is sometimes abundant (for example in Calakmul, S Campeche, Mexico, and Tikal, Guatemala).

Habits. Roosts in small groups in vine tangles and dense foliage. Activity starts soon after sunset but is curtailed around full moon. In deciduous forest, it is often caught in mist nets set over small pools of water. This strange-looking bat feeds on fruit, possibly by biting ripe fruits and sucking the juice. The facial folds may be used to direct juice to the mouth. Captives will accept green fruits, however, and little is known of their feeding behavior in the wild. Biology reviewed by Snow et al. (1980).

Vampire Bats
Subfamily Desmodontinae

There are 3 species of vampire bats, each in its own genus, found from Mexico to Chile and Argentina. Although vampires are included in the leaf-nosed bat family (Phyllostomidae), they do not have a free noseleaf. In place of a noseleaf, the nostrils are surrounded by an enlarged, flattened nose pad and a secondary fold of skin between the eyes and nose. The lower lip is deeply grooved at the center. The inner upper incisors have sharply pointed tips and are greatly enlarged, about the same size as the upper canines (the outer incisors, if present, are tiny). Dental formula: i 1/2 (2/2 in *Diphylla*), c 1/1, p 1/2, m 1/1 (*Desmodus*), m 2/1 (*Diaemus*), or m 2/2 (*Diphylla*). There is no tail, and the tail membrane is reduced to a narrow U-shaped band around the legs. The hind feet and thumbs are large and well developed.

Vampire bats are the only mammals to feed exclusively on blood of live animals. They do not drink water and do not take solid food. To feed, they make a small incision with the razor sharp incisor teeth, and blood is lapped up, not sucked. Anticoagulants in the saliva inhibit blood clotting. The bats usually feed at a wound until they are bloated with blood and take only one meal per night. Vampire bats, Common Vampires in particular, are extremely adept at walking and leaping, and usually approach their prey by crawling along the underside of branches or walking on the ground. They roost on vertical walls of caves, mines, or hollow trees, and grip the surface with feet and thumbs. Only one species regularly exploits livestock and may be a pest in some areas. A good reference to vampire bats is Greenhall and Schmidt (1988).

COMMON VAMPIRE BAT
Desmodus rotundus

Plate 7
Map 114

Spanish: vampiro, murciélago vampiro.

HB 68–93, T 0, HF 13–20, E 15–20, FA 53–65, Wt 19–43 g.

Description. Moderately large. Upperparts usually gray-brown, sometimes orangish; underparts gray-brown, well frosted with white, sharply demarcated from upperparts. Fur short, coarse, and shiny. Ears triangular, length greater than width. Eyes relatively small. **M**-shaped nosepad above nostrils. Upper incisors long and pointed. Tail membrane reduced to a narrow **U**-shaped band, lightly haired. Wing membranes blackish, leading edge often white; wingtips sometimes pale, but not pure white. Forearms nearly naked. *Thumbs very long, with 2 well-developed pads on underside near base.* **Similar Species.** Other vampire bats are much less common; *Diaemus* has pure white wing tips and one pad at base of thumb. See *Diphylla.*

Distribution. Sonora and Tamaulipas, Mexico, through Central and South America to N Chile and N Argentina; Trinidad. Lowlands to 2700 m (in Central America).

Status and Habitat. Common to abundant in a variety of habitats; most numerous in cattle country, uncommon or rare in extensive areas of mature forest.

Habits. Roosts in caves, sink holes, mines, and hollow trees during the day. In caves and mines, it occupies deep, dark recesses, in numbers of up to 2000 (Medellín and Lopez-Forment, 1986). Separate night roosts, such as under bridges, may be used. Activity is greatest 2 hours or more after sunset. This bat has long wings and is a fast flier, but is also agile on the ground. The long, well-developed thumbs and large hind feet enable it to walk, run, and jump with great dexterity. In confined spaces where it cannot take flight, it moves with tremendous leaps and hops to escape capture. The Common Vampire feeds on vertebrate

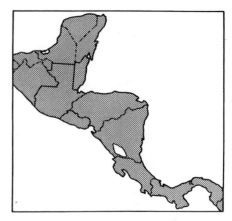

Map 114. Common Vampire Bat, *Desmodus rotundus*

blood from a variety of hosts and seems to favor blood of large mammals (in addition to livestock and wild mammals, humans are sometimes bitten). It usually approaches prey on the ground and crawls onto the legs, shoulders, rump, or neck of livestock before biting. Several individuals may feed from the same bite. Anticoagulants in the saliva result in a tell-tale streak of blood on the victim. Females roost in stable groups of 8–12 and cooperate with one another; if one fails to eat, others will feed her by regurgitating part of their meal. Breeding may occur year-round, and a single young is born after 7 months of gestation. Females suckle the young for 7–10 months and supplement milk with regurgitated blood after the first 3 months.

Common Vampires are well known and often feared or hated, both by residents and biologists. There is some justification for such feelings: these bats may be abundant around cattle ranches and do act as vectors of rabies and other diseases; for the bat netter they are agile, slippery, and difficult to handle and can easily inflict a deep bite (although with practice they pose no real problem); and they also have a negative impact on populations of other bats, as they may displace other species from suitable hollow tree roosts. Nonspecific control efforts (such as the use of explosives in roost sites, for example) have caused the demise of many beneficial bats. Research into vampire bat behavior has led to the development of a more specific control of these bats: anticoagulants are applied to livestock (usually to an animal that has been bitten previously) and are ingested by a vampire. On returning to the roost, mutual grooming among bats transfers the anticoagulant via their saliva throughout the colony. This eventually leads to the demise of the vampires without affecting other species of bats.

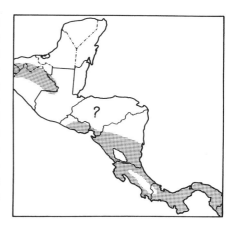

Map 115. White-winged Vampire Bat, *Diaemus youngi*

WHITE-WINGED VAMPIRE BAT
Diaemus youngi

Plate 7
Map 115

HB 77–115, T 0, HF 16–20, E 16–18, FA 48–54, Wt 32–40 g.

Description. Moderately large. Upperparts brown or reddish brown; underparts gray-brown, lightly frosted. Fur sparse and silky. Ears triangular, length greater than width. Eyes relatively small. M-shaped nosepad above nostrils. Upper incisors long and pointed; 2 large glands inside corners of mouth. Tail membrane reduced, U-shaped, lightly haired. Forearms almost naked; *wings blackish with sharply contrasting white tips* and white leading edge; *thumbs long, single pad on underside at base.* **Similar Species.** *Desmodus* is similar (and much more common), but lacks white wingtips, has longer thumbs with 2 pads, and no glands in the mouth. See *Diphylla.*

Distribution. Tamaulipas, E Mexico, patchily through Central America to N Argentina and E Brazil; Trinidad. Lowlands only.

Status and Habitat. Rare and local in Central America; found in evergreen or semideciduous lowland forest.

Habits. Roosts in caves and hollow trees in mixed-sex colonies of up to 30 individuals. In confined spaces, captive individuals successfully attacked and fed on the blood of several species of live wild birds weighing 15–200 g. This vampire will accept chicken blood but not bovine blood, and it has physiological modifications for digesting avian rather than mammalian blood. Although this bat is usually considered to be a bird-blood specialist, the diet in the wild also includes blood of goats, pigs, cattle, and unidentified mammals. This variety may reflect a recent change in dietary preference in response to an abundant food source. Prey is defended from other vampires by high pitched cries and baring of teeth. When handled, the White-winged Vampire may emit an offensive-smelling secretion from the mouth glands. Audible vocalizations include hisses, screams, and chirps. Most studies of this bat have taken place in Trinidad (Goodwin and Greenhall, 1961; Greenhall and Schmidt, 1988), and little is known of its ecology in Central America.

Comment. *Diaemus* is closely related to *Desmodus* and is sometimes included within that genus.

HAIRY-LEGGED VAMPIRE BAT Plate 7
Diphylla ecaudata   Map 116

HB 69–82, T 0, HF 15–18, E 16–18, FA 49–56 Wt 18–33 g.

Description. Medium sized. Upperparts gray-brown; underparts gray. Fur long and soft. *Ears short, broad, and rounded (width greater than length). Eyes very large.* M-shaped nosepad above nostrils. Upper incisors long and pointed. No tail and *almost no tail membrane; hind legs thickly haired.* Forearms well-haired; wing membranes blackish. **Similar Species.** Other vampires (*Desmodus* and *Diaemus*) have thinly haired legs, narrower ears, and smaller eyes.

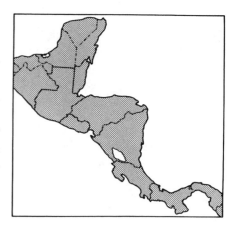

Map 116. Hairy-legged Vampire Bat, *Diphylla ecaudata*

Distribution. S Texas, USA, and E Mexico through Central America to Venezuela, Peru, and E Brazil. Lowlands to 1900 m.

Status and Habitat. Uncommon and local; found in all types of forest, mainly at low elevations.

Habits. Roosts in caves and mines, rarely in hollow trees. Individuals are well spaced in the roost, and group size is usually small, although a group of more than 500 was found in a cave in Puebla, Mexico (Medellín and Lopez-For-ment, 1986). The numbers in this cave were much reduced in January, perhaps indicating seasonal movements or migration. Captives will bite and feed on the blood of live chickens, but refuse mammalian blood and do not bite live mammals. Chickens are usually bitten on the legs or anal region, sometimes on the neck (Hoyt and Altenbach, 1981). Avian blood may predominate in the diet of wild individuals, although cattle are occasionally exploited. Unlike other vampires, this attractive bat is gentle and easy to handle. Reproduction may occur year-round.

FUNNEL-EARED BATS
Family Natalidae

The Natalidae includes 5 species in a single genus. Several species are found only on islands in the Bahamas and West Indies; one species occurs in Mexico, Central America, and N South America. These delicate bats have tiny bodies with long legs and tails and extensive, pale membranes. Dental formula: i 2/3, c 1/1, p 3/3, m 3/3.

Fairly common in suitable habitat, funnel-eared bats are remarkably agile fliers, moving with rapid, fluttery flight through the understory. They roost in large caves, and their distribution may be restricted by lack of suitable roost sites.

MEXICAN FUNNEL-EARED BAT
Natalus stramineus

Plate 14
Map 117

HB 38–46, T 47-52, HF 8-9, E 14-16, FA 36-39, Wt 3-5 g.

Description. Very small, delicate, and long-limbed. Upperparts pale orange-brown or yellowish; underparts yellow. Fur soft and slightly woolly. Ears broad, cream-colored with blackish edges; angled forward. Eyes tiny. Face triangular, facial skin pale pink; mustache over sides of mouth. *Legs and tail very long* (tibia about 20 mm); tail longer than head and body length, extending to tip of extensive tail membrane; edge of membrane fringed with short hair. Legs, tail, and arm bones pink, membranes pale brown. Wings long and narrow.
Similar Species. No other tiny bats have tail longer than head and body.

Distribution. Sonora and Nuevo León, Mexico, through Central America (including Yucatán Peninsula, but patchily distributed from Honduras to Panama) to E Brazil; Lesser Antilles; Hispaniola; Jamaica. Lowlands to 2400 m (usually below 300 m).

Status and Habitat. Uncommon to fairly common; usually recorded in dry and semideciduous forest and second growth, occasionally in evergreen forest.

Habits. Roosts in deep caves, often in large numbers (up to 300). Individuals hang widely spaced in dark caverns. Groups leave the roost

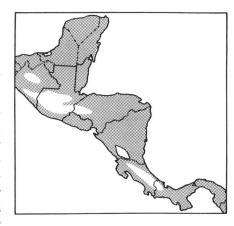

Map 117. Mexican Funnel-eared Bat, *Natalus stramineus*

about 30 minutes after sunset to feed on small, flying insects. Although flight is usually at the understory level, these bats are seldom taken in mist nets, even when nets are set near roost entrances. They dip, twist, and dodge in and around understory vegetation (and mist nets) with impressive speed and agility. Greatest activity occurs within 2 hours after sunset; later in the evening, night roosts distinct from daytime retreats are used. Colony size may vary considerably in a period of a few days and northern populations sometimes migrate in winter (Ceballos and Galindo, 1984). High-frequency echolocation calls (over 85 kHz) are used. Single young are born once a year, late in the dry season. Separate maternity colonies are established during the breeding season.

THUMBLESS BATS
Family Furipteridae

The Furipteridae family consists of 2 genera, each with a single species. One species is restricted to South America. These tiny bats have greatly reduced thumbs, mostly contained within the wing membrane. Dental formula: i 2/3, c 1/1, p 3/3, m 3/3 (same as for *Natalus*). They are rare in collections, and their habits are poorly known.

THUMBLESS BAT Plate 14
Furipterus horrens Map 118

HB 33–39, T 21–27, HF 7–9, E 8–12, FA 33–37, Wt 3–4 g.

Description. Very small and delicate. Fur *smoky gray,* underparts slightly paler than upperparts. Ears short and rounded, directed forward. Eyes tiny, hidden in fur. Mustache over sides of mouth; nose upturned. Tail enclosed in and shorter than tail membrane; tail membrane extensive, translucent, marked with transverse lines. Legs long, *femur as long as tibia* (about15 mm); *thumb tiny,* clawless, almost entirely enclosed in wing membrane (free portion is 1 mm or less). **Similar Species.** Superficially similar to some sac-winged bats (*Balantiopteryx* spp.), which have longer thumbs, large eyes, and tip of tail free. The only other adult gray bat with tiny thumbs is the Smoky Bat (*Cyttarops alecto*), which is much larger.

Distribution. Costa Rica to Peru and E Brazil; Trinidad. Lowlands only.

Status and Habitat. Apparently rare and local; known in Central America from few localities in lowland, evergreen forest.

Habits. Usually roosts in hollow, humid logs, but has also been found in caves and rock

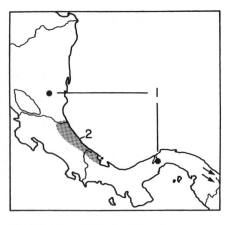

Map 118. 1. Peter's Disk-winged Bat, *Thyroptera discifera*
2. Thumbless Bat, *Furipterus horrens*

crevices (Timm et al., 1989). In Costa Rica, 59 individuals, all males, were recorded roosting in a large, hollow log on the forest floor. The bats were hanging in small clusters and were alert but reluctant to leave the roost (LaVal, 1977). A group of 4 found under a hollow log in Ecuador immediately vacated the roost when approached, then circled nearby and attempted to reenter. This small bat forages for insects, Lepidoptera in particular, flying close to the ground with a slow, fluttery, mothlike flight. It is seldom caught in mist nets.

DISK-WINGED BATS
Family Thyropteridae

The Thyropteridae consists of a single genus with 3 species, 2 of which occur in Central America. These tiny bats have "suction cups" at the base of the thumb and under the heel. No other bats in the New World have such cups. Sucker-footed bats of the Old World family Myzopodidae have similar, but less well-developed suction pads. Dental formula: i 2/3, c 1/1, p 3/3, m 3/3 (the same as for *Natalus*).

Disk-winged bats use their suction cups to cling to smooth surfaces. They can move rapidly along a pane of glass or inside a coiled leaf, the natural roost of one species. The toes of the tiny feet are fused together and are not used when crawling.

PETER'S DISK-WINGED BAT Plate 14
Thyroptera discifera Map 118

HB 37–47, T 24–33, HF 4–6, E 10–12, FA 31–35, Wt 3–4 g.

Description. Very small and delicate. Upperparts brown or rufous; *underparts slightly paler, gray-brown or yellowish.* Fur long and fluffy. Ears pale brown. Face triangular, with a rather long, pointed muzzle. *Tail long, extends 2–4 mm beyond tail membrane.* Tail membrane well-haired on upper surface for about half its length. *Suction cups on heels and thumbs;* feet tiny; *calcar long, with one indistinct bump* on its edge. **Similar Species.** *T. tricolor* usually has a white belly, 2 bumps on the calcar, and its tail extends more than 4 mm beyond the tail membrane.

Distribution. SE Nicaragua; C Panama (Handley et al., 1991); Colombia and the Guianas to NE Brazil and Peru. Lowlands only.

Status and Habitat. Known from 2 records in Central America; rare but widespread in South America, in evergreen forest and banana plantations.

Habits. Poorly known. In Venezuela, 2 groups of 10 and 7 were caught by hand from under dead banana leaves; a specimen from Guyana was found under an "eate" palm leaf. Seldom caught in mist nets. Biology reviewed by Wilson (1978).

SPIX'S DISK-WINGED BAT Plate 14
Thyroptera tricolor Map 119

HB 37–46, T 24–33, HF 5–7, E 11–14, FA 34–38, Wt 3–5 g.

Description. Very small and delicate. Upperparts (and occasionally throat) dark brown or reddish brown; *underparts white* or yellowish, rarely buffy. Fur long and fluffy. Ears pale brown. Face triangular, with a rather long, pointed muzzle. *Tail long, extends 5–8 mm be-*

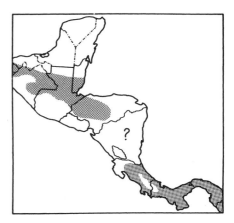

Map 119. Spix's Disk-winged Bat, *Thyroptera tricolor*

yond tail membrane. Tail membrane almost naked. *Suction cups under heels and thumbs;* feet tiny; *calcar long, with 2 distinct bumps on its edge.* **Similar Species.** See *T. discifera.* Other bats lack suction cups.

Distribution. Veracruz, Mexico, patchily distributed through Central America (not recorded in El Salvador or Nicaragua) to SE Brazil. Lowlands to 1300 m (usually below 800 m; 1300 m at Monteverde, Costa Rica).

Status and Habitat. Uncommon to locally common in evergreen forest and tall second growth. Not found in areas with a prolonged dry season.

Habits. Roosts in young, rolled up leaves of heliconia, *Calathea,* and banana. Unlike most species, this bat roosts upright, and individuals line up one above another inside the leaf. The suction cups on the thumbs and feet are kept moist and enable the bats to run up the slippery leaf surface. Suitable leaves are in the form of vertical tubes with openings of 50–100 mm diameter, located in shady areas, not in direct contact with other vegetation. Such leaves unroll rapidly and are usually only used as roosts for one day. Tree falls, stream banks, and other small, natural forest gaps provide good conditions for host plants and bats. These delicate, gentle bats can be captured by pinching the tops of occupied leaf roosts and extracting them one at a time. When released, groups usually fly together to a different roost, but sometimes circle and return to the original roost. Stable groups of 1-9 with approximately equal numbers of males and females occupy fixed territories and change roosts every day (Findley and Wilson, 1974). This species is seldom caught in mist nets, even in areas where it is known to be common and its roost sites are abundant, due to its agile and highly maneuverable flight. The diet is presumed to consist of small insects caught in flight. Biology reviewed by Wilson and Findley (1977).

Where to See. Occupied roosts can be located easily at Tortuguero and Corcovado national parks, Costa Rica (permits are required to capture wild bats, even if they are released immediately).

PLAIN-NOSED BATS
Family Vespertilionidae

The Vespertilionidae is the largest family of bats in the world, with 37 genera and more than 320 species. There are few places on the globe unoccupied by one or more species of plain-nosed bats, which are widely distributed on all continents and many islands. Most of the bats in the United States and Canada are vespertilionids. Members of the family range in size from tiny to large; Central American species are very small to medium sized. New World vespertilionids have small eyes and no flaps, folds, or nose-leafs on the mouth or nostrils, although a few have lumps on the snout. They have long tails that extend to the tip of the extensive tail membrane; the tail is entirely enclosed in the tail membrane. Wing and tail membranes are papery and appear crinkled when the bats are at rest. In most species, the wings attach to the base of the toes, and the calcar is much longer than the foot.

Almost all plain-nosed bats are aerial insectivores, using the legs and tail membrane as a scoop to capture flying moths and other insects. A few species glean insect prey from the ground or vegetation, and one specializes on fish. Most are agile fliers; some fly fast with reduced maneuverability. Loud echolocation calls are given through the mouth and can be easily picked up with a bat detector. Unlike other Neotropical bats, which usually have single offspring, some plain-nosed bats have twins, and a few species have litters of 3–5.

Following is an outline of the genera:

Myotis. Small. Fur on the back darker or same color at base as at tip. Ears fairly long, narrow, and pointed; *tragus held erect, narrow and tapered to a point.* Usually 3 upper premolars; *2 small premolars separate the large canine tooth from the equally large third premolar* (forming an apparent gap in tooth row). Dental formula: i 2/3, c 1/1, p 3/3 (p 2/3 in *M. fortidens*), m 3/3.

Pipstrellus. Very small. Fur on back darker at base than tip. Ears fairly long and narrow; *tragus curved forward, not tapered, tip rounded.* Two premolars, one small premolar between large canine and large second premolar (appears similar to *Myotis* unless greatly magnified). Dental formula: i 2/3, c 1/1, p 2/2, m 3/3.

Eptesicus. Small to medium sized. Fur on back darker at base than tip. Ears fairly long and narrow; tragus held curved forward, slightly tapered toward the tip. Muzzle tapered;

nostrils open on sides of muzzle. *One large premolar tooth next to large canine tooth* (no gap in tooth row). Dental formula: i 2/3, c 1/1, p 1/2, m 3/3.

Plecotus. Medium sized. Woolly, gray fur. *Huge ears* and long, narrow tragus. Prominent lumps on snout. Dental formula: i 2/3, c 1/1, p 2/3, m 3/3.

Rhogeessa. Very small. *Fur on the back paler at base than tip.* Ears fairly long, narrow, and pointed, with glands (in males) on outer surface facing crown of head; tragus erect, narrow, and pointed. One large premolar tooth next to larger canine tooth (no gap in tooth row). Dental formula: i 1/3, c 1/1, p 1/2, m 3/3.

Bauerus. Medium sized. Ears long and narrow; tragus long, narrow, and pointed. *Muzzle blunt, piglike*; nostrils open forward, on tip of muzzle. Dental formula: i 1/3, c 1/1, p 1/2, m 3/3.

Lasiurus. Small to medium sized. Fur on back *brightly colored* or banded. Ears short and rounded or somewhat elongated; tragus rather short, tip rounded. *Upper surface of tail membrane thickly furred.* Dental formula: i 1/3, c 1/1, p 1/2 or 2/2, m 3/3.

CALIFORNIA MYOTIS
Myotis californicus

Plate 14
Map 120

HB 38–53, T 28–41, HF 5–7, E 12–15, FA 31–37, Wt 4–6 g.

Description. Tiny. Upperparts *yellowish*; underparts cream or buffy; *base of hairs black, strongly contrasting with pale tips.* Fur long (7–8 mm) and silky. Ears and tragus narrow and pointed. Membranes, face, and ears black. *Tail membrane lightly haired below knee* (visible with a hand lens); wings naked. **Similar Species.** One of the smallest *Myotis* in the region. Only *M. keaysi* and Eastern Pipistrelle (*Pipistrellus subflavus*) have tail membranes haired below the knee; *M. keaysi* also has hair on wing membrane below knee level and has shorter, less contrasting fur; *Pipistrellus* has a broader, rounded tragus. Central American Yellow Bat (*Rhogeessa*) has fur paler at base than at tip.

Distribution. SE Alaska to Guatemala (McCarthy et al., 1993). Lowlands to 2300 m.

Status and Habitat. Rare and local in Central America and SE Mexico, at higher elevations only (1500–2300 m); found in open areas and pine–oak forest. Common in desert scrub and riparian woodland in SW United States.

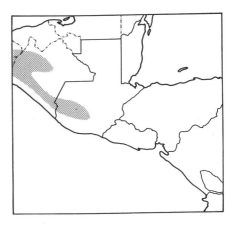

Map 120. California Myotis, *Myotis californicus*

Habits. Day roosts include buildings, mine tunnels, hollow trees, rock crevices, among dead leaves, under bridges, beneath bark, and behind sign boards. Different roosts are used from day to day. Night roosts are usually in buildings. Activity begins soon after sunset; flight is slow and fluttery, usually within 3 m of the ground. In the United States, small groups hibernate together in mines, and single young are born in May–June (Barbour and Davis, 1969).

CINNAMON MYOTIS

Myotis fortidens

Plate 14
Map 121

HB 47–63, T 30–43, HF 7–10, E 13–15, FA 35–40, Wt 5–8 g.

Description. Fairly small. Upperparts *yellow-orange or cinnamon-colored*; underparts cream or buffy; base of hairs *blackish, strongly contrasting with pale tips*. Fur 5–7 mm long, slightly woolly. Ears and tragus narrow and pointed. Tail membrane naked below knee, with a few stray hairs on edge; membranes blackish. **Similar Species.** All other *Myotis* spp. have 2 small premolar teeth between the large canine and large third premolar; *M. fortidens* has one small premolar (can be seen with a hand lens). Other yellowish myotis bats (*M. thysanodes* and *M. californicus*) occur in highlands, not lowlands; *M. elegans* is smaller.

Distribution. Sonora and Veracruz to Chiapas, Mexico (Medellín et al., 1986), and Guatemala (Dickerman et al., 1981). Lowlands only.

Status and Habitat. Uncommon to fairly common in dry and semideciduous forest and forest edge.

Habits. Roosts in hollow trees and holes in thistle stems (Villa-R., 1966), under palm-thatched roofs (Hall and Dalquest, 1963), and in a coiled heliconia leaf (Medellín et al., 1986). Group size is small, and individuals are well spaced when roosting. This species is sometimes seen flying around buildings and may use roofs as night roosts. Foraging flight is slow and erratic, at heights of about 2–4 m. It probably eats insects caught in flight, but feeding habits and diet are unknown. The few data available indicate that young are born in May.

CAVE MYOTIS

Myotis velifer

Plate 14
Map 122

HB 41–65, T 31–48, HF 8–11, E 13–17, FA 41–47, Wt 8–13 g.

Description. Relatively large. Upperparts *gray-brown*, often with a *bare patch between shoulder blades*; base of hairs slightly darker, contrasting little with tips; underparts buffy or cream, hairs darker at base than tip. Fur 6–7 mm long, woolly and even. Facial skin pinkish; ears gray-brown, narrow, and pointed. Tail membrane naked below knee. Membranes brown; legs, tail, and forearms pinkish brown. **Similar Species.** Most myotis bats in its range are smaller; of those that approach it in size, *M. thysanodes* has black ears, facial skin and membranes and a fringe of hair on the tail mem-

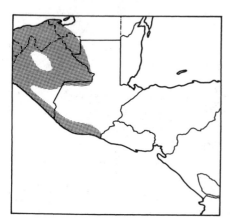

Map 121. Cinnamon Myotis, *Myotis fortidens*

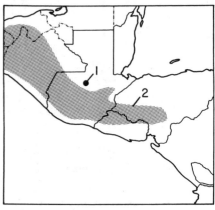

Map 122. 1. Guatemalan Myotis, *Myotis cobanensis*
2. Cave Myotis, *Myotis velifer*

brane; *M. auriculus* has long ears and longer fur. See *M. cobanensis.*

Distribution. S United States to Honduras and El Salvador (Hellebuyck et al., 1985). Lowlands to 3300 m.

Status and Habitat. Uncommon in Central America; usually found in evergreen or pine–oak forest at 1000–1800 m elevation. Common at lower elevations in riparian habitat near desert scrub in SW United States, and in pine forest at middle to high elevations in S Mexico.

Habits. Roosts in tight clusters in caves, mine tunnels, buildings, and under bridges. Colonies number 50–15,000. This bat leaves the roost about 30 minutes after sunset and flies directly to water to drink before foraging. It usually forages just above the vegetation, with fast, direct flight. Females return to the day roost within 2–3 hours and feed again before dawn. Insects eaten include beetles, flying ants, and moths. Some northern populations hibernate in winter, others migrate. In Kansas, single young are born in June–July. In Veracruz, Mexico, pregnant females were caught in March and December (Hall and Dalquest, 1963). Biology reviewed by Fitch et al. (1981).

GUATEMALAN MYOTIS
Myotis cobanensis   Map 122

HB 35, T 36, HF 9, E 13, FA 41, Wt ?

Description. Relatively large. Very similar to *M. velifer,* fur slightly darker, with a few stray hairs on the edge of the tail membrane. **Similar Species.** See *M. velifer* for comparisons with other myotis bats.

Distribution. Known only from one specimen from Alta Verapaz, C Guatemala, at about 1300 m.

Status and Habitat. Unknown.

Habits. The type specimen was caught in the cathedral in Cobán, Guatemala.

Comment. Sometimes treated as a subspecies of *M. velifer.*

BLACK MYOTIS   Plate 14
Myotis nigricans   Map 123

HB 39–52, T 28–39, HF 6–9, E 10–13, FA 33–38, Wt 3–6 g.

Description. Fairly small. Upperparts usually *blackish or dark brown,* occasionally reddish brown; underparts cream, buffy, or brown; base of hairs blackish. Fur 6–8 mm long, silky, hairs not all equal in length. Ears and tragus narrow and pointed. Membranes, face, and ears blackish. *Tail membrane naked below level of knee* and not fringed on edge. **Similar Species.** Color variable but usually darker than other myotis bats in Central America; *M. riparius* and *M. elegans* have shorter, slightly woolly, even-length fur (the 3 species can be easily confused; see *M. riparius* for additional differences). *M. keaysi* has hair on the tail membrane below knee level. See *M. albescens* and *M. oxyotus.*

Distribution. Nayarit, Mexico, through Central America (absent from Belize and Yucatán Peninsula) to Peru and N Argentina; Trinidad and Tobago; Grenada. Lowlands to 3150 m.

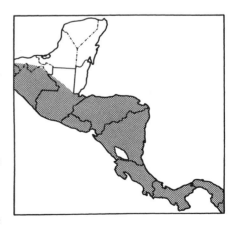

Map 123. Black Myotis, *Myotis nigricans*

Status and Habitat. Common and widespread in most lowland habitats (uncommon or absent in very dry regions); fairly common at high elevations.

Habits. Roosts in caves, hollow trees and attics. Large groups (sometimes more than 1000 individuals) consist of tight clusters of females with young and separate, unclustered males. Other roosts may contain small bachelor groups. Activity starts at sunset; all individuals leave the roost within an hour and do not return until dawn (separate night roosts may be used). This species may be caught in mist nets set across forest trails, over streams, and in clearings, although numbers caught this way are usually low compared to numbers seen or caught at roosts. The diet includes moths. In Panama, birth peaks occur in February, April–May, and August, resulting in young weaned only during the rainy season. Natural history reviewed by Wilson (1983b).

ELEGANT MYOTIS

Myotis elegans

Plate 14
Map 124

HB 39–49, T 27–35, HF 6–7, E 12–13, FA 32–34, Wt 3–5 g.

Description. Very small. Upperparts *reddish brown or orangish* (rarely, gray-brown); underparts buffy or pale orange; base of hairs dark brown, contrasting slightly with paler tips. Fur rather short (4–5 mm), even in length, and slightly woolly. Ears gray-brown, narrow, and pointed. Facial skin pinkish brown, with a thick mustache over lips. Membranes blackish. Tail membrane naked below level of knee. **Similar Species.** Usually smaller than other lowland myotis bats. See *M. nigricans, M. riparius, M. albescens,* and *M. keaysi.* Central American Yellow Bat (*Rhogeessa*) has fur paler at the base than tip and blackish ears.

Distribution. San Luis Potosí, Mexico, to Costa Rica. Lowlands to 750 m (seldom above 150 m).

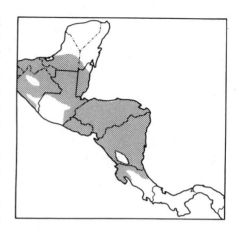

Map 124. Elegant Myotis, *Myotis elegans*

Status and Habitat. Uncommon to locally common in deciduous and evergreen lowland forest and openings.

Habits. Poorly known. Most often caught in harp traps (LaVal, 1977) or in mist nets set over water. Activity starts early, soon after sunset.

SILVER-HAIRED MYOTIS

Myotis albescens

Plate 14
Map 125

HB 48–62, T 31–39, HF 8–11, E 12–15, FA 33–38, Wt 5–8 g.

Description. Small. *Upperparts blackish, with tips of hairs conspicuously frosted white or cream;* underparts gray, paling to almost white on lower belly and around legs. Fur 5–7 mm long and silky. Facial skin and ears brown. Ears and tragus narrow and pointed. Tail membrane nearly naked below level of knee, with a sparse, inconspicuous fringe of short hairs along edge; membranes black. Feet rather large. **Similar Species.** The silver frosting is usually diagnostic; occasionally, tips of hairs are yellowish or buffy (approaching color of some *M. nigricans*), then note short fringe of hair on tail membrane and relatively large feet.

Distribution. S Veracruz, and Chiapas, Mexico, through Central America (mainly on the

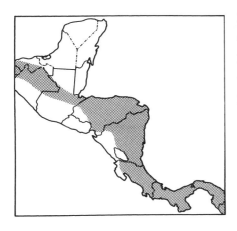

Map 125. Silver-haired Myotis, *Myotis albescens*

Caribbean Slope) to N Argentina, Uruguay, and Peru. Lowlands to 1500 m (usually below 500 m).

Status and Habitat. Rare and local from Nicaragua northward, rather common in Costa Rica, Panama, and parts of South America; found in evergreen forest and forest edge.

Habits. Roosts in buildings, caves, hollow trees or logs, and among rocks. Small groups roost together, often in relatively exposed situations with some natural light, such as on outer walls of buildings and open-sided attics. Activity starts at sunset. Although these bats can be found by day on buildings at 2 of the most intensively netted sites in Central America (La Selva, Costa Rica, and Barro Colorado Island, Panama), they have not been reported from mist net captures at either locality. Almost all individuals caught in mist nets elsewhere were taken over rivers or streams (Gardner et al., 1970; Handley, 1976). This species probably forages for insects over water or may feed high in the canopy. The diet of one individual included Lepidoptera, Coleoptera, Diptera, and fish (Whitaker and Findley, 1980). Pregnant females have been recorded in January and July (Dolan and Carter, 1979; LaVal, 1977).

RIPARIAN MYOTIS   Plate 14
Myotis riparius   Map 126

HB 40–54, T 31–43, HF 7–9, E 11–14, FA 32–38, Wt 4–7 g.

Description. Small. Upperparts *dark brown* to *orange-brown*, base of hairs slightly darker, but *barely contrasting with tips*; underparts buffy, base of hairs darker than tips. *Fur rather short* (5–6 mm), even in length, and slightly woolly. Facial skin pinkish brown; ears dark brown, narrow, and pointed. Membranes blackish; tail membrane naked below level of knee. **Similar Species.** Difficult to distinguish from *M. nigricans*, which is usually darker, with longer, silky fur. *M. nigricans* has 2 small upper premolars visible in tooth row, the second slightly smaller than the first; *M. riparius* has the second small premolar crowded to inside the tooth row and barely visible in live animals. *M. elegans* is usually smaller, brighter orange in color, with hair on the back clearly darker at base than tip. See *M. keaysi* and *M. albescens*.

Distribution. E Honduras to Uruguay and E Brazil; Trinidad. Lowlands to 2000 m (usually below 1000 m).

Status and Habitat. Fairly common in evergreen and semideciduous forest and clearings.

Map 126. 1. Fringed Myotis, *Myotis thysanodes*
2. Riparian Myotis, *Myotis riparius*

Habits. Poorly known. More easily captured in harp traps than in mist nets (LaVal, 1977). Each individual appears to occupy a small home range. In Costa Rica, pregnant females have been reported in April, May, and July (LaVal and Fitch, 1977).

HAIRY-LEGGED MYOTIS   Plate 14
Myotis keaysi   Map 127

HB 41–53, T 33–41, HF 7–9, E 10–14, FA 32–39, Wt 4–6 g.

Description. Small. Variable in size and color; extremes are (a) Yucatán Peninsula: upperparts pinkish gray or dark gray-brown, size small (FA 32–34 mm). (b) Costa Rica: upperparts reddish brown or orangish, size larger (FA 36–39 mm). Fur 5–7 mm long, slightly woolly; slightly darker at base than tip, but not strongly contrasting; underparts paler than upperparts. Facial skin and base of ears pinkish brown. *Tail membrane, legs, and adjoining portion of wings lightly haired below level of knees* (to at least halfway from knee to ankle); membranes blackish. **Similar Species.** Although variability in size and color can cause confusion, this species' hairy legs and tail membrane are usually diagnostic: only *M. californicus* has a hairy tail membrane, but it has no hair on upper surface of wing or on leg below the knee and has longer, yellow fur which is black at the base.

Distribution. Tamaulipas, Mexico, through Central America (absent from most of Panama) to SE Peru, N Argentina, and Venezuela; Trinidad. Lowlands to 2500 m.

Status and Habitat. Fairly common in dry forest, second growth, and scrub at low elevations in Mexico, Belize, Guatemala, and Honduras; locally common to abundant in evergreen and semideciduous forest, second growth, and forest edge in foothills and highlands throughout its range (seldom found below 1000 m from El Salvador to W Panama).

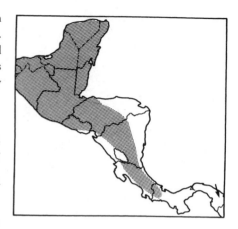

Map 127. Hairy-legged Myotis, *Myotis keaysi*

Habits. Roosts in limestone caves and may use hollow trees. A night roost of about 200 individuals was found under a bridge in Costa Rica (Timm et al., 1989). Activity begins at sunset or soon after. This species flies low along forest trails, streams, or in clearings and is easily caught in mist nets. In Costa Rica, a birth peak occurs in May–June, although breeding may occur throughout the wet season (LaVal and Fitch, 1977).

MONTANE MYOTIS   Plate 14
Myotis oxyotus   Map 128

HB 41–52, T 37–42, HF 7–10, E 11–15, FA 38–43, Wt 4–6 g.

Description. Relatively large. Upperparts *dark brown*, sometimes tinged orange-brown; underparts yellow-brown; base of hairs blackish brown. Fur long (7–9 mm), hairs even in length and woolly. Facial skin and ears dark brown. Ears and tragus narrow and pointed. Membranes blackish; tail membrane naked below knee, but with sparse hairs along its edge. Feet well haired. **Similar Species.** Usually larger than other myotis bats in its range; *M. nigricans* (may approach it in size) has silky, uneven-length fur and edge of the tail membrane naked. See *M. keaysi* and brown bats (*Eptesicus* spp.).

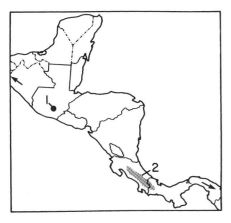

Map 128. 1. Southwestern Myotis, *Myotis auriculus*
2. Montane Myotis, *Myotis oxyotus*

Distribution. Costa Rica to W Panama; Andean corridor from Venezuela to Bolivia. 1400–3200 m (in Central America).

Status and Habitat. Uncommon to fairly common in evergreen highland forest and forest edge.

Habits. Poorly known. Pregnant females have been recorded in February and July (Gardner et al., 1970).

FRINGED MYOTIS
Myotis thysanodes   Map 126

HB 47–56, T 29–41, HF 9–10, E 16–20, FA 40–44, Wt 5–8 g.

Description. Relatively large. Upperparts *yellow* or *cream*; underparts white or cream; base of hairs *black, strongly contrasting with pale tips*. Fur 6–8 mm long, slightly woolly. Membranes, facial skin, and long ears black. Tail membrane lightly haired just below knee and *clearly fringed from tip of calcar to tail tip*. **Similar Species.** This species is larger than most myotis bats in SE Mexico, and its black ears and pale yellow fur are distinctive, but it is most easily recognized by the clearly fringed tail membrane. See *M. auriculus*.

Distribution. British Columbia, Canada, and South Dakota, USA, to Chiapas, Mexico. Lowlands to 3400 m.

Status and Habitat. Known in Chiapas from one specimen taken in pine–oak forest at 2400 m. Common in mid-elevation oak woodland in Arizona; also found in piñon, juniper, and desert scrub.

Habits. Roosts by day and night in caves, mines, and buildings; night roosts are distinct from day roosts. During summer, groups are divided by sex, and maternity colonies may contain 200–300 individuals. Northern populations migrate south; their destination is unknown (the specimen from Chiapas was caught in February and could have been a migrant). Activity begins soon after sunset, with greatest activity about an hour later. Food consists mainly of beetles, which may be gleaned from vegetation. Flight is slow and highly maneuverable. Captures are usually from nets set at roost entrances or over water. In New Mexico, single young are born in late June and early July. Biology reviewed by O'Farrell and Studier (1980).

SOUTHWESTERN MYOTIS
Myotis auriculus   Map 128

HB 46–54, T 39–49, HF 8–11, E 18–21, FA 36–40, Wt 4–6 g.

Description. Medium sized. Upperparts yellowish brown; underparts cream; base of hairs blackish. Fur 8–10 mm long, slightly woolly. Facial skin and base of ears pink; tips of ears brown. *Ears and tragus long.* Tail membrane naked below level of knee; membranes brown. **Similar Species.** Long ears and relatively large size distinguish it from all but *M. thysanodes*, which has black ears and a fringed tail membrane.

Distribution. Arizona and New Mexico, USA, to Jalisco, W Mexico; Nuevo León to Veracruz, E Mexico; and S Guatemala (Hoffmann et al., 1987). Lowlands to 2200 m.

Status and Habitat. Known in Guatemala from one specimen taken in wet pine–oak forest at 1800 m. Fairly common farther north in a variety of habitats including desert scrub, dry forest, and ponderosa pines.

Habits. Day roosts have not been reported; night roosts include buildings, mines, and caves (Barbour and Davis, 1969). Activity usually begins 1–2 hours after sunset, later than most myotis bats. Food consists mainly of moths gleaned from tree trunks or walls of buildings. Echolocation calls are short and of low intensity, with maximum energy at 60 kHz. In Arizona, single young are born in late June or July. Biology reviewed by Warner (1982).

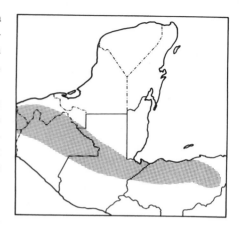

Map 129. Eastern Pipistrelle, *Pipistrellus subflavus*

EASTERN PIPISTRELLE Plate 14
Pipistrellus subflavus Map 129

HB 40–55, T 34–44, HF 7–10, E 11–14, FA 31–35, Wt 3–7 g.

Description. Very small. Upperparts dark brown, peppered with long, yellowish hairs; underparts brown, tips of hairs buffy (color different from subspecies in United States). Fur long and shaggy. *Tragus rather broad, tip rounded. Tail membrane sparsely covered with yellowish hair from base to below level of knee*; membranes blackish. **Similar Species.** Other small, plain-nosed bats (*Rhogeessa, Myotis*) have a narrow tragus with a pointed tip. See introduction to plain-nosed bats for other differences between genera.

Distribution. SE Canada and E United States to Guatemala and E Honduras (McCarthy et al., 1993). Lowlands to 2600 m.

Status and Habitat. Rare and local in SE Mexico and Central America; known from a few specimens taken in or near lowland, evergreen forest. In the United States and Canada, it is locally common at forest edge and in clearings.

Habits. Roosts singly or in small groups in foliage and in relatively exposed situations in buildings. Northern populations hibernate in caves. Activity begins early; it typically forages over water or at treetop level of forest edge, with a slow, erratic flight. Individuals may repeatedly patrol a limited area for small, flying beetles, bugs, ants, flies, or moths. Life span in the United States is up to 15 years. Biology reviewed by Fujita and Kunz (1984).

BIG BROWN BAT Plate 15
Eptesicus fuscus Map 130

HB 63–75, T 40–52, HF 9–16, E 12–19, FA 46–52, Wt 10–17 g.

Description. Relatively large. Upperparts *orange-brown, yellowish, or brown*, underparts orangish or buffy; base of hairs black. Fur long (8–10 mm) and glossy. Ears triangular, tragus curved forward. *Facial skin, ears, and membranes black*. Sides of muzzle appear slightly inflated. Tail extends to tip of long tail membrane. **Similar Species.** Most brownish, plain-nosed bats are smaller. See *E. brasiliensis* and Van Gelder's Bat (*Bauerus dubiaquercus*).

Distribution. Alberta and Ontario, Canada, through Mexico and Central America to Colombia and Venezuela; Greater Antilles; Bahamas; Dominica and Barbados. Lowlands to 2700 m.

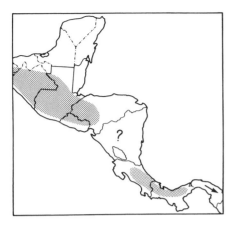

Map 130. Big Brown Bat, *Eptesicus fuscus*

Status and Habitat. Rare and local in SE Mexico and Central America, primarily at higher elevations; in forest gaps, plantations, and cleared areas. Common and widespread in Canada and the United States.

Habits. Roosts in buildings in the United States and in hollow trees and caves in tropical regions (Handley, 1966; Jones, 1966). Northern populations hibernate during the coldest winter months and do not migrate. Activity begins about 30 minutes after sunset; flight is direct, with sallies after insects. Open areas with scattered trees are favored, and 2–3 individuals may forage together. Beetles, ants, flies, and other insects are captured in flight. Echolocation calls have maximum intensity at 30–35 kHz, and audible chatters are often given in flight. Females give birth to 1–2 young, which are left at the roost while foraging. Mothers recognize their own young and will retrieve them if they fall to the floor of the roost (Barbour and Davis, 1969).

ANDEAN BROWN BAT Plate 15
Eptesicus brasiliensis Map 131

HB 52–72, T 35–46, HF 9–12, E 12–17, FA 39–48, Wt 7–14 g.

Description. Medium sized. Upperparts dark orange-brown to *blackish*; underparts orangish or buffy-brown; base of hairs black. Fur long (7–9 mm) and silky. Ears triangular; tragus usually held curved forward. *Facial skin pinkish brown*, membranes black. Sides of muzzle slightly inflated. Tail long, extends to tip of tail membrane. **Similar Species.** *E. fuscus* averages much larger, with paler fur and blackish facial skin. See *E. furinalis*. For comparisons with myotis bats (e.g., similar-sized *M. oxyotus*) see introduction to plain-nosed bats.

Distribution. San Luis Potosí to Chiapas, Mexico; Costa Rica to N Argentina and Uruguay; Trinidad and Tobago. Lowlands to 3000 m (usually above 1000 m).

Status and Habitat. Uncommon; found in evergreen forest and forest edge.

Habits. Roosts in houses and hollow trees. It is sometimes caught in mist nets set over streams in cloud forest. Activity begins about 30 minutes to 1 hour after sunset. Individuals may be seen foraging around lights, flying at heights of 5–7 m above ground and repeatedly patrolling a circular path.

Comment. The subspecies in the region, *E. b. andinus*, is sometimes treated as a distinct

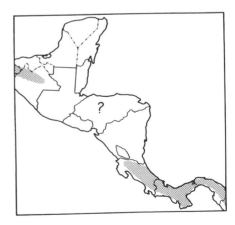

Map 131. Andean Brown Bat, *Eptesicus brasiliensis*

species (but see Jones et al., 1988, and Koopman, 1993).

ARGENTINE BROWN BAT
Eptesicus furinalis

Plate 15
Map 132

HB 48–64, T 29–43, HF 7–9, E 11–15, FA 37–41, Wt 4–8 g.

Description. Small. Upperparts *blackish or dark brown*, tips of hairs sometimes frosted buffy; underparts buffy gray; base of hairs black. Fur medium length (5–6 mm). Ears triangular, dark brown. Tragus sometimes held curved forward; narrow but not greatly tapered. Muzzle slightly inflated; facial skin pinkish brown. Membranes blackish; tail membrane naked. **Similar Species.** Easily confused with similar-sized myotis bats (*M. nigricans, M. albescens*). *Myotis* spp. have a narrower, tapered tragus and less inflated muzzle, but are best distinguished by teeth, which in *Myotis* show a gap (occupied by 1–2 tiny premolar teeth) between the large upper canine and the next large tooth (third premolar); in *Eptesicus* there is no gap, as the large canine is adjacent to another large tooth. *E. brasiliensis* is larger and longer-haired (usually at higher elevations).

Distribution. Jalisco and San Luis Potosí, Mexico, through Central America to N Argentina. Lowlands to 1800 m (usually below 500 m).

Status and Habitat. Uncommon to locally common and widespread in deciduous and evergreen forest and partially cleared areas.

Habits. Roosts in caves, buildings, and hollow trees. An unusually large group of about 100,000 was found roosting in a Mexican cave (Villa-R., 1966). Smaller roosts in buildings (behind shutters and in walls or floors) have been noted in Belize (McCarthy, 1987b). Activity begins early, soon after sunset. It is sometimes caught in mist nets set over water, near

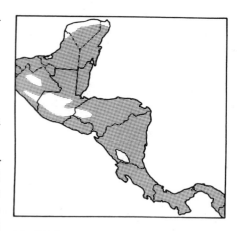

Map 132. Argentine Brown Bat, *Eptesicus furinalis*

cave entrances, or in forest clearings. During the breeding season in Belize, roosting groups form harems, with the harem male roosting apart from the female cluster. The male marks the roost site and his females with his chin. Females give birth to twins in late May. Some females breed again in July–August and have one young at that time (McCarthy, 1980).

MEXICAN LONG-EARED BAT
Plecotus mexicanus

Plate 15
Map 133

HB 38–62, T 40–50, HF 9–12, E 28–36, FA 40–45, Wt 5–10 g.

Description. Medium sized with *huge ears.* Upperparts gray or gray-brown; underparts slightly paler. Fur long and woolly. Enormous ears are translucent gray-brown; tragus very long and narrow. Two large lumps on upper surface of snout. Tail long, extends to tip of long tail membrane; membranes pale brown. **Similar Species.** No other plain-nosed bat in SE Mexico has such large ears.

Distribution. N Sonora and N Coahuila to Veracruz; Yucatán State and Cozumel Island, Mexico. Lowlands to 3200 m (usually above 1500 m outside Yucatán).

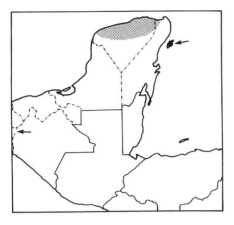

Map 133. Mexican Long-eared Bat, *Plecotus mexicanus*

Status and Habitat. Rare in SE Mexico, known from few specimens collected in dry, lowland areas. Elsewhere uncommon to locally common in highland pine–oak forest.

Habits. Roosts in caves and mine tunnels. Individuals hang well apart from one another, clinging to vertical surfaces with feet and thumbs, ears coiled back, and tail curled under to cover the lower belly. Numbers present in caves may vary throughout the year, and hibernating groups have been found in deep caves. Most southern and lowland records were obtained in the winter and may be due to seasonal migrations from cold, highland regions (Hall and Dalquest, 1963; Koopman, 1974). Diet probably consists of small, flying insects. Single young are born in May or June. Biology reviewed by Tumlinson (1992).

CENTRAL AMERICAN
YELLOW BAT   Plate 14
Rhogeessa tumida   Map 134

HB 37–50, T 27–33, HF 5–8, E 11–14, FA 27–31, Wt 3–5 g.

Description. Tiny. Upperparts *yellowish brown, hairs yellow at base, tipped brown;* underparts pale yellow or cream. Fur rather short

and smooth. Face and ears dark brown or black; tragus long and narrow, tip pointed. Prominent glands on ears (shiny, swollen areas on the outer surface of the ears above the crown of the head) most pronounced in males during breeding season. Tail membrane naked, tail extends to tip of membrane; membranes blackish. **Similar Species.** Sometimes recognizable by small size; no other tiny, plain-nosed bats have fur on back paler at base than at tip.

Distribution. Tamaulipas, Mexico, through Central America (see Comment) except high mountains, to Ecuador, Bolivia, and NE Brazil; Trinidad and Tobago. Lowlands to 1500 m.

Status and Habitat. Uncommon to locally common in a variety of habitats, including evergreen and deciduous forest, open areas, and villages. It appears to favor slightly disturbed, deciduous forest.

Habits. Roosts in buildings and hollow trees. This is one of the first bats to appear at sunset, often flying low to the ground along wide trails or roads. There are 2 peaks of activity, for an hour after sunset and within an hour of dawn. It feeds on small flying insects. Echolocation calls are short, with maximum energy at 50–60 kHz. In Belize, synchronized births

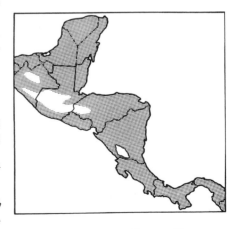

Map 134. Central American Yellow Bats, *Rhogeessa* spp.

occur once a year early in the rainy season, and litter size is usually 2 (McCarthy, 1980).

Comment. Other species of *Rhogeessa* occur in SE Mexico that are almost indistinguishable from *R. tumida* (Baker et al., 1985). *Rhogeessa genowaysi*, separated only by chromosomal differences, occurs on the Pacific Slope of Chiapas, Mexico, where it was found with *R. tumida* (Baker, 1984). *R. aeneus* is slightly smaller than *R. tumida*; it occupies the Yucatán Peninsula, N Belize, and NW Guatemala and does not appear to overlap in range with *R. tumida* (Audet et al., 1993).

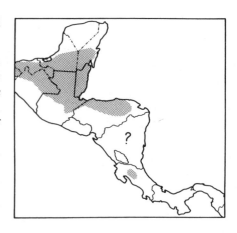

Map 135. Van Gelder's Bat, *Bauerus dubiaquercus*

VAN GELDER'S BAT

Bauerus dubiaquercus

Plate 15

Map 135

HB 55–78, T 43–57, HF 12–14, E 20–27, FA 49–56, Wt 10–24 g.

Description. Relatively large. Upperparts yellowish brown; underparts buffy or dull yellow; base of hairs dark brown. Fur fairly long (7–9 mm), dull, and slightly woolly. *Ears long*, extending beyond nose when laid forward; tragus long and narrow. *Muzzle blunt; openings of nostrils face forward*, piglike. Membranes blackish, tail membrane extensive and hairless, wings relatively short and broad. **Similar Species.** Big Brown Bat (*Eptesicus fuscus*) is about the same size and color, but has a tapered muzzle with nostrils opening to the sides, shorter ears, and glossy fur.

Distribution. Known distribution is patchy: Tres Marías Islands; Jalisco; Guerrero (Juárez-G. et al., 1988); Veracruz, Mexico, to E Honduras; Costa Rica (Dinerstein, 1985). Lowlands to 2300 m (usually below 1300 m).

Status and Habitat. Apparently uncommon and local (seldom caught in nets) in a variety of forested habitats from lowland deciduous to montane pine–oak and cloud forest.

Habits. One individual was caught in a building, but most records are from captures in mist nets, and little is known of the roosting habits of this species. It is active within an hour of sunset and flies low to the ground along forest trails. Large ears and short, broad wings suggest that this bat may feed by gleaning insects from the ground or vegetation. In captivity, it readily consumes large insects such as cockroaches and katydids. Biology reviewed by Engstrom et al. (1987).

Comment. Formerly in the genus *Antrozous* (Engstrom and Wilson, 1981; but also see Koopman, 1993).

WESTERN RED BAT

Lasiurus blossevillii

Plate 15

Map 136

HB 49–65, T 37–54, HF 7–10, E 8–13, FA 38–42, Wt 7–12 g.

Description. Small. Upperparts *bright orange-red*; hairs black at base, with a cream midsection and red toward the tip, sometimes with extreme tips frosted whitish; underparts buffy yellow or orange-brown, brightest on throat; *white patches on shoulders* at attachment point of wings. Fur long and thick. Ears short and rounded. Facial skin and ears pinkish. *Upper surface of long tail membrane thickly covered with reddish fur almost to tip of tail.* Mem-

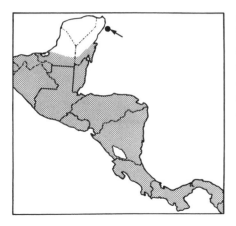

Map 136. Western Red Bat, *Lasiurus blossevillii*

branes brownish, with paler bands around fingers. Cream-colored patches of fur at base of thumb and on wrist. **Similar Species.** *L. egregius* is much larger, with longer ears, orange-red underparts, and no white patches on shoulders or thumbs; *L. castaneus* has deep-red fur on the back, blackish ears, and brown underparts.

Distribution. S British Columbia, Canada, and W United States through Mexico and Central America to Argentina and Chile. Lowlands to 2500 m.

Status and Habitat. Poorly known in Central America and SE Mexico, from few records obtained in a variety of habitats. Found in forested and disturbed habitats in both wet and dry regions.

Habits. Poorly known, probably similar to Eastern Red Bat (*L. borealis*), described here. Roosts singly in foliage of broadleaf trees, often along edges of fields or near urban areas. Roost sites are open below, with dense shade and cover above and on the sides. Roosts are usually located on the south side of the tree, 1–5 m above ground. Northern populations migrate southward in fall and may travel in groups. At low temperatures, individuals become torpid and probably hibernate for ex-

tended periods in S United States. Foraging begins 1–2 hours after sunset; activity is often concentrated around street lamps. Moths, flies, and some ground-dwelling insects are eaten. It is a fast, high-flying species that is seldom caught in mist nets, except when nets are set over water and the bat descends to drink. Mating apparently takes place in flight; litter size is 1-5, usually 3. This bat and other *Lasiurus* spp. are unusual in having 4 nipples, enabling females to raise rather large litters. Biology of *L. borealis* reviewed by Shump and Shump (1982a); see also Barbour and Davis (1969).

Comment. Genetic studies by Baker et al. (1988b) and Morales and Bickham (1995) indicate that the red bats (all formerly known as *Lasiurus borealis*) are a composite of at least 2 species, with *L. borealis* limited to E-C United States and Canada, and NE Mexico. All other mainland populations are included in *L. blossevillii*; Antillean populations may represent a third species (but see Koopman, 1993).

TACARCUNA BAT   Plate 15
Lasiurus castaneus   Map 137

HB 59–61, T 47–52, HF 10, E 14–17, FA 43–46, Wt 10–17 g.

Description. Medium sized. Upperparts *deep mahogany-red*, darkest on tail membrane; underparts dark brown frosted with buffy yellow; whitish patches on shoulders at attachment point of wings. Fur long and thick. Ears short and rounded; ears and facial skin blackish. Tail membrane thickly furred for about 2/3 of tail length. Membranes black. **Similar Species.** See *L. blossevillii*.

Distribution. Costa Rica (Dinerstein, 1985) to E Panama. Lowlands to 1500 m.

Status and Habitat. Rare; known from very few specimens found in evergreen forest.

Habits. Poorly known. It has been caught in mist nets set over streams through tall, lowland

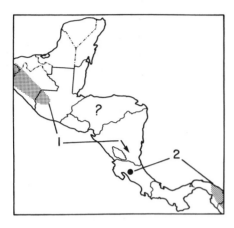

Map 137. 1. Hoary Bat, *Lasiurus cinereus*
2. Tacarcuna Bat, *Lasiurus castaneus*

evergreen forest in Panama and in nets across a trail through elfin forest on an exposed ridge of the Continental Divide in Costa Rica.

HOARY BAT
Lasiurus cinereus

Plate 15
Map 137

HB 71–90, T 46–62, HF 9–13, E 15–19, FA 50–57, Wt 19–26 g.

Description. Relatively large and distinctively colored. Upperparts and belly gray-brown with *contrasting white frosting* on tips of hair, yellowish band around face and throat. Tufts of whitish fur at base of thumbs and on wrists. Fur long and thick. Ears short and rounded, lined with yellow fur; facial skin and edges of ears black. *Upper surface of tail membrane thickly furred like the back for its entire length.* Fingers, forearms, and adjoining portions of wing membranes yellowish pink, remainder of membrane black, creating a scalloped pattern. **Similar Species.** No other hairy-tailed bat is gray with white frosting.

Distribution. Hudson Bay, Canada, through United States and Mexico to Guatemala; Colombia and Venezuela to Chile and Argentina; Hawaii; many islands in the Caribbean, Atlantic, and Pacific oceans. Lowlands to 4400 m.

Status and Habitat. Rare winter visitor in Central America, known only from 2 localities in the highland pine–oak zone of Guatemala. Widespread, sometimes fairly common, in a variety of forested and open habitats in the United States.

Habits. Roosts singly 3–5 m above ground on leafy branches of spruces, pines, and deciduous trees, resembling a piece of lichen-covered bark. This camouflage is effective, and the bat is difficult to detect when roosting. Long migrations take place in spring and fall; large numbers may appear in certain areas during this time. Activity usually begins well after sunset, and flight is swift and direct. Forest edges and clearings are favored foraging areas, where it preys on moths, beetles, other large flying insects and, occasionally, small bats. Individual foraging territories are maintained by aggressive chases and audible calls. Echolocation calls consist of loud, long, low-frequency pulses (maximum energy about 28 kHz), suitable for long-range prey detection. The calls can be used in identification and ecological studies of this bat (Belwood and Fullard, 1984). When captured in a mist net, it makes a forceful, "popping" alarm call or a nasal hiss and can be aggressive to handle. Litter size is 1–4, usually 2, and young are born from May–July in the United States. Biology reviewed by Shump and Shump (1982b).

BIG RED BAT
Lasiurus egregius

Plate 15
Map 138

HB 70, T 60, HF 12, E 20, FA 50, Wt 20 g.

Description. Fairly large and strikingly colored. Upperparts *bright orange-red, darkest on tail membrane*; hair banded, with cream midsection conspicuous on head and neck; *underparts bright orange.* Fur long and soft. Ears relatively long and narrow; facial skin and ears pinkish. Upper surface of tail membrane thickly haired at the base for 1/2 its length, then naked. **Similar Species.** This distinctive bat is similar to *L. blossevillii* in color (but much larger); in size, ear shape, extent of hair on tail membrane and lack of white tufts on wrists, it resembles the yellow bats (*L. intermedius* and *L. ega*).

Distribution. Known from single localities in E Panama, French Guiana, and S Brazil. Lowlands only.

Status and Habitat. Rare; known from 3 specimens.

Habits. Poorly known. Caught in a mist net set across a stream through tall evergreen forest in Panama.

NORTHERN YELLOW BAT
Lasiurus intermedius

Plate 15
Map 138

HB 60–89, T 47–64, HF 11–13, E 17–20, FA 48–58, Wt 17–28 g.

Description. Very similar to *L. ega*, differing only in larger size. **Similar Species.** See *L. ega* for comparisons with other yellowish bats.

Distribution. E United States, E and W coasts of Mexico to SE Honduras and NW El Salvador (Hellebuyck et al., 1985). Lowlands to 1600 m.

Status and Habitat. Uncommon to locally common in coniferous and broadleaf forest and dry thorn scrub.

Habits. Roosts in Spanish moss in SE United States, and under dead palm leaves or dry corn stalks in Mexico. This species appears to be more social than other *Lasiurus* spp. and may form nursery colonies. It usually forages 3–4 m above ground over open, grassy areas, and 100 or more bats may aggregate when feeding (Barbour and Davis, 1969). Northern populations reproduce in May–June, and litter size is 2–4. Biology reviewed by Webster et al. (1980).

SOUTHERN YELLOW BAT
Lasiurus ega

Plate 15
Map 139

HB 62–75, T 40–53, HF 8–11, E 14–19, FA 43–47, Wt 7–15 g.

Description. Medium sized. *Upperparts dull yellow* or buffy gray; fur bright yellow or pale orange on tail membrane; underparts cream or pale yellow. Fur long and thick. Face and ears pinkish, length of ears greater than width. Tail extends to tip of long tail membrane; *tail membrane thickly haired at the base for about half its length.* **Similar Species.** *L. intermedius* is al-

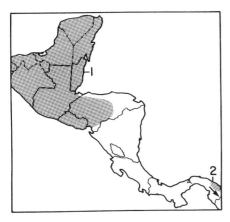

Map 138. 1. Northern Yellow Bat, *Lasiurus intermedius* 2. Big Red Bat, *Lasiurus egregius*

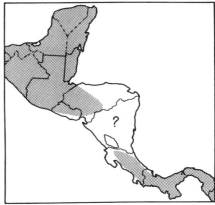

Map 139. Southern Yellow Bat, *Lasiurus ega*

161

most identical but larger. Shaggy Bat (*Centronycteris maximiliani*) has tail much shorter than tail membrane and sickle-shaped ears.

Distribution. S Texas, USA, and E Mexico through Central America (except Nicaragua) to Argentina and Uruguay; Trinidad. Lowlands to 1500 m (Dinerstein, 1985).

Status and Habitat. Uncommon but widespread in a variety of habitats from lowland desert scrub to evergreen forest.

Habits. Roosts in broadleaf trees and hibernates under dead palm fronds in the United States. Possibly migratory in parts of its range. Most records in Mexico and Central America are from mist-net captures over swimming pools or other large bodies of water.

Comment. Chromosomal and genetic studies (Baker et al., 1988b; Morales and Bickham, 1995) indicate that *Lasiurus xanthinus*, formerly a subspecies of *L. ega*, is a distinct species. *L. xanthinus* is found in the SW United States, W Mexico, and the Mexican Plateau.

FREE-TAILED BATS
Family Molossidae

The Molossidae consists of about 13 genera and 86 or more species, distributed worldwide. Relationships between species and genera are not well understood for several New World groups. The family and certain genera were revised by Eger (1977), Freeman (1981), and Dolan (1989). In these accounts, I follow Koopman (1993), who incorporated some, but not all, of the revisions proposed by these authors.

Molossids in Central America can be recognized by the stout, long tail, which is enclosed in a short tail membrane for about half its length, the remainder projecting freely. For all other bats in the region in which the tail tip projects beyond or above the tail membrane, the enclosed portion is much longer than the free portion. Free-tailed bats have velvety fur, rather flat heads and bodies, stocky limbs, leathery membranes, and very narrow wings (the long bone of the fifth finger is about half the length of the forearm, whereas in leaf-nosed bats it is about the same length). The broad ears point forward and outward and often meet over the head. At the base of the ear there is a blunt fold of skin called the antitragus. The tragus is very small and usually concealed by the ear and antitragus. There are no flaps or folds of skin around the nose. The sides of the stout toes are fringed with hair, and long, curved hairs project beyond the claws. The lower margin of the forearm is usually furred. Some species have long, fine bristles on the rump, and there may be some short hairs along the edge of the calcar. Males are larger than females in most species and have well-developed throat (gular) glands that secrete a musky oil. The coloration of these bats changes after specimen preparation, probably as a result of the glandular secretions, and most species are paler in life than when preserved as dried study skins.

Free-tailed bats occur in a variety of habitats, usually at lower elevations. Many species roost in buildings, crawling into crevices under roofs or into attics. Several species are common occupants of houses and old buildings. Tree holes, caves, and bridges are also used. These bats usually cluster in large groups crowded into small spaces and are adept at scurrying forward or backward, using sensory hairs on the feet and rump for guidance. Most rest in a horizontal position. They leave the roost at dusk to forage for flying insects with a very fast, erratic flight, similar to that of swifts. Most free-tails require a roost from which they can drop some distance before gaining lift. This is due to the long, very narrow wings that enable these bats to fly at great speed but limit their ability to take flight from a sitting position. In addition, their maneuverability in a cluttered environment is reduced. In forested regions, they typically fly above the canopy. These bats feed on insects caught in flight, usually several meters above ground. As a result of their high flight, free-tailed bats are rarely captured in mist nets set at ground level. They descend to drink from large, unobstructed bodies of water and can sometimes be netted in such situations. Most species appear to be rare or patchily distributed in Central America, but this is probably a consequence of few studies of these bats rather than actual rarity.

Identification of species of free-tails can be difficult, and some genera are easily confused. The following outline gives important characteristics of the genera:

Molossops. Small. Ears small and *not joined over crown of head.* Antitragus square. Snout broad and flat, not steeply ridged. Lips not wrinkled. Dental formula: i 1/1 or 1/2, c 1/1, p 1/2, m 3/3.

Tadarida. Medium sized. Ears fairly large, joined over crown, *do not extend beyond nose when laid forward.* Antitragus low and broad, top rounded. Snout rather broad, not steeply ridged. *Short, thick, black bristles on snout. Lips deeply creased and wrinkled.* Dental formula: i 1/3, c 1/1, p 2/2, m 3/3.

Nyctinomops. Medium sized. Ears large, joined over crown, *extend slightly beyond nose when laid forward.* Antitragus same height as width, top rounded. Snout rather broad, not steeply ridged. *No thick bristles on snout. Lips deeply creased and wrinkled.* Dental formula: i 1/2, c 1/1, p 2/2, m 3/3.

Eumops. Medium sized to very large. *Ears large,* joined over crown, extend almost to or slightly beyond nose when laid forward. Antitragus low and broad, roughly semicircular. *Snout broad and flat,* not steeply ridged. Nostrils widely spaced, surrounded by hard pads. Lips not deeply wrinkled. Dental formula: i 1/2, c 1/1, p 2/2, m 3/3.

Promops. Rather large. *Ears medium sized,* joined over crown, do not extend to tip of nose when laid forward. Small crest of hair on crown between ears. Antitragus same height as width, compressed at base, roughly circular. *Snout narrow, steeply ridged.* Nostrils closely spaced. Lips not wrinkled. No bristles on rump. Dental formula: i 1/2, c 1/1, p 1/2, m 3/3.

Molossus. Small to rather large. *Ears medium sized,* joined over crown, do not extend to tip of nose when laid forward. No crest of hair on crown. Antitragus same height as width, compressed at base, roughly circular. *Snout narrow, steeply ridged.* Nostrils closely spaced. Lips not wrinkled. Long, fine bristles on rump. Dental formula: i 1/1, c 1/1, p 1/2, m 3/3.

GREENHALL'S DOG-FACED BAT
Molossops greenhalli

Plate 16
Map 140

HB 55–76, T 25–34, HF 9–12, E 14–17, FA 34–38, Wt 11–29 g.

Description. Small. Upperparts dark brown to blackish; *underparts gray-brown.* Fur short (2–3 mm) and velvety. *Ears short and rounded, not joined* over forehead. Antitragus square-topped. Snout flat and broad, not ridged. Tail

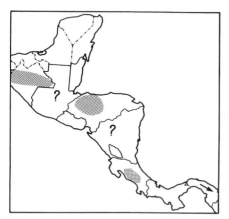

Map 140. Greenhall's Dog-faced Bat, *Molossops greenhalli*

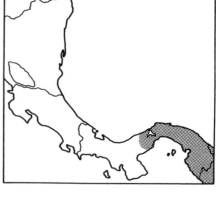

Map 141. Southern Dog-faced Bat, *Molossops planirostris*

length about half head and body length. **Similar Species.** See *M. planirostris*. All other free-tails have ears joined over the forehead.

Distribution. W coast of Mexico from Nayarit to Chiapas, patchily distributed through Central America to NE Brazil and Ecuador; Trinidad. Lowlands to 1500 m.

Status and Habitat. Uncommon; found in deciduous and evergreen forest and clearings, often near water.

Habits. Small groups roost in hollow branches and buildings. Activity begins soon after sunset. Most records are from individuals caught in mist nets set over streams or ponds (Gardner et al., 1970; Valdez and LaVal, 1971).

Comment. Included in the genus *Cynomops* by Freeman (1981); but see Koopman (1993).

SOUTHERN DOG-FACED BAT
Molossops planirostris

Plate 16
Map 141

HB 50–66, T 22–30, HF 5–10, E 13–17, FA 31–36, Wt 10–17 g.

Description. Small. Upperparts reddish brown to dark brown; *underparts white on neck and midline of belly*, gray-brown on sides of belly.

Fur short (2–3 mm) and velvety. Ears short and separated. Snout flat and broad, without a median ridge. Tail about half head and body length. **Similar Species.** This is the smallest free-tail in Central America. *M. greenhalli* is larger, with entirely gray-brown underparts.

Distribution. C Panama to Peru and N Argentina. Lowlands to 700 m.

Status and Habitat. Uncommon and poorly known in Panama; in South America it occurs in deciduous and evergreen forest, savannah, and swamps.

Habits. Roosts in houses, rotting snags, fence posts, and hollow trees. Group size is usually small (1–8) but may number several hundred. This bat appears to prefer wet areas and may forage over water (Handley, 1976).

Comment. Includes *M. paranus*. Included in the genus *Cynomops* by Freeman (1981); but see Koopman (1993).

BRAZILIAN FREE-TAILED BAT
Tadarida brasiliensis

Plate 16
Map 142

HB 52–62, T 30–39, HF 9–11, E 15–19, FA 41–45, Wt 8–13 g.

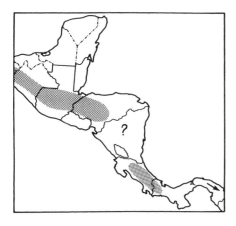

Map 142. Brazilian Free-tailed Bat, *Tadarida brasiliensis*

Description. Medium sized. Upperparts gray, gray-brown, or dark brown to base of hair (occasionally orangish); underparts paler, tips of hair frosted whitish. Fur short (3–4 mm) and velvety. *Ears moderately large but not extending beyond nose when laid forward*; ears meet over forehead, edges marked with small warts from forehead to tip. Antitragus low, width greater than height; tragus visible. Snout not steeply ridged; short, stiff, black bristles on upper surface. *Upper lips conspicuously grooved and wrinkled.* Tail length more than half head and body length; a few short hairs along edge of calcar. **Similar Species.** Most molossids have smooth upper lips. Broad-eared Bat (*Nyctinomops laticaudatus*) also has wrinkled upper lips but has larger ears, no stiff black bristles on nose, no hair on calcar, and the second long bone of fourth finger measures 3–4 mm (about 10 mm in *Tadarida*). See Dwarf Bonneted Bat (*Eumops bonariensis*).

Distribution. Oregon and S Carolina, USA, through Mexico (except Yucatán Peninsula) and patchily through Central and South America to Argentina and Chile; Greater and Lesser Antilles. Lowlands to about 3000 m (usually above 1200 m in Central America).

Status and Habitat. Uncommon to locally common in dry, open areas, thorn scrub, mountains, and populated regions. Not found in undisturbed forest.

Habits. Roosts in caves, buildings, under bridges, and in mine tunnels. Groups are usually large and may number several million. Partial segregation of sexes occurs at the roost; the largest aggregations are maternity colonies of females and their young, with a few males present. Northern populations migrate south to Mexico. Separate night roosts are sometimes used: a group of about 50 roosted at night under a bridge in a dry valley in Guatemala, but abandoned this site before dawn. This bat is well known in the United States for the spectacular sunset emergences of thousands of individuals from a large roost. Each bat flies considerable distances to feed, mainly on small moths. Echolocation calls have greatest intensity at about 35 kHz. In Texas, females give birth to single young in June. Females leave the young at the roost and are able to recognize their own offspring among several thousand when they return from foraging. Biology reviewed by Wilkins (1989).

BROAD-EARED BAT   Plate 16
Nyctinomops laticaudatus   Map 143

HB 50–64, T 35–48, HF 10–12, E 19–21, FA 41–45, Wt 9–16 g.

Description. Medium sized. Upperparts dark reddish brown or grayish, extreme base of hairs white; underparts gray-brown, tips of hairs frosted buff or cream. Fur short (4–5 mm) and velvety. *Ears large, extend beyond nose when laid forward*; ears meet over forehead, edges marked with small warts from forehead to tip. Height of antitragus equal to width, concealing tiny tragus. Snout broad, with no thick, black bristles. *Upper lips conspicuously grooved and wrinkled.* Tail length about 2/3 head and body length; no hairs along edge

165

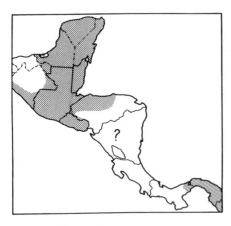

Map 143. Broad-eared Bat, *Nyctinomops laticaudatus*

of calcar. **Similar Species.** See Brazilian Free-tailed Bat (*Tadarida brasiliensis*) and Dwarf Bonneted Bat (*Eumops bonariensis*).

Distribution. Tamaulipas and Guerrero, Mexico, patchily distributed through Central America (present on Yucatán Peninsula, but not recorded in Nicaragua and Costa Rica; McCarthy et al., 1993) to Peru, Paraguay, and SE Brazil; Trinidad; Cuba. Lowlands to 1500 m.

Status and Habitat. Rare to locally common in dry and semideciduous forest, thorn scrub, and open areas.

Habits. Roosts in wall crevices of old buildings, cracks in tree trunks, and among palm leaves. On the Yucatán Peninsula, Maya ruins are favored, and colony size may be 500–1000. The bats are usually visible when roosting and make audible chirps but will retreat backward, deep into narrow crevices, if disturbed. Pregnant females have been recorded in June (Bowles et al., 1990).

Where to See. A large colony can be found in one of the temples at Uxmal, Yucatán, Mexico.

Comment. Previously placed in the genus *Tadarida* (see Freeman, 1981). Two other species, *N. macrotis* and *N. aurispinosus*, occur in S Mexico and in South America but have not yet been recorded in Central America. Both are larger than *N. laticaudatus*.

BLACK BONNETED BAT   Plate 16
Eumops auripendulus   Map 144

HB 75–92, T 43–54, HF 12–18, E 19–25, FA 57–63, Wt 25–35 g.

Description. Large. Upperparts *dark chocolate-brown* to *black*, hair dark to base (whitish at extreme base in some); no long bristles on rump; underparts dark gray-brown. Fur rather long (6–7 mm) and shiny. Ears large, extending to nose when laid forward. *Antitragus roughly semicircular*, width greater than height. Head broad and flat, *with no ridge on the snout*. No hair on edge of calcar. **Similar Species.** Other large bonneted bats, *E. glaucinus* and *E. underwoodi*, are gray-brown with fur white at base and have long bristles on rump. See Black Mastiff Bat (*Molossus ater*).

Distribution. Oaxaca and Tabasco, Mexico, through Central America to Bolivia and N Argentina; Trinidad. Lowlands to 2000 m.

Status and Habitat. Uncommon to rare (known from few records in Central America); occurs in deciduous and semideciduous forest and savannah.

Habits. Roosts in hollow trees, attics, and under corrugated tin roofs. Single young are born in March.

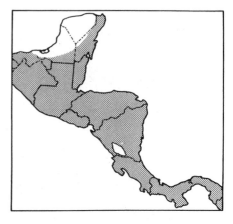

Map 144. Black Bonneted Bat, *Eumops auripendulus*

UNDERWOOD'S BONNETED BAT

Eumops underwoodi

Plate 16
Map 145

HB 85–112, T 50–64, HF 15–20, E 24–33, FA 66–74, Wt 58–59 g.

Description. Very large. Upperparts gray-brown or reddish brown, base of hair white; long bristles (about 15 mm) on rump; underparts pale gray-brown. Fur fairly long (6–8 mm) and soft. Ears large, extending to tip of nose when laid forward. Short hairs on edge of calcar. **Similar Species.** Largest free-tail in Central America. The 2 other large bonneted bats can usually be distinguished by size (males are larger than females in all *Eumops* spp.).

Distribution. SE Arizona, USA, and Sonora, Mexico, to Nicaragua, except Yucatán Peninsula (Dolan and Carter, 1979). Lowlands to 1300 m.

Status and Habitat. Uncommon or rare; usually in dry forest and arid regions, sometimes in semideciduous forest.

Habits. Poorly known. It has been caught in mist nets set over ponds or watering holes in deserts. Echolocation calls are audible to humans and are loud and high-pitched. In Arizona, single young are born in June or July (Barbour and Davis, 1969).

Comment. The largest species in the genus, *E. perotis* (FA 73–80 mm), is known from the United States, N Mexico, and South America, but has not yet been recorded in Central America or SE Mexico.

WAGNER'S BONNETED BAT

Eumops glaucinus

Plate 16
Map 146

HB 75–95, T 40–54, HF 10–15, E 22–29, FA 55–63, Wt 34–42 g.

Description. Large. Upperparts dark gray or gray-brown, base of hair white; long bristles (about 10 mm) on rump; underparts grayish. Fur medium length (5–6 mm) and soft. Ears large, but do not reach tip of nose when laid forward. Snout broad and flat. No hair on edge of calcar. **Similar Species.** See *E. underwoodi* and *E. auripendulus*.

Distribution. Florida, USA; Cuba; Jamaica; Jalisco and Morelos, Mexico, patchily distributed through Central America (not recorded in Guatemala or El Salvador) to SE Brazil and Bolivia. Lowlands to 900 m.

Status and Habitat. Rare to locally common in evergreen and deciduous forest, thorn scrub, towns, and clearings.

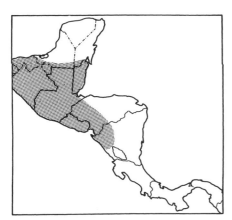

Map 145. Underwood's Bonneted Bat, *Eumops underwoodi*

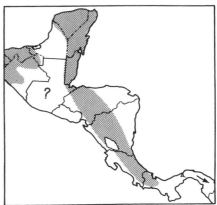

Map 146. Wagner's Bonneted Bat, *Eumops glaucinus*

Habits. Roosts in hollow trees and roofs of buildings. It is occasionally caught in mist nets set over large bodies of water. In a 12-year study in Yucatán State, Mexico, 262 of these bats were caught over a shallow pond in an open area, but only 4 were recorded from waterholes surrounded by vegetation or buildings (Bowles et al., 1990). In Miami, Florida, bats leave the roost after dark and fly at heights of 10 m or more. Echolocation calls are audible, and the loud, piercing calls can be heard above other city sounds (Barbour and Davis, 1969). Young are born in June or July.

SANBORN'S BONNETED BAT Plate 16
Eumops hansae Map 147

HB 61–75, T 24–39, HF 8–12, E 17–23, FA 37–42, Wt 16–21 g.

Description. Medium sized. *Upperparts dark brown or blackish, hair dark to base;* fine bristles (8 mm) on rump; underparts dark gray-brown, slightly paler than upperparts. Fur short (2–3 mm) and velvety. Ears large, extend to tip of nose when laid forward. *Antitragus roughly semicircular,* width greater than height. Head broad and flat, *with no ridge on the snout.* No hair on edge of calcar. **Similar Species.** Superficially similar to Miller's Mastiff Bat (*Molossus pretio-*

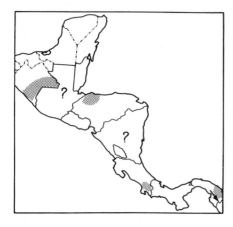

Map 147. Sanborn's Bonneted Bat, *Eumops hansae*

sus), which has a narrow, ridged snout and a square antitragus. *E. bonariensis* is about the same size, but its fur is longer, paler, and whitish at the base.

Distribution. Chiapas, Mexico (Medellín et al., 1992) to NW Honduras (Lee and Bradley, 1992); SW Costa Rica to SE Brazil and N Peru. Lowlands to 1000 m.

Status and Habitat. Rare; recorded in evergreen forest and forest edge.

Habits. Poorly known. One individual was found roosting in a rotting snag in Venezuela (Handley, 1976). Occasionally caught in mist nets set over water.

DWARF BONNETED BAT Plate 16
Eumops bonariensis Map 148

HB 49–68, T 28–47, HF 6–11, E 12–19, FA 39–48, Wt 7–13 g.

Description. Medium sized. Upperparts gray-brown or brown, base of hair pale; underparts gray-brown, tips of hairs frosted. Fur relatively long (5 mm) and soft. Ears large, extend to tip of nose when laid forward. *Antitragus roughly semicircular,* width greater than height. Snout broad and flat. A few shallow, inconspicuous grooves on lips. No bristles on rump; a few short hairs along edge of calcar. **Similar Species.** Easily confused with Brazilian Free-tail (*Tadarida brasiliensis*) and Broad-eared Bat (*Nyctinomops laticaudatus*), which have deeply grooved upper lips and square-topped antitraguses. See *E. hansae.*

Distribution. Veracruz, Mexico, patchily recorded through Central America to Argentina and Bolivia. Lowlands only.

Status and Habitat. Uncommon or rare; found in dry forest and thorn scrub.

Habits. Roosts in tree holes and roofs of houses. A long-term study in Yucatán State, Mexico (Bowles et al., 1990) found this poorly

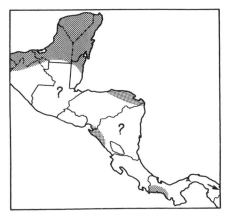

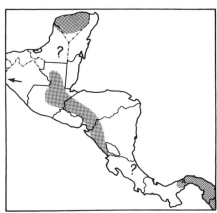

Map 148. Dwarf Bonneted Bat, *Eumops bonariensis*   Map 149. Big Crested Mastiff Bat, *Promops centralis*

known species to be fairly common. A group of about 20 occupied roof tiles of a house near Mérida, with 1–3 bats under single tiles. Almost 200 individuals were captured in mist nets set over natural and artificial bodies of water during the study. An activity peak occurred within 2 hours of sunset and a lesser peak before dawn. The diet includes moths, beetles, and other insects. In Yucatán, a birth peak occurs in late June, and lactation lasts 6–8 weeks.

BIG CRESTED MASTIFF BAT   Plate 16
Promops centralis   Map 149

HB 56–88, T 45–62, HF 10–13, E 14–16, FA 51–57, Wt 18–25 g.

Description. Moderately large. Upperparts *dark brown, reddish brown or blackish*, hair slightly paler at extreme base, but not white; *no bristles on rump*; underparts dark gray-brown. Fur medium length (6–7 mm), thick, and velvety. Thick, long hair starts abruptly at meeting point of ears. Ears short; antitragus large, compressed at base, and roughly circular in shape. Snout narrow and steeply ridged. Tail length more than half head and body length. No hair along edge of calcar; inner edge of forearm thickly furred. **Similar Spe-**

cies. Most similar to *Molossus* spp., which have shorter fur (especially between ears) and long rump bristles.

Distribution. Jalisco and Puebla, Mexico (Jones et al., 1988), patchily distributed through Central America (not reported from Belize, El Salvador, or Costa Rica) to Peru and N Argentina; Trinidad. Lowlands to 1800 m.

Status and Habitat. Uncommon to rare; found in a variety of low to high elevation habitats, including dry, deciduous forest, evergreen and pine–oak forest, towns and clearings.

Habits. Roosts in small groups of 1–6 under palm leaves (Goodwin and Greenhall, 1961); also found under bark, in tree hollows, and under roof tiles. Although most records are of solitary animals or small groups, Bowles et al. (1990) caught 59 individuals over a shallow, artificial pond near Mérida, Yucatán. These bats did not exhibit a peak activity period. A birth peak occurred in June in this population.

BLACK MASTIFF BAT   Plate 16
Molossus ater (= *rufus*)   Map 150

HB 71–98, T 38–54, HF 10–15, E 16–19, FA 47–54, Wt 28–37 g.

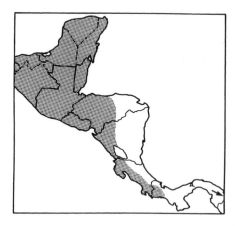

Map 150. Black Mastiff Bat, *Molossus ater*

Colonies number 30–50 or more and are the common larger "house bat" in some areas. The bats are active in the roost shortly before dusk, squeaking and scurrying over the walls and floor. The diet includes ground beetles and flying ants. Pregnant females have been recorded from March to June in Yucatán, Mexico (Bowles et al., 1990).

MILLER'S MASTIFF BAT   Plate 16
Molossus pretiosus   Map 151

HB 65–78, T 38–46, HF 9–12, E 14–17, FA 42–47, Wt 14–22 g.

Description. Medium sized (males larger than females). *Upperparts reddish brown, dark brown, or black to base of hair;* rump bristles 8–9 mm long; underparts dark gray-brown. Fur short (2–3 mm) and velvety. Ears short, do not extend to nose if laid forward, meet over crown. Antitragus compressed at the base, roughly circular in shape. Snout narrow, steeply ridged. Tail length slightly more than half head and body length. No hair on edge of calcar. **Similar Species.** This species is a small version of *M. ater* (forearm measurements are usually diagnostic, taking into account the size difference between the sexes of 1–2 mm). See *M. sinaloae.*

Description. Fairly large (males larger than females). *Upperparts black, dark chocolate-brown, or deep orange, hair uniformly colored to base; fine bristles (8–9 mm) on rump;* underparts slightly paler than upperparts, dark gray-brown. Fur short (2–4 mm) and velvety. Facial skin, ears, and membranes black. Ears short, do not extend to nose if laid forward, meet over crown. Antitragus compressed at the base, roughly circular in shape. Snout narrow, tapered, and steeply ridged. Tail length about half head and body length. No hair on edge of calcar. **Similar Species.** Averages much larger than other *Molossus* spp. and has blacker facial skin and membranes; *M. sinaloae* has fur white at base. See Black Bonneted Bat (*Eumops auripendulus*) and Big Crested Mastiff Bat (*Promops centralis*).

Distribution. Tamaulipas and Sinaloa, Mexico, through Central America, mainly on the Pacific Slope, to Peru and N Argentina; also Trinidad. Lowlands to 1500 m.

Status and Habitat. Locally common in deciduous and evergreen forest, thorn scrub, towns, and rural areas.

Habits. Roosts under corrugated roofs or attics of houses, in woodpecker holes in coconut palms, hollow logs and trees, and rock crevices.

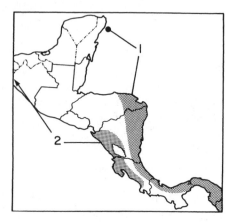

Map 151. 1. Bonda Mastiff Bat, *Molossus bondae* 2. Miller's Mastiff Bat, *Molossus pretiosus*

Distribution. Guerrero and Oaxaca, Mexico; W Nicaragua and W Costa Rica; also Colombia, Venezuela, and Guyana. Lowlands only.

Status and Habitat. Apparently uncommon; found in dry and semideciduous forest.

Habits. Roosts in caves, buildings, and hollow trees (Marinkelle and Cadena, 1972). LaVal (1977) noted a large group flying from riparian forest at dusk. The bats appeared in single file, flying about 20 m above ground. Pregnant females have been recorded in May, June, and October in Costa Rica.

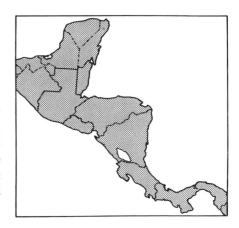

Map 152. Sinaloan Mastiff Bat, *Molossus sinaloae*

SINALOAN MASTIFF BAT   Plate 16
Molossus sinaloae   Map 152

HB 69–85, T 41–52, HF 10–13, E 13–17, FA 45–52, Wt 14–28 g.

Description. Medium sized. Upperparts black, dark brown, or reddish brown, *base of hair white*; rump bristles 11–12 mm long; underparts gray-brown. Fur short (3–5 mm) and velvety. Ears short, do not extend to nose if laid forward, meet over crown. Antitragus compressed at the base, roughly circular in shape. Snout narrow, steeply ridged. Tail length slightly more than half head and body length. No hair on edge of calcar. **Similar Species.** *M. pretiosus* is similar in size, but it has hair dark to the base and has shorter bristles on the rump. See *M. ater.*

Distribution. W Mexico from Jalisco to Chiapas, Yucatán Peninsula and Central America to Colombia and Surinam; Trinidad. Lowlands to 2400 m (usually below 1000 m).

Status and Habitat. Uncommon to locally common in evergreen and dry deciduous forest, pasture, and populated areas.

Habits. Roosts in caves and houses, often in large groups. In Costa Rica, 76 were captured from a single roost (Timm et al., 1989). A long-term study in Yucatán, Mexico, found this species to be the most commonly encountered molossid in the region (Bowles et al., 1990). Individuals are most active during the first 2 hours after sunset and again before dawn. The diet consists mainly of moths, with some beetles and other insects taken. In Yucatán, pregnant females have been recorded from March to June.

BONDA MASTIFF BAT   Plate 16
Molossus bondae   Map 151

HB 65–75, T 34–44, HF 9–13, E 13–16, FA 38–43, Wt 16–21 g.

Description. Small. Upperparts bright orange, dark brown, or black, slightly paler but *not white at base of hair*; longest rump bristles 5–6 mm; underparts slightly paler than upperparts. Fur short (2–3 mm) and velvety. Ears short, do not extend to nose if laid forward, meet over crown. Antitragus compressed at the base, roughly circular in shape. Snout narrow, steeply ridged. Tail length slightly more than half head and body length. No hair on edge of calcar. **Similar Species.** *M. pretiosus* averages larger, with much longer bristles on rump. See *M. molossus.*

Distribution. Cozumel Island, Mexico; Caribbean Slope of Central America from NE

Honduras to E Panama, south to Ecuador and Venezuela. Lowlands to 1000 m.

Status and Habitat. Uncommon; found in evergreen forest and forest edge.

Habits. Roosts in roofs, including thatch. It is sometimes caught in mist nets set over streams or pools. Pregnant females have been recorded in January and August in Costa Rica (Timm et al., 1989).

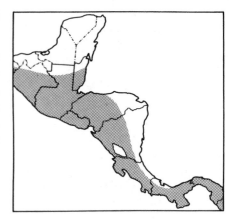

Map 153. Little Mastiff Bat, *Molossus molossus*

LITTLE MASTIFF BAT	Plate 16
Molossus molossus	Map 153

HB 59–65, T 30–39, HF 8–11, E 12–14, FA 36–40, Wt 10–14 g.

Description. Small. Upperparts *pale gray-brown to dark brown, base of hair white*; longest rump bristles 8–10 mm (bristles shorter and inconspicuous on some individuals); underparts gray-brown. Fur short (3 mm) and velvety. Ears short, do not extend to nose if laid forward, meet over crown. Antitragus compressed at the base, roughly circular in shape. Snout narrow, steeply ridged. Facial skin and ears brown. Tail length slightly more than half head and body length. No hair on edge of calcar. **Similar Species.** This is the smallest species in the genus; *M. bondae* is usually larger and does not have fur white at the base.

Distribution. Oaxaca, Mexico, through Central America (not recorded on the Yucatán Peninsula) to N Argentina and Peru; Trinidad and Tobago; Greater and Lesser Antilles. Lowlands to 1300 m.

Status and Habitat. Uncommon to locally common in dry and semideciduous forest and towns.

Habits. Roosts in houses, hollow trees, and under palm leaves. Large colonies of 300 or more occupy spaces between eaves and corrugated roofs and tolerate extremely high daytime temperatures. This species is the common smaller "house bat" in some areas. Before sunset, they can be heard moving toward small openings in beams or rafters. Individuals usually emerge one at a time at sunset and can be easily seen in flight. The diet consists largely of beetles.

Comment. There are 2 subspecies in the region that are sometimes treated as separate species (Dolan, 1989): *M. m. aztecus* is found in the foothills and highlands of Mexico to Costa Rica and *M. m. coibensis* occurs on the Pacific Slope from Chiapas, Mexico, to Panama. The form on mainland South America may also represent a distinct species.

MONKEYS

Order Primates

Primates are mainly tropical in distribution and are native throughout the world except Australia. They include primitive lemurs, lorises, tarsiers, and bushbabies, in addition to the more familiar monkeys and apes. Higher primates are divided into 2 ancient lineages, the New World monkeys and the Old World monkeys and great apes, including woman. New World monkeys were confined to South America when it was an island continent. A few species have since dispersed northward and are now among the more conspicuous Middle American mammals.

New World monkeys are arboreal; only a few species regularly feed on the ground, and some never leave the trees. They are threatened by deforestation throughout the Neotropics, and many suffer from overexploitation by hunters and live-animal traders.

MARMOSETS AND TAMARINS
Family Callitrichidae

Marmosets and tamarins are found mainly in South America, with only 1 of about 25 species entering Central America. These small monkeys have long, nonprehensile tails, and claws, rather than nails, on the hands and feet. The dental formula is: i 2/2, c 1/1, p 3/3, m 2/2.

GEOFFROY'S TAMARIN Plate 17
Saguinus geoffroyi Map 154

Red-crested bare-face tamarin; Panama: tití; Chocó: bichichí.

HB 225–285 (10"), T 331–390 (14"), Wt 400–680 g (1 lb).

Description. Smallest monkey, about the size of a squirrel, with a long, narrow, nonprehen- sile tail. Upperparts mottled black and buff; *nape dark orange-red;* stripe of white fur on crown of otherwise naked-looking, dark gray head. *Chest, underparts, and limbs cream-white.* Dark face contrasts with pale chest and limbs. Tail mainly black, dark red at the base; hangs below body. **Similar Species.** Much smaller than other diurnal monkeys in Panama.

Distribution. C Panama to NW Colombia (see Comment). Lowlands to 900 m.

Map 154. Geoffroy's Tamarin, *Saguinus geoffroyi*

Status and Habitat. CITES Appendix I. Many are illegally captured for the pet trade. Often common in secondary and disturbed forest; rare in mature evergreen forest. It favors dense, viney vegetation at forest edge, especially along river banks or roadsides. This is the most common monkey in remnant forests.

Habits. During the day, this small monkey is usually seen in the subcanopy or shrub level of the forest, about 3 m above ground. Although mainly arboreal, it sometimes searches for insects in the leaf litter. It runs on all fours along branches, but jumps and lands with the body in an upright position. This species is most active in the morning and mid-afternoon, spending the middle of the day resting and grooming. Groups spend the night in tall, emergent trees, retiring about an hour before sunset. They sleep huddled together on a nest pad of twigs situated away from the trunk, 10–20 m above ground. The diet consists of about equal parts of fruit and insects (mainly grasshoppers) and small amounts of plant exudates, particularly the gum of *Anacardium excelsum*. Geoffroy's Tamarins live in small, stable groups of 2–9 individuals consisting of one breeding female, one or more adult males, subadults, and young. Groups are territorial and occasionally fight. They signal neighbor-

ing groups with long, descending whistles and by scent marking. Low intensity, birdlike twitters and shrill chatters are given between group members. Females give birth to 1–2 young at the beginning of the rainy season. Young are carried on the back of either parent or another group member for the first few weeks of life. Reviewed by Snowdon and Soini (1988).

Where to See. Fairly common near Panama City and in the Canal Area: at Metropolitan Park, Gigante Peninsula, and along Achiote Road. Also in second growth in and around Darién National Park. Sometimes located by its shrill calls.

Comment. Formerly considered a subspecies of the Cotton-top Tamarin (*S. oedipus*) by some authors. Groves (1993) listed *S. oedipus* and *S. geoffroyi* from Panama; however there are no records of Cotton-tops (*S. oedipus*) from Central America.

Geoffroy's Tamarin has been reported from S Costa Rica and W Panama based on a sight record by Carpenter (1935), who merely noted that tamarins were "very scarce" in the Coto Region (a Pacific lowland site on the border of Panama and Costa Rica). Carpenter may have been confused by local reports of "titís," a name used for both squirrel monkeys and tamarins in Panama. Given the absence of subsequent documentation, specimens, or additional sight records in W Panama, the original record is questionable and in any case does not reflect the species' current distribution. Panamanian zoogeographer F. Delgado (D. Engleman, in litt.) verified that the range of Geoffroy's Tamarin is limited to C and E Panama and probably did not extend into W Panama prior to deforestation.

COLOR PLATES AND
FACING PLATE TEXTS

All measurements are given in millimeters.

Species are drawn to scale on most of the plates. Two scales are indicated by a line across the plate.

For several species, front (F) and hind (H) tracks are shown. Tracks are to scale with one another on a page, and most are shown at 50% of actual size. Very large tracks are shown at about 40% actual size. The tracks are usually of the right feet; "thumbs" face left.

The undersides of feet of some small rodents, opossums, and shrews are portrayed actual size. Left feet are shown; "thumbs" on left.

Representative bat silhouettes are included to illustrate wing shapes, tail membranes, and relative tail lengths.

PLATE 1 • LARGE OPOSSUMS

1 Water Opossum (*Chironectes minimus*), p. 45.
Boldly patterned. Long, sturdy tail with a short white tip; webbed hind feet.

2 Virginia Opossum (*Didelphis virginiana*), p. 44.
Fur whitish, blackish, or gray; cheeks and cheek whiskers white. Tail shorter than or equal to head and body length; black portion usually longer than white portion.

3 Common Opossum (*Didelphis marsupialis*), p. 43.
Size and color similar to 2 (often blackish, but can be gray or whitish); cheeks yellowish, cheek whiskers black. Tail usually longer than head and body, black portion shorter than white portion.

Tracks: Five toes on each foot; widely splayed, opposable thumb on hind foot. Shown at 50% actual size.

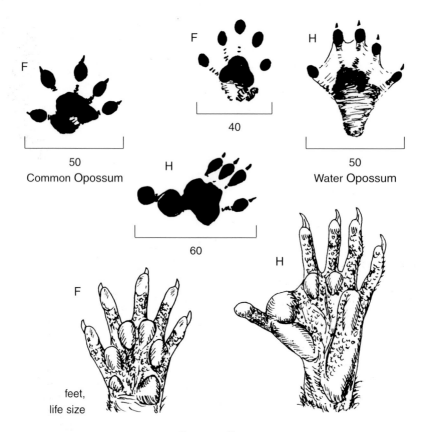

F

F

H

40

50
Common Opossum

H

60

50
Water Opossum

H

F

feet,
life size

Common Opossum

PLATE 2 • MEDIUM SIZED OPOSSUMS

1 Alston's Mouse Opossum (*Micoureus alstoni*), p. 50.
Largest mouse opossum (also see Plate 3). Grayish, woolly fur; black mask. Tail thickly furred at base, with a long, white tip.

2 Central American Woolly Opossum (*Caluromys derbianus*), p. 51.
Reddish or grayish, woolly fur; dark line down face; pale ears. Tail thickly furred for half its length, with a long, white tip.

3 Gray Four-eyed Opossum (*Philander opossum*), p. 45.
Back dark gray; pale spots above eyes. Tail furred at base, then half black, half white.

4 Brown Four-eyed Opossum (*Metachirus nudicaudatus*), p. 46.
Back brown; small pale spots above eyes. Tail nearly naked at base, mainly bi-color, fading to white at tip.

Tracks: Five toes on each foot; widely splayed, opposable thumbs. Shown at 55% actual size.

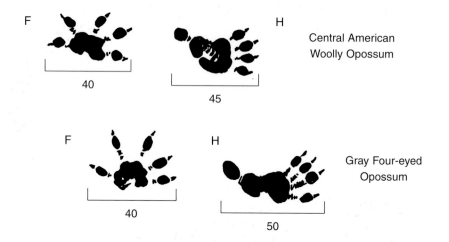

PLATE 3 • SMALL OPOSSUMS

1 **Sepia Short-tailed Opossum** *(Monodelphis adusta)*, p. 50.
Small; tail shorter than head and body (E Panama).

2 **Grayish Mouse Opossum** *(Marmosa canescens)*, p. 47.
Pale gray; tail about equal to head and body (Mexico).

3 **Slaty Mouse Opossum** *(Marmosops invictus)*, p. 49.
Belly silvery gray (Panama).

4 **Mexican Mouse Opossum** *(Marmosa mexicana)*, p. 47.
Orangish; fur short.

5 **Robinson's Mouse Opossum** *(Marmosa robinsoni)*, p. 48.
Similar to 4, but slightly larger and longer haired.

6 **Highland Mouse Opossum** *(Marmosops impavidus)*, p. 49.
Dark brown (Panama).

7 **Alston's Mouse Opossum** *(Micoureus alstoni)*, p. 50.
Largest species; grayish; tail furred at base, tip white (also see Plate 2).

F   H

Mexican Mouse Opossum
(actual size)

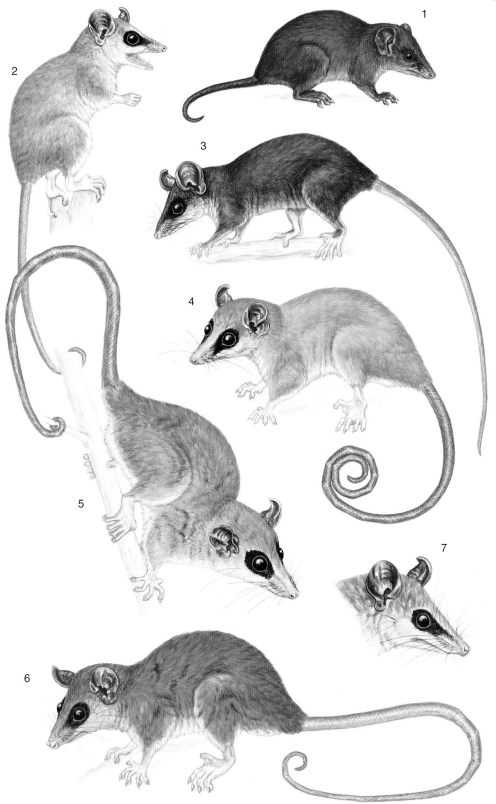

PLATE 4 • ANTEATERS

1 Silky Anteater (*Cyclopes didactylus*), p. 56.
Small. Fully furred, prehensile tail and 2 large claws on forefeet distinguish it from other mammals of similar size.

2 Northern Tamandua (*Tamandua mexicana*), p. 55.
Contrasting black vest; prehensile tail.

3 Giant Anteater (*Myrmecophaga tridactyla*), p. 54.
(a) Head.
(b) Large and long bodied; distinctive markings (different scale).

Tracks: Large claws of forefoot print in reverse or at right angles to direction of smaller claws of hind foot. Shown at 50% actual size.

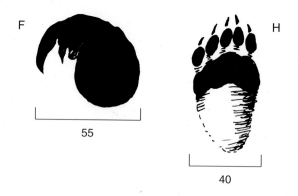

Northern Tamandua

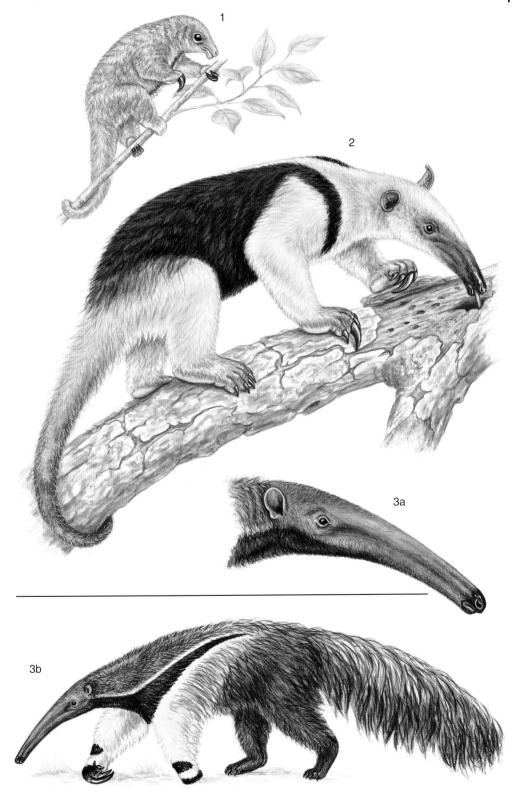

1

2

3a

3b

PLATE 5 • SLOTHS AND ARMADILLOS

1 Brown-throated Three-toed Sloth (*Bradypus variegatus*), p. 58.
Grayish; black mask and small nose; 3 claws on each foot; stumpy tail.
(a) Sleeping male showing orange and black patch on back (different scale).

2 Hoffmann's Two-toed Sloth (*Choloepus hoffmanni*), p. 57.
Brownish; white or greenish fur on head; piglike nose; 2 claws on forefoot; no tail.
(a) Sleeping (different scale).

3 Northern Naked-tailed Armadillo (*Cabassous centralis*), p. 59.
Small; flat-looking back; broad head. Tail pinkish, not armored.

4 Nine-banded Armadillo (*Dasypus novemcinctus*), p. 60.
Larger; rounded back; narrow head. Long, armored tail.

Tracks: Forefoot of armadillo often shows only two toes, parallel and almost equal in length; hind foot usually shows three toes and has a birdlike shape. Shown at 50% actual size.

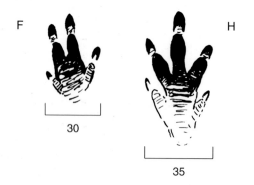

F

H

30

35

Nine-banded Armadillo

PLATE 6 • SAC-WINGED BATS

5

Tail about half length of tail membrane, tip projects above membrane at rest; several species with wing sacs (upper surface of wing of male shown in details); nose plain, eyes rather large.

1 Proboscis Bat (*Rhynchonycteris naso*), p. 74.
Tiny; grizzled; faint wavy lines on back; pale tufts of fur on forearms. **(a)** Profile showing long proboscis.

2 Lesser White-lined Bat (*Saccopteryx leptura*), p. 75.
Small; back brown, stripes buffy; wing sacs as in 3. **(a)** Profile.

3 Greater White-lined Bat (*Saccopteryx bilineata*), p.74.
Larger than 2; back blackish, stripes cream. **(a)** Wing sacs parallel to forearm.

4 Gray Sac-winged Bat (*Balantiopteryx plicata*), p. 78.
Gray; forearms pinkish brown. **(a)** Wing sacs small, open toward body, do not reach wing edge.

5 Least Sac-winged Bat (*Balantiopteryx io*), p. 78.
Tiny, brown; wing sacs as in 4.

6 Chestnut Sac-winged Bat (*Cormura brevirostris*), p. 77.
Snout mostly furred. Wings attach to base of toes. **(a)** Wing sacs large, open away from body, reach wing edge.

7 Greater Doglike Bat (*Peropteryx kappleri*), p. 77.
Head. Similar to 8 but larger, longer haired, often darker. Wing sacs as in 8.

8 Lesser Doglike Bat (*Peropteryx macrotis*), p. 76.
Snout nearly naked. Wings attach to ankles. **(a)** Wing sacs small, open away from body, reach wing edge.

9 Northern Ghost Bat (*Diclidurus albus*), p. 79.
Large, white. No wing sacs. **(a)** Gland around tail.

10 Shaggy Bat (*Centronycteris maximiliani*), p. 75.
Fuzzy, yellowish; sickle-shaped ears. Wings attach to base of toes. No wing sacs.

11 Smoky Bat (*Cyttarops alecto*), p. 79.
Dark gray; tiny thumbs. No wing sacs.

Greater White-lined Bat

PLATE 7 • LEAF-CHINNED, FISHING, AND VAMPIRE BATS

6

Pteronotus. Narrow, pointed ears; thick lips with a small flap on chin. Tail shorter than tail membrane, tip sticks out at rest. Wings attach on sides of body or meet on back, which then appears to be naked.

1 **Davy's Naked-backed Bat** (*P. davyi*), p. 84.
   Small; back naked; fur usually brown.

2 **Big Naked-backed Bat** (*P. gymnonotus*), p. 85.
   Similar to 1 but larger; fur orange or brown.

3 **Lesser Mustached Bat** (*P. personatus*), p. 84.
   Small; back furred; brown or orange.

4 **Common Mustached Bat** (*P. parnellii*), p. 83.
   Similar to 3 but larger; fur usually brown. **(a)** Calling.

5 **Ghost-faced Bat** (*Mormoops megalophylla*), p. 83.
   Several prominent chin flaps; rounded ears. **(a)** Profile.

6 **Greater Fishing Bat** (*Noctilio leporinus*), p. 81.
   Large and bony; drooping, split upper lips; fur gray to orange; huge feet and claws. **(a)** Fishing (smaller scale).

7 **Lesser Fishing Bat** (*Noctilio albiventris*), p. 82.
   Similar to 6 but smaller, with much smaller feet.

8 **Hairy-legged Vampire Bat** (*Diphylla ecaudata*), p. 142.
   Thick nosepad; short, rounded ears; big eyes. Hairy legs and almost no tail membrane.

9 **White-winged Vampire Bat** (*Diaemus youngi*), p. 141.
   Thick nosepad; triangular ears. Legs lightly haired, no tail and narrow tail membrane; wingtips pure white; one pad under base of thumb.

10 **Common Vampire Bat** (*Desmodus rotundus*), p. 140.
   Similar to 9 but wingtips grayish; 2 pads under base of thumb.

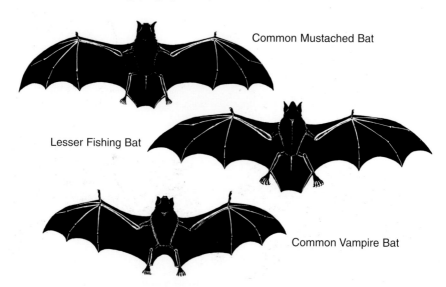

Common Mustached Bat

Lesser Fishing Bat

Common Vampire Bat

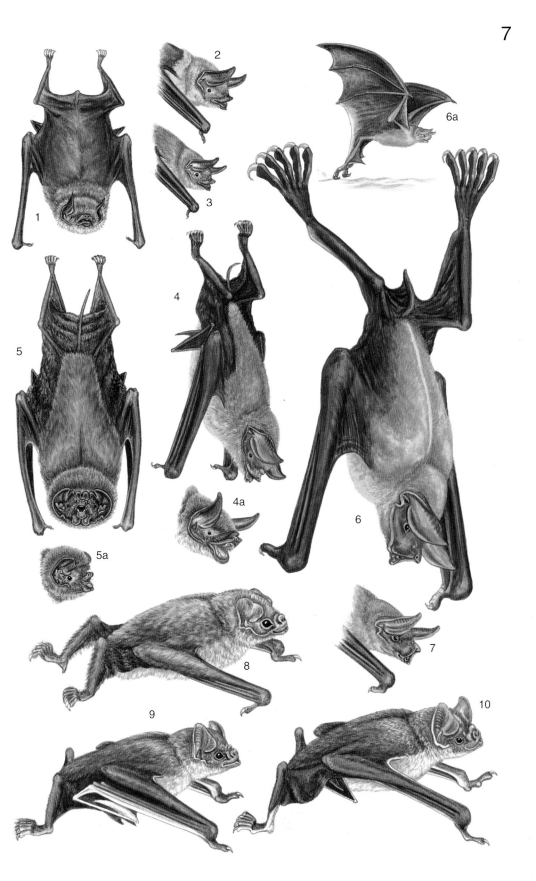

PLATE 8 • SMALL LEAF-NOSED BATS

7

Mostly short-tailed and big-eared; forearms 32–46 mm.

1 Long-legged Bat (*Macrophyllum macrophyllum*), p. 95.
Ears pointed; large noseleaf. Long tail, warts on underside of tail membrane; long legs and feet.

2 Pygmy Round-eared Bat (*Tonatia brasiliense*), p. 97.
Horseshoe of noseleaf fused to upper lip; small warts on chin groove. Wings attach to feet at base of toes.

Micronycteris. Smooth, V-shaped chin pad; wings attach to ankles (also see *M. daviesi*, Plate 9).

3 Common Big-eared Bat (*M. microtis*), p. 89.
Belly gray-brown, calcar longer than foot.

4 Tiny Big-eared Bat (*M. minuta*), p. 90.
Belly white; calcar shorter than foot. See *M. schmidtorum*, p. 90.

5 Hairy Big-eared Bat (*M. hirsuta*), p. 91.
Larger than other round-eared *Micronycteris*; fur long.

6 Tricolored Bat (*M. sylvestris*), p. 93.
Fur clearly banded, black at base; calcar shorter than foot.

7 Orange-throated Bat (*M. brachyotis*), p. 92.
Bright orange throat; calcar longer than foot.

8 Niceforo's Bat (*M. nicefori*), p. 92.
Fur faintly banded; some individuals with faint, gray back stripe; calcar short.

Carollia. U-shaped row of small warts with larger central wart on chin. Fur usually banded.

9 Seba's Short-tailed Bat (*C. perspicillata*), p. 118.
Largest species; fur short, tricolor, brown at base.

10 Chestnut Short-tailed Bat (*C. castanea*), p. 116.
Small; reddish brown or brown; fur not strongly banded.

11 Gray Short-tailed Bat (*C. subrufa*), p.116.
Fur clearly tricolor; short, black base, longer white midsection.

12 Silky Short-tailed Bat (*C. brevicauda*), p. 117.
Similar to 11, but black section at base of fur longer.

Seba's Short-tailed Bat

15–32 cm wide. Platform nests of shredded bark, often with several nests stacked on older nests, were occupied by females and young. When nests were disturbed, females ran out with young clinging to their nipples. This species is usually silent in the wild; mating pairs give birdlike, twittering calls. In captivity, individuals hiss and squeak if caged with strangers, although a male and female pair soon tolerate each other. Litter size is 1–4, averaging 2, and reproduction may take place year-round. Young are precocial at birth.

YUCATAN VESPER MOUSE
Otonyctomys hatti

Plate 30
Map 200

HB 90–116, T 97–127, HF 21–23, E 14–15, Wt 30–36 g.

Description. Small. *Upperparts bright orange, finely peppered with black on midback; underparts white to base of fur.* Ears pale brown and nearly naked. Eyes large, with a conspicuous black eye ring. *Tail all dark, well haired, with a terminal tuft* (hair 11 mm at tip). Feet short and stocky, soles pink, tops brown with white toes. **Similar Species.** This small, brilliant orange mouse is one of the most spectacular rodents in the region. The hairy, tufted tail is diagnostic in the Mexican portion of its range; in Belize and Guatemala it approaches the range of Vesper Rat (*Nyctomys sumichrasti*), which is larger (cf. hind foot length).

Distribution. Yucatán Peninsula of SE Mexico, N Guatemala, and N Belize. Lowlands only.

Status and Habitat. Rare; known from few specimens. It has been found in deciduous and semideciduous forest and second growth.

Habits. This poorly known mouse is highly arboreal. It has been trapped (usually with banana as bait) in thatched roofs, in a coconut palm, and in trees or dead branches (Jones et al., 1974; Peterson, 1966). In captivity it is nocturnal, extremely shy, and prefers seeds to fruit. It is not known to vocalize.

MEXICAN WOOD RAT
Neotoma mexicana

Plate 31
Map 201

HB 152–205, T 133–216, HF 33–41, E 25–30, Wt 151–253 g.

Description. Very large and stocky. Back reddish brown (with some black hairs); sides orangish; underparts grayish white. Fur thick and somewhat coarse. Ears nearly naked, large, and brown. Eyes large, with a narrow, dark eye ring. Whiskers long and thick. *Tail well haired,* faintly to clearly bicolor. *Hind feet long and broad,* tops whitish. **Similar Species.** See *N. chrysomelas.* Few species of large rats occur within its range and elevation: house rats (*Rattus* spp.) have sparsely haired, more uniformly colored tails.

Distribution. Colorado, USA, south to W Honduras and W El Salvador. 1100–4000 m (in SE Mexico and N Central America).

Status and Habitat. Generally uncommon and local; found in highland pine–oak forest and open woodland. It favors dry, rocky areas in coniferous forest and forest openings but also occurs in cool, evergreen forest.

Habits. Poorly known in Central America. This wood rat is nocturnal and mainly terrestrial, but it climbs well. In Colorado, the diet

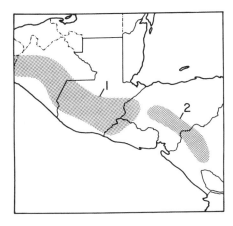

Map 201. 1. Mexican Wood Rat, *Neotoma mexicana*
2. Nicaraguan Wood Rat, *Neotoma chrysomelas*

consists primarily of green plant material (including *Yucca*), supplemented with fruit, seeds, and fungi. Unlike other wood rats, this species seldom constructs large stick nests, although piles of sticks may be found at den entrances. Dens are usually located in rock crevices and house spherical or cup-shaped nests of shredded bark (Finley, 1958). Litter size is 1–4, averaging about 2.

NICARAGUAN WOOD RAT

Neotoma chrysomelas   Map 201

HB 184–220, T 150–181, HF 33–36, E 25–30, Wt 152–187 g.

Description. Externally almost identical to *N. mexicana*, sometimes brighter orange. The species are distinguished by skull characters.

Distribution. Higher elevations in Honduras and NW Nicaragua. About 1000 m.

Status and Habitat. Rare and local; known from very few specimens.

Habits. Poorly known. Two pregnant females, each with a single embryo, were caught in September and February.

Comment. Possibly a subspecies of *N. mexicana*.

SOUTHERN PYGMY MOUSE   Plate 25

Baiomys musculus   Map 202

HB 65–80, T 41–54, HF 14–16, E 11–13, Wt 8–12 g.

Description. Tiny and short-tailed. Back *gray-brown*, sides dull ochre, grading to grayish white below. Fur short and smooth. Ears short and rounded, lightly haired. Eyes small. Whiskers fine and short. *Tail about 65% of head and body length*, faintly bicolor, lightly haired. Feet small, tops whitish. **Similar Species.** This is the smallest short-tailed mouse in SE Mexico and Central America. Alston's Singing Mouse

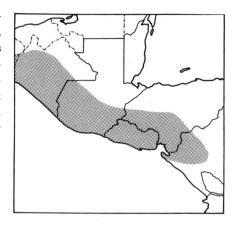

Map 202. Southern Pygmy Mouse, *Baiomys musculus*

(*Scotinomys teguina*) is only slightly larger, but much darker in color. House Mouse (*Mus musculus*) is similar in size and color, but has a longer tail and hind feet (and an unpleasant odor).

Distribution. Nayarit and Veracruz, Mexico, mainly on the Pacific Slope and dry central valleys to N Nicaragua. Lowlands to 1700 m.

Status and Habitat. Fairly common in dense grass and weedy fields. It is usually found in seasonally dry areas, often near rocks, fence rows, and along streams.

Habits. It is active by day or in the early evening. The presence of this diminutive, terrestrial mouse is often indicated by tiny runways through grass and weeds, littered with piles of small, green droppings. Underground burrows are used in grassy areas; rocks provide shelter in more open, arid regions. In Chiapas, Mexico, the diet consists of about 50% insects, 25% seeds (including Solanaceae), and 25% green plant material (Alvarez et al., 1984). A nest of finely chewed plant material was found under a large kapok (*Ceiba*) tree (Packard and Montgomery, 1978). This species appears to be social and may nest communally. Breeding may occur year-round, and litter size is 1–4, averaging 2.9 (Packard, 1960).

ALSTON'S SINGING MOUSE   Plate 25
Scotinomys teguina   Map 203

HB 66–86, T 48–60, HF 16–19, E 12–15, Wt 10–13 g.

Description. Tiny, dark, and short-tailed. Upperparts *dark chocolate-brown*; sides dark, tinged with orange; underparts dark gray-brown or orange-brown. *Fur smooth and shiny.* Ears black, lightly haired. *Tail blackish,* about *70% of head and body length,* lightly haired. Feet black. **Similar Species.** See *S. xerampelinus* and Southern Pygmy Mouse (*Baiomys musculus*). Small-eared shrews (*Cryptotis* spp.) have velvety fur and concealed ears (easily confused when seen crossing a path).

Distribution. Oaxaca, Mexico, through the highlands to W Panama. 900–2900 m.

Status and Habitat. Common to abundant in highland forest (mostly in cloud forest), forest edge, and grassy clearings.

Habits. This mouse is generally diurnal and is most active in the morning. It is mainly terrestrial, using runways and well-trodden paths through grass and under logs (Hooper, 1972). It sometimes climbs and has been caught 1–3 m above ground after feeding on nectar of the melastome, *Blakea austin-smithii* (Lumer and Schoer, 1986). Insects make up about 80% of the diet (adult beetles are preferred); some seeds and fruit are also taken (Hooper and Carleton, 1976). In captivity this mouse is a voracious insectivore and will immediately attack and kill a large number of insects, which are later consumed. Its common name refers to its insectlike, trilling call, which is made frequently by both sexes. The mouse usually stands up on its hind legs to call, and each song lasts up to 10 seconds. Initially, the song is fast-paced and almost inaudible, gradually dropping to a lower pitch, slower pace, and louder volume, and ending abruptly. Although insectlike in pitch and volume, the song can be

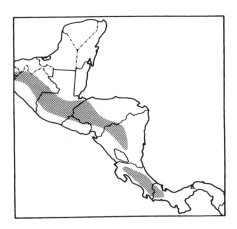

Map 203. Alston's Singing Mouse, *Scotinomys teguina*

distinguished from the steady trill of an insect by its gradual start and abrupt end. Once learned, the calls are often heard in suitable habitat, but it is extremely difficult to locate and observe singing mice in the field. Elaborate and well-constructed nests are made by both sexes in captivity. Breeding occurs year-round, and litter size is 1–3, averaging 2.3. Both males and females tend the young in captivity, and young are weaned in about 3 weeks. Both species of singing mice have a strong, distinctive musky odor.

CHIRIQUI SINGING MOUSE   Plate 25
Scotinomys xerampelinus   Map 204

HB 68–90, T 60–72, HF 18–20, E 15–18, Wt 14 g.

Description. Similar to *S. teguina*, it differs as follows: *fur long,* appears fuzzy rather than smooth; *tail proportionally longer,* 80–85% of head and body length; eyes smaller.

Distribution. C Costa Rica to W Panama. 2100–3400 m.

Status and Habitat. Fairly common in wet, montane forest, forest edge, dense grass, and

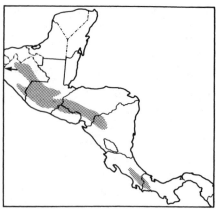

Map 204. Chiriquí Singing Mouse, *Scotinomys xerampelinus*

Map 205. Sumichrast's Harvest Mouse, *Reithrodontomys sumichrasti*

páramo. This species favors colder, wetter areas than *S. teguina.*

Habits. This mouse is terrestrial, traveling in runways under logs and among rocks or through dense vegetation. Almost entirely insectivorous in diet, it prefers larval beetles, which are probably located by smell. Little nest-building activity occurs in captivity, and nests have not been found in the wild. Vocalizations are similar to those of *S. teguina,* but the song is shorter (2–4 seconds) and not modulated in frequency or volume. It appears to breed year-round; litter size is 2–4, averaging 2.7.

SUMICHRAST'S HARVEST MOUSE   Plate 26
Reithrodontomys sumichrasti   Map 205

HB 64–93, T 65–98, HF 16–20, E 12–16, Wt 8–13 g.

Description. Small, dark, and rather short-tailed. *Usually blackish brown on upper back* (sometimes orange-brown grizzled with black), sides yellowish brown, grading to buff or grayish white on belly. Ears blackish, moderately haired. No eye rings. Whiskers rather short and sparse. *Tail relatively short, about equal to head and body length, somewhat bicolor.* Tops of hind feet off-white. **Similar Species.** Most other highland harvest mice are larger, and all have tails longer than head and body length.

Distribution. Jalisco and Queretaro, Mexico, south through mountains to W Panama. 1200–4000 m.

Status and Habitat. Widespread, often common at forest edge or among brush and pastures in cold, wet montane regions. This species favors more open habitats than other harvest mice; it is fairly common in coniferous forest, but rare in mature, broadleaf forest.

Habits. Although this harvest mouse can climb, it is mainly terrestrial and is usually trapped on the ground. A rounded nest of grass was found under a log in a coffee field in Nicaragua (Jones and Genoways, 1970). Breeding may occur year-round, and litter size is 3–5 (Anderson and Jones, 1960).

FULVOUS HARVEST MOUSE   Plate 26
Reithrodontomys fulvescens   Map 206

HB 57–82, T 84–118, HF 17–20, E 12–16, Wt 10 g.

Description. Small, with *grizzled fur.* Back buffy brown peppered with black, grading to

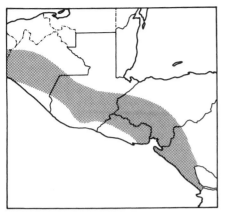

Map 206. Fulvous Harvest Mouse, *Reithrodontomys fulvescens*

in diameter and 5 cm wide inside. Adult pairs are often found in the same nest. Although this harvest mouse is usually silent, Svihla (1930) reported males making "a tiny, clear, high-pitched bugling sound" when sexually excited. A 2-note whistle (similar to the call of *R. gracilis*) was given by a lone male after a year in captivity. Litter size in Texas is 2–4, averaging 3 (Cameron, 1977). Pregnant females with 4–5 embryos were taken in San Luis Potosí, Mexico, where breeding occurred year-round (Dalquest, 1953).

ochre or pale orange on sides; belly whitish or buff. *Orange hair inside and at base of ears.* No eye ring. Whiskers short and sparse. *Tail bicolor,* longer than head and body. Tops of hind feet whitish. **Similar Species.** In all other harvest mice the ears are naked looking or are lined with dark hair. See Northern Pygmy Rice Rat (*Oligoryzomys fulvescens*) and House Mouse (*Mus musculus*).

Distribution. Missouri, USA, to S Nicaragua. Lowlands to 1700 m (in SE Mexico and Central America).

Status and Habitat. Uncommon in Central America; found in dry thorn scrub, gaps in deciduous forest, and grassy areas.

Habits. It is mainly terrestrial, but often travels above ground through low vegetation. Burrows are used in hot, dry areas, and small runways are made through grass. The diet consists of seeds, insects, and shoots; in the United States, insects make up the bulk of diet in spring, and seeds predominate in fall (Spencer and Cameron, 1982). In Chiapas, Mexico, its preference for seeds or insects varies with locality (Alvarez et al., 1984). Nests are usually built among vegetation, within 1 m of the ground. A ball-shaped nest is woven from grasses and shredded leaves and is about 10 cm

SLENDER HARVEST MOUSE Plate 26
Reithrodontomys gracilis Map 207

HB 67–80, T 91–112, HF 17–20, E 13–15, Wt 9–15 g.

Description. Small. Back *orange-brown peppered* with *black,* grading to bright orange or ochraceous on sides; underparts white. Fur soft and smooth. *Ears medium sized, pale brown;* thinly lined with dark hair. Narrow, black eye ring. Whiskers fairly thick and long. *Tail uniformly dark or faintly bicolor.* Ankles dusky, tops of hind feet entirely white, or dusky to base of toes. **Similar Species.** Easily confused with *R. mexicanus,* which averages larger, with darker ears and a longer tail. See *R. fulvescens, R. paradoxus,* and Northern Pygmy Rice Rat (*Oligoryzomys fulvescens*).

Distribution. SW Chiapas and Yucatán Peninsula, Mexico, south on Pacific Slope to Monteverde, N Costa Rica. Lowlands to 1800 m.

Status and Habitat. Locally common and widespread in a variety of habitats: from dry thorn scrub to wet highland forest. It is found in mature forest, second growth, and clearings.

Habits. It is mainly nocturnal, but may be active in the late afternoon. This species is arboreal and terrestrial; in tall, mature forest it is rarely trapped on the ground and has been caught in the canopy at 15 m; in scrub and

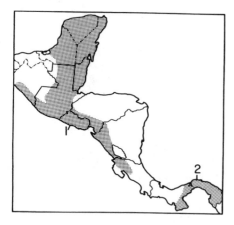

Map 207. 1. Slender Harvest Mouse, *Reithrodontomys gracilis*
2. Darién Harvest Mouse, *Reithrodontomys darienensis*

grassy areas it is largely terrestrial and is often trapped on the ground. The diet includes insects and seeds. This mouse makes spherical nests in hollows and sometimes uses bird nestboxes attached to trees. It often invades houses and buildings near forested areas, nesting on rafters or in gaps between roofs and ceilings. In some areas, this species is known as *el ratoncito rojo que canta* (the little red singing mouse) for its whistled calls given from the rafters. The calls consist of 2 (rarely 1 or 3) high-pitched, constant-frequency notes, the first note longer than the second, "eeee, ee". Both males and females call; these calls are heard most often at dusk, near the end of the dry season or early in the wet season. Reproduction occurs throughout the wet season and sporadically in the dry season. Litter size is 2–5, averaging 3. These small mice can live for more than 2 years in the wild, although normal life span is probably 6–9 months (C.A. Langtimm, personal communication).

Comment. This species was described by Hooper (1952) as an inhabitant of dry lowland regions. Its presence in cloud forest in Monteverde, Costa Rica, was noted by Reid and Langtimm (1993). The mice in this re-

gion were formerly identified as *R. mexicanus*, and the exact distributional limits of the 2 species are still unresolved.

COZUMEL HARVEST MOUSE
Reithrodontomys spectabilis   Map 208

HB 76–95, T 124–138, HF 21–22, E 16–18, Wt 14–23 g.

Description. Similar to *R. gracilis* in color and proportions, but larger. **Similar Species.** No other harvest mice occur on Cozumel Island. White-footed Mouse (*Peromyscus leucopus*) is larger, with a proportionally shorter, bicolor tail. Young Coues' Rice Rat (*Oryzomys couesi*) has hairy ears.

Distribution. Cozumel Island, Mexico.

Status and Habitat. Fairly common in dense, viney second growth and forest edge. It may be threatened by development and deforestation.

Habits. It is nocturnal and semiarboreal. This species gives 2-note whistling calls at dusk, much like the calls of *R. gracilis*.

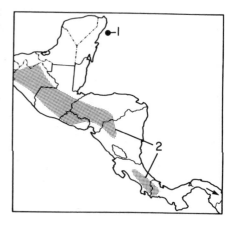

Map 208. 1. Cozumel Harvest Mouse, *Reithrodontomys spectabilis*
2. Mexican Harvest Mouse, *Reithrodontomys mexicanus*

DARIEN HARVEST MOUSE
Reithrodontomys darienensis   Map 207

HB 64–85, T 90–116, HF 16–20, E 12–16, Wt?

Description. Small. Back *reddish brown*, sides orangish; belly white. Fur short and even. Ears brown, sparsely haired. Narrow, dark eye ring. Whiskers rather long and thick. Tail uniformly dark, longer than head and body length. Tops of hind feet brown, toes white. **Similar Species.** Similar to *R. gracilis*, but sometimes brighter orange (ranges do not overlap). See Bicolored Arboreal Rice Rat (*Oecomys bicolor*).

Distribution. Azuero Peninsula, Panama, east to Panama–Colombia border. Lowlands to 900 m.

Status and Habitat. Uncommon; found in evergreen forest, forest edge, and openings.

Habits. Poorly known. It is mainly arboreal (Handley, 1966). A harvest mouse heard calling with a 3-note whistle on the slopes of Mount Pirre, Darién, Panama, was presumably this species. The call was similar to that of *R. gracilis*, although that species commonly makes a 2-note call. A female with 4 embryos was caught in February.

MEXICAN HARVEST MOUSE   Plate 26
Reithrodontomys mexicanus   Map 208

HB 69–100, T 92–134, HF 18–22, E 14–18, Wt 14–18 g.

Description. Fairly small and long tailed (averages larger south of Honduras). Back *rich orange-brown* peppered with black; sides bright orange; underparts white or buff. *Fur long*, thick, and *slightly woolly*. Ears large (most specimens), *blackish*, and moderately haired. Narrow black eye ring. Whiskers long and thick. *Tail long, usually uniformly dark, occasionally faintly bicolor*. Tops of hind feet dusky, usually to base of toes. **Similar Species.** See *R. gracilis*, *R. brevirostris*, and *R. fulvescens*, all of which

average smaller. *R. sumichrasti* has a shorter tail.

Distribution. Tamaulipas and Jalisco, Mexico, through the highlands to W Panama; Andes of W Colombia to N Ecuador. 500–3300 m (usually 1000–2000 m).

Status and Habitat. Uncommon to locally common in a wide variety of habitats, from montane oak forest to dry lowland forest and arid scrub. Found both within mature forest and in clearings and cultivated areas.

Habits. It is semiarboreal and may be trapped on logs, vines, or on the ground. The diet consists of green plant material and occasional insects (Alvarez et al., 1984; Dalquest, 1953). In Veracruz, Mexico, a nest was found on top of a bromeliad, about 2.5 m above ground. The nest was a loosely woven ball of grasses and plant fibers, about 23 cm in diameter (Hall and Dalquest, 1963). Litter size is 3–4.

SHORT-NOSED HARVEST MOUSE
Reithrodontomys brevirostris   Map 209

HB 62–78, T 97–114, HF 16–20, E 14–16, Wt 11–15 g.

Description. Small. Back *dark reddish brown*, sides orangish; underparts cream-white. Fur long and slightly woolly. Ears brown, naked looking. Narrow, dusky eye ring. Whiskers thick and long. Tail uniformly dark. Tops of hind feet brown with white toes. **Similar Species.** About the same size and proportions as *R. gracilis*, but darker in color (ranges do not overlap). *R. mexicanus* averages larger and is usually brighter orange. *R. sumichrasti* has a shorter, bicolor tail.

Distribution. Known only from the Cordillera Dariense, Nicaragua, 1100–1250 m; and the Cordillera Central, Costa Rica, 1700–2300 m.

Status and Habitat. Rare and local; found in or near evergreen forest. Recorded in Nicaragua from a shaded coffee field; in Costa Rica from deep rocky canyons and cloud forest.

Habits. Poorly known. It was trapped along fallen logs and at the bases of large trees in Nicaragua (Jones and Genoways, 1970). Two pregnant females, with 3 and 4 embryos, were caught in June.

NICARAGUAN HARVEST MOUSE

Reithrodontomys paradoxus   Map 210

HB 71–72, T 96–107, HF 18–19, E 13–15, Wt?

Description. Small. *Back dark buffy brown*, grading to buffy ochre on sides; underparts white. Tops of hind feet blackish, toes white. **Similar Species.** *R. gracilis* is brighter orange, with whitish or dusky hind feet. *R. fulvescens* has hairy ears.

Distribution. W Nicaragua (Diriamba, Carazo), 660 m; and W Costa Rica (San Ramón, Alajuela), 750 m (Jones and Baldassarre, 1982).

Status and Habitat. Rare; known from very few specimens taken in deciduous forest.

Habits. Unknown.

SMALL-TOOTHED HARVEST MOUSE

Reithrodontomys microdon

Plate 26
Map 209

HB 61–73, T 102–112, HF 19–21, E 16–17, Wt 8–11 g.

Description. Small. Upperparts *brown* or *reddish brown*, heavily peppered with *long, black hairs*, sides bright orange; underparts whitish or buff. Fur long and thick. Ears large and dark, lined with black hair. Narrow, black eye ring. Whiskers thick and long. *Tail long*, faintly bicolor, sometimes marked with pinkish blotches. *Hind feet relatively long, tops blackish* to base of toes. **Similar Species.** *R. mexicanus* averages larger (compare weights)

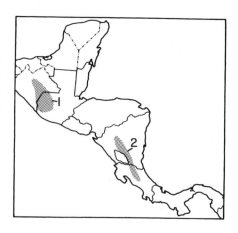

Map 209. 1. Small-toothed Harvest Mouse, *Reithrodontomys microdon*
2. Short-nosed Harvest Mouse, *Reithrodontomys brevirostris*

and is usually found at lower elevations. *R. sumichrasti* has a shorter tail. See *R. tenuirostris*.

Distribution. Isolated populations in mountains of Distrito Federal and Michoacán; Oaxaca; Chiapas, Mexico, and WC Guatemala. 2200–3100 m (in Chiapas and Guatemala).

Status and Habitat. Local but not uncommon in suitable habitat; possibly threatened by habitat loss. Restricted to mature montane forest with numerous ferns, mosses, and fallen trees.

Habits. This species is semiarboreal. It may be trapped on logs or on the ground at the base of large trees. It has also been found in a *Microtus* runway in dense ground cover in a pine forest and in a "tree top" (Hooper, 1952).

NARROW-NOSED HARVEST MOUSE

Reithrodontomys tenuirostris

Plate 26
Map 211

HB 80–110, T 116–129, HF 23–25, E 15–21, Wt 18–27 g.

Description. Relatively large and long tailed. Upperparts reddish brown; orange line on sides; *underparts cinnamon-buff.* Fur long and slightly woolly. Ears blackish. Narrow, black eye ring. Snout relatively long. *Tail long,* uniformly dark. Hind feet long, tops brown. **Similar Species.** *R. microdon* and *R. sumichrasti* are smaller; *R. mexicanus* (in region of overlap) is usually smaller, with a white belly.

Distribution. SE Chiapas, Mexico, to E Guatemala. 2400–2900 m (Rogers et al., 1983).

Status and Habitat. Rare and local; restricted to mature, broadleaf montane forest and may be threatened by habitat loss. It favors the coldest, wettest slopes, with abundant epiphytes and mosses.

Habits. This poorly known species is apparently semiarboreal.

RODRIGUEZ'S HARVEST MOUSE

Reithrodontomys rodriguezi   Map 210

HB 65–85, T 110–127, HF 21–22, E 15–17, Wt 15 g.

Description. Small and long-tailed. Back reddish brown peppered with long, black hairs, sides orangish; underparts whitish. Fur long and slightly woolly. Ears dark, lined with black-

Map 210. 1. Nicaraguan Harvest Mouse, *Reithrodontomys paradoxus*
2. Rodriguez's Harvest Mouse, *Reithrodontomys rodriguezi*

ish hair. Narrow, dusky eye ring. Snout relatively long. Whiskers long and thick. Tail very long, uniformly dark. Tops of hind feet blackish, toes white. **Similar Species.** *R. microdon* is similar in color but slightly smaller (ranges do not overlap). *R. creper* is larger with a buffy orange belly; *R. mexicanus* is brighter orange with a shorter snout (difficult to distinguish in the field); *R. sumichrasti* has a much shorter tail.

Distribution. C Costa Rica (known only from Volcán Barva, Heredia; Volcán Irazu and Cerro Asunción, Cartago). 1500–3400 m.

Status and Habitat. Rare and local; found in wet, mature highland forest and in pastures at forest edge.

Habits. Poorly known. It has been trapped on the ground in grass at the edge of wet forest on Irazu (Goodwin, 1946), in the "crotch" of a tree about 3 m above ground (P. Myers, personal communication), and in low vegetation in elfin forest. This mouse was caught feeding on the nectar of a melastome (*Blakea* sp.), and may be one of several mouse pollinators for this plant (Lumer and Schoer, 1986). A pregnant female was captured in July.

CHIRIQUI HARVEST MOUSE   Plate 26

Reithrodontomys creper   Map 211

HB 90–104, T 115–160, HF 22–25, E 17–19, Wt 19–28 g.

Description. Largest species of harvest mouse. *Back dark reddish brown, sides orange-brown, grading to buffy orange on belly.* Fur long and slightly woolly. Ears blackish, relatively small, moderately haired. Prominent, black eye ring. Whiskers long and thick. *Tail very long,* uniformly dark or faintly bicolor, often with a white tip. Tops of hind feet dark. **Similar Species.** Easily distinguished from other harvest mice in its range by its large size and orangish underparts. Could be confused with small rice rats (*Oryzomys* spp.), which have un-

Map 211. 1. Narrow-nosed Harvest Mouse,
Reithrodontomys tenuirostris
2. Chiriquí Harvest Mouse, *Reithrodontomys creper*

grooved upper incisors (see family account for other differences between the genera).

Distribution. N Costa Rica to W Panama. 1300–3300 m (Timm et al., 1989).

Status and Habitat. Locally common in highland and montane forest, forest edge, and clearings.

Habits. Poorly known. It is mainly terrestrial but is sometimes caught on logs or low branches. It may be found among patches of bamboo near creeks.

YELLOW DEER MOUSE
Isthmomys flavidus   Map 212

HB 127–165, T 163–208, HF 31–35, E 23–27, Wt?

Description. Large. Back *bright tawny brown*, sides *orange*; underparts grayish white (fur slate-colored at base). Fur long and thick. Ears large, lightly haired. Eye ring narrow or absent. Whiskers long and thick. Tail long, faintly bicolor or entirely dark, somewhat blotchy; sparsely haired. Tops of hind feet dark about halfway to toes, then white; hind feet rather broad, fifth toe extends beyond joint of fourth

toe. **Similar Species.** *Peromyscus mexicanus* is smaller, with a much shorter tail. Rice rats (*Oryzomys* spp.) have long, narrow hind feet, with fifth toe not reaching joint of fourth toe.

Distribution. W Panama (Chiriquí, Bocas del Toro, and Azuero Peninsula) only. 1000–1500 m (Carleton, 1989).

Status and Habitat. Apparently rare and local; found in mature forest.

Habits. Poorly known; nocturnal and terrestrial.

MOUNT PIRRI DEER MOUSE   Plate 27
Isthmomys pirrensis   Map 212

HB 153–176, T 178–214, HF 33–36, E 27–30, Wt 92–116 g.

Description. Large. Similar to *I. flavidus*: upperparts slightly darker, some black hairs interspersed with orange. Ears moderately haired. **Similar Species.** No other deer mice occur in E Panama. Montane Rice Rat (*Oryzomys albigularis*) is about the same size and color, but has narrow hind feet, with the middle toes much longer than the outer toes.

Distribution. E Panama (Cerro Pirre, Cerro Malí, and Tacarcuna Village, Darién); possibly N Colombia. 600–1600 m.

Map 212. 1. Yellow Deer Mouse, *Isthmomys flavidus*
2. Mount Pirri Deer Mouse, *Isthmomys pirrensis*

Status and Habitat. Uncommon to locally common in a small range. It is found in mature evergreen forest and favors wet elfin forest on ridges, with numerous epiphytes and deep leaf litter.

Habits. This large deer mouse is nocturnal and mainly terrestrial. It is trapped on the ground near burrows under tree roots or on low, mossy logs. A nest with 2 young was found 2 m above ground at the base of a palm frond. The nest was made of "pulverized bark and plant fibers" (Goldman, 1920).

CRESTED-TAILED DEER
MOUSE   Plate 27
Habromys lophurus   Map 213

HB 91–118, T 103–123, HF 23–25, E 19–20, Wt 22–31 g.

Description. Medium sized. Back *gray-brown*, grading to tawny-ochre on sides; underparts whitish. *Fur long*, thick, and *woolly*. Ears large, brown, and lightly haired. *Eyes small*, with a narrow, dark eye ring. Whiskers numerous, thick, and long; many extend beyond ear. *Tail faintly bicolor for about half its length, all dark toward tip; well haired with a terminal tuft* (hairs 6–7 mm at tip). *Tops of hind feet usually dark to base of toes*, toes white. **Similar Species.**

Other wet forest, highland deer mice do not have clearly tufted tails and are usually larger. Southern Brush Mouse (*Peromyscus levipes*) has a slight tail tuft, but tail is bicolor, tops of hind feet white, fur short and smooth, not woolly, and its eyes are larger.

Distribution. Mountains of Chiapas, Mexico, to NW El Salvador. 1900–3000 m (Musser, 1969).

Status and Habitat. Uncommon to locally common in wet montane forest in the pine–oak belt. It favors mature oak forest with numerous epiphytes, mosses, and fallen trees.

Habits. Nocturnal and semiarboreal; it is usually trapped on fallen logs or low branches. Females were nonreproductive in December in Guatemala.

WHITE-FOOTED MOUSE   Plate 27
Peromyscus leucopus   Map 214

HB 79–95, T 68–78, HF 19–21, E 14–16, Wt 13–24 g: Yucatán Peninsula.

HB 90–107, T 75–88, HF 21–23, E 16–18, Wt 19–28 g: Cozumel.

Description. Small and rather short tailed. Larger and browner on Cozumel than on main-

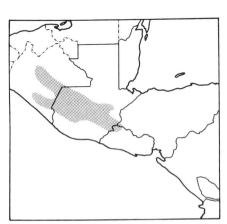

Map 213. Crested-tailed Deer Mouse, *Habromys lophurus*

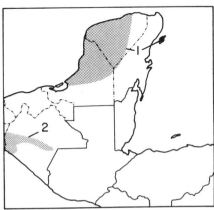

Map 214. 1. White-footed Mouse, *Peromyscus leucopus* 2. Plateau Mouse, *Peromyscus melanophrys*

land. *Back gray,* tinged with ochre on sides; *belly white,* clearly demarcated from sides. Fur short and smooth. Ears medium sized. Dark eye ring narrow or absent. *Tail bicolor, shorter than head and body length,* sparsely haired. Feet white. **Similar Species.** This is the smallest deer mouse in SE Mexico. See *P. yucatanicus.* House Mouse (*Mus musculus*) has an all dark tail, and underparts are not sharply demarcated from upperparts. In harvest mice (*Reithrodontomys* spp.) and Northern Pygmy Rice Rat (*Oligoryzomys*), the tail is much longer than head and body length.

Distribution. Canada and United States through Mexico to Oaxaca and Yucatán Peninsula; Cozumel Island. Lowlands only (in SE Mexico).

Status and Habitat. Common, but rather local in SE Mexico, mainly on roadsides, brushy areas, and weedy fields, sometimes at edges of deciduous forest.

Habits. It is nocturnal and mainly terrestrial. Berries, seeds, fruits, and insects are eaten. In Veracruz, Mexico, nests made of grass and inner bark were found under loose bark of fallen trees in an old cornfield (Hall and Dalquest, 1963). Reproduction may occur year-round; litter size is 2–5, mean 3.3.

other deer mouse with a tufted tail is Crested-tailed Deer Mouse (*Habromys lophurus*); it has smaller ears and is found in wet forest. *P. levipes* is much smaller with a shorter tail; *P. mexicanus* is darker, with a nearly naked tail. Big-eared Climbing Rat (*Ototylomys*) has a naked, shiny tail and white spots at base of ears.

Distribution. Coahuila and Durango, Mexico, through Mexican Plateau to E Chiapas. 100–2600 m. (Baker, 1952; Carleton et al., 1982).

Status and Habitat. Apparently rare in Chiapas, where it is known from very few specimens taken in the late 1800s. It is sometimes common farther north, in dry, rocky, desert areas.

Habits. This attractive deer mouse is semiarboreal. In San Luis Potosí, Mexico, it emerges at dusk to climb and feed on the fruit of Joshua trees and prickly pear cacti. Ball-like nests of woven grasses are made in thorny terminal branches of Joshua trees; a nest in a *Cholla* cactus 1.5 m above ground was lined with plant down and contained 3 young. Unlike most deer mice, "they are rather noisy and can be located by their constant squeaking" (Dalquest, 1953). Breeding takes place from June to January; litter size is about 3.

PLATEAU MOUSE

Peromyscus melanophrys   Map 214

HB 106–123, T 130–155, HF 25–29, E 22–25, Wt 38 g.

Description. Medium sized and long tailed. *Back pale gray* washed with tan, grading to ochre on sides; underparts white. Fur short, smooth, and even. *Ears large,* naked-looking, and pale brown. Face pale gray above and below eye. Whiskers long and moderately thick. *Long tail bicolor,* pale brown above, white below; *well haired with a terminal tuft* (hairs 5 mm at tip). Tops of feet buff. **Similar Species.** The only

AZTEC MOUSE   Plate 27

Peromyscus aztecus   Map 215

HB 109–126, T 108–140, HF 23–26, E 18–21, Wt 33–57 g.

Description. Medium sized. Back *dark reddish brown, sides orange;* underparts whitish. Fur long and thick. Narrow, dark eye ring. Snout relatively short. *Tail moderately bicolor, lightly haired* (hairs 2 mm at tip). Tops of hind feet dusky to bases of toes or all white. **Similar Species.** Adult is more brightly colored than other deer mice in its range, but subadult and juvenile closely resemble several other species.

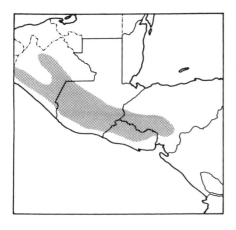

Map 215. Aztec Mouse, *Peromyscus aztecus*

See *P. mexicanus, P. grandis,* and especially *P. levipes.*

Distribution. Jalisco, and Veracruz, Mexico, to SE Honduras. 800–3100 m (Carleton, 1979).

Status and Habitat. Locally common; favors edges and second growth of wet highland forest.

Habits. Probably terrestrial. It is largely insectivorous and includes ants, weevils, crickets, and beetles in the diet; a few seeds (*Solanum* sp. and others) and green plant material are also eaten (Alvarez et al., 1984).

SOUTHERN BRUSH MOUSE Plate 27
Peromyscus levipes Map 216

HB 93–108, T 91–114, HF 21–24, E 18–23, Wt 18–28 g.

Description. Fairly small (larger, darker, and grayer in highlands than in lowlands). Back tawny mixed with black (blackish brown in highlands), grading to tawny-ochre on sides. Underparts white; white extends rather high onto sides. *Fur smooth and even.* Ears lightly haired. Narrow, dark eye ring. Eyes large, with moderately bright, reddish eyeshine. Snout relatively short. *Tail clearly bicolor, lightly haired,*

with a slight terminal tuft (hairs 3–5 mm at tip). Tops of hind feet usually white, or dark for less than half their length. **Similar Species.** Adult *P. aztecus* is larger and reddish brown, but juvenile is almost identical (*P. aztecus* prefers wetter forest). *P. mexicanus* and *P. gymnotis* have nearly naked tails and longer snouts. *P. stirtoni* has a thickly haired, stout tail and longer snout. See Crested-tailed Deer Mouse (*Habromys lophurus*).

Distribution. Nuevo León, Mexico, through Mexican Plateau and mountains to SE Honduras. 700–2800 m (Carleton, 1989).

Status and Habitat. Widespread and sometimes common in thorn scrub, forest edge, and clearings; favors rocky areas with brush and scattered trees. It is found in stands of conifers, but rarely enters in mature broadleaf forest.

Habits. This species is nocturnal, as are all deer mice. Its preference for relatively open areas makes it easier to observe at night than related species, and it can be located by eyeshine. It is mainly terrestrial but climbs well, traveling with speed and agility both on the ground and on branches and vertical tree trunks. Stomachs of 11 individuals from Chiapas, Mexico, contained 91% arthropods (beetles, crickets, ants, caterpillars, and spiders),

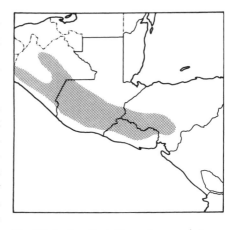

Map 216. Southern Brush Mouse, *Peromyscus levipes*

6% seeds, and 3% green plant material (Alvarez et al., 1984). Acorns are also consumed, and piles of acorn shells may be found at burrow entrances or in small hollows under roots or stones (Carleton et al., 1982). Burrows are located under rocks or tree roots, but nests may be made above ground or in burrows. A leaf nest was found 1 m above ground in a hollow oak tree (Dalquest, 1953). Breeding can take place year-round; mean litter size is 2.3 in Oaxaca, Mexico (Millar, 1989).

Comment. Previously considered a subspecies of *P. boylii.*

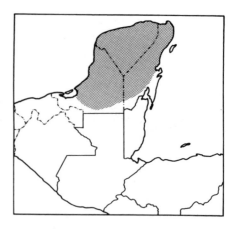

Map 217. Yucatán Deer Mouse, *Peromyscus yucatanicus*

YUCATAN DEER MOUSE Plate 27
Peromyscus yucatanicus Map 217

HB 93–103, T 91–104, HF 21–22, E 18–20, Wt 18–25 g.

Description. Fairly small. Variable in color: tawny-brown on back grading to bright tawny ochre on sides (as illustrated) in north (Yucatán State); farther south (Campeche), gray-brown on back grading to brownish ochre on sides (similar to illustration of *P. mexicanus*); underparts white. Ears large. Narrow, dark eye ring. Tail clearly bicolor, sometimes blotchy below; almost naked. Tops of feet white. **Similar Species.** Juvenile resembles *P. leucopus,* which has a proportionally shorter tail and smaller ears. No other deer mice overlap its range.

Distribution. Yucatán Peninsula, Mexico. Lowlands only.

Status and Habitat. Common in deciduous and semideciduous forest and second growth.

Habits. It is mainly terrestrial and can be trapped on the ground or on logs and low branches. Breeding occurs year-round, but reproductive activity is greatest in the wet season. Litter size is 1–4, mean 2.8 (Lackey, 1976).

MEXICAN DEER MOUSE Plate 27
Peromyscus mexicanus Map 218

HB 108–137, T 105–140, HF 25–28 (26–30, *P. m. nudipes*), E 19–24, Wt 29–50 g (40–57 g, *P. m. nudipes*).

Description. Medium sized to fairly large. Body size, fur length, and coat color vary with elevation, humidity, and season. Back dark gray or gray-brown grading to ochre-brown on sides (highlands and cool, humid areas); tawny-brown grading to bright ochre on sides (warm, humid areas); pale orange-brown grading to buff ochre on sides (warm, dry areas);

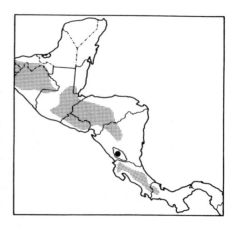

Map 218. Mexican Deer Mouse, *Peromyscus mexicanus*

underparts off-white. Ears large, naked look-ing. Moderate to broad dark eye ring. *Tail usu-ally somewhat bicolor and blotchy below,* some-times uniformly dark; *almost naked.* Tops of hind feet dark for about 1/3 or less of length, toes white. **Similar Species.** *P. aztecus* is usually reddish and has a bicolor, lightly haired tail. *P. levipes* and *P. stirtoni* are smaller and have bi-color, haired tails. *P. melanophrys* is pale gray with a long, tufted tail. Difficult to distinguish from *P. gymnotis* and *P. guatemalensis* (see those accounts).

Distribution. San Luis Potosí and Oaxaca, Mexico, through Central America (except Yu-catán Peninsula and Caribbean lowlands) to W Panama. Lowlands to 3000 m (usually 600–1500 m).

Status and Habitat. Widespread and often common or abundant, especially in semidecid-uous, secondary forest and along streams. Also found in rocky thorn scrub, evergreen and highland forest, coffee groves, and brush.

Habits. This deer mouse climbs well but is largely terrestrial in habits. It does not swim and is reluctant to enter water. It is shy and se-cretive and is seldom seen at night, even where abundant. Stomachs of 27 individuals from Chiapas, Mexico, contained 67% arthropods (primarily spiders, ants, crickets, and beetles), 23% seeds (Solanaceae and Compositae), and 10% green plant material (Alvarez et al., 1984). Caches of coffee beans and other seeds were found under rocks, logs, and near bur-rows in San Luis Potosí, Mexico (Dalquest, 1953). Its burrows are located among the roots of trees, under logs, or in open areas of the forest floor (by trapping and releasing this com-mon species, the burrows can be located). Bur-row entrances are angled at 45°, unlike those of pocket mice (*Heteromys* and *Liomys*), which are usually vertical. In captivity it often drums with the forefeet, but it is usually silent in the wild. Breeding can take place year-round, although populations in seasonally dry areas are usually nonreproductive early in the dry season. Litter size is usually 2–3, mean 2.5 (Lackey, 1976).

Comment. The large subspecies, *P. m. nudipes* (N Costa Rica to W Panama), is sometimes considered a separate species. Additional species may be included in *P. mexicanus* in Chiapas and Guatemala.

NAKED-EARED DEER MOUSE

Peromyscus gymnotis   Map 219

HB 101–120, T 95–120, HF 23–25, E 18–21, Wt 29–42 g.

Description. Fairly small. Back gray-brown, tawny brown, or blackish; sides tawny ochre; underparts grayish white. *Fur short and even.* Moderate eye ring. *Tail usually uniformly dark or faintly bicolor and blotchy below,* almost naked. Tops of hind feet usually white or dark for 1/3 length. **Similar Species.** This species is easily confused with lowland forms of *P. mexi-canus* but *P. gymnotis* is usually smaller, shorter haired, and slightly darker, with a uniformly dark tail (they are often indistinguishable in the field, but compare ranges). See *P. mexi-canus* for comparisons with other deer mice.

Distribution. SE Chiapas, Mexico, along Pa-cific Slope lowlands to SW Nicaragua (Jones and Yates, 1983; Musser, 1971). Lowlands to 1700 m (usually below 1000 m).

Status and Habitat. Common in suitable habitat; present distribution spotty due to in-tensive agricultural development. Found in tall evergreen forest, riparian areas in deciduous forest, second growth, and shaded coffee fields.

Habits. Terrestrial, it is often trapped near fallen logs and around the roots of trees or by rocks. Pregnant females were found from March to August in Nicaragua; litter size is 2–4, mean 2.7 (Jones and Yates, 1983).

GUATEMALAN DEER MOUSE

Peromyscus guatemalensis   Map 220

HB 124–139, T 125–154, HF 29–32, E 22–25, Wt 40–68 g.

Description. Large and dark. Upper back blackish brown, grading to dark gray-brown or ochre-brown on sides; *underparts off-white or buff,* often with a buffy orange pectoral stripe. *Fur long, thick, and slightly woolly. Prominent black eye rings,* sometimes extending to ears to form "spectacles." Tail usually longer than head and body; uniformly dark to strongly bicolor, often blotchy below; lightly haired. Tops of hind feet partially or entirely dark to base of toes; toes white. **Similar Species.** One of the largest deer mice in SE Mexico and Guatemala (similar to *P. zarhynchus,* illustrated; ranges do not overlap). *P. mexicanus* is usually smaller, shorter-haired, and paler in color (and is usually found at lower elevations). See *P. mayensis.*

Distribution. Sierra Madre mountains of S Chiapas, Mexico, east to SC Guatemala (Huckaby, 1980). 1300–3000 m (seldom below 2000 m).

Status and Habitat. Common to abundant in wet highland oak forest with numerous epiphytes; rare or absent from highly disturbed or logged areas.

Habits. It is mainly terrestrial and is often trapped on the ground near fallen logs or at the base of trees, occasionally along low branches or logs. Captive mice often drum with the forefeet.

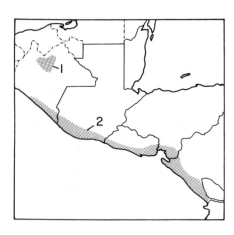

Map 219. 1. Chiapan Deer Mouse, *Peromyscus zarhynchus*
2. Naked-eared Deer Mouse, *Peromyscus gymnotis*

thick, and slightly woolly. Narrow, dark eye ring. Snout long and narrow. *Tail long, usually clearly bicolor, blotchy below,* rarely uniformly dark; very lightly haired. Tops of hind feet dark to base of toes or mainly white. **Similar Species.** Much larger than other deer mice in its range. Similar to a giant *P. mexicanus,* but easily distinguished by hind foot length.

Distribution. Highlands of NC Chiapas, Mexico. 1700–2900 m.

Status and Habitat. Locally common in wet highland forest; found in mature forest, second growth, and brushy, cutover areas. Below 2200 m, it is restricted to tall forest.

Habits. Poorly known. It is terrestrial and is usually trapped on the ground near large trees. Mean litter size is 2.0 (Lackey, 1976).

CHIAPAN DEER MOUSE   Plate 27

Peromyscus zarhynchus   Map 219

HB 135–151, T 135–178, HF 31–34, E 22–27, Wt 50–78 g.

Description. Large. Back *dark gray-brown,* darkest on midline, grading to yellow-brown on sides; underparts whitish or buff. Fur long,

GIANT DEER MOUSE

Peromyscus grandis   Map 220

HB 121–152, T 127–177, HF 28–35, E 24–26, Wt 48–82 g.

Description. Large. *Back blackish brown,* grading to ochre-brown on sides; underparts whitish or buffy brown, often with a buffy or-

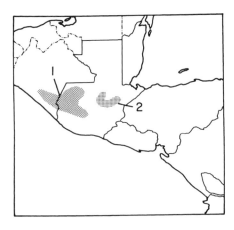

Map 220. 1. Guatemalan Deer Mouse, *Peromyscus guatemalensis*
2. Giant Deer Mouse, *Peromyscus grandis*

ange pectoral stripe. Fur thick and shiny. Narrow, dark eye ring. *Tail long,* uniformly dark or somewhat bicolor and blotchy below; very lightly haired. Tops of hind feet usually dark about halfway to toes, then white. **Similar Species.** Similar to *P. guatemalensis* and *P. zarhynchus,* which do not overlap in range. *P. aztecus,* the only deer mouse known in the same range, is much smaller.

Distribution. C Guatemala only (between Purulhá and Tucuru, Alta and Baja Verapaz; and Sierra de las Minas, Zacapa). 1500–2200 m.

Status and Habitat. Very local but fairly common in mature cloud forest. It is most common along steep banks of streams and in low-lying areas with numerous tree ferns and mosses.

Habits. Like other large deer mice, this species is usually trapped on the ground, occasionally on low logs or fallen trees. Stomach contents of one individual contained well-chewed green plant material only. Of 6 adult females caught in December, 1 was pregnant, with 2 embryos.

STIRTON'S DEER MOUSE   Plate 27
Peromyscus stirtoni   Map 221

HB 83–109, T 87–104, HF 22–25, E 18–20, Wt 24–36 g.

Description. Medium sized, with a *hairy, bicolor tail.* Back gray-brown or tan grizzled with black; sides buffy orange; underparts white. Fur long and soft. Narrow, dark eye ring. Snout relatively long. *Tail about equal to head and body length, stout; strongly bicolor* (black above, white below) and thickly haired, with a slight terminal tuft (hairs 3 mm at tip). Tops of feet white. **Similar Species.** *P. levipes* is similar in size, but has a narrower, lightly haired tail and a rather short snout. *P. mexicanus* has an almost-naked tail and is slightly larger. Other deer mice are not known to occur in the same habitat.

Distribution. Known from scattered localities in SE Guatemala, El Salvador, S Honduras, and W Nicaragua. 200–1000 m (Huckaby, 1980).

Status and Habitat. Local, usually uncommon, occasionally common; restricted to dry or semiarid rocky hills and valleys in dry, deciduous forest, brush, and thorn scrub.

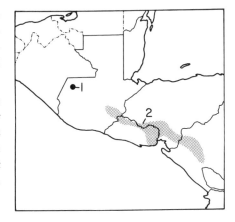

Map 221. 1. Maya Mouse, *Peromyscus mayensis*
2. Stirton's Deer Mouse, *Peromyscus stirtoni*

Habits. This poorly known terrestrial species is always trapped near rocks or boulders. In Nicaragua, a female with 3 embryos was caught in April (Jones and Yates, 1983). Females were nonreproductive in December and January in Guatemala.

MAYA MOUSE   Plate 27
Peromyscus mayensis   Map 221

HB 97–119, T 102–118, HF 26–28, E 21–23, Wt 26–38 g.

Description. Medium sized, with a relatively short tail. Upperparts *dark charcoal gray,* washed with ochre on sides; underparts silvery gray. *Fur long,* thick, and *fluffy-looking.* Ears blackish brown, lightly haired; usually held forward. *Eyes small,* eye ring narrow or absent. Snout long (face looks broadly triangular due to thick fur). *Tail about equal to head and body length; dark,* slightly paler below, almost naked. *Hind feet narrow,* tops dark to base of toes. **Similar Species.** Young *P. guatemalensis* looks similar but has a proportionally longer tail and larger eyes with a prominent black mask.

Distribution. W Guatemala (between Santa Eulalia and San Mateo Ixtatán, Huehuetenango) only. 2900–2950 m.

Status and Habitat. Locally common, but highly threatened due to intensive logging in its small known region of occurrence. This may be the most endangered species of mammal in Central America. It is found in mature, highland forest, where it seems to be restricted to cold, wet oak forest with scattered pines, abundant epiphytes and fallen trees, and a deep layer of leaf litter.

Habits. This poorly known mouse is terrestrial; it burrows through the leaf litter under and along decaying logs and tree roots. It appears to require a deep layer of litter, as it was not found in similar forest without deep litter at a slightly lower elevation (2800 m). At 2900 m, nightly frosts slow decomposition of litter, while at 2800 m the litter layer is shallower due to warmer conditions. Unlike most deer mice, this species is aggressive in captivity, often sitting with one forefoot raised in a fist, in the manner of a mouse opossum (*Marmosa*). Its shrewlike appearance and aggressive behavior suggest an insectivorous diet. Vocalizations include short clicks and snapping noises. Pregnant females were taken in May, with 1–3 embryos, mean 1.8 (Carleton and Huckaby, 1975). All individuals caught in December were nonreproductive.

Voles and Lemmings
Subfamily Arvicolinae

This large subfamily of rodents is distributed throughout the Northern Hemisphere and in parts of the Southern Hemisphere. Grazers or browsers, most arvicolines are terrestrial, with stocky bodies, short tails, and short legs and ears concealed in long fur. A few species, such as the muskrats (*Ondatra* and *Neofiber*) and water voles (*Arvicola*) are semiaquatic grazers. The red tree voles (*Phenacomys*), found in the northwestern United States, are the only arboreal members of the family. Most species are active day and night, and all are active throughout the winter. In tropical zones, voles are restricted to high mountains, and in the New World the southern limit of their distribution is Guatemala, where a single species is found.

GUATEMALAN VOLE
Microtus guatemalensis

Plate 29
Map 222

HB 93–118, T 28–42, HF 19–21, E 14–17, Wt 23–44 g.

Description. Medium sized with a very short tail. *Back dark blackish brown,* tinged with ochre; underparts dark buffy gray. Fur long, thick, and *fuzzy looking.* Ears short, well haired, almost hidden in fur. *Eyes tiny.* Snout blunt, with short, fine whiskers. *Tail about 30% of head and body length,* all dark, fairly well haired. Feet small and dark. **Similar Species.** The very short tail is diagnostic in its limited range.

Distribution. Chiapas, Mexico (Cerro Tzontehuitz), and S Guatemala. 2600–3100 m.

Status and Habitat. Uncommon to locally common in montane forest and pasture. It favors low-lying, damp areas in pine–oak forest and small clearings.

Habits. Possibly diurnal or crepuscular and terrestrial. Unlike most voles, which travel on run-

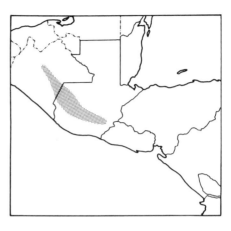

Map 222. Guatemalan Vole, *Microtus guatemalensis*

ways through grassy areas, this species can be found in deep forest and does not appear to use runways. It probably eats plant material, although details of the diet have not been reported. A pregnant female, caught in January, had one embryo (Smith and Jones, 1967).

Comment. Sometimes placed in the genus *Pitymys.*

Old World Rats and Mice
Subfamily Murinae

There are about 529 species in 122 genera in the Murinae. Native to the Old World, several species become commensal with humans within their natural range, but 3 species have followed the movements of humans and have become established in cities throughout the world. These rodents spread disease and cause considerable losses to stored grain and foodstuffs. They have created a bad image for all rats and mice around the world. Nonetheless, innumerable scientific and medical advances have resulted from use of laboratory colonies of the House Mouse and Norway Rat.

ROOF RAT
Rattus rattus

Plate 31

Spanish: rata de la casa; Belize: Charlie Price.

HB 158–196, T 164–244, HF 34–39, E 22–24, Wt 85–165 g.

Description. Medium sized to large in Central America (can be very large elsewhere). Upper-

parts usually dark brown, occasionally black, grizzled with black and white hairs on back and sides; *underparts buff, pale gray or whitish, not sharply demarcated from upperparts;* hairs gray at base. Fur long and rather coarse. Ears large, brown, and naked. Snout long and pointed, with long, thick whiskers. Eyeshine moderate, reddish. *Tail robust, slightly longer* than head and body; all brown, naked looking, and scaly. Feet long and broad, tops brown or gray. Female has 5–6 pairs of mammae. **Similar Species.** *R. norvegicus* is larger, with a relatively shorter tail and small ears. The naked tail, grayish underparts, and relative toe lengths (fifth toe reaches joint of fourth toe; thumb reaches base of middle toes) of hind foot distinguish it from other large rats.

Distribution. Introduced worldwide; originally from India and SE Asia.

Status and Habitat. Common and widespread; it is a serious agricultural pest and carrier of disease. This rat may kill or displace native species and can be especially harmful on islands. It is found in and around human habitations, both in cities and rural areas, and less commonly in forest or at forest edge.

Habits. It is mainly nocturnal but sometimes active by day. This house rat climbs well and usually occupies roofs or attics, where it may be heard running around and feeding at night. In agricultural areas it is largely terrestrial. The diet includes grain, fruit, garbage, and all kinds of household materials of dubious edibility. It is a prolific breeder with a mean litter size of 8; breeding can occur year-round.

NORWAY RAT   Plate 31
Rattus norvegicus

Local names as for Roof Rat.

HB 186–240, T 122–215, HF 30–45, E 15–20, Wt 195–485 g.

Description. Large to very large. Upperparts yellowish brown, darkest on midback; *underparts grayish white or yellowish, not sharply demarcated from upperparts;* hairs gray at base. Fur long and coarse. *Ears short, lightly haired.* Snout blunt, with short, thick whiskers. *Tail shorter than head and body, robust, moderately bicolor, thinly covered with coarse hairs.* Feet large and broad, tops whitish. Female has 5–6

pairs of mammae. **Similar Species.** See *R. rattus.* Other large rats do not occur in cities.

Distribution. Introduced worldwide; originally from SE Siberia and China.

Status and Habitat. Abundant in some urban areas, but less widespread than *R. rattus* in Central America. It is confined to towns and cities, where it favors sewers and wet areas.

Habits. Mainly nocturnal in habits, but where common, this large, ugly rat is often seen by day. It swims well and is largely terrestrial, but can climb well on occasion. The diet is catholic and includes any available foodstuffs. It is more carnivorous than *R. rattus* and may kill hens and young livestock. This species is social and constructs complex burrow systems. The colonies formed consist of several females and their young and one male. Breeding can occur year-round, and litter size is 2–22, with a mean of 8.5.

HOUSE MOUSE   Plate 25
Mus musculus

Spanish: ratone de la casa.

HB 66–91, T 69–93, HF 16–19, E 12–16, Wt 7–15 g.

Description. Small. Upperparts gray-brown or yellowish brown; *underparts slightly paler or grayish, not well demarcated from upperparts;* hairs gray at base. Fur short and even. Head rather small. Ears fairly large and naked. Whiskers short and sparse. *Tail robust, about equal to head and body length, all brown, and naked looking.* Tops of feet pale brown or whitish. Female has 5 pairs of mammae. **Similar Species.** Usually recognized by lack of demarcation between back and belly, tail length, and rank, musty odor. See Southern Pygmy Mouse (*Baiomys*) and harvest mice (*Reithrodontomys* spp.).

Distribution. Introduced worldwide. Found throughout Central America and SE Mexico.

Status and Habitat. Common and widespread. This species is a pest that may displace native species and often damages stored grain. It is found in agricultural areas, fields, and roadsides, usually near human settlements; also in urban areas.

Habits. It is nocturnal and mainly terrestrial, but climbs well. It sometimes makes runways through grass or uses those of other species. The diet includes grains, seeds, and insects. Nests are made of soft fiber, shredded paper, or cloth. Faint twitters and squeaks may be heard from the nest, but adults are usually silent when foraging. Breeding can occur year-round, and litter size averages 6.

NEW WORLD PORCUPINES (Spanish: puercoespines)
Family Erethizontidae

The Erethizontidae consists of about 15 species in 4 genera. These porcupines are more closely related to other cavylike rodents (such as agouti and paca) than to Old World porcupines. New World porcupines are primarily South American in distribution; only 2 species occur in Central America and one other in North America. Porcupines are well known for their long, sharp spines. The spines are barbed at the tip and are easily shed, although never thrown. All New World porcupines are spiny, but in some species the spines are concealed by long hair. Young of all species are hairy. The Central American species are stocky looking, with short limbs and long, prehensile tails. The tail is thick at the base and tapers sharply to the tip. The naked, grasping surface of the tail is on the upper side, unlike all other prehensile-tailed mammals in the region, in which the grasping surface is on the underside of the tail. There are 4 toes on each foot, equipped with long, sharp claws. The hind feet have large, rounded pads that produce a distinctive track. These porcupines have large, pink noses, small eyes, and barely visible ears, giving them a somewhat homely appearance.

MEXICAN PORCUPINE
Plate 32
Coendou mexicanus
Map 223

Spanish: puercoespín; Honduras: zorro espín, mistacuaz.

HB 320–457 (16"), T 200–358 (12"), Wt 1.4–2.6 kg (5 lb).

Description. Stocky, with a *black body* and a *contrasting pale head.* Long, black fur conceals the *yellowish spines* on most of the body but is absent on the head. Some are less hairy, and some spines may be visible on shoulders, back, and rump. Spines pale yellow with black tips. *Nose large*, pink, and *bulbous.* Eyes rather small; eyeshine moderately bright, reddish. *Tail pre-*

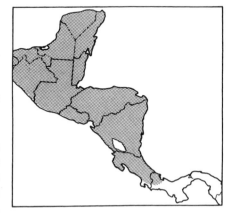

Map 223. Mexican Porcupine, *Coendou mexicanus*

hensile, thick and spiny at the base, tapering to the tip. **Similar Species.** Rothschild's Porcupine is entirely spiny, not hairy (ranges probably do not overlap).

Distribution. San Luis Potosí, Mexico, through Yucatán Peninsula and Central America to W Panama. Lowlands to 3200 m.

Status and Habitat. CITES Appendix III (Honduras). Locally common and widespread; hunted in some areas and often killed by traffic. It is found at middle and high elevations in all forest types, including disturbed forest and second growth. At low elevations it seems to favor seasonally dry habitats (Pacific Slope and Yucatán Peninsula); this species is generally uncommon or rare in wet evergreen forest of the Atlantic lowlands.

Habits. Nocturnal in habit, this porcupine seems to be most active on dark nights. When caught in a spotlight, it usually scrambles hastily away through the treetops, but occasionally sits and stares at the observer. The prehensile tail is usually coiled around a large branch. The Mexican Porcupine is mainly arboreal, but descends to the ground to cross roads and clearings. During the day it sleeps in hollow trees or on leafy branches. In highland forest it sometimes dens in bamboo thickets on the ground. Because the same den is used day after day, a characteristic pile of pellet-shaped droppings accumulates in the base of the hollow (or on the branch), along with a strong, musty odor. It feeds on seeds, fruit, buds, and young leaves, particularly those of *Inga, Cecropia, Ficus,* and *Brosimum* trees. This porcupine is usually solitary and silent, but during the breeding season it calls with loud yowls and screams, and breeding pairs may share a den. Females usually have one young. Young mew like kittens if separated from the mother. Ecology reviewed by Janzen (1983a), and Coates-Estrada and Estrada (1986).

Where to See. Most often seen at night in riparian forest in seasonally dry regions (especially N Belize, NW Costa Rica); check fruiting *Inga* and *Cecropia* trees (e.g., at Monteverde, Costa Rica). Ask locals for whereabouts of den sites.

Comment. This species and other hairy porcupines are sometimes placed in a separate genus, *Sphiggurus.*

ROTHSCHILD'S PORCUPINE Plate 32
Coendou rothschildi Map 224

Panama: puercoespín, gato de espinas; Chocó: pimini gli.

HB 332–420 (14"), T 290–413 (13"), HF 62–77, E 20–26, Wt 2 kg (4 lb).

Description. *Entirely spiny.* Spines are blackish in midsection with pale yellow tips and are evenly spaced over the body. Eyes rather small; nose pink, bulbous. *Tail prehensile,* broad at base, greatly tapered. **Similar Species.** Mexican Porcupine is hairy looking.

Distribution. Panama; possibly west of Andes in Colombia, Ecuador, and Peru. Lowlands only.

Map 224. Rothschild's Porcupine, *Coendou rothschildi*

Status and Habitat. Uncommon; found in deciduous and evergreen forest.

Habits. Poorly known, probably similar to Mexican Porcupine. Nocturnal and arboreal, it sleeps during the day in vine tangles near the tops of trees. The diet includes fruit and leaves (Goldman, 1920).

Comment. May be a subspecies of *C. bicolor* (Emmons, 1990).

CAPYBARAS
Family Hydrochaeridae

There is only one genus in the Hydrochaeridae. Most authorities recognize a single species, although some consider the smaller Capybaras from west of the Andes (in Panama, NW Venezuela, and N Colombia) to be a separate species, *H. isthmius.* Biology of South American Capybaras reviewed by Mones and Ojasti (1986).

CAPYBARA   Plate 32
Hydrochaeris hydrochaeris   Map 225

Panama: poncho; Kuna: cuini; Chocó: tocoriba, tocorigua.

HB 0.8–1.0 m (3'), SH 0.5–0.6 m (2'), Wt 25–45 kg (60 lb).

Description. Largest rodent in the world. Semiaquatic, with a *stocky body*, a *large, rectangular head*, and rounded rump. Fur dull orange or reddish brown. Male has a scent gland (raised area of bare, shiny skin) on the nose. Eyeshine moderate, reddish. Tail tiny, not visible. *Feet webbed*, with 4 toes on front foot and 3 on hind. **Similar Species.** Unmistakable if seen well. *Peccaries (Tayassu* spp.) are about the same size, but have triangular heads and are grayish or black, not reddish.

Distribution. C Panama to NE Argentina. Lowlands to 800 m.

Status and Habitat. Uncommon and local in Panama; hunted for meat and hides. Always found near water, along the edge of lakes, rivers, and marshes.

Habits. In areas where it is not hunted, it is active during the day and night, but if hunted, it

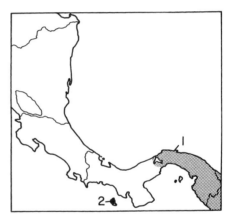

Map 225. 1. Capybara, *Hydrochaeris hydrochaeris*
2. Coiba Island Agouti, *Dasyprocta coibae*

becomes mainly nocturnal. When resting, this large rodent often sits on its haunches like a dog, or flops on its side. When disturbed, the Capybara barks in alarm and jumps into the water with a loud splash. It swims well and submerges completely if pursued. It feeds mostly on grass and aquatic vegetation but may enter agricultural areas at night to eat soybean plants or other crops. Small groups of 2–6 individuals occupy forested regions, larger groups of 20 or more are found in more open habitats.

Mating takes place in the water at any time of year. Females give birth to 2–8 young after 4 months of gestation. The young are born well developed and travel with their mother.

Where to See. Rather scarce and shy in Panama (unlike in Venezuela or Argentina).

Small groups can be seen at dusk around Gamboa pond; Capybara may be seen on shores of islands in the Panama Canal at dawn or dusk; elsewhere it is mostly nocturnal. Look for the characteristic, star-shaped tracks of the forefeet and piles of oval droppings (similar to those of deer, but larger).

AGOUTIS AND ACOUCHIS
Family Dasyproctidae

The Dasyproctidae consists of 2 genera and about 14 species. There are 4 species in one genus in Mexico and Central America, the other species occur in South America. They are terrestrial forest dwellers.

MEXICAN BLACK AGOUTI	Plate 33
Dasyprocta mexicana	Map 226

Mexico: serete, guaqueque negro.

HB 446–557 (20"), T 20–30 (1"), Wt 2–4 kg (6 lb).

Description. Large, with a *rounded back* and *long, skinny legs. Dark; blackish fur* finely grizzled with white; long, black hairs on rump. Underparts paler. Pink skin around eyes and at base of naked ears. Forefoot with 4 toes, hindfoot with 3 toes; claws hooflike. **Similar Species.** Central American Agouti (*D. punctata*) is reddish brown, not black.

Distribution. SE Mexico only: Veracruz, N Oaxaca, NW Chiapas, and W Tabasco. Gulf lowlands to 600 m.

Status and Habitat. Probably uncommon; hunted for meat and considered an agricultural pest. Found in lowland evergreen forest and second growth.

Habits. This agouti is mainly diurnal, although sometimes it is seen at night. Like other agoutis, it is terrestrial. This species eats fruit, soft seeds, and new growth of forest plants. In Veracruz, fruits eaten include figs, hog plums (*Spondias mombin*), and *Brosimum*

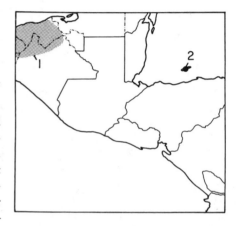

Map 226. 1. Mexican Black Agouti, *Dasyprocta mexicana*
2. Roatán Island Agouti, *Dasyprocta ruatanica*

alicastrum. The Mexican Black Agouti may be seen alone or in pairs. Pairs occupy territories of 1–2 ha. If alarmed, it gives a series of sharp, nasal barks, stamping the feet as it runs off. One or 2 young are born during the dry season. Young are precocious and follow their mother soon after birth. Reviewed by Coates-Estrada and Estrada (1986).

CENTRAL AMERICAN AGOUTI

Plate 33

Dasyprocta punctata

Map 227

Mexico: guaqueque alazán; Belize: indian rabbit; Honduras, Costa Rica: guatusa; Panama: ñeque.

HB 450–570 (20"), T 20–40 (1"), Wt 3–4 kg (8 lb).

Description. Large; *orange-brown* with a *rounded back* and *long, skinny legs.* Color varies from entirely yellowish or orange, finely grizzled with black, to dark brown foreparts, orange midback, and cream/black rump (on the Atlantic Slope of Costa Rica and Panama). Rump hairs long, sometimes erected into a fan. Ears naked, pinkish, with rounded tips. Forefoot with 4 toes, hind foot with 3 toes and hooflike claws. **Similar Species.** See Mexican Black Agouti. Paca (*Agouti paca*) is spotted, stocky, and nocturnal.

Distribution. Chiapas and Tabasco, Mexico, through Yucatán Peninsula and Central America to S Bolivia and N Argentina. Lowlands to 2400 m.

Status and Habitat. CITES Appendix III (Honduras). Although widespread and often common in parks and reserves, this agouti is heavily hunted for meat, and populations are much reduced in many areas with suitable habitat. It is reluctant to leave its territory and so can be run to ground by dogs and killed with machetes. It occurs in deciduous and evergreen forest, second growth, and plantations.

Habits. The Central American Agouti is diurnal; activity starts early in the morning and continues on and off throughout the day. It is sometimes seen at night as it is easily disturbed when sleeping, and it may continue feeding after sunset. It sleeps in hollow logs, under buttress roots, or in tangles of vegetation. Burrows in banks may be used in some regions.

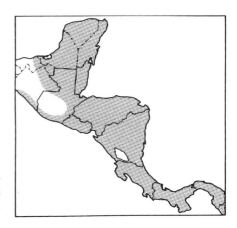

Map 227. Central American Agouti, *Dasyprocta punctata*

Each individual has several sleeping sites that are used repeatedly. The diet consists mainly of seeds and fruits; small amounts of plant material and fungi are included when supplies of fruit are low. This agouti can sometimes be located by the rasping sounds made as it chews on hard seeds and nuts. When food is abundant, it carries seeds away and buries them for future use, depositing each seed in a different place. Since not all seeds are recovered, this rodent is an important seed disperser for a number of tree species including Guapinol (*Hymenaea courabil*; Hallwachs 1986) and Almendro (*Dipteryx panamensis*). Agoutis live in stable pairs that remain together until one of the pair dies. Often only one individual may be seen, as members of the pair do not stay in close contact with each other. Pairs maintain territories but are fairly tolerant of other agoutis if food is plentiful. In aggressive interactions, the long rump hairs are raised to form a fan-shaped crest. When startled, an agouti will give a few low grunts, followed by one or more sharp, high-pitched barks as it runs off. It may drum with the forefeet if mildly alarmed. Females give birth to 1–2 well-developed young. Soon after birth, the mother leads the young to a small nest hole. The babies enter the nest, emerging only when the mother calls them out

243

to nurse at the entrance. The entrance to the nest hole is too small for the mother and large predators to enter. After a few weeks the young outgrow the nest and move to another hole. They gradually spend more time above ground and eventually leave the nest to travel with the mother. Young are independent at 4–5 months. For a detailed account of natural history, see Smythe (1978).

Where to See. Most easily found in small, well-protected forest tracts, where it habituates to people and probably has few predators. Good sites are Tikal, Guatemala; La Selva and Manuel Antonio national parks, Costa Rica; and Barro Colorado Island, Panama.

COIBA ISLAND AGOUTI
Dasyprocta coibae   Map 225

HB 435–520 (18"), T 30–40 (1").

Description. Similar to Central American Agouti, differing mainly in characters of the skull. Upperparts uniformly yellow-brown, grizzled with black; underparts paler.

Distribution. Coiba Island, Panama.

Status and Habitat. Poorly known. Found in forested regions, which are mainly deciduous on Coiba.

Habits. Not reported, probably similar to Central American Agouti.

ROATAN ISLAND AGOUTI
Dasyprocta ruatanica   Map 226

HB 435 (17").

Description. A small version of the Central American Agouti. Upperparts uniformly orange-brown grizzled with black.

Distribution. Roatán Island, Honduras.

Status and Habitat. Threatened. Presumably occurs in forest and second growth.

Habits. Not reported, probably similar to Central American Agouti.

PACAS
Family Agoutidae

This family consists of 2 species in one genus. Unfortunately, the scientific name of pacas, *Agouti*, is not matched with the common name, but refers to these less familiar, nocturnal, spotted rodents. One species occurs in the region, the other one is restricted to South America.

PACA   Plate 33
Agouti paca   Map 228

Spanish: tepezcuintle; Mexico: tuza real; Belize and Caribbean coast: gibnut; Panama: conejo pintado.

HB 500–774 (27"), T 13–23 (1/2"), SH 270–310 (12"), Wt 5–12 kg (18 lb).

Description. Large and stocky; piglike body shape. Upperparts *reddish brown*, marked with *rows of white spots*; underparts white. Legs short, 4 toes on forefoot, 5 toes on hind foot (track usually shows 3 toes, 2 outer toes very small). Eyeshine very bright, yellow-orange.

Similar Species. The only other spotted mammals in the region are young deer and tapir. Deer (*Mazama, Odocoileus*) have very different body proportions (long legs, smaller head, etc.). Young Baird's Tapir (*Tapirus*) is brown-black, not reddish, has striped legs, more prominent ears, and is less commonly encountered than Paca.

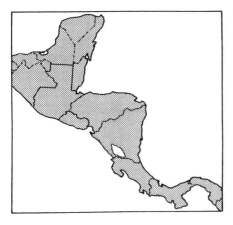

Map 228. Paca, *Agouti paca*

Distribution. Atlantic Slope of Mexico from San Luis Potosí to Chiapas, then throughout the Yucatán Peninsula and Central America to Paraguay and S Brazil. Lowlands to 2000 m.

Status and Habitat. CITES Appendix III (Honduras). Widespread and locally common, but heavily hunted for meat, and rare or absent from much suitable habitat as a result. Found in evergreen and deciduous forest, second growth, and gardens. It is usually found near water, along small creeks, swamps, riversides, and in low-lying areas. This species is surprisingly common in small strips of riparian forest in agricultural zones.

Habits. The Paca is strictly nocturnal and seldom emerges until a few hours after sunset. It is most active on dark nights. It walks slowly across the forest floor, in the dry season accompanied by sound of rustling leaves. If caught in a light it may freeze, and so can be easily shot by hunters. When pursued, it may run into water and submerge completely. During the day this rodent sleeps in burrows, often dug on steep banks. Burrows have several entrances, some of which are plugged with leaves. The diet consists of fruit, seeds, and young plants. Monogamous pairs occupy exclusive territories. Single individuals are most often encountered, as members of the pair den and travel alone most of the time, but 2 may be seen feeding together under a fruiting tree. This large rodent is usually silent, though it can produce deep barks and ominous grinding sounds; the greatly enlarged cheek bones act as resonating chambers. Sounds are probably used in aggression between males. Females give birth to single young. Reviewed by Smythe (1983).

Where to See. Scarce and wary where hunted; it is easily seen in small, well-protected forest tracts such as Manuel Antonio National Park, Costa Rica, and Barro Colorado Island, Panama. Often seen along shores of lakes and rivers, near forested creeks, or under fruiting trees.

SPINY RATS AND TREE RATS
Family Echimyidae

The Echimyidae is a complex and diverse family of large rats. There are about 70 species in 15 genera. Most are restricted to South America, but 3 species range northward into Central America. Despite their ratlike form, echimyids are more closely related to cavylike rodents (agoutis, Capybaras, and porcupines) than to true rats. The most conspicuous external characteristic that these groups share is the ear shape, which is indented on the posterior edge, where it is roughly M-shaped. Central American echimyids are forest dwellers; some are strictly arboreal and others are terrestrial. They have few offspring in a litter, and the young are born well developed, fully furred, and with their eyes open (another feature shared with larger cavylike rodents).

TOMES' SPINY RAT
Proechimys semispinosus

Plate 31
Map 229

Map 229. Tomes' Spiny Rat, *Proechimys semispinosus*

Spanish: rata espinosa, casiragua; Panama: mocangué.

HB 221–279, T 175–192, HF 50–60, E 22–27, Wt 320–536 g.

Description. Very large, with *sleek, reddish brown upperparts and pure white underparts.* Spines on the back are narrow, mixed with fur, and inconspicuous in the field. Head long and narrow, with large eyes and erect, slender ears. Feet long and narrow; claws long and broad. *Tail shorter than head and body, nearly naked, and clearly bicolor.* About 1 in 5 individuals seen are tailless and look like long-nosed guinea pigs. Eyeshine bright, reddish. **Similar Species.** See Armored Rat (*Hoplomys gymnurus*). Other terrestrial rats are much smaller, with weaker eyeshine, and most have tail longer than head and body.

Distribution. E Honduras to NE Peru and Amazonian Brazil. Lowlands to about 800 m.

Status and Habitat. Common, often abundant, in lowland evergreen forest and second growth. Also found in deciduous forest, where it favors riparian corridors and low-lying areas.

Habits. This large, sleek rat is nocturnal and mainly terrestrial. It travels along fallen logs or old walls but does not climb trees. At night it is often seen sitting quietly near buttress roots or logs. It walks slowly and sometimes freezes in a spotlight. This rat may use burrows during the day but often occupies shallow depressions under roots and hollow logs, or in dense vegetation. The diet consists mainly of fruit and seeds, with lesser amounts of plant material, insects, and fungi. Palm nuts and other large seeds are carried to a sheltered spot to be eaten. It is usually silent. Females give birth to 1–5 precocious young and may breed 4 times a year.

Where to See. Abundant and conspicuous in forests of the Panama Canal area: on Barro Colorado Island, Gigante Peninsula, and in secondary palm forest near Gamboa. Often seen in forest camps in Darién National Park. North of Panama, it seems much less common, though it can be seen at night at La Selva, Costa Rica.

ARMORED RAT
Hoplomys gymnurus

Plate 31
Map 230

Spanish: rata espinosa.

HB 205–295, T 126–195, HF 51–60, E 22–27, Wt 230–680 g.

Description. Very large, with *prominent, thick spines on back and sides.* Upperparts vary from entirely black to reddish brown, grading to ochraceous on sides. Underparts pure white. Tail naked, bicolor, easily broken or lost. Eyeshine moderately bright, reddish. **Similar Species.** Similar in shape and size to Tomes' Spiny Rat (*Proechimys semispinosus*) and can be confused at a distance. Armored Rat has slightly smaller eyes, less conspicuous eyeshine, and a longer snout. Even at some distance, the spines give the back a bristly, uneven outline, unlike the smooth, sleek look of *Proechimys.*

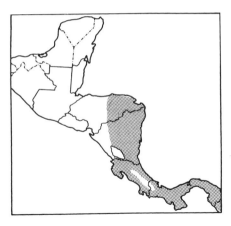

Map 230. Armored Rat, *Hoplomys gymnurus*

Distribution. N Honduras (McCarthy et al., 1991) to NW Ecuador. Lowlands to 800 m.

Status and Habitat. Uncommon to locally abundant in evergreen, lowland forest; usually near creeks or streams, or in low-lying areas such as palm swamps.

Habits. The Armored Rat is nocturnal and terrestrial. During the day it occupies burrows, usually located on steep banks near water. Burrows are roughly horizontal and extend about 2 m to a nest chamber lined with shredded vegetation (Buchanan and Howell, 1965). This large rat can be easily detected at night as it has good eyeshine, and, when disturbed, it usually runs swiftly to a burrow. It may remain at the burrow entrance, where it can be closely observed or even captured by hand. The diet includes fruit, insects (beetle and orthopteran remains have been found in its burrows), and some green plant matter. Litter size is 1–3; young are precocious at birth and have soft fur. Spines develop after 1 month (Tesh, 1970a).

Where to See. Most often located by walking along creeks or canoeing along forested rivers at night. Population size often fluctuates greatly from year to year; streams crossing Pipeline Road, near Gamboa, Panama, can be productive.

RUFOUS TREE RAT   Plate 31
Diplomys labilis   Map 231

Panama: gato bruja, ratón marañero.

HB 212–340, T 175–249, HF 44–48, E 15–17, Wt 300–492 g.

Description. Very large; arboreal. Upperparts *reddish brown*; underparts *pale orange*. Fur thick and coarse, but not spiny. *Head grayish* with white patches at base of whiskers and behind ears. Ears short and broad. Tail *shorter than head and body length*, skin pinkish, thickly *covered in brown hair*. Feet short and broad, tops buff. Eyeshine moderately bright, reddish. **Similar Species.** Other arboreal rats in Panama are smaller, with proportionally longer tails, head same color as back, and no white facial markings.

Distribution. Coclé Province (Villa-R., 1993) and Isla del Rey (formerly known as San Miguel Island), Panama, to W Colombia and possibly N Ecuador. Lowlands to 1500 m.

Status and Habitat. Poorly known but probably not uncommon; found in evergreen and deciduous forest, mangroves, plantations, and second growth. Common on Isla del Rey.

Habits. Although this rat is nocturnal on the mainland, those on Isla del Rey may be diurnal

Map 231. Rufous Tree Rat, *Diplomys labilis*

(Goldman, 1920). It is strictly arboreal and has not been trapped on the ground. Tree rats move slowly and may remain motionless for long periods, but climb swiftly if pursued. This species can be detected at night by its moderate eyeshine. During the day, adult pairs or lone individuals sleep in holes in trees. If disturbed by banging on the trunk of an occupied tree, they sticks their heads out, showing the characteristic facial markings. This behavior is well known to rural residents, who report that "gato bruja" (witch cat) usually occupy trees near water and are always in pairs. Pairs may travel and forage together at night. The diet probably includes fruit and young leaves. Litter size is 1–2 and breeding may occur year-round (Tesh, 1970b).

RABBITS AND HARES

Order Lagomorpha, Family Leporidae

The lagomorphs are distributed worldwide and include 2 families, 1 of which is represented in the Neotropics. With about 44 species in 10 genera, this family is known in SE Mexico and Central America by only 4 species in 2 genera. Originally classified as rodents because of their constantly growing incisors, lagomorphs differ in having a second pair of small incisors behind the long upper incisors. The dental formula is: i 2/1, c 0/0, p 3/2, m 3/3. Rabbits and hares have long, narrow ears, slitlike nostrils, soft fur, short tails, and long, fully furred hind feet. There are 5 toes on the forefoot and 4 on the hind foot. Both jackrabbits and hares are members of the genus *Lepus* (with one representative in SE Mexico); other Central American rabbits are in the genus *Sylvilagus*.

Most rabbits and hares are nocturnal. They are herbivores and have a modified digestive system for handling large amounts of vegetation. Several species eat their feces, allowing the food to pass through the intestines twice and increasing the efficiency of nutrient extraction. Rabbits and hares are found in a wide variety of habitats, from deserts to forest and tundra. Many species occur in open areas and rely on speed to escape predators, traveling with a hopping or bounding gait. Long-legged hares can reach speeds of 80 km/hour. Rabbits and hares differ in their breeding biology. Rabbits build elaborate nests and give birth to blind, naked, helpless young; hares use a shallow depression as a nest and give birth to well-developed young that are independent soon after birth.

TEHUANTEPEC JACKRABBIT Plate 34
Lepus flavigularis Map 232

Spanish: liebre, liebre tropical.

HB 420–556 (19"), T 57–91 (3"), HF 127–136, E 121–130, Wt 2–3.5 kg (6 lb).

Description. Large, pale, and *long legged*, with *very long, white-tipped ears*. Upperparts pale buff grizzled with dark brown, rump and legs pale gray. Dark line on nape of neck to base of each ear. *Sides and belly white*, chest and neck buff. Tail black above, white below. **Similar Species.** No other jackrabbits occur in its range; Eastern Cottontail (*Sylvilagus floridanus*) is smaller and more compact, with much shorter legs and ears.

Distribution. Coastal region of the Gulf of Tehuantepec, from Salina Cruz, Oaxaca, to the border of Chiapas, Mexico. Lowlands only.

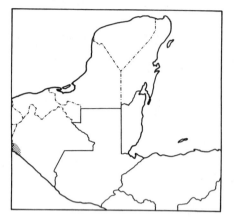

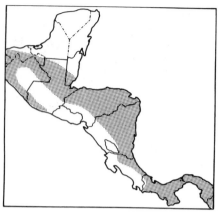

Map 232. Tehuantepec Jackrabbit, *Lepus flavigularis*

Map 233. Forest Rabbit, *Sylvilagus brasiliensis*

Status and Habitat. Rare and local; restricted to sand dunes and scrubby, riparian vegetation in a narrow strip (4–5 km or less) along the shores of coastal lagoons. It is threatened by habitat loss and excessive hunting pressure throughout its limited range and is presumed to be highly endangered (Flux and Angermann, 1990).

Habits. Poorly known; probably similar to other jackrabbits. It is mainly nocturnal and feeds at night on a variety of green plant material and seeds. It is solitary in habit. Jackrabbits rest and raise their young in shallow depressions lined with dry leaves, usually situated in a shady spot. Pregnant females, one carrying 2 embryos, have been recorded in February. Biology reviewed by Cervantes (1993).

FOREST RABBIT   Plate 34
Sylvilagus brasiliensis   Map 233

Spanish: conejo, conejo tropical, conejo de monte; Belize: bush rabbit; Panama: muleto.

HB 289–400 (13"), T 13–35 (1"), HF 63–92, E 40–52, Wt 0.68–1.25 kg (1.7 lb).

Description. Small, with an *inconspicuous tail* and relatively *short ears* (highland populations have shorter ears than those in the lowlands).

Upperparts buffy-orange grizzled with black, small orange patch on nape, legs and feet orange-brown. Throat orangish, belly whitish with gray underfur. *Underside of tail brownish* or orange. Eyeshine bright, reddish. **Similar Species.** Dice's Rabbit (*S. dicei*) is distinguished mainly by larger size; it may also have darker fur (the 2 species have not been found together). Eastern Cottontail (*S. floridanus*) has a conspicuous, white tail, longer ears, and a larger orange patch on the nape.

Distribution. S Tamaulipas, Mexico, through wetter parts of Central America (except El Salvador) to Peru, Bolivia, S Brazil, and N Argentina. Lowlands to at least 1500 m (to 4500 m in Andes of South America).

Status and Habitat. Fairly common and widely distributed in edges bordering evergreen forest, such as tree-fall gaps, roadsides, pastures, clearings, and brushy second growth. It is absent from areas with a prolonged dry season.

Habits. Mainly nocturnal, this rabbit is sometimes seen early in the morning or at dusk. During the day it rests under logs or in dense cover. Soon after sunset it may be located by reddish eyeshine from a single eye if in profile, feeding on short grass in clearings near forest. When feeding it can often be approached closely. If discovered it will remain motionless for some time and then dash to a nearby shelter. The Forest Rabbit is solitary. The female builds aboveground nests of dry grass, with a central chamber and several small chambers at the end of a runway system. In Chiapas, Mexico, it breeds throughout the year, and litters of 2–8 are born after 1 month of gestation. Biology reviewed by Chapman and Ceballos (1990).

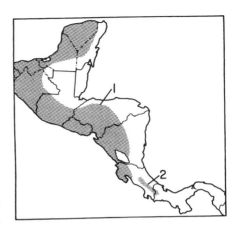

Map 234. 1. Eastern Cottontail, *Sylvilagus floridanus* 2. Dice's Rabbit, *Sylvilagus dicei*

DICE'S RABBIT
Sylvilagus dicei

Plate 34
Map 234

HB 344–448, T 7–34, HF 85–103, E 45–57, Wt?

Description. Similar to Forest Rabbit, but slightly larger and sometimes darker, with a blackish back and tail. **Similar Species.** See Forest Rabbit and Eastern Cottontail.

Distribution. Cordillera de Talamanca of Costa Rica and W Panama. 1100–3500 m.

Status and Habitat. Poorly known; probably not uncommon in highland forest and páramo.

Habits. Poorly known; presumably similar to Forest Rabbit.

Comment. Formerly considered a subspecies of *S. brasiliensis*, Diersing (1981) elevated it to a species based on size differences.

EASTERN COTTONTAIL
Sylvilagus floridanus

Plate 34
Map 234

Spanish: conejo, conejo de campo, conejo de monte, conejo castellano.

HB 337–423 (14"), T 47–66 (2"), HF 87–102, E 50–71, Wt 0.63–1.4 kg (2 lb).

Description. Medium sized, with a cottony, white tail. Upperparts buff grizzled with black, sides paler; *nape* and legs *orange; feet whitish.* Throat buff, belly white. *Ears and legs moderately long. Tail* brown above, *white below* (un-derside visible). Eyeshine bright, reddish. **Similar Species.** Forest and Dice's Rabbit have inconspicuous tails (both appear tailless in the field), slightly shorter ears, and are usually darker than Eastern Cottontail.

Distribution. Canada and United States through Mexico to NW Costa Rica; N Colombia and Venezuela. Lowlands to 3300 m.

Status and Habitat. Common and widespread in arid areas, farmland, deciduous forest, mountains, and wetlands. It is not found in mature evergreen forest. This species can be a pest of corn and other crops. In some areas it is heavily hunted for meat.

Habits. This rabbit is mainly nocturnal but may be seen in the late afternoon or early morning. It travels by hopping and can leap 4 m. It sometimes stands on its hind legs to scan its surroundings. When pursued, the Eastern Cottontail circles its home range, making occasional erratic zigzag movements. It also may freeze and flatten down, concealing the white tail. Although usually silent, if captured it makes a loud, high-pitched scream; squeals and grunts are occasionally given. This rabbit eats a wide assortment of green vegetation and woody plants and is often seen at night feeding in short grass or along roadsides. Although it is usually solitary when not breeding, it is not territorial, and home ranges of several individuals may overlap. During the breeding season males fight over females, and only a few dominant males in an area breed. Females may have 5–7 litters per year, usually with 3–5 young per litter. Females make nests in tall grass or in shallow holes in the ground. Nests are composed of plant material and lined with fur from the mother's belly. Young reach breeding age at 3 months, and life span is usually less than 1 year. Biology reviewed by Chapman et al. (1980).

CARNIVORES

Order Carnivora

The 7 families of carnivores, with about 240 species in 92 genera, occur worldwide. There is considerable debate on the taxonomy of several groups of carnivores at all levels of classification. Carnivores are adapted to catch and kill animal prey and have teeth designed for tearing and slicing. All but the cats have rear molars designed for crushing. Not all members of the order are strict meat-eaters, however; the 4 families in SE Mexico and Central American include the omnivorous skunks, raccoons, and foxes (mustelid, procyonid, and canid families) and fruit specialists such as the Kinkajou (procyonid family). The largest and smallest carnivores in the region, Jaguar (felid family) and Long-tailed Weasel (mustelid family), are both strictly carnivorous and can kill prey larger than their body size.

Most carnivores are opportunistic hunters, eating whatever prey is most common or easily obtained. Although carnivores are almost always less abundant than their herbivorous prey species, the lack of specialization in diet allows them to occupy a range of habitats, and most species also have broad geographic ranges. Carnivores are often hunted for fur or for sport, and forest species also suffer from loss of habitat. Many species may not be at risk of extinction throughout their range, but the continued survival in Central America of the more vulnerable species is questionable.

DOGS AND FOXES (Spanish: perros, zorros)
Family Canidae

There are 16 genera and about 36 species in the canid family, which has a worldwide distribution. Only 3 species occur in Central America. Canids have elongate muzzles, flat backs, and bushy tails. Their tracks show 4 toes on each foot; the front foot has a fifth toe that does not carry weight. The dental formula for species in the region is: i 3/3, c 1/1, p 4/4, m 2/3, or m 1/2 in the Bush Dog (*Speothos*). Most species are omnivorous; they lack powerful jaws to bring down large prey and only do so when hunting in packs.

COYOTE
Canis latrans

Plate 35
Map 235

Spanish: coyote; Mexico: perro de monte, Maya: pek'i'cash.

HB 750–1150 (35"), T 300–400 (15"), Wt 10–15 kg (26 lb).

Description. *Rangy,* doglike form. Upperparts dull yellow-brown grizzled blackish; underparts cream-yellow. Ears large, triangular, held erect, backs of ears rufous. Eyeshine bright yellow. *Tail long,* bushy or straggly with a *dark tip.* Runs with tail down. Long, orangish legs. **Similar Species.** Gray Fox is much smaller and grayer; it runs with tail horizontal. Domestic dogs in area have shorter legs and fur.

Distribution. Canada and Alaska, USA, through Mexico and Central America to W Panama (Vaughan, 1983). Lowlands to 3000 m.

Status and Habitat. Widespread and often common in agricultural areas, grassland, lowland deciduous forest, arid regions and highlands. Not found in mature evergreen forest. This species benefits from habitat disturbance and has recently expanded its range south to Panama, as a result of deforestation.

Habits. The Coyote may be active night or day, but is most active soon after dusk and before and after dawn. It rests in caves, under fallen trees, or in burrows. This species is the fastest of the canids and can run at 65 km/hour. It travels long distances at a steady trot and often follows small roads or trails, leaving scat and tracks as signs of its presence. In Costa Rica the diet includes carrion (road-killed mammals, birds, and reptiles), small rodents (chiefly *Sigmodon hispidus* and *Liomys salvini*), agoutis, rabbits, sea turtle eggs, lizards, and fruit (Janzen, 1983b). Individuals travel singly, in pairs, or in small groups. The Coyote has a number of vocalizations including barks, growls, and whimpers, but is best known for its howls. These loud cries consist of a series of high yips fol-

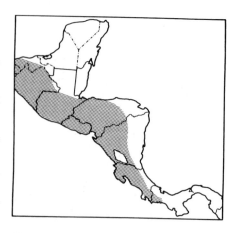

Map 235. Coyote, *Canis latrans*

lowed by a longer howl and ending with short, sharp yaps. Howls are given during the night in Costa Rica, and seem to be heard more often in wet season than in dry season. Several animals call in chorus and may be answered by neighboring groups. Litters of 2–12, usually 5–6, are born after a 2-month gestation.

Where to See. Santa Rosa National Park (at night on dirt roads in and around the park), Costa Rica; and elsewhere in the Pacific lowlands.

GRAY FOX
Urocyon cinereoargenteus

Plate 35
Map 236

Spanish: zorro/zorra gris, gato de monte; Maya: w'ash, ch'amak; Costa Rica: tigrillo; Panama: micho de cerro.

HB 481–718 (2'), T 277–400 (13"), Wt 1.8–3.5 kg (6 lb).

Description. Small, slender, and bushy tailed. Upperparts *gray,* legs, sides, and line from chest to ears rufous to buff; belly, throat, and cheeks white. Large, triangular ears held erect. *Tail black on upper surface* and at tip; held horizontally when running. Legs relatively sort. Eyeshine bluish white. **Similar Species.** See Coyote. Unmistakable when seen well; note

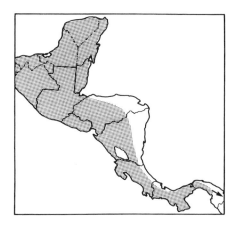

Map 236. Gray Fox, *Urocyon cinereoargenteus*

bushy tail, flat back, tapered muzzle, and large ears.

Distribution. SE Canada and Oregon, USA, through Mexico and Central America to N Colombia and Venezuela. Lowlands to 2600 m.

Status and Habitat. Common and widespread in deciduous and semideciduous forest, agricultural areas, and arid regions. Less common in evergreen forest (not found in wet forest in the Caribbean lowlands). It favors edges of forest and farmland, especially in rocky country, at low to moderately high elevations.

Habits. Mainly nocturnal in hot, dry areas (and in the United States); the Gray Fox may be active day or night in forested and highland regions. It is rather easily seen and observed, trotting down wide trails or dirt roads or sitting on rocks and logs. Although almost always seen on the ground, this species climbs well and sometimes dens high in trees, unlike other canids. Dens are also located in abandoned burrows, under brush, in hollow logs, or in rocky cavities. This fox is an omnivorous and opportunistic feeder; it eats large quantities of fruit when available, at other times it specializes on small mammals or insects, and it occasionally eats birds, small reptiles, and

carrion. During the dry season in Belize, the diet consisted mainly of fruits and arthropods; some birds, small rodents, and other vertebrates were also taken (Novaro et al., 1995). Although reported to remain in family groups, single individuals are most often encountered. This fox is usually silent in the wild; captives may bark and whine. Litter size is 1–7, usually 4, and life span in the wild is about 4–5 years. Biology reviewed by Fritzell and Haroldson (1982).

Where to See. Common and easily seen at night along roads in dry regions such as NW Costa Rica and the northern half of the Yucatán Peninsula, Mexico. Some have habituated to humans and may be approached closely in Tikal, Guatemala, and Monteverde, Costa Rica (by night or day).

BUSH DOG	Plate 35
Speothos venaticus	Map 237

Panama: perro de monte; Chocó: usa.

HB 600–750 (26"), T 110–130 (5"), Wt 5–7 kg (13 lb).

Description. Long, stocky body, *short legs and tail.* Body reddish brown; head and neck paler, yellowish brown. Muzzle short; ears short and rounded. Legs and tail dark brown; feet large; front feet broad, toes partially webbed. Tail held upright. **Similar Species.** None.

Distribution. E Panama to N Bolivia, SE Brazil and Paraguay. Lowlands to 1500 m.

Status and Habitat. CITES Appendix I. Very rare and local throughout its range, usually found in evergreen forest near water. Little known in Panama.

Habits. Poorly known. Probably diurnal, it dens in burrows (Goldman, 1920) or at the base of hollow trees. It is terrestrial and swims well. The Bush Dog is thought to be strictly carnivorous and probably eats a variety of medium sized vertebrates. In Brazil, 2 instances have been reported of this canid hunting Paca (*Agouti paca*) during the day: one report was of a lone Bush Dog chasing its prey into water (Deutsch, 1983); the second account was a group of 4–6 individuals running through forest in pursuit of the Paca, "yapping like puppies" (Peres, 1991). The few observations or captures in the wild have usually been of pairs or small groups (Strahl et al., 1992). Captives form strong pair-bonds and can be kept in large groups. Barks, whines, and yelps may be heard from such groups; short, doglike barks, low whines, and high-pitched squeaks have been noted in the wild. Reproduction is not seasonal in captivity, and litter size is 1–6.

Map 237. Bush Dog, *Speothos venaticus*

RACCOONS AND ALLIES
Family Procyonidae

The procyonid family consists of 6 genera and 10–15 species, all restricted to the New World. The Lesser Panda was placed in this family but is now considered to be more closely related to the bears. Procyonids have 5 toes on each foot and leave 5-toed tracks. The dental formula is: i 1/1, c 1/1, p 4/4, m 2/2, except for the Kinkajou (*Potos*) which has p 3/3. They are omnivorous, and most species climb well.

CACOMISTLE
Bassariscus sumichrasti

Plate 37
Map 238

Central American Ringtail; Spanish: cacomistle/cacomixtle, olingo; Mexico: mico de noche; Guatemala: guia de león, guayanoche; Maya: uayuc; El Salvador: uyo, muyuxe; Honduras: mico rayado, rintel, gato de monte.

HB 380–470 (17"), T 390–530 (18"), Wt 0.6–1.6 kg (3 lb).

Description. Catlike and bushy tailed. Body gray-brown, darkest on midline of back; underparts pale yellow. Fur long and soft. Ears erect, broadly rounded, edged white. Face blackish with prominent, whitish eye rings; muzzle short and pointed. Eyes large; eyeshine

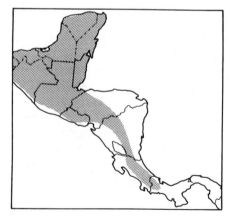

Map 238. Cacomistle, *Bassariscus sumichrasti*

bright, red-orange. *Tail very long and bushy, clearly banded black and white*, terminal 1/3 entirely black to tip. Legs short, feet blackish. **Similar Species.** Olingo (*Bassaricyon*) is similar in shape and size but has a less bushy, indistinctly banded tail and smaller ears. Kinkajou (*Potos*) has a tapered, uniformly colored tail and smaller ears. White-nosed Coati (*Nasua*) has a less bushy, faintly banded tail and a long nose; it is seldom seen in treetops at night.

Distribution. Guerrero and Veracruz, Mexico, to W Panama. Lowlands to 2700 m.

Status and Habitat. CITES Appendix III (Costa Rica). Apparently uncommon to rare and patchily distributed; locally common in some areas in the northern part of its range. Found in evergreen and deciduous forest, tall second growth, and wet montane forest.

Habits. Strictly nocturnal, it dens high in trees, in holes or on shaded branches, during the day, and becomes active at dusk. This species is highly arboreal and is usually seen near the tops of trees or at middle levels. It travels rapidly, following established routes through the canopy. The diet consists of fruits (*Cecropia, Ficus, Poulsenia, Pseudolmedia*, and *Brosimum* spp.), insects, and small vertebrates (Coates-Estrada and Estrada, 1986; Estrada and Coates-Estrada, 1985). The Cacomistle is easily located by the loud, wailing calls heard after sunset and intermittently during the night. Calls are given in 2–3 repeated syllables: "uyoo-whaa", or "boyo-baa-wow" (several local names are based on these sounds). Individuals are usually solitary, but pairs are sometimes seen; the loud calls may be used to maintain territorial spacing. Marking branches with urine may serve a similar function. The home ranges of 4 individuals (2 males and 2 females) in Costa Rica were 16–32 ha. The home range of each male overlapped with a female's range but did not overlap with the other male. Similarly, a female's home range was distinct from that of the other female (Vaughan et al., 1994).

Where to See. Surprisingly common in El Salvador, where it can be seen and heard in forest remnants and protected areas, including El Imposible and Montecristo national parks. Sometimes seen at El Triunfo National Park, Chiapas, Mexico. Recently reported from the Maya Mountains, Belize (Parker et al., 1993). Also in Altos de Escazu and Braulio Carrillo National Park, Costa Rica.

Comment. The Ringtail (*B. astutus*) is found from SW United States to Tehuantepec, Mexico (approaching, but not entering, the region covered by this book). It is paler in color, with buff, not blackish, feet, and the tail is clearly banded for its entire length. It has narrower, more pointed ears (often incorrectly said to have more rounded ears). The Ringtail is usually found in dry, rocky terrain and is less arboreal than the Cacomistle.

NORTHERN RACCOON
Procyon lotor

Plate 36
Map 239

Spanish: mapache, mapachín; Mexico: tejón; Maya: culu; Miskito: suksuk; Panama: gato manglatero; Chocó: touaru.

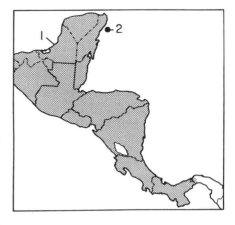

Map 239. 1. Northern Raccoon, *Procyon lotor*
2. Cozumel Raccoon, *Procyon pygmaeus*

HB 392–620 (20"), T 259–332 (11"), Wt 3.3–7.8 kg (12 lb).

Description. The familiar "masked bandit" of the United States (although usually smaller, darker, and shorter-haired in Central America). Back arched, rump higher than shoulders, head and tail held low; moves with a bouncing gait. Upperparts *grizzled gray-brown*; underparts buff. Fur thick, with short underfur and longer guard hairs (including some very long, white hairs). Ears edged white. Face with *distinctive black mask extending onto cheeks*, bordered by white eyebrows and sides of muzzle. Tail about half head and body length, clearly ringed orangish and black. *Legs* and *tops of feet pale gray* (rarely blackish); feet long and narrow. Bright, yellowish eyeshine. **Similar Species.** Crab-eating Raccoon (*P. cancrivorous*) is similar, but has legs and tops of feet blackish and lacks long, white guard hairs on legs and body; difficult to distinguish in the field. At close range, the Crab-eating Raccoon has a strong, distinctive odor, which the Northern Raccoon lacks. Observed in the hand, hair on the nape of the neck is reversed (angled toward the head) in Crab-eating Raccoon, but normal in Northern Raccoon.

Distribution. S Canada and United States through Mexico to C Panama. Lowlands to 2800 m.

Status and Habitat. Widespread and common in coastal regions, mangroves, towns, and rural areas with mixed habitat. Uncommon in mature evergreen forest. It sometimes damages corn crops or raids chicken coops.

Habits. Nocturnal in habit, the Northern Raccoon is usually seen on the ground at night; it escapes by loping away to a tree and may climb high to avoid a spotlight. During the day it sleeps in hollow trees, under rocks, in burrows, or in buildings. This omnivore eats whatever is available, including invertebrates (crabs and crayfish), vertebrates (turtle eggs, birds and bird eggs, frogs, and fish), fruits, seeds, vegetables, and garbage. Individuals often dabble in water in search of food, and manipulate but do not wash their food. Usually solitary and silent; males fight noisily and both sexes give loud, high-pitched squeals and shrieks during the breeding season. Litter size is 2–5; young stay with their mothers for about 9 months. Life span is usually about 3 years, although captives have lived for 17 years. Biology reviewed by Lotze and Anderson (1979).

COZUMEL RACCOON
Procyon pygmaeus   Map 239

Mexico: tejón enano, Maya: chichan culu.

HB 357–437 (15"), T 220–250 (9"), Wt 2.2 kg (5 lb).

Description. Similar in shape and color to Northern Raccoon, but much smaller. **Similar Species.** Cozumel Coati (a race of White-nosed Coati, *Nasua*) is similar in size, but has a much longer nose and tail.

Distribution. Endemic to Cozumel Island, Mexico.

Status and Habitat. Uncommon or rare; threatened by habitat loss, hunting, and poisoning. It favors mangroves on sandy soils, but has been recorded in inland forest. Apparently it is most common on Isla la Pasión and Punta Chunchacab, on the north and south coasts of Cozumel.

Habits. Probably similar to Northern Raccoon. The diet includes crabs, ants, possibly lizards, and some fruit (Navarro and Suarez, 1989). Lactating females have been recorded May–July.

Where to See. Boat trips to Isla la Pasión can be arranged from hotels in San Miguel, Cozumel.

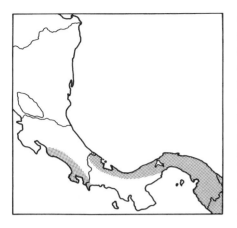

Map 240. Crab-eating Raccoon, *Procyon cancrivorus*

CRAB-EATING RACCOON

Plate 36

Procyon cancrivorus Map 240

Spanish: mapache, mapachín; Panama: gato manglatero.

HB 550–762 (24"), T 250–381 (13"), Wt 3–7 kg (11 lb).

Description. Upperparts grizzled gray-brown or reddish brown; underparts orangish or whitish. Fur rather short and coarse; *no long, white guard hairs on belly or legs.* Ears edged white. Face with *distinctive black mask*; mask extends beyond eyes but only part-way across cheeks. Tail about half head and body length, clearly ringed orangish and black. *Legs and feet blackish.* Bright, yellowish eyeshine. **Similar Species.** See Northern Raccoon.

Distribution. SW Costa Rica to NE Argentina. Lowlands to 600 m (in Central America).

Status and Habitat. Uncommon; along rivers, coasts, and swamps, in relatively undisturbed regions. Seldom found in close association with humans.

Habits. Nocturnal, this raccoon sleeps in hollow trees during the day. It is mainly terrestrial but climbs well. The diet consists of invertebrates (mainly crayfish, snails, crabs, and in-

sects) and fish (Bisbal, 1986). Some fruit and other vertebrates may be eaten, but this species appears to be less omnivorous than the Northern Raccoon. Individuals are usually solitary but are sometimes seen in pairs or family groups.

Where to See. Not easily found; Caribbean lowlands of the Canal Area and inland rivers and hills in Darién National Park, Panama. Reported from Manuel Antonio National Park, Costa Rica, but recent studies indicate that the Northern Raccoon is much more common in the park, while the Crab-eating Raccoon is rare or absent.

WHITE-NOSED COATI

Plate 36

Nasua narica Map 241

Coatimundi; Mexico: tejón, coatí; Maya: chiic; Belize: quash; Miskito: wistiting; Honduras, Costa Rica: pizote, pizote solo; Panama: gato solo; Chocó: susuma.

HB 439–680 (21"), T 472–600 (22"), Wt 2.7–6.5 kg (10 lb).

Description. Long, low profile; usually seen with head down and *long tail held upright.* Body *dark brown, reddish orange,* or yellow-brown; *grizzled* with cream *on shoulders.* Throat, spots above and below eyes, and lower portion of muzzle whitish; *muzzle very long.* Snout mobile, blackish. Tail narrow and tapered, colored like body, with or without indistinct dark bands. Legs and feet dark brown or blackish; feet with long, strong claws. Eyeshine bluish-white. **Similar Species.** Long nose and upright tail distinctive (may be seen in groups, all with tails held up). If high in trees could be confused with Tayra (*Eira*), which has a darker, bushier tail, or a large monkey; monkeys of similar size have prehensile tails and short faces.

Distribution. SW United States through Mexico and Central America to E Panama and adjacent N Colombia. Lowlands to 3000 m.

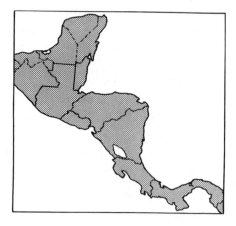

Map 241. White-nosed Coati, *Nasua narica*

Status and Habitat. CITES Appendix III (Honduras). Widespread and common where not hunted; found in deciduous and evergreen forest, second growth, and arid scrub.

Habits. Mainly diurnal, it sleeps at night and rests during the day on tree branches. Both terrestrial and arboreal; this coati often feeds on the ground but may climb into the canopy of a fruiting tree. It feeds on invertebrates found in the leaf litter and under rotting logs, using the strong claws to dig, then rooting with the long, sensitive nose. Disturbance of the leaf litter and shallow digging over a wide area may indicate the recent activity of a coati group. Small vertebrates are eaten, and fruits are taken when available. A large fruiting fig tree may be occupied by a group for several days; *Dipteryx* and *Spondias* fruits are also heavily exploited. Males are solitary except during the breeding season ("Coatimundi" is a South American term for a lone male). Females, juveniles, and males younger than 2 years live in stable groups of 4–65 individuals (usually 10–20). Groups of coatis are especially conspicuous as they slowly wave their erect tails while parading through the forest. Soft calls, barks, and whines are given between group members. A short, sharp bark given in alarm will cause an entire group to run to nearby trees and climb

1–2 m. In Panama, the White-nosed Coati breeds once a year. A male joins a group of females in January or February and stays with them for a month. Pregnant females leave the group and make tree nests, where litters of 2–5 are born in April–May. After about 5 weeks the female and her young rejoin the group. Natural history reviewed by Kaufmann (1983).

Where to See. Common and conspicuous. Especially abundant on Barro Colorado Island and Pipeline Road, Panama; Rincón de la Vieja National Park, Costa Rica; and Tikal, Guatemala. Highly visible at Santa Rosa and Palo Verde national parks, Costa Rica.

Comment. In a taxonomic revision of the genus, Decker (1991) included the Cozumel Coati, *Nasua nelsoni,* as a subspecies of *N. narica* (*N. n. nelsoni*). The Cozumel Coati is much smaller than the mainland form but is similar in other respects.

KINKAJOU   Plate 37
Potos flavus   Map 242

Spanish: mico león, mico de noche; Mexico: martucha; Belize and E Nicaragua: night walker; Honduras: kinkaju; Miskito: uyuk; Costa Rica: martilla; Panama: cusumbí.

HB 430–740 (21"), T 390–570 (20"), Wt 2–4.6 kg (7 lb).

Description. Upperparts usually *golden brown,* less commonly pale gray-brown (in dry areas) or dark brown (in humid areas), sometimes with dark brown line down spine. Underparts creamy yellow or orangish. Fur dense and woolly, with a slight sheen. Head broad; muzzle short and blunt. Tongue long and narrow. Ears short and rounded, on sides of head. *Prehensile tail long and tapered,* tip dark brown (some in Panama have a small white tip). Legs and feet short and sturdy, with short, curved claws. Eyeshine bright, orange. Male has a bare

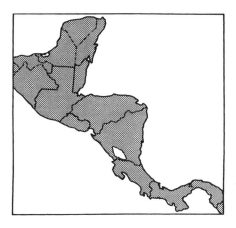

Map 242. Kinkajou, *Potos flavus*

patch on the throat and is larger than female. **Similar Species.** Can be difficult to distinguish from Olingo (*Bassaricyon*) at night; Olingo is smaller and slimmer, with a bushier, nonprehensile tail, a more pointed muzzle, and is usually grayer. Western Night Monkey (*Aotus*) has a patterned face and nonprehensile tail.

Distribution. Tamaulipas and Guerrero, Mexico, through Central America to S Brazil. Lowlands to at least 2200 m.

Status and Habitat. CITES Appendix III (Honduras). Common and widespread in evergreen and deciduous forest; also found in second growth, dry scrub, and agricultural areas with scattered trees.

Habits. The Kinkajou is the most commonly seen nocturnal, arboreal mammal in the region. Its bright eyeshine and noisy movements through the trees make it easy to locate, and when found, it often remains motionless for long periods, staring at the observer. At times this species moves rapidly and climbs with agility; the tail is held horizontally or lower, and the tip is often curled around a branch. It can hang freely from the tail to reach fruit, but often holds on with hind legs and tail. Although primarily arboreal and nocturnal, the Kinkajou sometimes descends to the ground

to cross fields or roads and is occasionally active during the day, especially in February or March (in Costa Rica). Daytime dens are in tree holes or on crotches of trees. When feeding in the canopy, its movements are accompanied by sounds of falling fruit and twigs. Fruits make up most of the diet; figs, hog plums (*Spondias mombin*), mangos, passion fruit, and fruits of *Inga* sp., *Goldmania macrocarpa*, *Dipteryx panamensis*, and *Pouteria campechiana* are eaten (Bisbal, 1986; Walker and Cant, 1977). It will climb trunks of spiny palms, with great care and deliberation, to reach the fruits. Some insects (including ants) and small vertebrates are taken. It has been reported to capture and eat bats visiting fruiting trees (Coates-Estrada and Estrada, 1986). Nectar is also consumed (Janson et al., 1981). This species is an important seed disperser of several forest trees and probably also acts as a pollinator. Individuals are usually solitary in habits but sometimes travel in pairs, and several may gather in a fruiting tree. Calls include whistles, screams, grunts, barks, and low moans. A fast-repeated, high-pitched bark, "wick-a-wick-a-wick," seems to be given in alarm and in aggressive interactions between males. Females give birth to one young, rarely twins, during the dry season. Captives have lived 23 years. Biology reviewed by Ford and Hoffmann (1988).

Where to See. Most forested parks (including Calakmul, Mexico; Tikal, Guatemala; Cockscomb Basin, Belize; El Imposible, El Salvador; Tortuguero, La Selva, and Monteverde, Costa Rica; Barro Colorado Island and Soberania, Panama); also in unprotected areas. Best views are in areas with a low canopy or along rivers. Check fruiting figs, mangos, and guavas, or flowering balsa trees.

OLINGO Plate 37
Bassaricyon gabbii Map 243

Costa Rica: martilla; Panama: olingo.

HB 360–420 (15"), T 380–480 (17"), Wt
1.1–1.4 kg (3 lb).

Description. Upperparts *gray-brown*, brown or
golden, darker on midline; underparts creamy
yellow. Face grayer than body and broad, with a
short, pointed muzzle. Ears short and rounded,
widely spaced, angled forward. *Tail long* and
faintly banded; not tapered or prehensile,
slightly bushy, tip darker than base (sometimes
white tipped). Legs short; feet broad with
short, curved claws. Eyeshine bright orange.
Similar Species. Kinkajou (*Potos*) has a tapered,
prehensile tail; it is larger and usually golden
brown, with a blunt muzzle. See Cacomistle
(*Bassariscus*).

Distribution. C Nicaragua to W Colombia
and W Ecuador. Lowlands to 1700 m.

Status and Habitat. CITES Appendix III
(Costa Rica). Uncommon to locally common in
evergreen forest and forest edge. Seems to favor
cloud forest at middle elevations. Seldom found
in deciduous forest or highly disturbed regions.

Habits. This species is often confused with the
Kinkajou (*Potos*), which is similar in appearance and habits. It is nocturnal, though may
be seen by day, and it is arboreal. The Olingo is
much more active than Kinkajou, and quickly
moves away from a spotlight, running from
branch to branch with great agility. The tail is
held straight out from the body, or arched up,
and is not prehensile. During the day it dens
in tree holes or sleeps on branches. The diet includes fruits of *Cecropia* sp., *Quararibea costa-
ricensis, Inga* sp., and figs. Invertebrates and
small vertebrates are probably taken; an Olingo
was observed catching and eating a Mexican
Deer Mouse (*Peromyscus mexicanus*). Nectar of
balsa (*Ochroma* sp.) and *Quararibea cordata* is
consumed in Peru (Janson et al., 1981). Indi-

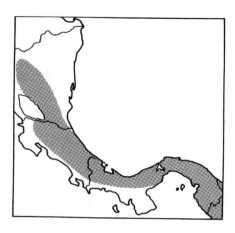

Map 243. Olingo, *Bassaricyon gabbii*

viduals are usually solitary, but may be seen in
pairs or small groups and may feed in the same
tree with Kinkajous. A range of vocalizations
is given; a repeated, 2-note bark: "whey-chuck,
whey-chuck" may be an alarm call. This call
is slower and lower in pitch than a Kinkajou
bark. Little is known of the reproductive cycle;
young are seen late in the dry season in Costa
Rica.

Comment. Two additional species have been
described from Central America: *B. lasius* from
Cartago, Costa Rica; and *B. pauli,* from Cerro
Pando, Panama. Both are known only from the
type localities and may be conspecific with *B.
gabbii.*

Where to See. At Monteverde, Costa Rica, an
Olingo has visited a hummingbird feeder (at
the Hummingbird Gallery) for several years. It
usually comes during the afternoon, leaping
on the feeder and lapping nectar that spills
out. At night Olingos can be seen in trees in
and around the Monteverde Reserve. They are
sometimes seen at Tortuguero National Park,
Costa Rica, although Kinkajous are much more
common. They are also found along Pipeline
Road and in forest throughout the Canal Area,
Panama (check flowering balsa trees).

WEASELS, SKUNKS, AND ALLIES
(Spanish: comadrejas, zorillos)
Family Mustelidae

The Mustelidae contains about 64 species in 23 genera, distributed worldwide. Weasels, skunks, river and sea otters, badgers, and wolverines are members of the family. There are 8 species in Central America. Mustelids typically have long bodies and short legs. They have 5 toes on each foot. Anal scent glands are usually well developed. These mammals have powerful jaws, and most are strictly carnivorous, although some tropical species also eat fruit. The dental formula of species in the region is: i 3/3, c 1/1, p 3/3 (p 4/3 in river otters, p 2/3 in hog-nosed skunks), m 1/2. Their sense of smell is acute and is used to locate prey.

Skunks are well known for their odoriferous anal secretions, which are discharged in defense. Several warnings, including lifting the tail, turning the rump to face the aggressor, stamping the front feet, and, in the case of the Spotted Skunk, a series of handstands, are usually given before the skunk sprays. As a consequence of their built-in defense system, skunks are much less wary than most mammals, and, where common, are often killed by cars on roads. Skunks are omnivorous, eating a variety of plant and animal food. At least 3 species of skunks employ a similar method of opening large eggs: the body is arched, with the egg grasped in the forelegs then hurled backwards between the legs, sometimes receiving an extra kick from a hind leg en route. If the egg does not hit a hard surface and break, the process is repeated (Janzen and Hallwachs, 1982; Van Gelder, 1953). Natural history of the 3 Central American species that also occur in the United States is summarized in Rosatte (1987).

LONG-TAILED WEASEL   Plate 38
Mustela frenata   Map 244

Spanish: comadreja; Mexico: hurón, onzita, oncilla; Maya: sabín.

HB 230–325 (11"), T 130–235 (7"), Wt 108–450 g (8 oz).

Description. Very small, with a *long body* and *short legs.* Variable in color; generally *dark brown* with some *white facial markings.* SE Mexico to Nicaragua: back reddish brown; belly cream; head blackish with throat white; M-shaped white stripe extending from throat over eyes, sometimes broken into 3 white spots, one over each eye and one on muzzle. Costa Rica and Panama: upperparts dark brown to blackish; belly pale orange; head black with lower jaw white, sometimes with narrow white spots above eyes and thin white stripe on fore-

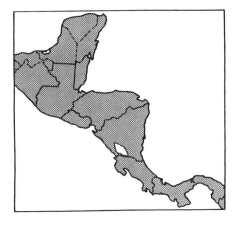

Map 244. Long-tailed Weasel, *Mustela frenata*

head. *Tail narrow,* slightly more than half head and body length, tipped black. Males are much larger than females. Eyeshine bluish. **Similar**

Species. Much smaller than other weasel-shaped carnivores; body longer and narrower and tail less bushy than a similar-sized squirrel.

Distribution. S Canada through the United States, Mexico, and Central America to Venezuela and west of the Andes to Bolivia. Lowlands to 4100 m.

Status and Habitat. Uncommon to locally common and widespread; found in lowland deciduous and highland evergreen forest, second growth, and agricultural areas. Rare in lowland evergreen forest.

Habits. Mainly diurnal, but sometimes active at night. It dens under rocks or buildings or in burrows made by other mammals. Small rodents weighing about 50 g are the chief component of the diet, although larger prey, including rabbits and pocket gophers, may be taken. Snakes, birds, and bird eggs are also consumed. The long, narrow body enables it to enter mouse burrows and find prey during the day. In the United States, home range size of males varies from 10 to 160 ha, depending on prey availability. Females occupy smaller ranges that overlap with those of males. Although solitary hunters, weasels are not strongly territorial. In the north, mating takes place in late summer and implantation is delayed; the young are born in spring after 27 days of gestation. Litter size is 3–9, usually 6. Biology in United States reviewed by Fagerstone (1987).

Where to See. Occasionally seen darting across trails or clearings in a variety of habitats. It can sometimes be attracted by "spishing" or squeaking sounds and may stop and stand up on its hind legs to locate the sound. Common in dry scrub on the Yucatán Peninsula, Mexico, and in elfin forest at Monteverde, Costa Rica.

GREATER GRISON
Galictis vittata

Plate 38
Map 245

Spanish: grisón, hurón; Belize: bushdog; Honduras: zabin; Panama: lobo gallinero, tigrillo rosillo.

HB 475–552 (20"), T 146–163 (6"), Wt 1.5–3.2 kg (5 lb).

Description. Long bodied and muscular. *Upperparts grizzled gray; legs, feet, and underparts black.* Face mostly black with a *white line across forehead* to ears and down sides of neck. *Tail short,* grayish. Feet broad, with long claws. Eyeshine bright, blue-green. **Similar Species.** No other long, low-bodied terrestrial mammals in Central America are gray in color.

Distribution. San Luis Potosí and Veracruz, Mexico, patchily distributed through Central America to Peru and S Brazil. Lowlands to 1500 m.

Status and Habitat. CITES Appendix III (Costa Rica). Rare and local. Poorly known in Central America from few, scattered records. Mostly in evergreen forest of lowlands and foothills, often near water; sometimes found in deciduous forest and pastures.

Habits. Poorly known. Active by day or night, mainly early in the morning and in late afternoon. It is terrestrial and rarely climbs, but

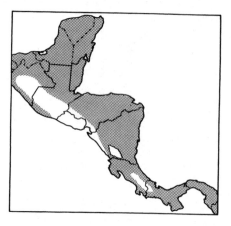

Map 245. Greater Grison, *Galictis vittata*

swims well. The Greater Grison dens in burrows, including those dug by armadillos. It eats reptiles, birds, and small mammals, including agoutis. Individuals may be seen alone or in pairs. A female in Venezuela had a home range of 4.2 km² (Sunquist et al., 1989). Litter size is usually 2.

Where to See. This is one of the most difficult species in the region to find; people who spend a lot of time in the field see one every 5 years or so. Most sightings are in forests in the Caribbean lowlands of Costa Rica and Panama (often near rivers); it has also been seen several times in dry fields near Carara, Costa Rica.

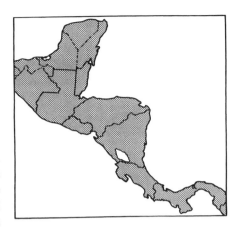

Map 246. Tayra, *Eira barbara*

TAYRA
Eira barbara

Plate 38
Map 246

Mexico: cabeza de viejo, viejo de monte; Maya: sanjor; Belize: bushdog; Honduras: lepasil; Costa Rica: tolomuco; Panama: gato negro, gato cutarra.

HB 601–705 (2'4"), T 382–460 (16"), Wt 3–6 kg (9 lb).

Description. Large, long-legged weasel with a *long, bushy tail*. Body, legs, and tail *blackish brown*, head and neck pale yellow or gray-brown (in Mexico, Belize, and Guatemala); or head and neck dark gray-brown, slightly paler than body (Honduras to Panama); usually with a white diamond on the throat. Feet large, with long, powerful claws. **Similar Species.** Unlike other mustelids. Jaguarundi (*Herpailurus*) has a long, narrow tail and moves flat backed at a sedate walk or graceful run; Tayra bounces or moves erratically, with back and tail arched.

Distribution. Sinaloa and Tamaulipas, Mexico, through Central and South America to Bolivia and N Argentina. Lowlands to 2400 m.

Status and Habitat. CITES Appendix III (Honduras). Fairly common and widespread in deciduous and evergreen forest, second growth, and plantations.

Habits. Mainly diurnal, sometimes crepuscular. At night the Tayra dens in hollow trees or in burrows. It is terrestrial and arboreal, traveling on the ground or along horizontal branches, and searching in crevices or among leaves with rather noisy movements. On the ground it travels with a bouncing gait, back and tail arched; movements in trees are more fluid. If alarmed on the ground, it gives a sharp snort, races to a tree, and climbs partway up. The diet includes fruit, invertebrates, mammals (rats, agoutis, rabbits, and monkeys), and lizards (Galef et al., 1976). It is usually silent in the wild; yowls, snarls, and clicking calls are sometimes given by groups (Kaufmann and Kaufmann, 1965). Tayra may be seen singly or in pairs; occasionally in groups of 3–4. Litter size is 2–3.

Where to See. Although wary, Tayras are fairly easy to see and can sometimes be observed for long periods. The blond-headed race can be seen at Tikal National Park, Guatemala (in the less traveled parts of the park). Dark-headed Tayras are common at La Selva and Monteverde, Costa Rica, and in the Canal Area, Panama.

HOODED SKUNK
Mephitis macroura

Plate 39
Map 247

Spanish: zorrillo; Mexico: zorrillo rayado; Maya: pay; Honduras: zorrillo común.

HB 195–295 (10"), T 220–305 (10"), Wt 0.4–2 kg (2 lb).

Description. *Small, all black or black and white with a long tail.* Fur long and thick. Size and color pattern are highly variable: (a) large, with a wide, whitish dorsal stripe from forehead to rump and a mostly white tail; (b) medium sized, with a white nape and 3 stripes (wide dorsal stripe and narrow side stripes); tail white above and at tip, black below; and (c) small, all black or with narrow, widely spaced white stripes on sides and a black tail. All variants may be seen in a single population, although individuals from SW Nicaragua and Costa Rica are usually small and dark (form c), while those from Guatemala and northward are usually larger (form a or b) with white tails. Some individuals have a narrow white stripe on midline of face. Eyeshine bright green. **Similar Species.** Other skunks have tails shorter than head and body length. Striped Hog-nosed Skunk (*Conepatus semistriatus*) is larger, with stripes close together on back, not on sides. See Common Hog-nosed Skunk (*Conepatus mesoleucus*).

Distribution. SW United States through Mexico and N Central America to NW Costa Rica. Lowlands to 2400 m.

Status and Habitat. Locally common in deciduous forest and forest edge, rocky canyons, pastures, and brush. Hunted in the drier parts of Guatemala for the scent glands, which are used in folk medicines.

Habits. Nocturnal in behavior, this skunk is active soon after dusk and travels on the ground along rock walls, streambeds, and in weedy fields. When foraging it moves slowly, snuffling among leaves and pouncing on grasshoppers or beetles, but does not dig deep into the soil in search of insect larvae and

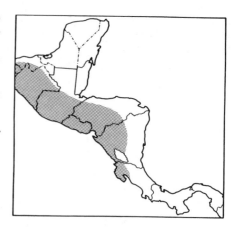

Map 247. Hooded Skunk, *Mephitis macroura*

leaves little sign of its activity. During the day it dens in rock crevices or burrows. This omnivore eats insects, fruit, small vertebrates, bird eggs, and garbage. Although generally solitary, several may gather at a feeding site without aggression. Litter size is 3–6.

Where to See. Although only recently reported from NW Costa Rica (Janzen and Hallwachs, 1982), the Hooded Skunk is hard to miss in this region. It can be seen easily at night along roads on the Nicoya Peninsula and in Guanacaste. It is numerous at Santa Rosa National Park, where many may be seen feeding together at the garbage dump behind the "comedor" after dark or around nearby buildings and the campsite.

SPOTTED SKUNK
Spilogale putorius

Plate 39
Map 248

Spanish: zorrillo manchado; Mexico: zorrito; Maya: payoch, pay.

HB 210–305 (10"), T 100–142 (5"), Wt 240–533 g (14 oz).

Description. Small, short legged, and slim bodied. *Black* with a *complex pattern of white stripes and spots.* Fur very soft. *Tail short,* about half head and body length, mostly black,

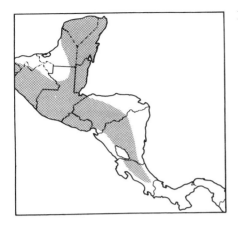

Map 248. Spotted Skunk, *Spilogale putorius*

white at base and tip. **Similar Species.** Size, short tail, and fur pattern distinctive.

Distribution. SW Canada and United States through Mexico to Costa Rica. Lowlands to 3000 m.

Status and Habitat. Uncommon but widespread in farmland, open woodland, and brush; often in dry, rocky terrain.

Habits. Nocturnal, it dens by day under rocks, in hollow logs, in or under buildings, and in burrows dug by other mammals. Although mainly terrestrial, this species climbs well and sometimes shelters high in trees. It is omnivorous, feeding on insects and insect larvae, small mammals, fruit, grain, birds, and bird eggs. In Durango, Mexico, the diet consists mainly of adult and larval beetles and moths (Baker and Baker, 1975). Usually solitary in habits, it sometimes sleeps in groups. Litter size is 2–9, usually 4–5.

COMMON HOG-NOSED SKUNK

Conepatus mesoleucus

Plate 39
Map 249

Texas: rooter skunk; Spanish: zorrillo; Mexico: zorrillo cadeno, zorrillo de espalda blanca; Maya: pay; Honduras: zorrillo de capucha.

HB 340–440 (16"), T 210–302 (10"), Wt 1.5–4 kg (6 lb).

Description. Large and stocky with a *short, entirely white tail.* Black with a *single, broad, white stripe* from forehead to tail, stripe widest on shoulders and midback, narrower on rump. Large, *naked, piglike snout.* Long, powerful claws. **Similar Species.** Striped Hog-nosed Skunk (*C. semistriatus*) has 2 narrow, white stripes on the back (ranges may not overlap). Hooded Skunk (*Mephitis*) sometimes has a single back stripe, but the stripe is not pure white; it is smaller and its tail is relatively longer and black on the underside.

Distribution. Colorado and S California, USA, through Mexico (except Yucatán Peninsula and Belize) to Nicaragua. Lowlands to 3200 m.

Status and Habitat. Uncommon to locally common and widespread; it favors rocky hills with scattered trees and brush, but also occurs in highland pine–oak forest. Not found in evergreen forest or hot deserts.

Habits. Although largely nocturnal, it sometimes forages during the day in cold weather. Dens are located in burrows, under rocks, in caves or mine shafts, and in wood rat (*Neotoma*) houses. Piles of dry grass may be stacked

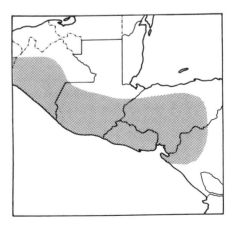

Map 249. Common Hog-nosed Skunk, *Conepatus mesoleucus*

to a height of 1 m in the den and used as a nest (Hoffmeister, 1986). This skunk digs for food, rooting in the soil and turning over rocks and logs with its powerful front claws, leaving characteristic "ploughed" areas. It feeds mainly on invertebrates (insects, spiders, and snails) in the soil; some small mammals, reptiles, and vegetation are also taken (Davis, 1960). Litter size is 2–4.

STRIPED HOG-NOSED SKUNK
Conepatus semistriatus

Plate 39
Map 250

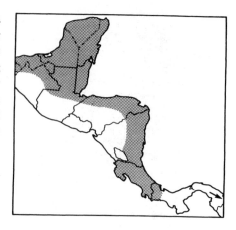

Map 250. Striped Hog-nosed Skunk, *Conepatus semistriatus*

Spanish: zorrillo; Mexico: zorro hediondo; Maya: pai och; Belize: polecat; Panama: gato cañero, gato de caña.

HB 340–500 (16"), T 166–310 (9"), Wt 1.4–3.5 kg (5.5 lb).

Description. Large and stocky. Body *black* with *2 narrow, white stripes* from forehead to upper rump; stripes are *separated by a thin black line down spine.* Large, naked, piglike snout. *Tail short,* about half head and body length, black at base, then *white;* tail often held up with short hair fanned out like a bottle brush. Eyeshine bright, greenish white. **Similar Species.** See Common Hog-nosed Skunk and Hooded Skunk.

Distribution. Veracruz and Yucatán Peninsula, Mexico, to W Panama; Venezuela to Peru; E Brazil. Lowlands to 4100 m (in South America).

Status and Habitat. Uncommon to locally common; favors tree fall gaps, clearings, and pastures adjacent to evergreen forest. Seldom found in areas with a pronounced dry season.

Habits. Nocturnal, it rests by day in burrows which it digs among tree roots or under tree falls. The burrows extend 1–2 m and are within 0.3 m of the surface (Hall and Dalquest, 1963). Burrow openings are about 15 cm in diameter. This skunk emerges about a half hour after dusk and travels on well-established pathways on the ground to foraging areas. The diet is mainly invertebrates, but this species does not root in the soil as much as the Common Hog-nosed Skunk. Some small vertebrates and possibly some fruits are also eaten. Individuals are solitary. Litter size is 3–5.

Where to See. In Costa Rica it is often seen soon after dark on the bridge or in clearings at La Selva; also seen in pastures with scattered trees at Monteverde; on the airstrip at Sirena Station, Corcovado National Park; and in secondary forest at Manuel Antonio National Park.

NEOTROPICAL RIVER OTTER
Lutra longicaudis

Plate 38
Map 251

Spanish: perro de agua, nutria; Belize: water dog.

HB 564–800 (2'3"), T 370–475 (16"), Wt 5–9.5 kg (15 lb).

Description. *Semiaquatic;* long, stocky body and short legs. Upperparts brown, paler on sides; underparts cream-colored. Fur short and shiny. Head small with a *short, broad muzzle* and small ears. *Tail long* and tapered, *thick at base.* Feet broad, *toes webbed.* Eyeshine reddish.

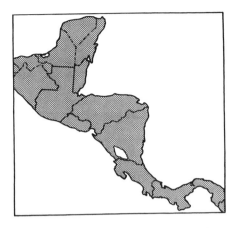

Map 251. Neotropical River Otter, *Lutra longicaudis*

Similar Species. None in region.

Distribution. Chihuahua and Veracruz, Mexico, through Central America to N Argentina and Uruguay. Lowlands to 3000 m.

Status and Habitat. CITES Appendix I. Hunted for fur; present status in region poorly known. Widespread but uncommon or rare; along rivers, streams, and coastal lagoons in relatively undisturbed habitats.

Habits. Mainly diurnal where not hunted; sometimes active at night. It dens in burrows on banks; the entrance may be above or below the water level. This semiaquatic mammal is always near water; it may be seen swimming with just the head visible or sunning on a log near the water's edge. It is a fast and graceful swimmer, but moves awkwardly on land. Feces are usually deposited in a prominent position on a rock and are characterized by a large proportion of invertebrate exoskeleton. Tracks and scat are sometimes seen along tiny streams and may mark the path of dispersing subadults. The diet is mainly fish, molluscs, and crustaceans (particularly crayfish); small mammals and birds are occasionally taken. It is usually solitary, although young remain with the mother for extended periods, and male–female pairs are sometimes seen. Groups may whistle, purr, or grunt; lone individuals are usually silent. Litter size is 1–5, usually 2.

Comment. New World otters, including this species, are sometimes placed in the genus *Lontra* (see Wozencraft, 1993).

Where to See. Fairly common at Tortuguero National Park and in the Río Corobicí near Cañas, Costa Rica; also in the Panama Canal near Gamboa.

CATS (Spanish: gatos)
Family Felidae

The cat family consists of 37 species in 5–12 genera distributed worldwide. There are 6 species in Central America. Higher levels of classification within the family are a subject of controversy. Some authors place all the small cats in the genus *Felis*, while others divide them into several separate genera. These accounts follow the taxonomy of Wozencraft (1993). Cats have lithe, muscular bodies and short, rounded heads. Males are larger than females in most species. Central American cats have 4 weight-bearing toes on each foot, with retractile claws. A small thumb is present on the forefoot but does not touch the ground. All tracks are 4-toed and almost always appear clawless. The dental formula is: i 3/3, c 1/1, p 2/2 or 3/2, m 1/1.

Cats in Central America occupy a wide variety of habitats but are generally uncommon or rare, as they require large, relatively undisturbed areas in which to forage. They suffer from habitat loss and hunting. These carnivores are killed for fur, sport, and as potential predators of livestock. All wild cats are in CITES Appendix II or Appendix I. Cats are seldom seen or heard; they move silently, and only Jaguars make loud roars. They travel long distances; their tracks may be found along dirt roads and trails and by riverbanks and waterholes. All cats in the region scratch on fallen logs; scratch marks are sometimes accompanied by dark stains of strongly scented urine. Cats are carnivorous, although most species eat some grass, which may aid in digestion. They prey on mammals, birds, reptiles, fish, amphibians, and even insects, depending on local availability. Most cats are solitary hunters; groups of 2 or more are usually a breeding pair or mother and her offspring.

OCELOT

Plate 41

Leopardus pardalis

Map 252

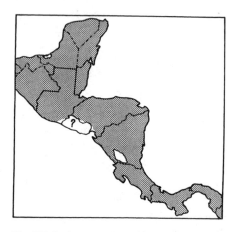

Map 252. Ocelot, *Leopardus pardalis*

Spanish: ocelote, tigrillo, manigordo; Maya: ek-sush; Belize: tiger cat; Miskito: kruhbu; Panama: gato tigre.

HB 640–838 (2'6"), T 260–419 (14"), Wt 7–14.5 kg (22 lb).

Description. Largest of the small spotted cats. *Tail narrow, not bushy; shorter than hind legs* (reaches ground but would not drag if relaxed). Upperparts sandy brown to pale yellow, patterned with black rosettes or long ovals with tawny brown centers. Underparts white with black spots. Fur rather short and even; fur reversed on nape of neck, slants toward head. Eyes medium sized, yellowish; eyeshine bright yellow. Feet large, forefoot broader than hind foot. **Similar Species.** See Margay (*L. wiedii*). Jaguar (*Panthera*) is much larger and heavier in build.

Distribution. S Texas, USA, through Mexico and Central America to N Argentina. Lowlands to 3700 m.

Status and Habitat. CITES Appendix I. Uncommon but widespread in evergreen and deciduous forest, second growth, and agricultural areas with sufficient cover.

Habits. Mainly nocturnal or crepuscular, the Ocelot sometimes hunts during the day in dense cover or when the weather is overcast. It is active for most of the night, traveling 3 km or more, often along trails or small roads. Chiefly terrestrial, it may climb trees to rest in the daytime. Other rest sites include culverts, under tree falls, or among tree buttresses in shady areas. This cat eats a variety of vertebrate and invertebrate prey. Small rodents (particularly spiny rats, *Proechimys* spp., in Peru and Panama), rabbits, opossums, iguanas, land crabs, and birds are favored; larger mammals (including porcupines, anteaters, and agoutis), turtles, snakes, and fish are occasionally taken (Emmons, 1987; Ludlow and Sunquist, 1987; Mondolfi, 1986). Large opossums and armadillos are the principal prey in Belize (Konecny, 1989). Individuals are usually solitary. Males have large home ranges that include the ranges of several females. Although captives growl and meow, wild Ocelots rarely vocalize and move silently. Females give birth to single young; litters of 2–3 are occasionally produced.

Where to See. Although shy and seldom common, Ocelots are the most easily seen spotted cat in Central America. As with all cats, sightings are more a matter of luck and persistence, rather than specific locality. Night boat or canoe trips through lowland forest may be productive. Their tracks may be found on muddy banks and along trails.

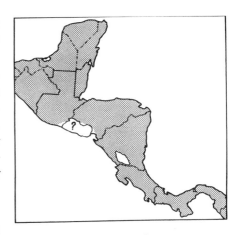

Map 253. Margay, *Leopardus wiedii*

MARGAY — Plate 41
Leopardus wiedii — Map 253

Spanish: tigrillo; Maya: chak'shikin; Belize: tiger cat; Honduras, Costa Rica: caucel; Miskito: limi wayata; Chocó: urigli.

HB 490–737 (2'), T 370–533 (17"), Wt 2.6–5 kg (8 lb).

Description. Medium sized, slim, and leggy. *Tail bushy, longer than hind legs*, drags on ground if hanging freely. Upperparts pale *gray-brown to tawny*, patterned with thick-edged black rosettes and long ovals with tawny-brown centers. Underparts whitish with black spots and stripes. Fur relatively long and thick; fur on neck reversed, slants toward head. Muzzle short. Eyes large, brownish; eyeshine bright yellow. Feet broad, forefoot same width as hindfoot. **Similar Species.** Ocelot is larger and stockier in build, with a shorter, narrower tail; it has a longer muzzle and yellow eyes. A young Ocelot is probably indistinguishable from a Margay in the field. See Oncilla (rare, smaller). The spotting pattern is highly variable in all 3 species and not reliable for identification.

Distribution. N Mexico through Central America to N Argentina. Lowlands to 3000 m.

Status and Habitat. CITES Appendix I. Uncommon and patchily distributed in relatively undisturbed forest. This cat does not adapt well to habitat alteration.

Habits. Poorly known. Mainly nocturnal; during the day it usually sleeps 7–10 m above ground in vine tangles or in hollow trees, occasionally in caves or dense cover. This is the most arboreal New World cat and probably hunts in trees, although it may travel on the ground. Unlike other cats, it can partially rotate the hind feet and run down trees head first, clinging like a squirrel. This cat feeds mainly on climbing mice, opossums, and squirrels (Konecny, 1989); monkeys, sloths, porcupines, and birds are sometimes taken. Individuals appear to be solitary. Litter size is usually 1, rarely 2 (Mondolfi, 1986).

ONCILLA — Plate 41
Leopardus tigrinus — Map 254

Spanish: tigrillo; Costa Rica: caucel.

HB 426–648 (20"), T 245–340 (12"), Wt 1.4–2.8 kg (5 lb).

Description. *Small and delicate*, not much larger than a domestic cat. Tail narrow, slightly longer than hind legs. Upperparts pale to *dark gray-brown* or *tawny*, with *small black spots or rosettes*. Spots are usually discrete black circles with dark brown centers, but sometimes form

Map 254. Oncilla, *Leopardus tigrinus*

narrow stripes or ovals. Underparts white with black spots. Fur on neck normal, slants toward body. Muzzle short. Eyes yellowish; eyeshine bright yellow. Feet small, forefoot broader than hindfoot. **Similar Species.** Easily confused with Margay, which is larger, with bigger feet and a proportionally longer and bushier tail; Margay usually has larger and more boldly defined spots or streaks (pattern is highly variable in both species). The few Central American specimens of Oncillas are darker in color than Margays (South American Oncillas range from all black to pale brown with black spots). Ocelot is much larger.

Distribution. In Central America, known only from Costa Rica; patchily distributed in South America, in Colombia, Venezuela and the Guianas, parts of E and SE Brazil and N Argentina. Lowlands to 3200 m.

Status and Habitat. CITES Appendix I. Rare. Usually found in wet evergreen forest, often at high elevations.

Habits. Poorly known. The Oncilla is probably nocturnal and mainly terrestrial, although it climbs well. Mice, shrews, and small birds are included in the diet (Gardner, 1971). Litter size in captivity is 1–2 (Mondolfi, 1986).

JAGUARUNDI Plate 40
Herpailurus yaguarondi Map 255

Otter cat, weasel cat; Spanish: yaguarundi; Mexico: leoncillo; Maya: ek-barum, ekmuch; Belize: halari; Honduras: gato cerban; Miskito: arari; Costa Rica: león breñero; Panama: tigrillo congo, tigrillo negro; Chocó: urigli paima.

HB 525–940 (2'4"), T 345–600 (19"), Wt 4–9 kg (15 lb).

Description. *Short legged*, with a long back and *long, narrow tail.* May be *entirely dark gray* (gray to chocolate brown) or *entirely reddish* (tawny yellow to chestnut). Gray individuals are more common. Head, ears, and feet small. Eyes rather small; eyeshine dull, reddish. **Similar Species.** Puma is much larger and has longer legs; other cats are spotted. Tayra (*Eira*) has a shorter, bushy tail and moves with a bouncy gallop, back arched, while Jaguarundi moves flat-backed at a sedate walk or graceful run.

Distribution. S Texas, USA, and N Mexico through Central America to N Argentina. Lowlands to 2000 m.

Status and Habitat. CITES Appendix I (North and Central America). Uncommon but widespread in a variety of habitats, from

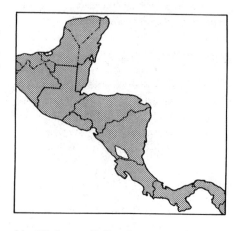

Map 255. Jaguarundi, *Herpailurus yaguarondi*

arid thorn scrub to evergreen forest and agricultural areas. Favors areas with dense, low cover near water and is less common in deep forest. This species adapts fairly well to human disturbance of habitat, and its fur is of less value than that of spotted cats. This is the only wild cat in Central America likely to be seen in open, highly disturbed habitats.

Habits. Mainly diurnal, the Jaguarundi is sometimes seen trotting across roads during the day and is the most commonly sighted cat in the region. It rests in dense thickets, in hollow trees, or under tree falls. Activity is greatest in the morning; it is also sometimes seen at night. This cat is mainly terrestrial but climbs well. In Belize, 3 radio-tracked individuals traveled about 6 km per day and occupied large home ranges: 100 km² for males and 20 km² for females (Konecny, 1989). These individuals fed mainly on arthropods, Hispid Cotton Rats (*Sigmodon hispidus*), and birds. In Venezuela, the diet consists mainly of small rodents and birds; rabbits, armadillos, and lizards are also eaten (Bisbal, 1986; Mondolfi, 1986). Jaguarundis sometimes raid chicken coops. Usually solitary and silent, captives give chirpy whistles and make screeching noises during the breeding season. Litter size is 2–4; gray and red kittens may occur in the same litter.

PUMA
Plate 40

Puma concolor
Map 256

Cougar, mountain lion; Spanish: león, puma, león de montaña; Maya: cha-barum, cabcoh; Belize: red tiger; Miskito: limi pauni; Kuna: achumicul; Chocó: imama-puru.

HB 860–1219 (3'3"), T 610–737 (2'2"), Wt 24–65 kg (100 lb).

Description. *Large*, with a relatively small head and *long legs* (body size smaller in Central America than in W United States or parts of South America). Upperparts yellow-brown to

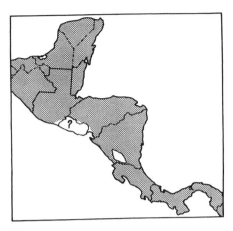

Map 256. Puma, *Puma concolor*

deep reddish; underparts cream or whitish. Ears large and pointed. *Tail long and narrow*, usually tipped black. Eyeshine bright, yellowish. Young are spotted; spots circular, dark brown, not forming open ovals or stripes. **Similar Species.** The only large, unspotted cat in Middle America. See Jaguar and Jaguarundi.

Distribution. S Canada and United States through Mexico and Central America to S Argentina and S Chile. Lowlands to over 5000 m (in the Andes).

Status and Habitat. CITES Appendix I (3 subspecies) or Appendix II (all other subspecies). Status in region poorly known; killed by sport hunters and as a predator of livestock, also threatened by loss of natural habitat. Uncommon but widespread in forests, deserts, and highlands. Absent from mangroves and flooded areas.

Habits. Active by day or night; Puma dens and resting areas are located among rocks, under tree falls, or on tree branches. This cat is shy and retiring and is seldom seen. It often travels great distances along dirt roads or trails but avoids deep mud or water. It is mainly terrestrial but climbs well. The Puma eats a wide variety of vertebrate prey and favors medium to large mammals such as deer, pacas, and agoutis. Uneaten portions of prey are often covered with sticks and debris and marked with strong-smelling urine. Home ranges in the United States are about 200–800 km² for males and 60–300 km² for females. Ranges of adult males seldom overlap, but several females may occupy portions of a male's home range. Adults are solitary. Vocalizations include whistles given between females and young; yowls of females in heat; grunts, and purrs. It is usually silent in the wild, but may vocalize when pursuing prey (Smallwood, 1993). Breeding may occur throughout the year; young are born in caves, thickets or tall grass. Litters of 1–6 have been reported. Biology (in United States) reviewed by Lindzey (1987).

JAGUAR
Panthera onca

Plate 40
Map 257

Spanish: tigre, jaguar; Maya: bolom, barum; Belize: tiger; Miskito: limi bulni; Kuna: achubarbat; Chocó: imama.

HB 1100–1600 (4'3"), T 450–550 (22"), Wt 30–100 kg (160 lb)

Description. Very large, powerful, and *big headed.* Upperparts golden yellow to sandy brown, marked with circular black rosettes, usually with a small black central spot. Underparts white with solid black spots. *Tail* narrow and *rather short,* less than half head and body length. Legs short and stocky; *feet broad.* **Similar Species.** Much larger and heavier than other spotted cats. At a distance, Jaguar silhouette is stockier, with a bigger head and shorter legs and tail than Puma.

Distribution. N Mexico through Central and South America to N Argentina. Lowlands to about 2000 m.

Status and Habitat. CITES Appendix I. Previously widespread, now uncommon and patchily distributed. This cat suffers from exploitation for

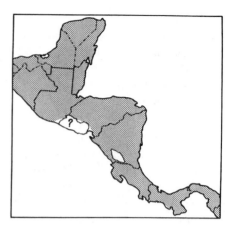

Map 257. Jaguar, *Panthera onca*

fur and sport and from deforestation. Favors undisturbed evergreen forest in the lowlands and foothills, but is also found in deciduous forest, mangroves, and grasslands.

Habits. Usually active at night for several hours after dusk and before dawn, but it may also be active during the day. The Jaguar rests during the day in shady areas, on stream banks, or on horizontal tree branches. This big cat is mainly terrestrial, but climbs and swims well. It feeds on a variety of vertebrates, depending on local availability: mammals (including armadillos, pacas, capybaras, deer, peccaries, tamanduas, and coatis) and reptiles (including turtles and iguanas) are preferred; some birds and fish are also taken. Small prey are killed by a smack of the forepaw. Large prey are killed with bites on neck or head which crush the spinal cord or break the skull; prey is then dragged into cover and eaten. This cat is remarkably strong and may carry prey of 3–4 times its weight for distances of 1 km or more. Although generally solitary, adults sometimes feed and travel in pairs; such associations are often breeding pairs, but occasionally are 2 females or 2 males. In Belize, males occupy home ranges of 28–40 km², and females use smaller areas within a male's range (Rabinowitz and Nottingham, 1986). Studies in

South America indicate larger home ranges. Grunting calls, marking with urine, and scratching trees are probably used in defining home ranges. Loud roars are given by males and females, and consist of series of hoarse coughs: "uh, uh, uh . . .," of increasing volume and duration. Softer grunts, purrs, and meows are also given. Breeding may occur throughout the year; litters of 1–4 have been recorded, with twins most commonly produced. Young stay with the mother for 1.5 years and may remain within her home range after this period. Biology and conservation reviewed by Mondolfi and Hoogesteijn (1986).

MANATEES AND DUGONGS

Order Sirenia, Family Trichechidae

There are 2 families of sirenians: the Dugongidae, with a single species found only in the Old World, and the Trichechidae, with 3 species, one of which occurs in Central America. These aquatic mammals are rotund, with bulbous, bristly noses, forelimbs modified into flippers, and horizontally flattened tails. They are placid herbivores that methodically browse on aquatic vegetation in shallow waters of rivers, estuaries, and coasts.

WEST INDIAN MANATEE   Plate 44
Trichechus manatus   Map 258

Caribbean manatee; Spanish: manatí, vaca marina; Belize: sea cow.

TL 2.5–4.5 m (11'), Wt 200–600 kg (900 lb).

Description. A bulky, *aquatic mammal* with no dorsal fin and a *paddle-shaped tail.* Body gray or brown; rolls of flesh on the neck. Head small and blunt, with a pair of round nostrils and short, stiff whiskers on the snout. There are 3–4 fingernails at the tip of each flipper. **Similar Species.** Unmistakable if seen well. Estuarine and coastal dolphins have dorsal fins and narrow beaks.

Distribution. Atlantic coast and estuaries from SE United States and E coast of Central America to Brazil; West Indies and Caribbean.

Status and Habitat. CITES Appendix I. Rare and local; numbers reduced by hunting, habitat loss, and incidental death through collision

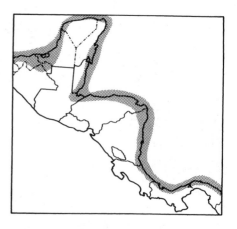

Map 258. West Indian Manatee, *Trichechus manatus*

with motor boats. Patchily distributed in Central America; in coastal marine, brackish, and fresh water.

Habits. Manatees are difficult to see because they cruise along below the water surface, exposing only the nostrils when breathing. Occasionally the finless, gray back appears. The diet

276

includes seagrasses, water hyacinth, and other aquatic vegetation. Individuals may be solitary or members of small groups. Females give birth to a single calf after gestation of about 1 year. Breeding may occur at any time of year but is often locally seasonal. In Tabasco, Mexico, reproduction occurs in the wet season, coinciding with higher water levels and increased food availability in inland lagoons and rivers (Colmenero-R., 1986). Biology reviewed by Caldwell and Caldwell (1985) and Husar (1978). For present status in Central America, see O'Shea and Salisbury (1991).

Where to See. One of the largest populations of West Indian Manatees is in Southern Lagoon, Belize, and boat trips to see the manatees can be arranged from Gales Point or Belize City. The water is often turbulent, and views may be disappointing. In Mexico, viable populations of manatees are present in Chetumal Bay, Quintana Roo (Colmenero-R. and Zárate, 1990), and along the Usumacinta River, Tabasco. Small numbers are protected in Cuero y Salado Wildlife Refuge, Honduras, and Tortuguero National Park, Costa Rica.

ODD-TOED UNGULATES

Order Perissodactyla

There are 3 families of odd-toed ungulates: horses, rhinoceroses, and tapirs. Although perissodactyls are externally similar to the artiodactyls (even-toed ungulates), the 2 orders may not be each other's nearest relatives. Some authors suggest that the closest living relative to the odd-toed ungulates in Central America may be the West Indian Manatee (Fischer and Tassy, 1993). Tapirs are the only members of the order that include living species native to the New World.

TAPIRS (Spanish: dantas)
Family Tapiridae

The tapir family contains 4 species in one genus. One species is found in Southeast Asia, and 3 are in South America, one of which ranges northward into Central America and S Mexico. Tapirs are large, stocky, hoofed mammals, with 3 weight-bearing toes on the forefoot (a small outer toe sometimes leaves a faint track), and 3 toes on the hind foot. The dental formula is: i 3/3, c 1/1, p 4/3–4, m 3/3.

BAIRD'S TAPIR Plate 42
Tapirus bairdii Map 259

Spanish: danta, tapir; Mexico: anteburro; Maya: cash-i-tzimin; Belize: mountain cow; Miskito: tilba; Costa Rica: macho de monte; Kuna: molí.

HB 1900–2200 (6'6"), T 100 (4"), SH 1150 (3'8") Wt 180–300 kg (550 lb).

Description. *Largest land mammal* in Central America. Solidly built, with a rounded back and rump, a thick neck, and large head with a *long, trunklike nose* and upper lip. Mostly *dark gray-brown*; whitish on cheeks and throat. Small, white-edged ears. *Short, stumpy tail.* Eyeshine reddish, moderately bright. Young reddish brown with bold white spots and stripes. **Similar Species.** Much larger and heavier than other hoofed mammals in the region. When seen running away, the tail is clearly visible; in peccaries (which are much smaller) the rump is narrower, and no tail is visible.

Distribution. S Veracruz and S Oaxaca, Mexico, to NW Ecuador and N Colombia. Lowlands to 3800 m.

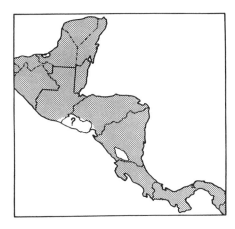

Map 259. Baird's Tapir, *Tapirus bairdii*

Status and Habitat. CITES Appendix I. Rare and local; heavily hunted for meat and suffering from deforestation throughout its range. Tapirs avoid people and leave areas of human activity, even when hunting is controlled. Found in evergreen and deciduous forest, second growth, and swamps.

Habits. Active by day or night. Baird's Tapir often spends part of the day resting in mud wallows or standing water or lying in shaded thickets. It uses well-worn trails through forest and favors stream banks and other forest gaps with low, dense vegetation. It travels long distances and follows ridges when crossing mountains (these ridge trails may later be modified into human paths). This large mammal moves quietly unless disturbed, when it runs crashing through vegetation, making a tremendous noise.

Baird's Tapir feeds on browse and favors new growth of shrubs or low trees, but it also eats some fruit, flowers, and grasses. It may knock over saplings to reach the upper leaves. Because it feeds mainly on secondary vegetation, selective logging may actually benefit this species if hunting is controlled (Fragoso, 1991). Tapir droppings, which look like coarse, dry, greenish horse droppings, are often defecated in water. Individuals are mainly solitary, although juveniles may travel with their mother long after they are weaned. Tapirs have an acute sense of smell and good hearing, but seem to have poor eyesight. They communicate over distance with long whistles; grunts, hiccups, and whimpers are used at close range. A low snort may be given in alarm. Single young are born after 13 months of gestation. Natural history studied by Terwilliger (1978).

Where to See. It is much easier to find the characteristic tracks, trails, and droppings of tapirs than to see the live animal, especially in areas where they are hunted. Tracks may lead to mud wallows that are visited on a regular basis. Stay downwind of recently used tapir trails if waiting at a mud wallow or water hole. Canoeing rivers through forest at night may be productive, and long whistles may elicit a response. Good sites are the Mountain Pine Ridge (along Macal River) and Maya Mountains, Belize; Santa Rosa National Park (waterholes not far from the beach), Rara Avis, and Corcovado National Park (near Sirena Station), Costa Rica.

EVEN-TOED UNGULATES

Order Artiodactyla

The Artiodactyla includes pigs, hippopotamuses, camels, giraffes, deer, antelope, and cattle and is the most diverse order of hoofed mammals. Even-toed ungulates have 2 weight-bearing toes on each foot. They probably are only distantly related to the odd-toed ungulates; but rather, within the region, are thought to be more closely related to cetaceans (whales and dolphins). Two families are native to Central America.

PECCARIES (Spanish: saínos, pecarís)
Family Tayassuidae

Peccaries are piglike mammals but are highly distinctive and are placed in a separate family from domestic pigs and wild boar (Family Suidae). There are 3 species of peccaries in 2 or 3 genera. Two species occur in Central and South America, the third is found only in South America. The classification of the 2 northern species is confusing. Some authors treat them as separate genera, while others place both in one genus. Further, the generic names *Dicotyles* and *Tayassu* have both been used for each species. The name *Pecari* is used by some authors for the Collared Peccary (see Grubb, 1993). Peccaries do at least have well-established common names. Scientific names used below follow Jones et al. (1992). There are 4 hooflike toes on the forefoot and 3 on the hind foot, but only 2 toes on each foot carry weight and leave tracks. Long, stiff hairs extending down the spine can be erected to give the impression of larger size. Peccaries have a tiny tail that is hidden in the fur. There is a large scent gland on the rump, which secretes an oily musk. The dental formula is: i 2/3, c 1/1, p 3/3, m 3/3.

Peccaries are highly social, living and traveling in herds. They have good senses of smell and hearing, which are used to maintain contact among group members, and have rather poor eyesight. Their strong, musky scent is also used in territorial spacing between neighboring groups. Peccaries are heavily hunted throughout their range for meat and hides. Although often considered ferocious, they usually avoid humans and run away when possible. Unlike domestic pigs, which have large litters of helpless young, peccaries have small litters, usually twins, and the young are precocial. A good general reference is Sowls (1984).

COLLARED PECCARY
Tayassu tajacu

Plate 42
Map 260

Spanish: javelina, pecari de collar, chancho de monte; Mexico: jabalí; Maya: kitam; Honduras: quequeo; Miskito: buksa; Costa Rica, Panama: saíno, zahino; Kuna: guatarra; Chocó: bidove.

HB 800–1000 (3'), SH 400–500 (18"), Wt 12–26 kg (44 lb).

Description. Relatively small, with a large, triangular head, *stocky body*, and *thin legs*. Coarse *fur* is *grizzled, dark gray-brown*, with a *cream-colored collar* from shoulders to chest. Eyeshine reddish, moderately bright. Young paler, pinkish. **Similar Species.** White-lipped Peccary (much less common) is larger, with ungrizzled, blackish fur and a white patch on cheek and lower jaw. Feral pig or wild boar (*Sus scrofa*) lacks pale collar and has a conspicuous tail and larger ears (young boar is spotted and striped).

Distribution. SW United States through Mexico and Central America to NW Peru and N Argentina. Lowlands to 3000 m.

Status and Habitat. CITES Appendix II. Widespread and common where not hunted, in all forest types, grassland, and deserts. Adapts well to disturbed habitat, but may be locally scarce due to hunting pressure.

Habits. Active by night or day, usually inactive at midday in hot, dry habitats; it may become entirely nocturnal where heavily hunted. When resting, groups shelter in abandoned burrows, caves, or under rocky outcroppings and logs. Dust baths and mud wallows are frequented regularly; these sites become permeated with the Collared Peccary's characteristic, musty-cheese odor. The diet consists mainly of fruits and seeds (including palm nuts, figs, guácimo, hog plum, zapote, and acorns). Vegetable matter, roots, and a few invertebrates are eaten when fruit is unavailable. In Venezuela, groups often associate with capuchins (*Cebus*

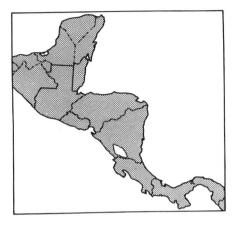

Map 260. Collared Peccary, *Tayassu tajacu*

sp.), eating fruit dropped or shaken down by the monkeys (Robinson and Eisenberg, 1985). Herds may number 2–50 (usually 15 or fewer), but they are usually seen in smaller feeding groups of 2–5. Groups travel quietly at a walk or trot, but when alarmed give a series of sharp barks or "whoofs" while noisily running off and may raise the long hairs on their backs. Individuals grunt, purr, or bark to remain in contact with one another. Herds have large home ranges (averaging 118 ha in Costa Rica; McCoy et al., 1990), although only a small portion of the range is used daily. Adults rub against rocks and trees, leaving dark, oily, odoriferous deposits from the scent gland. Litter size is 1–4, usually 2.

Where to See. Throughout SE Mexico and Central America; especially easy to find at water holes early or late in the day at Santa Rosa and Palo Verde national parks, Costa Rica; Barro Colorado Island (mainly at night), Pipeline Road in Soberanía National Park, and Darién National Park, Panama.

WHITE-LIPPED PECCARY
Dicotyles pecari

Plate 42
Map 261

Spanish: pecari de labios blancos; Mexico: jabalí, senso; Maya: hash-kekan; Belize: wari; Honduras: jaguilla, barbiblanco, baquira; Miskito: wuari; Costa Rica: chancho de monte, cariblanco; Panama: puerco de monte; Kuna: yanu; Chocó: bidó.

HB 900–1300 (4'), SH 500–600 (22"), Wt 27–40 kg (75 lb).

Description. Medium sized; large, triangular head and slim legs. *Mainly blackish brown; white patch along lower jaw, cheek, and throat* (sometimes whitish on chest). Fur long and coarse with long, erectile hairs along spine. Young paler, grizzled reddish brown, with an indistinct, pale throat patch (similar to young of Collared Peccary). **Similar Species.** See Collared Peccary. Feral pig (*Sus scrofa*) lacks white patch on lower jaw and has a conspicuous tail and larger ears.

Distribution. Oaxaca and Veracruz, Mexico, through Central America to W Ecuador and NE Argentina. Lowlands to 1900 m.

Status and Habitat. CITES Appendix II. Rare and local, suffering from habitat loss and excessive hunting. Patchily distributed in Central America; limited to extensive tracts of undisturbed, evergreen forest.

Habits. This large peccary may be active by day or night, but usually rests during the heat of the day. It is terrestrial and a good swimmer, but does not climb (attacks can be avoided by climbing 1 m off the ground). It feeds by noisily bulldozing through the leaf litter and topsoil with its snout, eating fruit, seeds, roots, vegetation, and small quantities of invertebrates. This species has very strong, interlocking jaws that enable it to open extremely hard seeds and nuts. Palm nuts are sought after, and crops such as maize, sweet potatoes, and manioc are sometimes exploited. These peccaries live in herds of 40–200, much larger than

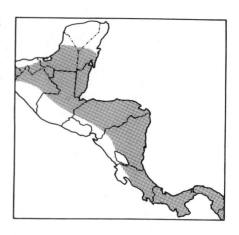

Map 261. White-lipped Peccary, *Dicotyles pecari*

Collared Peccary herds. Smaller herds may be remnants of a disappearing population. White-lipped Peccaries travel long distances, walking single file along paths or trails through forest. The herd may spread out in a wide swath to feed, with males at the periphery and females and young in the center (Hernandez et al., 1995). The home range of a large herd is poorly known, but has been estimated as up to 200 km² in Peru. Vocalizations include low rumbles and loud barks used as togetherness calls; grumbles, clicks, snorts, and wheezes are used in aggressive situations. Alarm barks are louder and lower in pitch than those of Collared Peccaries. If threatened, they may clash their canine teeth together, making a loud, clicking sound. Females usually give birth to twins (rarely 1–3) after 5 months of gestation. Biology reviewed by Mayer and Wetzel (1987).

Where to See. Because herds travel extensively, their presence in an area cannot be predicted, although when nearby they are hard to miss. They are seen fairly regularly in Corcovado National Park, Costa Rica, and Darién National Park, Panama.

DEER (Spanish: venados)
Family Cervidae

There are 16 genera of deer with about 42 species; 3 species in 2 genera occur in Central America. Deer have long, slim legs and necks. Males have antlers that are usually shed each year, although male brocket sometimes retain the antlers for 2 years or more. Each foot has 2 weight-carrying hooves and 2 small hooves that do not touch the ground. The dental formula is: i 0/3, c 0/0 (or 1/1), p 3/3, m 3/3.

Deer, like cattle, are ruminants, specialized for browsing on leafy plant growth. They rapidly chew and swallow food, which passes to the rumen, or first stomach; later they lie down in a sheltered spot and regurgitate the contents of the rumen. The food is chewed more thoroughly the second time and passed to the remaining 3 chambers of the stomach to complete digestion. Deer usually produce 1–2 young, which are precocial and can walk soon after birth. Females leave their spotted fawns in a secluded area while they feed. The fawns lie motionless, and the white spots provide a disruptive pattern, which serves as an effective camouflage in dappled light.

WHITE-TAILED DEER
Odocoileus virginianus

Plate 43
Map 262

Spanish: venado cola blanca; Maya: ke, jalal; Belize: savanna deer; Miskito: sula; Chocó: beguí torro; Kuna: coée pebenicat.

HB 900–1500 (3'6"), T 120–180 (6"), SH 700–1000 (3'), Wt 25–43 kg (77 lb).

Description. Medium sized; slim, with *long legs, a flat back*, and a long, narrow head. Upperparts *gray-brown* to *orange-brown* (darker, red-brown in C Panama); *belly*, inner thighs, chest, and throat *white*. Forehead dark brown; *conspicuous white facial markings* around eyes and on muzzle. Ears relatively long and narrow. Curved, branched antlers on male only. *Tail* brown above, *edge and underside white*. Eyeshine bright, pale yellow or bluish. Young reddish brown, with white spots and stripes. **Similar Species.** See Red and Gray Brockets (*Mazama* spp.).

Distribution. S Canada and United States through Mexico and Central America to Bolivia, the Guianas, and N Brazil. Lowlands to 2600 m.

Status and Habitat. CITES Appendix III (Guatemala). Widespread and fairly common

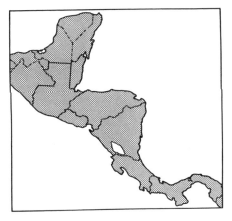

Map 262. White-tailed Deer, *Odocoileus virginianus*

where not hunted. Some populations have been eliminated by excessive hunting and deforestation (Méndez, 1984). Favors deciduous forest interspersed with grassland but is found in a variety of habitats; rarely in mature evergreen forest.

Habits. Active by day or night, this deer is most often seen at dawn or dusk and at night, when it ventures into fields and open areas to feed. It walks with the head held higher than the back. When disturbed, it gives a sharply exhaled whistling snort, raises and fans out the tail to expose the white "flag," and moves off with a bounding gait, head high. It may sneak away quietly if the disturbance is minor. At night it is easily detected by its bright eyeshine and will often freeze in a strong light. White-tailed Deer browse on leaves and twigs and eat fallen fruits and nuts. Fruits probably make up a significant portion of the diet when available. These deer are seen singly or in small groups. In Costa Rica, mating takes place during the wet season, and females give birth to 1–2 young during the dry season (February–May).

Comment. Central American White-tails are much smaller than those in the United States and have shorter tails that show less white when raised. The antlers of bucks are about half the size of those in the United States of comparable age.

Where to See. Abundant at Santa Rosa and Palo Verde national parks, Costa Rica; at night (on the airstrip), at Tikal, Guatemala; the small, reddish forest race (easily confused with Red Brocket) can be seen on Barro Colorado Island, Panama.

RED BROCKET
Mazama americana

Plate 43
Map 263

Spanish: venado colorado; Mexico: temezate; Maya: yuk; Belize: antelope; Miskito: snapuka; Costa Rica: cabro de monte; Panama: corzo; Chocó: beguí; Kuna: coeé.

HB 900–1200 (3'), T 95–145 (5"), SH 600–750 (2'4") Wt 12–32 kg (48 lb)

Description. Fairly small, with a *rounded body, arched back, and slim legs* and neck; head triangular in profile. Upperparts mostly *bright reddish brown*; head and neck dark gray-brown (or reddish); throat and chest usually whitish; *belly orangish*, paler than upperparts but not sharply contrasting. Fur short and shiny. Ears

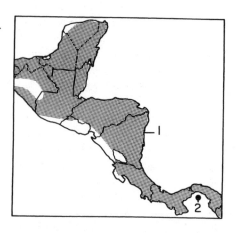

Map 263. 1. Red Brocket, *Mazama americana*
2. Gray Brocket, *Mazama gouazoubira*

relatively broad, naked inside. Male has a pair of short, straight, unbranched antlers (about same length as ears). Tail rather short, underside of tail and inner edge of thighs white. Eyeshine bright yellow-white. Young reddish with white spots. **Similar Species.** White-tailed Deer is usually larger and paler, but in forested areas (especially in C Panama), the 2 species are similar in size and color and are easily confused. The White-tail has a flat back, white belly, and white facial markings and a slimmer head with narrow ears. It runs with the head held high, while the Red Brocket usually runs with its head held at the level of its back or lower.

Distribution. S Tamaulipas, Mexico, through Central America to Bolivia, S Brazil, and N Argentina; Trinidad and Tobago. Lowlands to 2800 m.

Status and Habitat. CITES Appendix III (Guatemala). Fairly common and widespread in forested areas, except where heavily hunted. It favors mature evergreen forest and adjacent small clearings and seems to be most common at mid- to high elevations.

Habits. Active night or day, the Red Brocket is usually seen at dusk or during the night. It is more often found lying down digesting than a White-tail and will often remain motionless when approached. Brocket are forest dwellers; their small size, short antlers, and rounded backs enable them to move through dense vegetation. Their gait also reflects their habitat, as they usually walk with the head held low and run with head outstretched. When disturbed, the Red Brocket usually slips quietly away through dense vegetation but may raise its tail and run off, giving a whistling snort in alarm. It swims well and sometimes enters water when pursued by predators. It often forages in small clearings or along wide trails through forest. The diet includes fruits (such as figs and hog plums), flowers, fungi, and vegetation. Individuals are usually solitary but are occasionally seen in pairs. Females give birth to single young or, less often, twins.

Where to See. Río Bravo Conservation Area and Cockscomb Basin Wildlife Preserve, Belize; Monteverde, Costa Rica: Barro Colorado Island, Panama.

GRAY BROCKET
Mazama gouazoubira   Map 263

Spanish: venado plomo, venado cenizo; Panama: corzo chocolate.

HB 800–1100 (2'9"), T 80–150 (5"), SH 450–600 (21"), Wt 13–20 kg (35 lb).

Description. Relatively small and slim; back arched. Upperparts *buffy gray*, darker on spine, legs, and forehead; underparts whitish. Male has short, straight, unbranched antlers. Young gray with white spots. **Similar Species.** Similar in shape to Red Brocket, but gray, not reddish, and slightly smaller and slimmer (the 2 species do not overlap in Central America). White-tailed Deer (also found on San José Island) is larger, with a flat back, white markings on muzzle, and branched antlers on male.

Distribution. In Central America on San José Island, Panama, only; also Colombia and Venezuela to Peru, S Brazil, Paraguay, and N Argentina. Lowlands to 1000 m.

Status and Habitat. Apparently fairly common on San José Island, in deciduous forest and second growth. Widespread in South America, where common to abundant in dry scrub (such as the Chaco of Argentina and Paraguay); generally uncommon in evergreen forest.

Habits. The Gray Brocket is mainly diurnal and usually solitary. The diet is mostly fruit, with some vegetation (Stallings, 1984). Females give birth to single young, and reproduction does not appear to be seasonal.

WHALES, DOLPHINS, AND PORPOISES

Order Cetacea

Cetaceans are aquatic mammals that breathe air and suckle their young. As a result of modifications associated with life in water, they are fishlike in form. Many dolphins have upright, sharklike dorsal fins; however, the tail of a dolphin is flattened horizontally, whereas a shark's tail is vertical. Unlike fish, cetaceans breathe through blowholes (nostrils) located on the top of their head. Whales and dolphins do not resemble other orders of mammals, but are thought to be related to artiodactyls (progenitors of modern ungulates), based on similar fossil ancestors and other evidence. Cetaceans are divided into 2 major groups, the toothed whales (Suborder Odontoceti) and the baleen whales (Suborder Mysticeti).

There are a great many books on marine mammals. Useful general references are Evans (1987), Jefferson et al. (1993), Leatherwood and Reeves (1983), and Leatherwood et al. (1976). More technical information can be found in the series *Handbook of Marine Mammals*, edited by Ridgway and Harrison (1985, 1989, 1994). The following species accounts are largely derived from these sources, with additional information about distribution from Mead and Brownell (1993) and Schmidly (1981).

Toothed Whales
Suborder Odontoceti

Toothed whales range in size from small dolphins and porpoises to one of the largest cetaceans, the Great Sperm Whale. As the name implies, these whales have teeth (although the teeth may not be visible externally or may be present in one sex only) and have a single blowhole. All toothed whales may echolocate, although this has been established for only a few species. The diet of most species consists mainly of fish and squid.

OCEAN DOLPHINS (Spanish: delfines)
Family Delphinidae

There are 33 species in 17 genera in the family. Included are typical beaked dolphins and much larger, blunt-headed killer and pilot whales (the latter sometimes placed in the Family Globicephalidae). All delphinids have rows of conical teeth on upper and lower jaws, and most have a prominent dorsal fin and a beak (or rostrum). Delphinids are marine cetaceans, although a few species enter fresh water. Most have complex social behavior and long-term mother–offspring bonds.

ROUGH-TOOTHED DOLPHIN
Steno bredanensis

Plate 45

Spanish: esteno.

TL 2–2.75 m (8'), Wt 120–160 kg (300 lb).

Description. White-lipped, with *no demarcation between beak and forehead*. Upperparts *dark gray* or *brown, marked with white spots* and scratches; belly white. **Similar Species.** The unusual, conical head is distinctive at close range. White lips and blotches on sides distinguish it from Bottlenose (*Tursiops truncatus*) and Spinner Dolphins (*Stenella longirostris*).

Distribution. Worldwide in tropical and subtropical waters.

Status and Habitat. CITES Appendix II. Common in the Pacific Ocean off Central America and in the Gulf of Mexico. Thirteen adults were stranded on the coast of Belize in 1981 (Perkins and Miller, 1983). Three groups of 20–65 individuals were sighted in shallow water off the coast of Tabasco, Mexico (Delgado Estrella, 1994). In other parts of its range it is uncommon or poorly known. It is usually found in deep, offshore water.

Habits. This dolphin sometimes swims at high speeds, skimming with the snout and dorsal fin exposed; it may bowride. The diet includes squid, octopus, and large fish. It is usually seen in groups of 10–50, occasionally in association with other dolphin species.

TUCUXI
Sotalia fluviatilis

Plate 44

Estuarine dolphin; Spanish: bufeo negro, tonino.

TL 1.4–2.1 m (5'), Wt 35–50 kg (90 lb).

Description. Small and gray, with a *low, broad-based, triangular dorsal fin*. Flippers rather broad. **Similar Species.** This is the smallest dolphin in Central American waters. Bottlenose Dolphin (*Tursiops*) is much larger, with a tall, curved dorsal fin and a slightly shorter beak. Young spotted dolphins (*Stenella* spp.) are slimmer, with narrow dorsal fins and flippers.

Distribution. Nicaragua; Panama to SE Brazil on Atlantic coast, Amazon River, and its tributaries.

Status and Habitat. CITES Appendix I. Some are captured incidentally in fish nets. Known in Central America only from a stranding in Wounta Lagoon, Haulover, Nicaragua (Carr, 1994) and a sighting record in coastal water off C Panama (Borobia et al., 1991). Elsewhere uncommon to locally common in major rivers, estuaries, and inshore waters, both in fresh and salt water.

Habits. Active in the early morning or late evening, this small dolphin sometimes jumps, landing on one side, and lifts the tail before diving. Individuals travel close to one another in groups of 4–7 (larger groups of about 30 may be seen in marine environments), feeding on fish and crustaceans. It may use echolocation to navigate or communicate in muddy river water.

PANTROPICAL SPOTTED DOLPHIN
Plate 45
Stenella attenuata

Bridled dolphin; Spanish: estenela moteada.

TL 1.6–2.6 m (7'), Wt 100–120 kg (240 lb).

Description. Slender and spotted. Cape blackish, sides *gray, with white spots* (spots not always visible at a distance). Beak long and narrow, white at tip; lips may be white. *Dark mask from eye to beak and line from mouth to flipper.* Young and some adults are not spotted. **Similar Species.** The extent of spotting varies with age and population. Atlantic Spotted Dolphin (*S. frontalis*) is usually more heavily spotted, lacks a dark mask, and is more robust, with a shorter beak. Unspotted young resemble Bottlenose Dolphin (*Tursiops*), which is stockier with a shorter beak.

Distribution. In tropical and subtropical waters of all oceans.

Status and Habitat. CITES Appendix II. Large numbers drown in seine nets, and some are hunted. It may be the most abundant species of dolphin both in the Pacific off Central America and along the continental slope in the north–central and western parts of the Gulf of Mexico. It appears to be scarce in Caribbean waters. It is generally common and widespread, mainly offshore, but also in coastal regions with deep water.

Habits. This spotted dolphin is a fast, active swimmer, often seen bowriding. It hunts near the surface during the day. The diet includes flying fish and squid. It usually travels in groups of 100 or more, in association with yellowfin tuna and Spinner Dolphins (*S. longirostris*).

ATLANTIC SPOTTED DOLPHIN
Plates 44, 45
Stenella frontalis

Spanish: delfín pintado, delfín moteado del Atlantico; St. Vincent: speckly gammin fish.

TL 1.8–2.3 m (6'6"), Wt 100–140 kg (260 lb).

Description. Fairly stocky and heavily spotted. White spots on upperparts, *black spots on underparts.* Beak relatively short with a white tip. Young and some adults are unspotted. **Similar Species.** See Pantropical Spotted Dolphin (*S. Attenuata*). Unspotted young are similar to young Bottlenose Dolphins (*Tursiops*), but have a slightly larger beak.

Distribution. Tropical and warm temperate waters of the Atlantic Ocean.

Status and Habitat. CITES Appendix II. One of the most common offshore dolphins in the Gulf of Mexico and Caribbean. Found in offshore and coastal waters.

Habits. Similar to Pantropical Spotted Dolphin, but usually in smaller groups of 50 or fewer. Coastal groups may number 1–15.

Comment. This species was formerly known as *S. plagiodon*, with the common name Spotted Dolphin. It has often been confused with *S. attenuata.*

SPINNER DOLPHIN
Plate 45
Stenella longirostris

Spanish: estenela giradora.

TL 1.3–2.4 m (6'), Wt 70–95 kg (140 lb).

Description. Small and *slim bodied*, with a *very slender, long beak.* Tip of beak black. *Color plain gray* (Pacific Central America) or dark gray on upper back only, grading to white on the belly. Dorsal fin *narrow and triangular*, not curved backward in most Central American populations. **Similar Species.**

Other dolphins have shorter beaks, more robust bodies, and usually have curved dorsal fins. Spotted dolphins (which sometimes lack spots) have white-tipped beaks and dark saddles extending lower on the sides. Striped Dolphin (*S. coeruleoalba*) has a dark line on its side. See Clymene Dolphin (*S. clymene*).

Distribution. Tropical and subtropical waters worldwide.

Status and Habitat. CITES Appendix II. Large numbers are killed in seine nets. Common and widespread; one of the most abundant species in the Caribbean Sea. Usually found in deep, offshore water; also in inshore water near islands.

Habits. This species is a very fast, agile swimmer, often leaping out of the water, and sometimes spinning on its long axis while in the air. The Spinner is the most acrobatic of all dolphins. It feeds on small fish and squid caught at middle depths, mainly at night. Individuals travel in small to large groups and may associate with Pantropical Spotted Dolphins (*S. attenuata*) and yellowfin tuna.

CLYMENE DOLPHIN   Plate 45
Stenella clymene

Spanish: delfín clymene.

TL 1.8–2 m (6'), Wt 75–85 kg (180 lb).

Description. Relatively stocky. Dark gray saddle dips below dorsal fin. Beak short and broad; pale gray marked with *black on the lips, tip*, and along the *midline*. **Similar Species.** Color pattern of the beak is distinctive at close range; at a distance, note shape of the dark saddle. Spinner Dolphin is slimmer and lacks a dark saddle below the dorsal fin.

Distribution. Atlantic Ocean only, in tropical and subtropical zones.

Status and Habitat. CITES Appendix II. Not recorded from the Atlantic coast of Central

America. It is the fifth most abundant species along the continental slope of the Gulf of Mexico; there are a few records of this species from the Caribbean. Elsewhere it is generally rare; found in deep, offshore waters.

Habits. This poorly known dolphin is a fast, agile swimmer that sometimes spins. Groups of up to 50 have been recorded.

STRIPED DOLPHIN   Plate 45
Stenella coeruleoalba

Spanish: estenela listada.

TL 2.3–2.7 m (8'), Wt 100–150 kg (270 lb).

Description. Strikingly patterned. Back black with a *pale gray blaze from eye to dorsal fin; dark line from eye to anus* and another dark line from eye to flipper. **Similar Species.** Color pattern unique. Pale and dark blazes below dorsal fin are usually visible in the field. Common Dolphin (*Delphinus delphis*) has an hourglass pattern. See Fraser's Dolphin (*Lagenodelphis hosei*).

Distribution. Tropical and temperate waters worldwide.

Status and Habitat. CITES Appendix II. In the last 10 years, 1000–3000 have been killed annually by Japanese fishermen. Common and widespread in deep, offshore waters.

Habits. This dolphin is a fast swimmer, often jumping clear of the water. Groups occasionally bowride, but are usually wary of boats. It is a fairly deep diver, feeding on small fish and squid caught at middle depths. Group size is 30–500.

COMMON DOLPHIN   Plate 45
Delphinus delphis

Spanish: delfín común, bufeo.

TL 2–2.6 m (7'6"), Wt 70–135 kg (220 lb).

Description. Slim, with a *distinctive hourglass pattern on its sides*. Color variable, yellowish to tan flank-patch crisscrosses with pale gray patch on tail stock. Dark mask from beak to eye and from chin to flipper. Long, slim beak. **Similar Species.** Hourglass pattern diagnostic. See *Stenella* spp. and Bottlenose Dolphin (*Tursiops*).

Distribution. Tropical and warm temperate waters worldwide.

Status and Habitat. CITES Appendix II. Some populations are hunted, and others are caught incidentally in fish nets. Common and widespread in deep, offshore water (including Pacific off Central America); less common coastally. It does not appear to occur in the Gulf of Mexico.

Habits. Large groups of these bouncy, acrobatic dolphins churn up the water surface and often bowride for extended periods. Groups may hunt cooperatively, feeding at night on small fish and squid. Group size ranges from 20–10,000. This species is highly vocal and may whistle, squeak, click, and creak.

BOTTLENOSE DOLPHIN   Plate 44
Tursiops truncatus

Spanish: tursion, delfín hocico de botella.

TL 2–3.8 m (9'), Wt 200–650 kg (900 lb).

Description. The familiar "Flipper" and other captive performers. Stocky and *gray*; belly pale, pinkish or spotted in some populations. *Beak short.* Dorsal fin tall, slightly angled backward. **Similar Species.** Usually recognizable by the short beak and lack of a distinct color pattern. Spinner and young spotted dolphins (*Stenella* spp.) are smaller and slimmer, with longer beaks. See Tucuxi (*Sotalia*).

Distribution. Tropical and temperate waters worldwide, seldom far from land.

Status and Habitat. CITES Appendix II. Common and widespread; still hunted in some regions. In Central America this species is more likely to be seen from shore than any other dolphin. Most common in coastal waters, also in estuaries, major rivers, and offshore waters.

Habits. Although this well known dolphin is often trained to perform impressive leaps in captivity, in the wild it usually travels in rather slow, graceful formations, showing only the back and dorsal fin. It is attracted to boats and often bowrides or travels at the stern. The characteristic "smiling" beak is exposed occasionally. When feeding it may be more acrobatic. The Bottlenose Dolphin eats a wide variety of bottom-dwelling fish and invertebrates and sometimes follows fishing boats. It travels in groups of 1–50 and often associates with other species. Larger groups are sometimes seen offshore. Females bear a single young every 2–3 years. The calf is suckled for a year and may be tended by other adults while its mother hunts.

FRASER'S DOLPHIN   Plate 45
Lagenodelphis hosei

Short-snout dolphin; Spanish: delfín de Fraser.

TL 2.3–2.7 m (8'), Wt 100–210 kg (350 lb).

Description. *Short-beaked and stocky*, with *very small appendages.* Upperparts blackish; sides gray; belly white. Broad, dark stripe from eye to anus. Dorsal fin small, upright or slightly angled backward. **Similar Species.** All other dolphins have longer flippers and most have longer beaks. Bottlenose Dolphin (*Tursiops*) lacks a dark stripe on the sides. Striped Dolphin (*Stenella coeruleoalba*) has a pale blaze from eye to fin.

Distribution. Tropical waters worldwide.

Status and Habitat. CITES Appendix II. Sometimes caught in fish nets. Uncommon in waters off Central America; recently sighted in the Gulf of Mexico in association with Melon-headed Whales (*Peponocephala*). Some are taken by harpoon fisheries from St. Vincent, Lesser Antilles. Generally poorly known; it may be fairly common in deep, off-shore waters.

Habits. Frasers Dolphin is a splashy swimmer that bowrides in some regions and avoids ships in others. It feeds at night on squid, fish, and crustaceans. Groups may number 100–1000 and sometimes mix with other species.

Comment. Initially described from skeletal material, the first strandings were recorded in the early 1970s. Subsequently, the species has been found to be widespread and relatively common.

RISSO'S DOLPHIN Plate 46
Grampus griseus

Grampus; Spanish: delfín de Risso.

TL 3.5–4 m (12'), Wt 300–500 kg (900 lb).

Description. Large, *pale gray*, with a *blunt, nearly rectangular head* and a vertical crease down the forehead. Body *heavily scarred*. Dorsal fin and flippers long and narrow. **Similar Species.** Rectangular head, pale color, and heavy white scarring are distinctive.

Distribution. Worldwide, in tropical and temperate waters.

Status and Habitat. CITES Appendix II. Some are taken by hunters in the West Indies. Fairly common and widespread in deep, off-shore water.

Habits. Risso's Dolphin moves slowly at times, showing only the back and dorsal fin, but it also may be seen leaping and bowriding. It sometimes rears up vertically, with head and flippers out of the water. The diet includes squid and crustaceans. Normal group size is 3–30, although groups of 4000 or more have been seen. Groups often associate with other species of dolphins.

MELON-HEADED WHALE Plate 46
Peponocephala electra

Spanish: calderón pequeño, ballena melón.

TL 2–2.7 m (7'6"), Wt 150–275 kg (460 lb).

Description. Small, slim, and *blackish*, with *no beak*. Head pointed when viewed from above. White patches on lips, throat, and belly. *Flippers narrow*, with *pointed tips*. 20–25 pairs of teeth in upper and lower jaws. **Similar Species.** See Pygmy Killer Whale (*Feresa*).

Distribution. Worldwide in tropical and sub-tropical waters.

Status and Habitat. CITES Appendix II. Although generally rare and little known, this species is the fourth most abundant cetacean in continental slope waters of the Gulf of Mexico. A mass stranding was recorded on the Pacific coast of Central America. It is usually found in offshore waters.

Habits. Fast and active, it leaps without clearing the water and sometimes bowrides. The diet includes medium-sized squid and fish. It travels in groups of 100–500 and may associate with other dolphins.

PYGMY KILLER WHALE Plate 46
Feresa attenuata

Spanish: orca pigmea/pigmeo.

TL 2–2.6 m (7'4"), Wt 150–225 kg (400 lb).

Description. Small, *blackish*, with a *rounded head* (when viewed from above) and no beak. White patches of variable extent on lips, chin, and belly. *Tips of flippers rounded.* 8–13 pairs of teeth in upper and lower jaws. **Similar Species.** Easily confused with Melon-headed Whale (*Peponocephala*), which has flippers with pointed tips and a more tapered snout. Stranded individuals of the 2 species can be distinguished by tooth number. See False Killer Whale (*Pseudorca*).

Distribution. Worldwide in tropical and warm temperate waters.

Status and Habitat. CITES Appendix II. Uncommon but widespread in deep, offshore waters.

Habits. Poorly known, apparently less active than Melon-headed Whale. It usually travels in groups of 10–50 and eats squid and fish.

FALSE KILLER WHALE   Plate 46
Pseudorca crassidens

Spanish: orca falsa, falsa ballena asesina.

TL 4.5–6 m (17'), Wt 1–2.5 tons.

Description. Very *slender, large,* and *black. Flippers long,* with a *hump on the leading edge.* Dorsal fin tall and narrow, slightly arched backward. **Similar Species.** No other black whales have humps on the flippers. Short-finned Pilot Whale (*Globicephala*) and Killer Whale (*Orcinus*) are more robust; Pygmy Killer Whale (*Feresa*) and Melon-headed Whale (*Peponocephala*) are much smaller and have white lips.

Distribution. Worldwide in tropical to warm temperate waters.

Status and Habitat. CITES Appendix II. Fairly common and widespread; mainly in deep, offshore waters.

Habits. This slim whale is a fast and active swimmer. It behaves more like a smaller dolphin as it leaps and sprints, sometimes jumping completely out of the water. It feeds on large fish and squid. Groups number about 10–60, and mass strandings occur quite often.

KILLER WHALE   Plate 46
Orcinus orca

Orca; Spanish: ballena asesina, orca.

TL 6–9.8 m (26'), Wt 4–8 tons.

Description. Large, with *striking black and white coloration and a very tall dorsal fin.* Flippers large and rounded. Dorsal fin tall, narrow, and erect in males, smaller and arched backward in females. **Similar Species.** Usually unmistakable.

Distribution. Worldwide, in all seas.

Status and Habitat. CITES Appendix II. Not well known in Central American waters, elsewhere fairly common. It favors cold, inshore waters.

Habits. Killer Whales are usually seen cruising in groups, the large, black fins clearly visible. When approached it may rear up vertically with head and flippers above water. The diet includes marine mammals, fish, and other vertebrates. This species appears to migrate in response to food availability rather than on a seasonal basis. Stable groups of 1–50 travel together and may hunt communally.

SHORT-FINNED PILOT WHALE   Plate 46
Globicephala macrorhynchus

Spanish: ballena piloto, calderón de aletas cortas.

TL 4–6.5 m (17'), Wt 1–3 tons.

Description. Bulbous headed, with a *broad, low dorsal fin.* Almost entirely black. *Flippers long* and *sickle-shaped.* Dorsal fin set far forward on back and angled backward. **Similar Species.** Other black whales of similar size have more upright, slender dorsal fins. See False Killer Whale (*Pseudorca*).

Distribution. Worldwide in warm temperate to tropical waters.

Status and Habitat. CITES Appendix II. Hunted in waters off Japan and the West Indies. Common to abundant and widely distributed; usually in deep, offshore waters. Mass strandings are quite common on the Pacific coast of Costa Rica.

Habits. It may be seen lolling at the surface or traveling at slow speed and is easily approached. It eats squid and fish, feeding at night. Highly social in behavior, stable groups of these whales may number 10–200 or more. Groups often associate with other species such as Bottlenose Dolphins (*Tursiops*).

SPERM WHALES
Family Physeteridae

There are 2 genera and 3 species of sperm whales, all of which may occur in the region. The 2 small species are sometimes placed in a different family, Kogiidae, and appear only distantly related to the Great Sperm Whale. Sperm whales have teeth only on the lower jaw, which is narrow and underslung. In common with other toothed whales, they have a single blowhole. A good reference is Ridgway and Harrison (1989).

GREAT SPERM WHALE   Plate 47
Physeter catodon

Spanish: cachalote.

TL 10–18 m (50'), Wt 22–57 tons.

Description. Large and *square headed.* Male is much larger than female. Blowhole on left side near tip of rostrum. Peglike teeth on the lower jaw only. *Dorsal fin low* and *broad,* set far back on body, followed by a series of ridges extending to flukes. Flukes triangular with a straight trailing edge and a deep notch. The blow is a single spout, directed forward and to the left. **Similar Species.** The massive, blunt head and angled blow are distinctive.

Distribution. Worldwide, in tropical and temperate waters. Only large males venture into polar seas.

Status and Habitat. CITES Appendix I. Despite excessive whaling which continued into the 1970s and depleted some populations, this species is the most common of all the great whales. It has been sighted beyond the Belize Barrier Reef. Found in deep waters, usually in offshore regions.

Habits. Sometimes only the tip of the snout is visible when breathing, at other times the long, flat profile and low hump of this whale are exposed. Before a long dive, the tail flukes are flung high into the air in a vertical position. The Great Sperm Whale is a deep diver, sometimes reaching depths of 3000 m, and it may stay underwater for 2 hours. It eats a variety of deep-water prey, but favors cephalopods (squid and octopus). Groups of 20–50 are commonly seen, but lone males are sometimes encountered. The mating system is polygynous; adult males form harems and drive off younger males. Females reproduce every 3–6 years, calving in summer or fall.

Comment. The name is derived from the "spermaceti" oil, which fills most of the forehead. Its function is not known, but is probably related to deep diving in some way, perhaps to aid in buoyancy, or for removal of excess nitrogen or as an acoustic lens in echolocation.

PYGMY SPERM WHALE   Plate 46
Kogia breviceps

Spanish: cachalote pigmeo, ballena enana de esperma.

TL 2.7–3.4 m (10'), Wt 350–400 kg (800 lb).

Description. Small and dark, with a *bulbous, squared-off snout* and *underslung jaw.* There are

12–16 (rarely 10–11) pairs of teeth in the lower jaw, and no creases in the throat. A pale bracket-shaped mark, or "false gill" runs between eye and flipper. *Dorsal fin* is usually *small* (less than 20 cm high), arched backward, and *set more than halfway back* toward the tail. Flukes deeply notched. **Similar Species.** Very difficult to distinguish from Dwarf Sperm Whale (*K. simus*), which usually has a larger, more upright dorsal fin halfway down the back. There is variation in size and position of the dorsal fin in both species, and they may be indistinguishable in the field. Stranded *K. simus* has creases on the throat and fewer teeth. Both *Kogia* species can be distinguished from dolphins of similar size by their blunt snouts, underslung jaws, and relatively small dorsal fins.

Distribution. In warm temperate and tropical waters of all seas. Mostly near the continental slope.

Status and Habitat. CITES Appendix II. Poorly known; probably uncommon or rare. Sometimes caught in gill nets. A number of strandings and sightings have been recorded in the Gulf of Mexico, Cuba, and Florida. Found in deep, offshore waters.

Habits. It is a sluggish swimmer, producing no visible blow. Both *Kogia* species rest near the surface with the back of the head exposed and the tail hanging down. If startled, they may emit a reddish brown fluid. Although seldom seen at sea, they are often stranded. The Pygmy Sperm Whale travels in groups of 1–6 individuals and feeds on deep-sea fish and cephalopods.

DWARF SPERM WHALE   Plate 46
Kogia simus

Spanish: cachalote enano.

TL 2.3–2.7 m (8'), Wt 150–210 kg (400 lb).

Description. Similar to Pygmy Sperm Whale, but slightly *smaller*, with a *larger, more erect dorsal fin* (over 20 cm high) set *halfway down the back*. There are 8–11 (rarely 12–13) pairs of teeth in the lower jaw, up to 3 pairs of teeth in the upper jaw, and a pair of short creases in the throat. **Similar Species.** See Pygmy Sperm Whale (*K. breviceps*).

Distribution. Worldwide in warm temperate and tropical waters.

Status and Habitat. CITES Appendix II. Poorly known; probably rare. A few strandings have been recorded in the Gulf of Mexico and Baja California. Usually found in deep, offshore waters.

Habits. The Dwarf Sperm Whale is shy and unobtrusive, known mainly from strandings. It feeds on deep-sea fish and cephalopods. Occasionally sighted in groups of 2–10. Biology reviewed by Nagorsen (1985).

BEAKED WHALES
Family Ziphiidae

There are 19 species of beaked whales in 5 genera. At least 4 species in 2 genera occur in oceans around Central America. These whales have a pair of grooves forming an inverted **V** on the throat, and the beak is usually pronounced. There is no notch in the tail. Adult males of species in the region have 2 functional teeth in the lower jaw, but teeth are absent in females. Beaked whales are pelagic in habit and most are poorly known. A good reference is Ridgway and Harrison (1989).

CUVIER'S BEAKED WHALE   Plate 47
Ziphius cavirostris

Spanish: zifio de Cuvier.

TL 5–7 m (20'), Wt 3–4 tons.

Description. Rather *stocky* with a *concave forehead*. Body color varies from dark gray to pale brown, marked with white scratches and spots. Head paler, often whitish, with a V-shaped groove on throat. Adult *male* has *2 small teeth at the tip of the lower jaw*. Dorsal fin small, set about 2/3 of the way back toward the tail. **Similar Species.** Could be confused with other beaked whales (*Mesoplodon* spp.), which are usually darker in color and slimmer. Other beaked whales expose the beak when breathing, which Cuvier's seldom does.

Distribution. Worldwide, from tropical to cold temperate zones.

Status and Habitat. CITES Appendix II. Fairly common in some areas; known from sightings in Pacific Ocean off Central America and strandings in Baja California, the Gulf of Mexico, and Puerto Rico. Found in deep, offshore waters.

Habits. Inconspicuous and wary, it is seldom seen at sea but often stranded. When breathing, the rounded forehead is exposed, followed by the fin. The tail may be raised before a deep dive. It eats deep sea squid and fish. Groups of 1–10 have been seen.

BLAINVILLE'S BEAKED WHALE   Plate 47
Mesoplodon densirostris

Spanish: zifio de Blainville.

TL 3.5–4.6 m (13'), Wt 470–1030 kg (1500 lb).

Description. Upperparts usually *heavily marked with pale spots* and *scratches*. Underparts whitish in female and young; gray in male. Head small, *lower jaw arched*; in male extending over upper jaw with a *broad tusk* on top of each arch. **Similar Species.** Female may be indistinguishable from other *Mesoplodon* spp.; male recognized by shape and position of the tusks.

Distribution. Temperate and tropical waters of all oceans.

Status and Habitat. CITES Appendix II. Apparently uncommon but widely distributed, mostly in deep, offshore waters.

Habits. Poorly known. Feeds on deep sea squid and fish. Seen singly or in groups of 2–7.

GERVAIS' BEAKED WHALE   Plate 47
Mesoplodon europaeus

Spanish: zifio de Gervais.

TL 4–5 m (15'), Wt 560–1200 kg (1900 lb).

Description. *Dark gray* with a *few pale scars* or spots on body. *Jawline almost straight* in both sexes; male has a *small tooth* on each lower jaw, 1/3 of the way from snout to gape. **Similar Species.** Female probably indistinguishable from other *Mesoplodon* spp.; if visible, the small tooth set forward on the straight jawline distinguishes male from *M. densirostris*, the only other confirmed *Mesoplodon* in the Caribbean.

Distribution. Atlantic Ocean, mainly E United States, Gulf of Mexico, and Caribbean, a few records from Africa and Europe.

Status and Habitat. CITES Appendix II. Uncommon or rare; usually in warm, temperate waters.

Habits. Poorly known. Feeds on squid.

MESOPLODON
Species "A"

TL approx. 5.5 m (18')

Description. This species has not been named, as it is known only from sightings at sea. This account is based on Jefferson et al. (1993). There are 2 forms, one (probably male) has *black, heavily scarred upperparts with a broad pale band from nape to belly,* and white underparts; the other (probably female and young), is uniformly brown. Beak rather long. Dorsal fin low and triangular. **Similar Species.** Male distinguished by color of upperparts, female not easily recognized.

Distribution. Tropical E Pacific, from Baja California to Peru. May be endemic to this region.

Status and Habitat. The most frequently sighted *Mesoplodon* in its range; status unknown. Occurs in offshore waters.

Habits. Breaches occasionally. Seen in groups of 1–4.

Baleen Whales
Suborder Mysticeti

The baleen whales are large, with 2 blowholes and no teeth. Plates of baleen, a keratinous material, hang from the upper jaw. These whales use fringes on the inner edge of the baleen to trap plankton or small fish when mouthfuls of water are forced out through the plates.

RORQUAL WHALES (Spanish: ballenas)
Family Balaenopteridae

The Balaenopteridae consists of 2 genera and 6 species, all of which occur in oceans off the coast of Central America for at least part of the year. Rorquals are slender, streamlined baleen whales (although the Humpback is stockier) with a small dorsal fin set more than halfway down the back and a series of folds on the throat and chest. The blowholes are close together and produce a single, vertical spout. Their extensible throat and large gape enable these whales to engulf and then filter a large volume of water by closing the mouth, pushing the tongue up and forcing water out through the baleen. They usually feed by actively lunging open-mouthed into concentrations of prey. Most species are similar and can be difficult to identify in the field. A good reference is Ridgway and Harrison (1985).

MINKE WHALE   Plate 48
Balaenoptera acutorostrata

Little piked whale; Spanish: rorcual enano.

TL 8–10 m (30'), Wt 6–14 tons.

Description. Relatively small, with a pointed head and *white bands across the flippers.* Pronounced ridge on snout. Baleen mainly whitish. Dorsal fin relatively tall and slightly angled backward. **Similar Species.** Much smaller than other rorquals; white bands on flippers diagnostic and usually visible at close range (bands often lacking in animals from the Southern Hemisphere).

Distribution. Worldwide, from tropical to polar regions.

Status and Habitat. CITES Appendix I (except Greenland population, which is in Appendix II). Fairly common in cold waters of the Southern Hemisphere, less common in the Northern Hemisphere. Large numbers are present near the West Indies, and some have been recorded in the Gulf of Mexico; seldom encountered close to Central American coasts. Currently hunted by Japanese and Norwegian whalers. Favors coastal and inshore waters; rare in tropical, offshore regions.

Habits. The Minke often exhales underwater, so a blow may not be seen. After a deep dive, the blow and dorsal fin are visible simultaneously. It breaches occasionally. The diet is mainly krill and schooling fish. It is usually seen in groups of 1–3, but may form large aggregations on feeding grounds. Young are born in warmer seas in the winter, and females may breed every 18 months.

BRYDE'S WHALE   Plate 48
Balaenoptera edeni

Spanish: rorcual tropical.

TL 12–15 m (44'), Wt 13–25 tons.

Description. Medium sized, with *3 prominent ridges on the snout*. Baleen black. Dorsal fin small, slightly angled backward, often with a frayed rear margin. **Similar Species.** Sei Whale (*B. borealis*) has one ridge on the snout (often indistinguishable in the field). Fin Whale (*B. physalus*) is larger, and Minke (*B. acutorostrata*) is smaller.

Distribution. Tropical and subtropical zones of all seas, to about 40° in both hemispheres.

Status and Habitat. CITES Appendix I. Status poorly known due to confusion with Sei Whales by whalers. Known from strandings and sightings in the Gulf of Mexico and West Indies. It is found in coastal and offshore waters.

Habits. It breathes with the back and dorsal fin exposed, then dives, arching the back sharply as the dorsal fin disappears, not showing the tail. Bryde's Whale eats small fish by actively lunging and pursuing prey. It is usually seen singly or in pairs, occasionally in larger groups. Breeding can occur at any time of year.

SEI WHALE   Plate 48
Balaenoptera borealis

Spanish: rorcual del norte.

TL 14–20 m (56'), Wt 14–30 tons.

Description. Medium sized and slim-bodied. *Head narrow* and V-shaped, with a single ridge on the snout. Baleen black. *Dorsal fin small but prominent*, erect or slightly angled backward. **Similar Species.** Difficult to distinguish from Fin (*B. physalus*) and Bryde's Whales (*B. edeni*). Bryde's has 3 ridges on the snout and is slightly smaller. See Fin Whale.

Distribution. All oceans except coldest polar seas.

Status and Habitat. CITES Appendix I. Recovering slowly from previous hunting pressure, but not common. Known in the region from a stranding in Campeche, Mexico. It is found in deep, oceanic water, seldom near coasts, and favors temperate, mid-latitude regions.

Habits. It breathes with much of the back and dorsal fin visible at the same time, then dives without arching the back or exposing the tail. It eats copepods and other small prey by skimming the surface. This fast swimmer is usually seen in groups of 2–5. Mating usually occurs in autumn, and single young are born after 12 months of gestation.

FIN WHALE   Plate 48
Balaenoptera physalus

Spanish: rorcual común.

TL 20–27 m (75'), Wt 40–75 tons.

Description. Large, slim, and streamlined, with an *assymetrical color pattern. Lower jaw and* most of the *baleen white on the right side, dark gray on the left side. Head narrow and* **V**-*shaped* from above. Dorsal fin small but prominent and sharply angled backward. **Similar Species.** The assymetrical color pattern is unique among rorquals. Difficult to distinguish at a distance from Sei (*B. borealis*) and Bryde's Whales (*B. edeni*), both of which have more upright dorsal fins. See Blue Whale (*B. musculus*).

Distribution. Worldwide, in all oceans.

Status and Habitat. CITES Appendix I. Uncommon; numbers depleted by whaling. Small resident populations are known from the Gulf of California and Gulf of Mexico; winter migrants are possible in both oceans off Central America. Usually found in deep, offshore water, sometimes in coastal regions.

Habits. The breathing profile differs from that of Blue Whale in that the back is shorter and the dorsal fin appears more prominent. The tail flukes are not exposed before diving. The Fin Whale is a fast swimmer and is more social than other rorquals. It feeds on crustaceans, schools of small fish, or squid by lunging and gulping, often rolling on one side. Group size is usually 6–15. Single calves are born in warm waters after 12 months of gestation. Females breed every 2 years.

small, triangular, and set far back on the body. Tail flukes triangular, clearly notched, with a straight trailing edge. **Similar Species.** Fin Whale can be about the same size and is difficult to distinguish; it has a narrow, V-shaped head with an assymetrical color pattern and a larger dorsal fin.

Distribution. Worldwide, in all seas.

Status and Habitat. CITES Appendix I. Slowly recovering from excessive exploitation by whalers; uncommon. Known in the region from a stranding at San Cristóbal, Atlantic coast of Panama, and a resident population off the Pacific coast of Costa Rica and Panama. It is found mainly in open ocean, sometimes coming inshore to feed or breed.

Habits. The breathing/diving profile of this huge whale is distinctive: after the blow, a long expanse of back is seen, finally followed by the tiny dorsal fin. The tail may appear in a horizontal position, but is rarely raised vertically. The Blue Whale is usually seen singly or in small groups: up to a dozen may aggregate on feeding grounds. In spring it moves toward the polar icepacks and eats about 4 tons of krill and other crustaceans per day. After 4 months, as the ice pack advances southward, it moves to warmer waters and appears not to eat until the following spring. Females give birth to a single calf on tropical breeding grounds and normally breed every 3 years.

BLUE WHALE   Plate 48
Balaenoptera musculus

Spanish: ballena azul.

TL 23–33 m (92'), Wt 90–190 tons.

Description. The largest animal ever known. Entirely bluish or gray in color, often mottled on back and sides. *Head* **U** -*shaped from above,* with a prominent dorsal ridge on the midline of the snout. Baleen black. *Dorsal fin very*

HUMPBACK WHALE   Plate 47
Megaptera novaeangliae

Spanish: rorcual jorobado, ballena jorobado.

TL 11–16 m (46'), Wt 24–35 tons.

Description. Large, with *very long, white flippers* and a small dorsal fin. Raised knobs on snout, mouth, and chin. Flippers all white, or dark above, white below; leading edge bumpy. *Low, broad dorsal fin* on a raised hump. Tail flukes broad, with concave, serrated edges and white undersides. **Similar Species.** The long, whitish flippers are diagnostic. White patches on the tail flukes can be seen at some distance.

Distribution. Worldwide, from tropical to polar seas.

Status and Habitat. CITES Appendix I. Uncommon but widespread, numbers depleted by whaling in the first half of this century. Known in the region from sighting records off the Pacific coast and islands of Costa Rica (Acevedo and Smultea, 1995); the Gulf of Mexico and the Caribbean. Calving grounds are located in the Gulf of Panama and in the Pacific Ocean off South America. The Humpback favors shallow waters and coastal areas, but it may travel through open ocean during migration.

Habits. Highly acrobatic; it is often seen breaching, rolling, and slapping the surface with its flippers. The tail is thrown up vertically before a deep dive. Groups may herd prey or form large bubble nets to trap krill and small fish. The Humpback is usually seen in groups of 1–3, but it may aggregate in feeding grounds. In the Pacific Ocean, Northern Hemisphere populations migrate south into Mexican and Central American waters from December to April; calves are born from December to February. Southern Hemisphere populations migrate north into waters off Ecuador, Colombia and the Gulf of Panama from June to October, calving in July and August. Males compete for females and use a complex song as part of the breeding display. Females give birth to a single calf and usually breed every 2 years.

RIGHT AND BOWHEAD WHALES
Family Balaenidae

One of the 3 species in the Balaenidae may enter tropical waters of Central America, although right whales are usually found in cold water. These huge baleen whales have enormous heads and arched jaws and usually feed by skimming open-mouthed near the water surface. The baleen plates can be up to 4 m long and have very fine fringes for filtering small plankton. Right whales were so named as the "right" whales to hunt because they frequent inshore waters, swim slowly, and float when harpooned.

NORTHERN RIGHT WHALE   Plate 48
Eubalaena glacialis

Spanish: ballena franca.

TL 15–18 m (55'), Wt 60–106 tons.

Description. Very large and chunky, with a *massive head and no dorsal fin*. Mostly black, with pale gray patches of rough, horny skin (called callosities) above eyes and on snout. Flippers large and fan shaped. Tail flukes broad, smooth edged, and deeply notched. Blowholes widely separated, producing a V-shaped blow.

Similar Species. All other large whales in the region produce a single spout when blowing, and none have a smooth, black, finless back.

Distribution. Mainly in cold or temperate waters of the Northern Hemisphere; Alaska to Baja California, Siberia to China in the Pacific Ocean; Newfoundland to the Gulf of Mexico, and Scotland to Portugal in the Atlantic Ocean.

Status and Habitat. CITES Appendix I. Once widespread, but now rare and local as a result of excessive whaling in the 1800s. There are no records from Central America; however, a stranding from Galveston, Texas, in the Gulf of Mexico and sightings off Baja California suggest that this species might rarely stray into the region in either ocean. Found in shallow, coastal water, with winter migrations toward the equator.

Habits. It remains close to the surface while breathing, sometimes rolling over or slapping with the flippers or tail. The tail flukes are raised vertically out of the water before a deep dive. This species is usually seen in small groups of 1–6 or in family units. Mating takes place in early spring; several males may pursue a receptive female. A single calf is born in warm, shallow water after 9–10 months of gestation. Calves suckle for a year and remain with their mother for 3–4 years.

GLOSSARY

Adult. A sexually mature individual, with all permanent teeth erupted.

Altricial. Young born helpless (often naked and with eyes closed), requiring extensive parental care.

Antitragus. A flap of skin at the base of the ear, conspicuous in free-tailed bats (Molossidae), concealing the tragus.

Arboreal. Living and foraging in trees.

Arthropod. Invertebrates with a jointed exoskeleton, including insects, spiders, and crustaceans.

Broadleaf forest. Forest consisting of trees that may remain evergreen year-round, but are not conifers.

Browser. Animal that eats leaves and shoots of shrubs and trees, but not grass.

Buff, buffy. Pale yellowish brown.

Calcar. Cartilage or bone projecting from the ankle along the edge of the tail membrane of bats.

Cenote. Sinkhole in limestone.

Central America. The geographic area including the countries of Guatemala, Belize, El Salvador, Honduras, Nicaragua, Costa Rica and Panama (politically, Central America does not include Belize or Panama).

Character. A discrete feature or characteristic of an organism used to distinguish it from another similar organism.

Cloud forest. Highland evergreen forest that is almost always wet or misty.

Crepuscular. Active at dawn or dusk.

Deciduous forest. Forest in which most trees lose their leaves at the same time during the dry (or cold) season.

Dental formula. A short-hand enumeration of the type and number of teeth on one side of the jaw (see "How to use this book").

Diurnal. Active by day.

Endemic. Native to a specific region.

Epididymis. An organ on the posterior surface of the testis that houses the beginning of the vas deferens.

Evergreen forest. Forest that appears green year-round, as leaves are not lost on a strictly seasonal basis.

Eyeshine. Reflection from a membrane in the back of an animal's eyes, seen when illuminated at night. May only be visible if the light source is near the observer's eyes.

Feral. Domestic animals that have become established and are breeding in the wild.

Forearm. Arm from elbow to wrist (important in bat measurements).

Form. A general term describing a different race or population of a species. Used when specific or subspecific status is unclear.

Fossorial. Living underground.

Gestation. Pregnancy.

Grizzled. Fur with a mixture of dark and pale hairs, or individual hairs that have bands of color from base to tip.

Guard hairs. Hairs that are longer than the rest of the fur.

Harem. A group of females defended by one male.

Hispid. Fur that is coarse or spiny.

Home range. Area occupied by an individual over a period of time.

Infant. A baby animal dependent on its mother.

Juvenile. A young animal partially or totally independent of its mother; permanent teeth usually not fully in place.

Mammae. Nipples or teats.

Melanistic. Dark or black.

Middle America. Mexico and Central America (the West Indies is sometimes included, but not in this book).

Morph. A term used to describe a different form of a species, mainly used for color differences.

Morphology. Structure or form.

Nocturnal. Active by night.

Ochre, ochraceous. A yellow-brown color.

Olivaceous. A green-brown color.

Population. A local, freely interbreeding group of animals within a species.

Precocial. Young born well-developed, fully haired, and with eyes open; usually able to move independently at birth.

Prehensile tail. Tail with a tip that can curl and grip a branch, supporting all or part of the animal's weight.

Primary forest. Forest that has not been cut over or otherwise disturbed.

Procumbent. Angled forward. Used to describe the upper incisor teeth of some glossophagine bats; "bucktoothed."

Secondary forest. Forest that has been disturbed and has partially regenerated.

Subadult. Stage between juvenile and adult, after weaning but before sexual maturity.

Systematics. The study of the diversity and relationships among organisms.

Taxonomy. The identification, naming, and classification of organisms.

Terrestrial. Living on the ground.

Territory. Part or all of the home range that an animal actively defends against intruders of the same species.

Tibia. Bone between ankle and knee.

Tragus. A fleshy projection inside the external ear of most bats.

Type (=holotype). The specimen on which the name and description of a species is based.

Type locality. Place where the type specimen was obtained.

Underparts. Underside, including belly, throat, chin, and inside of limbs.

Upperparts. Upper surface of an animal, including outer sides of limbs.

BIBLIOGRAPHY

Acevedo, A., and M. A. Smultea. 1995. First records of humpback whales including calves at Golfo Dulce and Isla del Coco, Costa Rica, suggesting geographical overlap of northern and southern hemipshere populations. Marine Mammal Science, 11:554–560.

Adams, J. K. 1989. Pteronotus davyi. Mamm. Species, 346:1–5.

Altenbach, J. S. 1989. Prey capture by the fishing bats *Noctilio leporinus* and *Myotis vivesi*. J. Mamm., 70:421–424.

Alvarez, T., and S. T. Alvarez-C. 1990. Cuatro nuevos registros de murciélagos (Chiroptera) del estado de Chiapas, México. An. Esc. Cienc. Biol., Mex., 33:157–161.

Alvarez, T., P. Dominguez, and J. A. Cabrales. 1984. Mamíferos de la Angostura, región central de Chiapas, México. Instituto Nacional de Antropología e Historia, 24: 1–89.

Alvarez-Castañeda, S. T., and T. Alvarez. 1991. Los murciélagos de Chiapas. Instituto Politécnico Nacional, México, D.F. 211 pp.

Anderson, S. 1969. Macrotus waterhousii. Mamm. Species, 1:1–4.

Anderson, S., and C. E. Nelson. 1965. A systematic revision of *Macrotus* (Chiroptera). Amer. Mus. Novitates, 2212:1–39.

Anderson, S., and J. K. Jones, Jr. 1960. Records of harvest mice, *Reithrodontomys*, from Central America, with description of a new subspecies from Nicaragua. Univ. Kansas Publ., Mus. Nat. Hist., 9:521–529.

Aranda Sánchez, J. M. 1981. Rastros de los mamíferos silvestres de México. Manual de campo. Inst. Nac. Invest. Rec. Bioticos, Xalapa, Ver., México. 198 pp.

Aranda, M., and I. March. 1987. Guía de los mamíferos silvestres de Chiapas. Inst. Nac. Invest. Rec. Bioticos, Xalapa, Ver., México. 149 pp.

Arita, H. T. 1991. Spatial segregation in long-nosed bats, *Leptonycteris nivalis* and *Leptonycteris curasoae*, in Mexico. J. Mamm., 72:706–714.

Arita, H. T., and S. R. Humphrey. 1988. Revisión taxonómica de los murciélagos magueyeros del género *Leptonycteris* (Chiroptera: Phyllostomidae). Acta Zool. Mex. n.s., 29:1–60.

Arita, H. T., and J. A. Vargas. 1995. Natural history, interspecific association, and incidence of the cave bats of Yucatán, Mexico. Southwestern Nat., 40:29–37.

Armstrong, D. M., and J. K. Jones, Jr. 1971. Mammals from the Mexican state of Sinaloa. I. Marsupialia, Insectivora, Edentata, Lagomorpha. J. Mamm., 52:747–757.

Arroyo-Cabrales, J., R. R. Hollander, and J. K. Jones, Jr. 1987. Choeronycteris mexicana. Mamm. Species, 291:1–5.

Arroyo-Cabrales, J., and J. K. Jones, Jr. 1988. Balantiopteryx io and Balantiopteryx infusca. Mamm. Species, 313:1–3.

Audet, D., M. D. Engstrom, and M. B. Fenton. 1993. Morphology, karyology, and echolocation calls of *Rhogeessa* (Chiroptera: Vespertilionidae) from the Yucatán Peninsula. J. Mamm., 74:498–502.

Baker, R. H. 1952. Geographic range of *Peromyscus melanophrys*, with description of new subspecies. Univ. Kansas Publ., Mus. Nat. Hist., 5:251–258.

Baker, R. H., and M. W. Baker. 1975. Montane habitat used by the spotted skunk (*Spilogale putorius*) in Mexico. J. Mamm., 56:671–673.

Baker, R. H., and M. K. Petersen. 1965. Notes on a climbing rat, *Tylomys*, from Oaxaca. J. Mamm., 46:694–695.

Baker, R. J. 1984. A sympatric cryptic species of mammal: a new species of *Rhogeessa* (Chiroptera: Vespertilionidae). Syst. Zool., 33:178–183.

Baker, R. J., J. W. Bickham, and M. L. Arnold. 1985. Chromosomal evolution in *Rhogeessa* (Chiroptera: Vespertilionidae): possible speciation by centric fusions. Evolution, 39:233–243.

Baker, R. J., and C. L. Clark. 1987. Uroderma bilobatum. Mamm. Species, 279:1–4.

Baker, R. J., C. G. Dunn, and K. Nelson. 1988a. Allozymic study of the relationships of *Phylloderma* and four species of *Phyllostomus*. Occas. Papers Mus., Texas Tech Univ., 125:1–14.

Baker, R. J., C. S. Hood, and R. L. Honeycutt. 1989. Phylogenetic relationships and classification of the higher categories of the New World bat family Phyllostomidae. Syst. Zool., 38:228–238.

Baker, R. J., and J. K. Jones, Jr. 1975. Additional records of bats from Nicaragua, with a revised checklist of Chiroptera. Occas. Papers Mus., Texas Tech Univ., 32:1–13.

Baker, R. J., J. C. Patton, H. H. Genoways, and J. W. Bickham. 1988b. Genic studies of *Lasiurus* (Chiroptera: Vespertilionidae). Occas. Papers Mus., Texas Tech Univ., 17:1–15.

Baldwin, J. D., and J. I. Baldwin. 1976. Primate populations in Chiriqui, Panama. Pp. 20–31, *in* Neotropical primates: field studies and conservation (R. W. Thorington, Jr., and C. P. Groves, eds.). Natl. Acad. Sci., Washington. 135 pp.

Barbour, R. W., and W. H. Davis. 1969. Bats of America. Kentucky Univ. Press, Lexington, Kentucky. 286 pp.

Bateman, G. C., and T. A. Vaughan. 1974. Nightly activities of mormoopid bats. J. Mamm., 55:45–65.

Belwood, J. J., and J. H. Fullard. 1984. Echolocation and foraging behavior in the Hawaiian hoary bat *Lasiurus cinereus semotus*. Can. J. Zool., 62:2113–2120.

Belwood, J. J., and G. K. Morris. 1987. Bat predation and sexual advertisement in Neotropical katydids. Science, 238:64–67.

Benshoof, L., T. L. Yates, and J. W. Froehlich. 1984. Noteworthy records of mammals from eastern Honduras. Southwestern Nat., 29:511–514.

Best, T. L., H. A. Ruiz-Piña, and L. S. Leon-Paniagua. 1995. Sciurus yucatanensis. Mamm. Species, 506:1–4.

Bisbal, F. J. 1986. Food habits of some neotropical carnivores in Venezuela (Mammalia, Carnivora). Mammalia, 50:329–339.

Boinski, S., and P. E. Scott. 1988. Association of birds with monkeys in Costa Rica. Biotropica, 20:136–143.

Boinski, S., and R. M. Timm. 1985. Predation by squirrel monkeys and double-toothed kites on tent-making bats. Amer. Jour. Primatol., 9:121–127.

Bonaccorso, F. J. 1979. Foraging and reproductive ecology in a Panamanian bat community. Bull. Florida State Mus., Biol. Sci., 24:359–408.

Bonaccorso, F. J., W. E. Glanz, and C. M. Sandford. 1980. Feeding assemblages of mammals at fruiting *Dipteryx panamensis* (Papilionaceae) trees in Panama: seed predation, dispersal, and parasitism. Rev. Biol. Trop., 28:61–72.

Borobia, M., S. Siciliano, L. Lodi, and W. Hoek. 1991. Distribution of the South American dolphin *Sotalia fluviatilis*. Can. J. Zool., 69:1025–1039.

Bowles, J. B., P. D. Heideman, and K. R. Erickson. 1990. Observations on six species of free-tailed bats (Molossidae) from Yucatán, Mexico. Southwestern Nat., 35:151–157.

Bradbury, J. W. 1977. Social organization and communication. Pp. 1–72, *in* Biology of bats. III. (W. A. Wimsatt, ed.). Academic Press, Inc., New York. 651 pp.

Bradbury, J. W. 1983. Saccopteryx bilineata. Pp. 488–489, *in* Costa Rican natural history (D. H. Janzen, ed.). Univ. Chicago Press, Chicago. 816 pp.

Bradbury, J. W., and S. L. Vehrencamp. 1976. Social organization and foraging in emballonurid bats. I. Field studies. Behav. Ecol. Sociobiol., 1:337–381.

Brooke, A. P. 1987. Tent construction and social organization in *Vampyressa nymphaea* (Chiroptera: Phyllostomidae) in Costa Rica. J. Trop. Ecol., 3:171–175.

Brooke, A. P. 1990. Tent selection, roosting ecology and social organization of the tent-making bat, *Ectophylla alba*, in Costa Rica. J. Zool., Lond., 221:11–19.

Brooke, A. P. 1994. Diet of the fishing bat, *Noctilio leporinus* (Chiroptera: Noctilionidae). J. Mamm., 75:212–218.

Buchanan, O. M., and T. R. Howell. 1965. Observations on the natural history of the Thick-spined rat, *Hoplomys gymnurus*, in Nicaragua. Ann. Mag. Nat. Hist., ser. 13, 8:549–559.

Butcher, J. E., and R. S. Hoffmann. 1980. Caluromys derbianus. Mamm. Species, 140:1–4.

Caldwell, D. K., and M. C. Caldwell. 1985. Manatees-*Trichechus manatus*, *Trichechus senegalensis*, and *Trichechus inunguis*. Pp. 33–66, *in* Handbook of marine mammals. Volume 3: the sirenians and baleen whales (S. H. Ridgway and R. Harrison, eds.). Academic Press, London. 362 pp.

Cameron, G. N. 1977. Experimental species removal: demographic responses by *Sigmodon hispidus* and *Reithrodontomys fulvescens*. J. Mamm., 58:488–506.

Carleton, M. D. 1979. Taxonomic status and relationships of *Peromyscus boylii* from El Salvador. J. Mamm., 60:280–296.

Carleton, M. D. 1989. Systematics and evolution. Pp. 7–141, *in* Advances in the study of *Peromyscus* (Rodentia). (G. L. Kirkland and J. N. Layne, eds.). Texas Tech Univ. Press, 366 pp.

Carleton, M. D., and D. G. Huckaby. 1975. A new species of *Peromyscus* from Guatemala. J. Mamm., 56: 444–451.

Carleton, M. D., and G. G. Musser. 1995. Systematic studies of oryzomyine rodents (Muridae: Sigmodontinae): definition and distribution of *Oligoryzomys vegetus* (Bangs, 1902). Proc. Biol. Soc. Wash., 108:338–369.

Carleton, M. D., D. E. Wilson, A. L. Gardner, and M. A. Bogan. 1982. Distribution and systematics of *Peromyscus* (Mammalia: Rodentia) of Nayarit, Mexico. Smithsonian Contrib. Zool., 352:1–46.

Carpenter, C. R. 1935. Behavior of red spider monkeys in Panama. J. Mamm., 16:171–180.

Carr, T. 1994. The manatees and dolphins of the Miskito Coast Protected Area, Nicaragua. Caribbean Conservation Corporation, on contract to the Marine Mammal Commission, contract T94070376. 19 pp.

Ceballos, G., and C. Galindo L. 1984. Mamíferos silvestres de la cuenca de México. Editorial Limusa, S.A., México. 300 pp.

Ceballos, G., and R. A. Medellín. 1988. Diclidurus albus. Mamm. Species, 316:1–4.

Cervantes, F. A. 1993. Lepus flavigularis. Mamm. Species, 423:1–3.

Chapman, J. A., and G. Ceballos. 1990. The cottontails. Pp. 95–110, *in* Rabbits, hares and pikas. Status survey and conservation action plan (J. A. Chapman and J. E. C. Flux, eds.). IUCN, Gland, Switzerland. 168 pp.

Chapman, J. A., J. G. Hockman, and M. M. Ojeda C. 1980. Sylvilagus floridanus. Mamm. Species, 136:1–8.

Choate, J. R. 1970. Systematics and zoogeography of Middle American shrews of the genus Cryptotis. Univ. Kansas Publ., Mus. Nat. Hist., 19:195–317.

Choate, J. R. 1973. Cryptotis mexicana. Mamm. Species, 28:1–3.

Choate, J. R., and E. D. Fleharty. 1974. Cryptotis goodwini. Mamm. Species, 44:1–3.

Choe, J. C., and R. M. Timm. 1985. Roosting site selection by *Artibeus watsoni* (Chiroptera: Phyllostomidae) on *Anthurium ravenii* (Araceae) in Costa Rica. J. Trop. Ecol., 1:241–247.

Coates-Estrada, R., and A. Estrada. 1986. Manual de identificación de campo de los mamíferos de la estación de biología "Los Tuxtlas." Univ. Nac. Aut. México, México, D.F. 151 pp.

Coimbra-Filho, A., and R. A. Mittermeier, (eds.) 1981. Ecology and behavior of neotropical primates. Volume 1. Academia Brasileira de Ciências, Rio de Janeiro. 496 pp.

Colmenero-R., L. C. 1986. Aspectos de la ecología y comportamiento de una colonia de manatíes (*Trichechus manatus*) en el municipio de Emiliano Zapata, Tabasco. An. Inst. Biol. Univ. Nal. Autón. Mex., 56:589–602.

Colmenero-R., L. C., and B. E. Zárate. 1990. Distribution, status and conservation of the West Indian manatee in Quintana Roo, México. Biol. Conservation, 52:27–35.

Dalquest, W. W. 1953. Mammals of the Mexican State of San Luis Potosí. Louisiana State Univ. Studies, Biol. Ser., 1: 1–229.

Daugherty, H. E. 1972. The impact of man on the zoogeography of El Salvador. Biol. Conservation, 4:273–278.

Davis, W. B. 1960. The mammals of Texas. Texas Game and Fish Comm., Bull., 41:1–252.

Davis, W. B. 1968. Review of the genus *Uroderma* (Chiroptera). J. Mamm., 49:676–698.

Davis, W. B. 1980. New Sturnira (Chiroptera: Phyllostomidae) from Central and South America, with key to currently recognized species. Occas. Papers Mus., Texas Tech Univ., 70:1–5.

Davis, W. B. 1984. Review of the large fruit-eating bats of the Artibeus "lituratus" complex (Chiroptera: Phyllostomidae) in Middle America. Occas. Papers Mus., Texas Tech Univ., 93:1–16.

Davis, W. B., and D. C. Carter. 1964. A new species of fruit-eating bat (genus *Artibeus*) from Central America. Proc. Biol. Soc. Wash., 77:119–122.

Davis, W. B., and D. C. Carter. 1978. A review of the round-eared bats of the *Tonatia silvicola* complex, with descriptions of three new taxa. Occas. Papers, Mus., Texas Tech Univ., 53:1–12.

Decker, D. 1991. Systematics of the coatis, genus *Nasua* (Mammalia: Procyonidae). Proc. Biol. Soc. Wash., 104:370–386.

Delgado Estrella, A. 1994. Presencia del delfín de dientes rugosos o esteno (*Steno bredanensis*), en la costa de Tabasco, México. Anales Inst. Biol. Univ. Nac. Autón. México, Ser. Zool., 65:303–305.

Deutsch, L. A. 1983. An encounter between bushdog (*Speothos venaticus*) and paca (*Agouti paca*). J. Mamm., 64:532–533.

Dickerman, R. W., K. F. Koopman, and C. Seymour. 1981. Notes on bats from the pacific lowlands of Guatemala. J. Mamm., 62:406–411.

Diersing, V. E. 1980. Systematics of flying squirrels, *Glaucomys volans* (Linnaeus), from Mexico, Guatemala, and Honduras. Southwestern Nat., 25:157–172.

Diersing, V. E. 1981. Systematic status of *Sylvilagus brasiliensis* and *S. insonus* from North America. J. Mamm., 62:539–556.

Dinerstein, E. 1985. First records of *Lasiurus castaneus* and *Antrozous dubiaquercus* from Costa Rica. J. Mamm., 66:411–412.

Dinerstein, E. 1986. Reproductive ecology of fruit bats and the seasonality of fruit production in a Costa Rican cloud forest. Biotropica, 18:307–318.

Dolan, P. G. 1989. Systematics of Middle American mastiff bats of the genus *Molossus*. Spec. Publ. Mus., Texas Tech Univ., 29:1–71.

Dolan, P. G., and D. C. Carter. 1979. Distributional notes and records for Middle American Chiroptera. J. Mamm., 60:644–649.

Eger, J. L. 1977. Systematics of the genus *Eumops* (Chiroptera: Molossidae). Life Sci. Contr., R. Ont. Mus., 110:1–69.

Emmons, L. H. 1987. Comparative feeding ecology of felids in a neotropical rainforest. Behav. Ecol. Sociobiol., 20:271–283.

Emmons, L. H. 1990. Neotropical rainforest mammals: a field guide. Univ. Chicago Press, Chicago. 281 pp.

Enders, R. K. 1980. Observations on *Syntheosciurus*: taxonomy and behavior. J. Mamm., 61:725–727.

Engstrom, M. D. 1984. Chromosomal, genic, and morphological variation in the *Oryzomys melanotis* species group. Unpubl. PhD Thesis, Texas A & M Univ. 171 pp.

Engstrom, M. D., J. R. Choate, and H. H. Genoways. 1994a. Taxonomy. Pp. 179–199, *in* Seventy-five years of mammalogy (1919–1994) (E. C. Birney and J. R. Choate, eds.). Spec. Publ. 11. The American Society of Mammalogists. 433 pp.

Engstrom, M. D., T. E. Lee, and D. E. Wilson. 1987. Bauerus dubiaquercus. Mamm. Species, 282:1–3.

Engstrom, M. D., B. K. Lim, and F. A. Reid. 1994b. Two small mammals new to the fauna of El Salvador. Southwestern Nat., 39:281–306.

Engstrom, M. D., F. A. Reid, and B. K. Lim. 1993. New records of two small mammals from Guatemala. Southwestern Nat., 38:80–82.

Engstrom, M. D., and D. E. Wilson. 1981. Systematics of *Antrozous dubiaquercus* (Chiroptera: Vespertilionidae), with comments on the status of *Bauerus* Van Gelder. Ann. Carnegie Mus., 50:371–383.

Estrada, A., and Coates-Estrada, R. 1985. A preliminary study of resource overlap between howling monkeys (*Alouatta palliata*) and other arboreal mammals in the tropical rain forest of Los Tuxtlas, Mexico. Amer. J. Primatol., 9:27–37.

Evans, P. G. H. 1987. The natural history of whales and dolphins. Facts on File, New York. 343 pp.

Fagerstone, K. A. 1987. Black-footed ferret, long-tailed weasel, short-tailed weasel, and least weasel. Pp. 549–573, *in* Wild furbearer management and conservation in North America (M. Novak, J. A. Baker, M. E. Obbard, and B. Malloch, eds.). Ontario Trappers Assoc., Ontario. 1150 pp.

Fenton, M. B. 1992. Bats. Facts on File, New York. 207 pp.

Fenton, M. B., D. Audet, D. C. Dunning, J. Long, C. B. Merriman, D. Pearl, D. M. Syme, B. Adkins, S. Pedersen, and T. Wohlgenant. 1993. Activity patterns and roost selection by *Noctilio albiventris* (Chiroptera: Noctilionidae) in Costa Rica. J. Mamm., 74:607–613.

Ferrell, C. S., and D. E. Wilson. 1991. Platyrrhinus helleri. Mamm. Species, 373:1–5.

Findley, J. S., and D. E. Wilson. 1974. Observations on the Neotropical disk-winged bat, *Thyroptera tricolor* Spix. J. Mamm., 55:562–571.

Finley, R. B., Jr. 1958. The wood rats of Colorado: distribution and ecology. Univ. Kansas Publ., Mus. Nat. Hist., 10:213–552.

Fischer, M. S., and P. Tassy. 1993. The interrelation between Proboscidea, Sirenia, Hyracoidea, and Mesaxonia: the morphological evidence. Pp. 217–234, *in* Mammalian phylogeny: placentals (F. S. Szalay, M. J. Novacek, and M. C. McKenna, eds.). Springer-Verlag, New York. 321 pp.

Fitch, J. H., K. A. Shump, Jr., and A. U. Shump. 1981. Myotis velifer. Mamm. Species, 149:1–5.

Fleming, T. H. 1970. Notes on the rodent faunas of two Panamanian forests. J. Mamm., 51:473–490.

Fleming, T. H. 1971. Population ecology of three species of Neotropical rodents. Misc. Publ. Mus. Zool., Univ. Michigan, 143:1–77.

Fleming, T. H. 1972. Aspects of the population dynamics of three species of opossums in the Panama Canal Zone. J. Mamm., 53:619–623.

Fleming, T. H. 1973. The reproductive cycles of three species of opossums and other mammals in the Panama Canal Zone. J. Mamm., 54:439–455.

Fleming, T. H. 1974a. The population ecology of two species of Costa Rican heteromyid rodents. Ecol., 55:493–510.

Fleming, T. H. 1974b. Social organization in two species of Costa Rican heteromyid rodents. J. Mamm., 55:543–561.

Fleming, T. H. 1983a. *Heteromys desmarestianus* (Ratón Semiespinosa, Spiny Pocket Mouse). Pp. 474–475, *in* Costa Rican natural history (D. H. Janzen, ed.). Univ. Chicago Press, Chicago. 816 pp.

Fleming, T. H. 1983b. *Liomys salvini* (Ratón Semiespinosa, Guardafiesta, Spiny Pocket Mouse). Pp. 475–477, *in* Costa Rican natural history (D. H. Janzen, ed.). Univ. Chicago Press, Chicago. 816 pp.

Fleming, T. H. 1988. The short-tailed fruit bat: A study in plant-animal interactions. Univ. Chicago Press, Chicago. 365 pp.

Fleming, T. H., and G. J. Brown. 1975. An experimental analysis of seed hoarding and burrowing behavior in two species of Costa Rican heteromyid rodents. J. Mamm., 56:301–315.

Fleming, T. H., E. T. Hooper, and D. E. Wilson. 1972. Three Central American bat communities: structure, reproductive cycles, and movement patterns. Ecology, 53:555–569.

Flux, J. E. C., and R. Angermann. 1990. The hares and jackrabbits. Pp. 61–94, *in* Rabbits, hares and pikas. Status survey and conservation action plan (J. A. Chapman and J. E. C. Flux, eds.). IUCN, Gland, Switzerland. 168 pp.

Ford, L. S., and R. S. Hoffmann. 1988. Potos flavus. Mamm. Species, 321:1–9.

Fragoso, J. M. V. 1991. The effects of hunting on tapirs in Belize. Pp. 154–162, *in* Neotropical wildlife use and conservation (J. G. Robinson and K. H. Redford, eds.). Univ. Chicago Press, Chicago. 520 pp.

Freeman, P. W. 1981. A multivariate study of the family Molossidae (Mammalia: Chiroptera): morphology, ecology, evolution. Fieldiana Zool. n.s., 7:1–173.

Freese, C. H. 1983. *Cebus capucinus* (Mono Cara Blanca, White-faced Capuchin). Pp. 458–460, *in* Costa Rican natural history (D. H. Janzen, ed.). Univ. Chicago Press, Chicago. 816 pp.

Fritzell, E. K., and K. J. Haroldson. 1982. Urocyon cinereoargenteus. Mamm. Species, 189:1–8.

Froehlich, J. W., and P. H. Froehlich. 1987. The status of Panama's endemic howling monkeys. Primate Conservation, 8:58–62.

Fujita, M. S., and T. H. Kunz. 1984. Pipistrellus subflavus. Mamm. Species, 228:1–6.

Galef, B. G., Jr., R. A. Mittermeier, and R. C. Bailey. 1976. Predation by the tayra (*Eira barbara*). J. Mamm., 57:760–761.

Gardner, A. L. 1971. Notes on the little spotted cat, *Felis tigrina oncilla* Thomas, in Costa Rica. J. Mamm., 52:464–465.

Gardner, A. L. 1977. Feeding habits. Pp. 293–350, *in* Biology of bats of the New World family Phyllostomatidae, Part II (R. J. Baker, J. K. Jones, Jr., and D. C. Carter, eds.). Spec. Publ., Mus. Texas Tech Univ., 13:1–364.

Gardner, A. L. 1983a. *Didelphis marsupialis* (Raposa, Zarigüeya, Zorro Pelón, Zorra Mochila, Opossum). Pp. 468–469, *in* Costa Rican natural history (D. H. Janzen, ed.). Univ. Chicago Press, Chicago. 816 pp.

Gardner, A. L. 1983b. *Oryzomys caliginosus* (Ratón pardo, Ratón Arrocero Pardo, Costa Rican

Dusky Rice Rat). Pp. 483–485, *in* Costa Rican natural history (D. H. Janzen, ed.). Univ. Chicago Press, Chicago. 816 pp.

Gardner, A. L., and G. K. Creighton. 1989. A new generic name for Tate's *microtarsus* group of South American mouse opossums (Marsupialia: Didelphidae). Proc. Biol. Soc. Wash., 102:3–7.

Gardner, A. L., R. K. LaVal, and D. E. Wilson. 1970. The distributional status of some Costa Rican bats. J. Mamm., 51:712–729.

Gardner, A. L., and J. L. Patton. 1976. Karyotypic variation in Oryzomyine rodents (Cricetinae) with comments on chromosomal evolution in the neotropical Cricetine complex. Occas. Papers Mus. Zool., Louisiana State Univ., 49:1–48.

Genoways, H. H. 1973. Systematics and evolutionary relationships of spiny pocket mice, genus *Liomys*. Spec. Publ., Mus. Texas Tech Univ., 5:1–368.

Genoways, H. H., and J. H. Brown (eds.). 1993. Biology of the Heteromyidae. Spec. Publ. 10. The American Society of Mammalogists. 719 pp.

Genoways, H. H., and J. K. Jones, Jr. 1972. Variation and ecology in a local population of the vesper mouse (*Nyctomys sumichrasti*). Occas. Papers Mus., Texas Tech Univ., 3:1–21.

Giacalone, J., N. Wells, and G. Willis. 1987. Observations on *Syntheosciurus brochus* (Sciuridae) in Volcán Poás National Park, Costa Rica. J. Mamm., 68:145–147.

Glanz, W. E. 1984. Food and habitat use by two sympatric *Sciurus* species in central Panama. J. Mamm., 65:342–347.

Goldman, E. A. 1920. Mammals of Panama. Smithsonian Misc. Coll., 69:1–309.

Goodwin, G. G. 1946. Mammals of Costa Rica. Bull. Amer. Mus. Nat. Hist., 87:271–473.

Goodwin, G. G., and A. M. Greenhall. 1961. A review of the bats of Trinidad and Tobago. Bull. Amer. Mus. Nat. Hist., 122:187–302.

Greene, H. W. 1989. Agonistic behavior by three-toed sloths, *Bradypus variegatus*. Biotropica, 21:369–372.

Greenhall, A. M., and U. Schmidt (eds.). 1988. Natural history of vampire bats. CRC Press, Florida. 246 pp.

Gribel, R. 1988. Visits of *Caluromys lanatus* (Didelphidae) to flowers of *Pseudobombax tomento-sum* (Bombacaceae): a probable case of pollination by marsupials in central Brazil. Biotropica, 20:344–347.

Groves, C. P. 1993. Order Primates. Pp. 243–277, *in* Mammal species of the world: a taxonomic and geographic reference. Second edition (D. E. Wilson and D. M. Reeder, eds.). Smithsonian Institution Press, Washington. 1206 pp.

Grubb, P. 1993. Order Artiodactyla. Pp. 377–414, *in* Mammal species of the world: a taxonomic and geographic reference. Second edition (D. E. Wilson and D. M. Reeder, eds.). Smithsonian Institution Press, Washington. 1206 pp.

Hafner, M. S. 1991. Evolutionary genetics and zoogeography of Middle American pocket gophers, genus *Orthogeomys*. J. Mamm., 72:1–10.

Hafner, M. S., and D. J. Hafner. 1987. Geographic distribution of two Costa Rican species of *Orthogeomys*, with comments on dorsal pelage markings in the Geomyidae. Southwestern Nat., 32:5–11.

Hall, E. R. 1981. The mammals of North America. Vols. 1 and 2. John Wiley: New York. 1175 pp.

Hall, E. R., and W. W. Dalquest. 1963. The mammals of Veracruz. Univ. Kansas Publ., Mus. Nat. Hist., 14:165–362.

Hallwachs, W. 1986. Agoutis (*Dasyprocta punctata*), the inheritors of guapinol (*Hymenaea courbaril*: Leguminosae). Pp. 285–304, *in* Frugivores and seed dispersal (A. Estrada and T. H. Fleming, eds.). W. Junk, Dordrecht. 392 pp.

Handley, C. O., Jr. 1966. Checklist of the mammals of Panama. Pp. 753–795, *in* Ectoparasites of Panama (R. L. Wetzel and V. J. Tipton, eds.). Field Mus. Nat. Hist., Chicago. 861 pp.

Handley, C. O., Jr. 1976. Mammals of the Smithsonian Venezuelan project. Brigham Young Univ. Sci. Bull. Biol. Ser., 20:1–89.

Handley, C. O., Jr., D. E. Wilson, and A. L. Gardner, eds. 1991. Demography and natural history of the common fruit bat, *Artibeus jamaicensis*, on Barro Colorado Island, Panamá. Smithsonian Contrib. Zool., 511:1–173.

Hartshorn, G. S. 1983. Plants. Pp. 118–157, *in* Costa Rican natural history (D. H. Janzen, ed.). Univ. Chicago Press, Chicago. 816 pp.

Heaney, L. R. 1983. *Sciurus granatensis* (Ardilla Roja, Ardilla Chisa, Red-tailed Squirrel). Pp. 489–490, *in* Costa Rican natural history (D. H. Janzen, ed.). Univ. Chicago Press, Chicago. 816 pp.

Hellebuyck, V., J. R. Tamsitt, and J. G. Hartman. 1985. Records of bats new to El Salvador. J. Mamm., 66:783–788.

Helm, J. D. 1975. Reproductive biology of *Ototylomys* (Cricetidae). J. Mamm., 56:575–590.

Hensley, A. P., and K. T. Wilkins. 1988. Leptonycteris nivalis. Mamm. Species, 307:1–4.

Herd, R. M. 1983. Pteronotus parnellii. Mamm. Species, 209:1–5.

Hernandez, O. E., G. R. Barreto, and J. Ojasti. 1995. Observations of behavioral patterns of white-lipped peccaries in the wild. Mammalia, 59:146–148.

Hershkovitz, P. 1960. Mammals of northern Colombia, preliminary report no. 8: arboreal rice rats, a systematic revision of the subgenus *Oecomys*, genus *Oryzomys*. Proc. U.S. Nat. Mus., 110:513–568.

Hoffmann, R. S., J. K. Jones, Jr., and J. A. Campbell. 1987. First record of *Myotis auriculus* from Guatemala. Southwestern Nat., 32:391–413.

Hoffmeister, D. F. 1986. Mammals of Arizona. Univ. Arizona Press and Arizona Game and Fish Dept. 602 pp.

Honacki, J. H., K. E. Kinman, and J. W. Koeppl (eds.). 1982. Mammal species of the world. Allen Press and Association of Systematics Collections, Lawrence, Kansas. 694 pp.

Hood, C. S., and Jones, J. K., Jr. 1984. Noctilio leporinus. Mamm. Species, 216:1–7.

Hood, C. S., and J. Pitochelli. 1983. Noctilio albiventris. Mamm. Species, 197:1–5.

Hooper, E. T. 1952. A systematic review of the harvest mice (genus *Reithrodontomys*) of Latin America. Misc. Publ. Mus. Zool., Univ. Michigan, 77:1–255.

Hooper, E. T. 1968. Habitats and food of amphibious mice of the genus *Rheomys*. J. Mamm., 49:550–553.

Hooper, E. T. 1972. A synopsis of the rodent genus *Scotinomys*. Occas. Papers, Mus. Zool. Univ. Michigan, 665:1–32.

Hooper, E. T., and M. D. Carleton. 1976. Reproduction, growth and development in two contiguously allopatric rodent species, genus *Scotinomys*. Misc. Publ. Mus. Zool., Univ. Michigan, 151:1–52.

Horwich, R. H., and E. D. Johnson. 1986. Geographical distribution of the black howler (*Alouatta pigra*) in Central America. Primates, 27:53–62.

Howell, D. J. 1983. *Glossophaga soricina* (Murciélago Lengualarga, Nectar Bat). Pp. 472–474, *in* Costa Rican natural history (D. H. Janzen, ed.). Univ. Chicago Press, Chicago. 816 pp.

Howell, D. J., and D. Burch. 1974. Food habits of some Costa Rican bats. Rev. Biol. Trop., 21:281–294.

Hoyt, R. A., and J. S. Altenbach. 1981. Observations on *Diphylla ecaudata* in captivity. J. Mamm., 62:215–216.

Huckaby, D. G. 1980. Species limits in the *Peromyscus mexicanus* group (Mammalia: Rodentia: Muroidea). Contrib. Sci., Los Angeles Co. Mus. Nat. Hist., 326:1–24.

Humphrey, S. R., F. J. Bonaccorso, and T. L. Zinn. 1983. Guild structure of surface-gleaning bats in Panama. Ecology, 64:284–294.

Hunsaker, D., II. 1977. The biology of marsupials. Academic Press, New York. 537 pp.

Husar, S. L. 1978. Trichechus manatus. Mamm. Species, 93:1–5.

Hutterer, R. 1980. A record of Goodwin's shrew, *Cryptotis goodwini*, from Mexico. Mammalia, 44:413.

Janson, C. H., J. Terborgh, and L. H. Emmons. 1981. Non-flying mammals as pollinating agents in the Amazonian forest. Biotropica, Repro. Bot. Supp., 1–6.

Janzen, D. H. 1983a. *Coendou mexicanum* (Puercoespín, Prehensile-tailed Porcupine). Pp. 460–461, *in* Costa Rican natural history (D. H. Janzen, ed.). Univ. Chicago Press, Chicago. 816 pp.

Janzen, D. H. 1983b. *Canis latrans* (Coyote). Pp. 456–457, *in* Costa Rican natural history (D. H. Janzen, ed.). Univ. Chicago Press, Chicago. 816 pp.

Janzen, D. H., and W. Hallwachs. 1982. The hooded skunk, *Mephitis macroura*, in lowland northwestern Costa Rica. Brenesia, 19/20:549–552.

Jeanne, R. L. 1970. Note on a bat (*Phylloderma stenops*) preying on the brood of a social wasp. J. Mamm., 51:624–625.

Jefferson, T. A., S. Leatherwood, and M. A. Webber. 1993. FAO species identification guide. Marine mammals of the world. FAO, Rome. 320 pp.

Jones, J. K., Jr. 1966. Bats from Guatemala. Univ. Kansas Publ., Mus. Nat. Hist., 16:439–472.

Jones, J. K., Jr., J. Arroyo-Cabrales, and R. D. Owen. 1988. Revised checklist of bats (Chiroptera) of Mexico and Central America. Occas. Papers Mus., Texas Tech Univ., 120:1–34.

Jones, J. K., Jr., and G. A. Baldassarre. 1982. Reithrodontomys brevirostris and Reithrodontomys paradoxus. Mamm. Species, 192:1–3.

Jones, J. K., Jr., and M. D. Engstrom. 1986. Synopsis of the rice rats (genus *Oryzomys*) of Nicaragua. Occas. Papers Mus., Texas Tech Univ., 103:1–23.

Jones, J. K., Jr., and H. H. Genoways. 1970. Harvest mice (genus *Reithrodontomys*) of Nicaragua. Occas. Papers, Western Foundation of Vert. Zool., 2:1–16.

Jones, J. K., Jr., and H. H. Genoways. 1975. Sciurus richmondi. Mamm. Species, 53:1–2.

Jones, J. K., Jr., H. H. Genoways, and T. E. Lawlor. 1974. Annotated checklist of mammals of the Yucatan Peninsula, Mexico. II. Rodentia. Occas. Papers Mus., Texas Tech Univ., 22:1–24.

Jones, J. K., Jr., R. S. Hoffmann, D. W. Rice, C. Jones, R. J. Baker, and M. D. Engstrom. 1992. Revised checklist of North American mammals north of Mexico, 1991. Occas. Papers Mus., Texas Tech Univ., 146:1–23.

Jones, J. K., Jr., J. D. Smith, and H. H. Genoways. 1973. Annotated checklist of mammals of the Yucatan Peninsula, Mexico. I. Chiroptera. Occas. Papers Mus., Texas Tech Univ., 13:1–31.

Jones, J. K., Jr., and T. L. Yates. 1983. Review of the white-footed mice, genus *Peromyscus*, of Nicaragua. Occas. Papers Mus., Texas Tech Univ., 82:1–15.

Juárez-G., J., T. J. Jimenez-A. and D. N. Navarro-L. 1988. Additional records of *Bauerus dubiaquercus* (Chiroptera: Vespertilionidae) in Mexico. Southwestern Nat., 33:385.

Junge, J. A., and R. S. Hoffmann. 1981. An annotated key to the long-tailed shrews (genus *Sorex*) of the United States and Canada, with notes on Middle American *Sorex*. Occas. Papers, Mus. Nat. Hist., Univ. Kansas, 94:1–48.

Kalko, E. K. V., and C. O. Handley, Jr. 1994. Evolution, biogeography, and description of a new species of fruit-eating bat, genus *Artibeus* Leach (1821), from Panamá. Z. Säugetierk., 59:257–273.

Kaufmann, J. H. 1983. *Nasua narica* (Pizote, Coati). Pp. 478–480, *in* Costa Rican natural history (D. H. Janzen, ed.). Univ. Chicago Press, Chicago. 816 pp.

Kaufmann, J. H., and A. Kaufmann. 1965. Observations on the behavior of tayras and grisons. Z. Säugetierk., 30:146–155.

Kenyon, K. W. 1977. Caribbean monk seal extinct. J. Mamm., 58: 97–98.

Konecny, M. J. 1989. Movement patterns and food habits of four sympatric carnivore species in Belize, Central America. Pp. 243–264, *in* Advances in Neotropical mammalogy (K. H. Redford and J. F. Eisenberg, eds.). Sandhill Crane Press, Gainesville. 614 pp.

Koopman, K. F. 1974. Eastern limits of *Plecotus* in Mexico. J. Mamm., 55:872–873.

Koopman, K. F. 1993. Order Chiroptera. Pp. 137–241, *in* Mammal species of the world: a taxonomic and geographic reference. Second edition (D. E. Wilson and D. M. Reeder, eds.). Smithsonian Institution Press, Washington. 1206 pp.

Kunz, T. H. (ed.). 1988. Ecological and behavioral methods for the study of bats. Smithsonian Institution Press, Washington. 533 pp.

Kunz, T. H., M. S. Fujita, A. P. Brooke, and G. F. McCracken. 1994. Convergence in tent architecture and tent-making behavior among Neotropical and Paleotropical bats. J. Mamm. Evol., 2:57–78.

Lackey, J. A. 1976. Reproduction, growth and development in the Yucatan deer mice, *Peromyscus yucatanicus*. J. Mamm., 57:638–655.

Lassieur, S. and D. E. Wilson. 1989. Lonchorhina aurita. Mamm. Species, 347:1–4.

LaVal, R. K. 1977. Notes on some Costa Rican bats. Brenesia, 10/11:77–83.

LaVal, R. K., and H. S. Fitch. 1977. Structure, movements and reproduction in three Costa Rican bat communities. Occas. Papers, Mus. Nat. Hist., Univ. Kansas, 69:1–28.

LaVal, R. K., and M. L. LaVal. 1980. Prey selection by a neotropical foliage-gleaning bat, *Micronycteris megalotis*. J. Mamm., 61:327–331.

Lawlor, T. E. 1969. A systematic study of the rodent genus *Ototylomys*. J. Mamm., 50:19–42.

Lawlor, T. E. 1982. Ototylomys phyllotis. Mamm. Species, 181:1–3.

Leatherwood, S., D. K. Caldwell, and H. E. Winn. 1976. Whales, dolphins and porpoises of the Western North Atlantic. A guide to their identification. NOAA Technical Report NMFS CIRC–396. 176 pp.

Leatherwood, S., and R. R. Reeves. 1983. The Sierra Club handbook of whales and dolphins. Sierra Club Books, San Francisco. 302 pp.

Lee, T. E., and R. D. Bradley. 1992. New distributional records of some mammals from Honduras. Texas J. Sci., 44:109–111.

Leopold, A. S. 1959. Wildlife of Mexico: the game birds and mammals. Univ. Calif. Press, Berkeley. 568 pp.

Lewis, S. E., and D. E. Wilson. 1987. Vampyressa pusilla. Mamm. Species, 292:1–5.

Lim, B. K. 1993. Cladistic reappraisal of Neotropical Stenodermatine bat phylogeny. Cladistics, 9:147–165.

Linares, O. J. 1986. Murciélagos de Venezuela. Cuadernos Lagoven, Venezuela. 122 pp.

Lindzey, F. 1987. Mountain lion. Pp. 657–668, *in* Wild furbearer management and conservation in North America (M. Novak, J. A. Baker, M.E. Obbard, and B. Malloch, eds.). Ontario Trappers Assoc., Ontario. 1150 pp.

Lotze, J-H., and S. Anderson. 1979. Procyon lotor. Mamm. Species, 119:1–8.

Lubin, Y. D. 1983. *Tamandua mexicana* (Oso Jaceta, Hormiguero, Tamandua, Banded Anteater, Lesser Anteater). Pp. 494–496, *in* Costa Rican natural history (D. H. Janzen, ed.). Univ. Chicago Press, Chicago. 816 pp.

Ludlow, M. E., and M. E. Sunquist. 1987. Ecology and behavior of ocelots in Venezuela. Nat. Geog. Res., 3:447–461.

Lumer, C., and R. D. Schoer. 1986. Pollination of *Blakea austin-smithii* and *B. penduliflora* (Melastomataceae) by small rodents in Costa Rica. Biotropica, 18:363–364.

Marineros, L. and F. Martínez Gallegos. 1988. Mamíferos silvestres de Honduras. Asociación Hondureña de Ecología. 129 pp.

Marinkelle, C. J., and A. Cadena. 1972. Notes on bats new to the fauna of Colombia. Mammalia, 36:50–58.

Marshall, L. G. 1978. Chironectes minimus. Mamm. Species, 109:1–6.

Martinsen, D. L. 1969. Energetics and activity patterns of short-tailed shrews (*Blarina*) on restricted diets. Ecology, 50:505–510.

Mayer, J. J., and R. M. Wetzel. 1987. Tayassu pecari. Mamm. Species, 293:1–7.

McBee, K., and R. J. Baker. 1982. Dasypus novemcinctus. Mamm. Species, 162:1–9.

McCarthy, T. J. 1980. Aspects of reproduction in *Rhogeessa tumida* and *Eptesicus furinalis* from Belize. Abstract, Annual meeting, Amer. Soc. Mamm.

McCarthy, T. J. 1982. *Chironectes, Cyclopes, Cabassous* and probably *Cebus* in southern Belize. Mammalia, 46:397–400.

McCarthy, T. J. 1987a. Additional mammalian prey of the carnivorous bats, *Chrotopterus auritus* and *Vampyrum spectrum*. Bat Res. News, 28:1–3.

McCarthy, T. J. 1987b. Distributional records of bats from the Caribbean lowlands of Belize and adjacent Guatemala and Mexico. Fieldiana Zool., n.s., 39:137–162.

McCarthy, T. J., D. L. Anderson, and G. A. Cruz D. In press. Confirmation of tree sloths (Mammalia: Xenarthra) in Honduras, Central America. Southwestern Nat.

McCarthy, T. J., W. B. Davis, J. E. Hill, J. K. Jones, Jr., and G. A. Cruz. 1993. Bat (Mammalia: Chiroptera) records, early collectors, and faunal lists for northern Central America. Annals Carnegie Mus., 62:191–228.

McCarthy, T. J., B. Myton, G. A. Cruz D., and W. B. Davis. 1991. Mammal records for *Orthogeomys, Hoplomys*, and *Galictis* for Honduras. Texas J. Sci., 43:429–431.

McCoy, M. B., C. S. Vaughan, M. A. Rodriguez, and D. Kitchen. 1990. Seasonal movement, home range, activity and diet of collared peccaries (*Tayassu tajacu*) in Costa Rican dry forest. Vida Silvestre Neotropical, 2:6–20.

McCracken, G. F., and J. W. Bradbury. 1981. Social organization and kinship in the polygynous bat *Phyllostomus hastatus*. Behav. Ecol. Sociobiol., 8:11–34.

McPherson, A. B. 1985. A biogeographical analysis of factors influencing the distribution of Costa Rican rodents. Brenesia, 23:97–273.

Mead, J. G., and R. L. Brownell, Jr. 1993. Order Cetacea. Pp. 349–364, *in* Mammal species of the world: a taxonomic and geographic reference. Second edition (D. E. Wilson and D. M. Reeder, eds.). Smithsonian Institution Press, Washington. 1206 pp.

Medellín, R. A. 1983. *Tonatia bidens* and *Mimon crenulatum* in Chiapas, Mexico. J. Mamm., 64:150.

Medellín, R. A. 1988. Prey of *Chrotopterus auritus*, with notes on feeding behavior. J. Mamm., 69:841–844.

Medellín, R. A. 1994. Mammal diversity and conservation in the Selva Lacandona, Chiapas, Mexico. Conservation Biol., 8:780–799.

Medellín, R. A., and H. T. Arita. 1989. Tonatia evotis and Tonatia silvicola. Mamm. Species, 334:1–5.

Medellín, R. A., G. Cancino Z., A. Clemente M., and R. O. Guerrero V. 1992. Noteworthy records of three mammals from Mexico. Southwestern Nat., 37:427–429.

Medellín, R. A., and W. Lopez-Forment C. 1986. Las cuevas: un recurso compartido. An. Inst. Biol. Univ. Nal. Autón. Mex. 56, Ser. Zool. (3):1027–1034.

Medellín, R. A., D. Navarro L., W. B. Davis, and V. J. Romero. 1983. Notes on the biology of *Micronycteris brachyotis* (Dobson) (Chiroptera), in southern Veracruz, Mexico. Brenesia, 21:7–11.

Medellín, R. A., G. Urbano-Vidales, O. Sanchez-Herrera, G. Tellez-Giron S., and H. Arita W. 1986. Notas sobre murciélagos del este de Chiapas. Southwestern Nat., 31:532–535.

Medellín, R. A., D. E. Wilson, and D. Navarro L. 1985. Micronycteris brachyotis. Mamm. Species, 251:1–4.

Méndez, E. 1970. Los principales mamíferos silvestres de Panamá. E. Méndez, Panamá. 283 pp.

Méndez, E. 1984. Mexico and Central America. Pp. 513–524, in White-tailed deer: ecology and management (L. K. Halls, ed.). Stackpole Books, Harrisburg. 870 pp.

Miles, M. A., A. A. de Souza, and M. M. Povoa. 1981. Mammal tracking and nest location in Brazilian forest with an improved spool-and-line device. J. Zool. Lond., 195:331–347.

Millar, J. S. 1989. Reproduction and development. Pp. 169–232, in Advances in the study of Peromyscus (Rodentia) (G. L. Kirkland and J. N. Layne, eds.). Texas Tech Univ. Press. 366 pp.

Mittermeier, R. A., A. B. Rylands, A. F. Coimbra-Filho, and G. A. B. Fonseca (eds.). 1988. Ecology and behavior of Neotropical primates. Volume 2. World Wildlife Fund, Washington, D. C. 610 pp.

Molina U., H., C. Roldán C., A. Sáenz F., and S. Torres L. 1986. Hallazgo de Bradypus griseus y Choloepus hoffmanni (Edentata: Bradypodidae) en tierras altas de Costa Rica. Rev. Biol. Trop., 34:165–166.

Mondolfi, E. 1986. Notes on the biology and status of the small wild cats in Venezuela. Pp. 125–146, in Cats of the world: biology, conservation, and management (S. D. Miller and D. D. Everett, eds.). Nat. Wildlife Fed., Washington. 501 pp.

Mondolfi, E., and R. Hoogesteijn. 1986. Notes on the biology and status of the jaguar in Venezuela. Pp. 85–123, in Cats of the world: biology, conservation, and management (S. D. Miller and D. D. Everett, eds.). Nat. Wildlife Fed., Washington. 501 pp.

Mones, A., and J. Ojasti. 1986. Hydrochoerus hydrochaeris. Mamm. Species, 264:1–7.

Montgomery, G. G. 1983a. Bradypus variegatus (Perezoso de Tres Dedos, Three-toed Sloth). Pp. 453–456, in Costa Rican natural history (D. H. Janzen, ed.). Univ. Chicago Press, Chicago. 816 pp.

Montgomery, G. G. 1983b. Cyclopes didactylus (Tapacara, Serafin de Platanar, Silky Anteater). Pp. 461–463, in Costa Rican natural history (D. H. Janzen, ed.). Univ. Chicago Press, Chicago. 816 pp.

Montgomery, G. G. (ed.). 1985. The evolution and ecology of armadillos, sloths, and vermilinguas. Smithsonian Institution Press, Washington. 451 pp.

Montgomery, G. G., and M. E. Sunquist. 1978. Habitat selection and use by two-toed and three-toed sloths. Pp. 329–359, in The ecology of arboreal folivores (G. G. Montgomery, ed.) . Smithsonian Institution Press, Washington. 573 pp.

Mora, J. M., and I. Moreira. 1984. Mamíferos de Costa Rica. Editorial Universidad Estatal a Distancia, San José. 175 pp.

Morales, J. C., and J. W. Bickham. 1995. Molecular systematics of the genus Lasiurus (Chiroptera: Vespertilionidae) based on restriction-site maps of the motochondrial ribosomal genes. J. Mamm., 76: 730–749.

Morgan, G. S. 1989. Geocapromys thoracatus. Mamm. Species, 341:1–5.

Morrison, D. W. 1979. Apparent male defense of tree hollows in the fruit bat, Artibeus jamaicensis. J. Mamm., 60:11–15.

Morrison, D. W. 1980. Foraging and day-roosting dynamics of canopy fruit bats in Panama. J. Mamm., 61:20–29.

Murie, O. J. 1974. A field guide to animal tracks. Houghton Mifflin, Boston. 375 pp.

Musser, G. G. 1968. A systematic study of the Mexican and Guatemalan gray squirrel, Sciurus aureogaster F. Cuvier (Rodentia: Sciuridae). Misc. Pubs. Mus. Zool., Univ. Michigan, 137:1–112.

Musser, G. G. 1969. Notes on *Peromyscus* (Muridae) of Mexico and Central America. Amer. Mus. Novitates, 2357:1–23.

Musser, G. G. 1971. *Peromyscus allophylus* Osgood: a synonym of *Peromyscus gymnotis* Thomas (Rodentia, Muridae). Amer. Mus. Novitates, 2453:1–10.

Musser, G. G., and M. D. Carleton. 1993. Family Muridae. Pp. 501–755, *in* Mammal species of the world: a taxonomic and geographic reference (D. E. Wilson and D. M. Reeder, eds.). Smithsonian Institution Press, Washington. 1206 pp.

Musser, G. G., and M. M. Williams. 1985. Systematic studies of Oryzomyine rodents (Muridae): definitions of *Oryzomys villosus* and *Oryzomys talamancae*. Amer. Mus. Novitates, 2810:1–22.

Nagorsen, D. 1985. Kogia simus. Mammal. Species, 239:1–6.

Navarro, D., and M. Suarez. 1989. A survey of the pygmy raccoon (*Procyon pygmaeus*) of Cozumel, Mexico. Mammalia, 53:458–461.

Nikitman, L. Z. 1985. Sciurus granatensis. Mamm. Species, 246:1–8.

Novaro, A. J., R. S. Walker, and M. Suarez. 1995. Dry season food habits of the gray fox (*Urocyon cinereoargenteus fraterculus*) in the Belizean Peten. Mammalia, 59:19–24.

O'Connell, M. A. 1982. Population biology of North and South American grassland rodents: a comparative review. Pp. 167–185, *in* Mammalian biology in South America. (M. A. Mares and H. H. Genoways, eds.). Vol. 6, Spec. Pub. Ser. Pymatuning Lab. Ecol., Univ. Pittsburgh. 539 pp.

O'Connell, M. A. 1983. Marmosa robinsoni. Mamm. Species, 203:1–6.

O'Farrell, M. J., and E. H. Studier. 1980. Myotis thysanodes. Mamm. Species, 137:1–5.

O'Shea, T. J., and C. A. Salisbury. 1991. Belize—a last stronghold for manatees in the Caribbean. Oryx, 25:156–164.

Owen, R. D. 1987. Phylogenetic analysis of the bat subfamily Stenodermatinae (Mammalia: Chiroptera). Spec. Publ. Mus., Texas Tech Univ., 26:1–65.

Packard, R. L. 1960. Speciation and evolution of the pygmy mice, genus *Baiomys*. Univ. Kansas Publ., Mus. Nat. Hist., Vol. 9, 23:579–670.

Packard, R. L., and J. B. Montgomery, Jr. 1978. Baiomys musculus. Mamm. Species, 102:1–3.

Parker, T. A., III, B. K. Holst, L. H. Emmons, and J. R. Meyer. 1993. A biological assessment of the Columbia River Forest Reserve, Toledo District, Belize. Conservation International, RAP Working Papers, 3:1–81.

Patton, J. L. 1993. Order Geomyidae. Pp. 469–476, *in* Mammal species of the world: a taxonomic and geographic reference. Second edition (D. E. Wilson and D. M. Reeder, eds.). Smithsonian Institution Press, Washington. 1206 pp.

Perkins, J. S., and G. W. Miller. 1983. Mass stranding of *Steno bredanensis* in Belize. Biotropica, 15:235–236.

Peres, C. A. 1991. Observations on hunting by small-eared (*Atelocynus microtis*) and bush dogs (*Speothos venaticus*) in central-western Amazonia. Mammalia, 55:635–639.

Peterson, R. L. 1966. Notes on the Yucatan vesper rat, *Otonyctomys hatti*, with a new record, the first from British Honduras. Can. J. Zool., 44:281–284.

Peterson, R. L., and P. Kirmse. 1969. Notes on *Vampyrum spectrum*, the false vampire bat, in Panama. Can. J. Zool., 47:140–142.

Pine, R. H. 1971. A review of the long-whiskered rice rat, *Oryzomys bombycinus* Goldman. J. Mamm., 52:590–596.

Pine, R. H. 1972. The bats of the genus *Carollia*. Tex. Agric. Exp. Stn., Tech. Monogr., Texas A & M Univ., 8:1–125.

Rabinowitz, A. R., and B. G. Nottingham. 1986. Ecology and behavior of the jaguar (*Panthera onca*) in Belize, Central America. J. Zool. Lond., 210:149–159.

Redford, K. H. 1985. Feeding and food preference in captive and wild giant anteaters (*Myrmecophaga tridactyla*). J. Zool. Lond., 205:559–572.

Redford, K. H., and J. F. Eisenberg. 1992. Mammals of the Neotropics, Volume 2. The southern cone: Chile, Argentina, Uruguay, Paraguay. Univ. Chicago Press, Chicago. 430 pp.

Reid, F. A., and C. A. Langtimm. 1993. Distributional and natural history notes for selected mammals from Costa Rica. Southwestern Nat., 38:299–302.

Rick, A. M. 1968. Notes on bats from Tikal, Guatemala. J. Mamm., 49:516–520.

Ridgway, S. H., and R. J. Harrison (eds.). 1985. Handbook of marine mammals, Volume 3: the sirenians and baleen whales. Academic Press, London. 362 pp.

Ridgway, S. H., and R. J. Harrison (eds.). 1989. Handbook of marine mammals, Volume 4: river dolphins and the larger toothed whales. Academic Press, London. 442 pp.

Ridgway, S. H., and R. J. Harrison (eds.). 1994. Handbook of marine mammals, Volume 5: the first book of dolphins. Academic Press, London. 416 pp.

Robinson, J. G., and J. F. Eisenberg. 1985. Group size and foraging habits of the collared peccary *Tayassu tajacu*. J. Mamm., 66:153–155.

Rogers, D. S. 1989. Evolutionary implications of chromosomal variation among spiny pocket mice, genus *Heteromys* (Order Rodentia). Southwestern Nat., 34:85–100.

Rogers, D. S. 1990. Genic evolution, historical biogeography, and systematic relationships among spiny pocket mice (subfamily Heteromyinae). J. Mamm., 71:668–685.

Rogers, D. S., and M. D. Engstrom. 1992. Genic differentiation in spiny pocket mice of the *Liomys pictus* species-group (family Heteromyidae). Can. J. Zool., 70:1912–1919.

Rogers, D. S., E. J. Heske, and D. A. Good. 1983. Karyotypes and a range extension of *Reithrodontomys* (Cricetidae: subgenus Aporodon) from Mexico. Southwestern Nat., 28:372–374.

Rogers, D. S., and J. E. Rogers. 1992a. Heteromys nelsoni. Mamm. Species, 397:1–2.

Rogers, D. S., and J. E. Rogers. 1992b. Heteromys oresterus. Mamm. Species, 396:1–3.

Rogers, D. S., and D. J. Schmidly. 1982. Systematics of spiny pocket mice (genus *Heteromys*) of the *desmarestianus* species group from Mexico and northern Central America. J. Mamm., 63:375–386.

Rosatte, R. C. 1987. Striped, spotted, hooded, and hog-nosed skunk. Pp. 599–613, *in* Wild furbearer management and conservation in North America (M. Novak, J. A. Baker, M. E. Obbard, and B. Malloch, eds.). Ontario Trappers Assoc., Ontario. 1150 pp.

Rossan, R. N., and D. C. Baerg. 1977. Laboratory and feral hybridization of *Ateles geoffroyi panamensis* Kellogg and Goldman 1944 and *A. fusciceps robustus* Allen 1914 in Panama. Primates, 18:235–237.

Sanchez-H., O., G. Tellez-G., R. A. Medellín, and G. Urbano-V. 1986. New records of mammals from Quintana Roo, México. Mammalia, 50:275–278.

Sazima, I. 1976. Observations on the feeding habits of phyllostomatid bats (*Carollia, Anoura,* and *Vampyrops*) in southeastern Brazil. J. Mamm., 57:381–382.

Schlichte, H-J. 1978. A preliminary report on the habitat utilization of a group of howler monkeys (*Alouatta villosa pigra*) in the National Park of Tikal, Guatemala. Pp. 551–559, *in* The ecology of arboreal folivores (G. G. Montgomery, ed.). Smithsonian Institution Press, Washington. 573 pp.

Schmidly, D. J. 1981. Marine mammals of the Southeastern United States coast and the Gulf of Mexico. U.S. Fish and Wildlife Service, Office of Biological Services, Washington. FWS/OBS–80/41. 163 pp.

Schmidt, C. A., M. D. Engstrom, and H. H. Genoways. 1989. Heteromys gaumeri. Mamm. Species, 345:1–4.

Schmidt, C. A., and M. D. Engstrom. 1994. Genic variation and systematics of rice rats (*Ory-*

zomys palustris species group) in southern Texas and northeastern Tamaulipas, Mexico. J. Mamm., 75:914–928.

Shump, K. A., and A. U. Shump. 1982a. Lasiurus borealis. Mamm. Species, 183:1–6.

Shump, K. A., and A. U. Shump. 1982b. Lasiurus cinereus. Mamm. Species, 185:1–5.

Simmons, N. B. 1996. A new species of *Micronycteris* (Chiroptera: Phyllostomidae) from Northeastern Brazil, with comments on phylogenic relationships. Amer. Mus. Novitates, 3158:1–34.

Sisk, T., and C. Vaughan. 1984. Notes on some aspects of the natural history of the giant pocket gopher (*Orthogeomys* Merriam) in Costa Rica. Brenesia, 22:233–247.

Smallwood, K. S. 1993. Mountain lion vocalizations and hunting behavior. Southwestern Nat., 38:65–67.

Smith, J. D. 1972. Systematics of the chiropteran family Mormoopidae. Misc. Publ. Mus. Nat. Hist., Univ. Kansas, 56:1–132.

Smith, J. D., and J. K. Jones, Jr. 1967. Additional records of the Guatemalan vole, *Microtus guatemalensis* Merriam. Southwestern Nat., 12:189–191.

Smythe, N. 1978. The natural history of the Central American agouti (*Dasyprocta punctata*). Smithsonian Contrib. Zool., 257:1–52.

Smythe, N. 1983. *Dasyprocta punctata* and *Agouti paca* (Guatusa, Cherenga, Agouti, Tepezcuintle, Paca). Pp. 463–465, *in* Costa Rican natural history (D. H. Janzen, ed.). Univ. Chicago Press, Chicago. 816 pp.

Snow, J. L., J. K. Jones, Jr., and W. D. Webster. 1980. Centurio senex. Mamm. Species, 138:1–3.

Snowdon, C. T., and P. Soini. 1988. The tamarins, genus *Saguinus*. Pp. 223–298, *in* Ecology and behavior of Neotropical primates. Volume 2 (R. A. Mittermeier et al., eds.). World Wildlife Fund, Washington. 610 pp.

Sowls, L. K. 1984. The peccaries. Univ. Arizona Press, Tucson. 251 pp.

Spencer, S. R., and G. N. Cameron. 1982. Reithrodontomys fulvescens. Mamm. Species, 174:1–7.

Stallings, J. R. 1984. Notes on feeding habits of *Mazama gouazoubira* in the Chaco Boreal of Paraguay. Biotrop., 16:155–157.

Starrett, A. 1972. Cyttarops alecto. Mamm. Species, 13:1–2.

Starrett, A., and R. S. Casebeer. 1968. Records of bats from Costa Rica. Los Angeles Co. Mus. Contrib. Sci., 148:1–21.

Starrett, A., and G. F. Fisler. 1970. Aquatic adaptations of the water mouse, *Rheomys underwoodi*. Los Angeles Co. Mus. Contrib. Sci., 182:1–14.

Stirton, R. A. 1944. Tropical mammal trapping I: the water mouse *Rheomys*. J. Mamm., 25:337–343.

Strahl, S. D., J. L. Silva, and I. R. Goldstein. 1992. The bush dog (*Speothos venaticus*) in Venezuela. Mammalia, 56:9–13.

Sunquist, M. E., S. N. Austad, and F. Sunquist. 1987. Movement patterns and home range in the common opossum (*Didelphis marsupialis*). J. Mamm., 68:173–176.

Sunquist, M. E., F. Sunquist, and D. E. Daneke. 1989. Ecological separation in a Venezuelan llanos carnivore community. Pp. 197–232, *in* Advances in neotropical mammalogy (K. H. Redford and J. F. Eisenberg, eds.). Sandhill Crane Press, Gainesville. 614 pp.

Svihla, R. D. 1930. Notes on the golden harvest mouse. J. Mamm., 11:53–55.

Tamsitt, J. R., and D. Nagorsen. 1982. Anoura cultrata. Mamm. Species, 179:1–5.

Tate, G. H. H. 1933. A systematic revision of the marsupial genus *Marmosa*. Bull. Amer. Mus. Nat. Hist., 66:1–249.

Terwilliger, V. J. 1978. Natural history of Baird's tapir on Barro Colorado Island, Panama Canal Zone. Biotrop., 10:211–220.

Tesh, R. B. 1970a. Notes on the reproduction, growth, and development of echimyid rodents in Panama. J. Mamm., 51:199–202.

Tesh, R. B. 1970b. Observations on the natural history of *Diplomys darlingi*. J. Mamm., 51:197–199.

Thomas, O. 1905. New neotropical *Molossus, Conepatus, Nectomys, Proechimys*, and *Agouti*, with a note on the genus *Mesomys*. Ann. Mag. Nat. Hist., Ser. 7, 15:584–591.

Timm, R. M. 1985. Artibeus phaeotis. Mamm. Species, 235:1–6.

Timm, R. M. 1987. Tent construction by bats of the genera *Artibeus* and *Uroderma*. Pp. 187–212, *in* Studies in Neotropical mammalogy: essays in honor of Philip Hershkovitz (B. D. Patterson and R. M. Timm, eds.). Fieldiana Zool., n.s. 39:1–506.

Timm, R. M., D. E. Wilson, B. L. Clauson, R. K. LaVal, and C. S. Vaughan. 1989. Mammals of the La Selva-Braulio Carrillo complex, Costa Rica. North American Fauna. U.S. Fish and Wildlife Service Publ., 75:1–162.

Tumlinson, R. 1992. Plecotus mexicanus. Mamm. Species, 401:1–3.

Tuttle, M. D. 1970. Distribution and zoogeography of Peruvian bats, with comments on natural history. Univ. Kansas Sci. Bull., 49:45–86.

Tuttle, M. D., and M. J. Ryan. 1981. Bat predation and the evolution of frog vocalizations in the neotropics. Science, 214:677–678.

Valdez, R., and R. K. LaVal. 1971. Records of bats from Honduras and Nicaragua. J. Mamm., 52:247–250.

Van Den Bussche, R. A., R. J. Baker, H. A. Wichman, and M. J. Hamilton. 1993. Molecular phylogenetics of Stenodermatini bat genera: congruence of data from nuclear and mitochondrial DNA. Mol. Biol. Evol., 10:944–959.

Van Gelder, R. 1953. The egg-opening technique of a spotted skunk. J. Mamm., 34:255–256.

Vaughan, C. 1983. Coyote range expansion in Costa Rica and Panama. Brenesia, 21:27–32.

Vaughan, C., T. Kotowski, and L. Saénz. 1994. Ecology of the Central American Cacomistle, *Bassariscus sumichrasti*, in Costa Rica. Small Carnivore Conservation, 11:4–7.

Vehrencamp, S. L., F. G. Stiles, and J. W. Bradbury. 1977. Observations on the foraging behavior and avian prey of the Neotropical carnivorous bat, *Vampyrum spectrum*. J. Mamm., 58:469–478.

Villa-R., B. 1966. Los murciélagos de México. Inst. Biol., Univ. Nac. Aut. México. 492 pp.

Villa-R., B. 1993. Registros nuevos para algunos mamíferos de Panamá. Anales Inst. Biol. Nac. Autón. México. Ser. Zool., 64:79–85.

Voss, R. S. 1988. Systematics and ecology of Ichthyomyine rodents (Muroidea): patterns of morphological evolution in a small adaptive radiation. Bull. Amer. Mus. Nat. Hist., 188:260–493.

Voss, R. S., J. L. Silva L., and J. A. Valdes L. 1982. Feeding behavior and diets of Neotropical water rats, genus *Ichthyomys* Thomas, 1893. Z. Säugetierk., 47:364–369.

Walker, P. L., and J. G. H. Cant. 1977. A population survey of kinkajous (*Potos flavus*) in a seasonally dry tropical forest. J. Mamm., 58:100–102.

Wallace, D. R. 1995. Adventuring in Central America: Guatemala, Belize, El Salvador, Honduras, Nicaragua, Costa Rica, Panama. Sierra Club Books, San Francisco. 445 pp.

Warner, R. M. 1982. Myotis auriculus. Mamm. Species, 191:1–3.

Webster, W. D. 1993. Systematics and evolution of bats of the genus Glossophaga. Spec. Publ., Mus. Texas Tech Univ., 36:1–184.

Webster, W. D., and J. K. Jones, Jr. 1980. Taxonomic and nomenclatorial notes on bats of the genus *Glossophaga* in North America, with description of a new species. Occas. Papers Mus., Texas Tech Univ., 71:1–12.

Webster, W. D., and J. K. Jones, Jr. 1982. Artibeus aztecus. Mamm. Species, 177:1–3.

Webster, W. D., and J. K. Jones, Jr. 1984. Glossophaga leachii. Mamm. Species, 226:1–3.

Webster, W. D., and J. K. Jones, Jr. 1985. Glossophaga mexicana. Mamm. Species, 245:1–2.

Webster, W. D., J. K. Jones, Jr., and R. J. Baker. 1980. Lasiurus intermedius. Mamm. Species, 132:1–3.

Wells, N. M., and J. Giacalone. 1985. Syntheosciurus brochus. Mamm. Species, 249:1–3.

Wetzel, R. M. 1983. *Dasypus novemcinctus* (Cusuco, Armadillo). Pp. 465–467, *in* Costa Rican natural history (D. H. Janzen, ed.). Univ. Chicago Press, Chicago. 816 pp.

Whitaker, J. O., Jr. 1974. Cryptotis parva. Mamm. Species, 43:1–8.

Whitaker, J. O., Jr., and J. S. Findley. 1980. Foods eaten by some bats from Costa Rica and Panama. J. Mamm., 61:540–544.

Wilkins, K. T. 1989. Tadarida brasiliensis. Mamm. Species, 331:1–10.

Williams, S. L., M. R. Willig, and F. A. Reid. 1995. A review of the *Tonatia bidens*-complex (Mammalia: Chiroptera), with descriptions of two new subspecies. J. Mamm., 76:612–626.

Willis, K. B., M. R. Willig, and J. K. Jones, Jr. 1990. Vampyrodes caraccioli. Mamm. Species, 359:1–4.

Wilson, D. E. 1971. Food habits of *Micronycteris hirsuta* (Chiroptera: Phyllostomidae). Mammalia, 35:107–110.

Wilson, D. E. 1978. Thyroptera discifera. Mamm. Species, 104:1–3.

Wilson, D. E. 1979. Reproductive patterns. Pp. 317–378, *in* Biology of bats of the New World family Phyllostomatidae. Part III (R. J. Baker, J. K. Jones, Jr., and D. C. Carter, eds.). Spec. Publ., Mus. Tex. Tech Univ., 16:1–441.

Wilson, D. E. 1983a. Checklist of mammals. Pp. 443–447, *in* Costa Rican natural history (D. H. Janzen, ed.). Univ. of Chicago Press, Chicago. 816 pp.

Wilson, D. E. 1983b. *Myotis nigricans* (Murciélago Pardo, Black Myotis). Pp. 477–478, *in* Costa Rican natural history (D. H. Janzen, ed.). Univ. of Chicago Press, Chicago. 816 pp.

Wilson, D. E. 1991. Mammals of the Tres Marías Islands. Bull. Amer. Mus. Nat. Hist., 206:214–250.

Wilson, D. E., and J. S. Findley. 1977. Thyroptera tricolor. Mamm. Species, 71:1–3.

Wilson, D. E., and D. M. Reeder (eds.). 1993. Mammal species of the world: a taxonomic and geographic reference. Second edition. Smithsonian Institution Press, Washington. 1206 pp.

Woodman, N., and R. M. Timm. 1992. A new species of small–eared shrew, genus *Cryptotis* (Insectivora: Soricidae), from Honduras. Proc. Biol. Soc. Wash., 105:1–12.

Woodman, N., and R. M. Timm. 1993. Intraspecific and interspecific variation in the *Cryptotis nigrescens* species complex of small-eared shrews (Insectivora: Soricidae), with the description of a new species from Colombia. Fieldiana Zool., n.s., 74:1–30.

Wozencraft, C. W. 1993. Order Carnivora. Pp. 279–348, *in* Mammal species of the world: a taxonomic and geographic reference. Second edition. (D. E. Wilson and D. M. Reeder, eds.). Smithsonian Institution Press, Washington. 1206 pp.

INDEX TO SCIENTIFIC NAMES

Genus names used in the accounts are in boldface. Italicized numbers refer to an illustration on that page. Numbers following Pl. are plate numbers.

INDEX TO COMMON NAMES

Italicized numbers refer to an illustration on that page. Numbers following Pl. are plate numbers.